HOW TO DO just about ANYTHING ON A computer

Microsoft® Windows® 7™

READER'S DIGEST

HOW TO ANYTHING

DO just about ON A computer

Microsoft® Windows® 7™

Published by The Reader's Digest Association, Inc.

LONDON • NEW YORK • SYDNEY • MONTREAL

Contents

PRACTICAL HOME PROJECTS

TROUBLESHOOTING

How to use this book

Find out how this book will help you to make the most of your PC

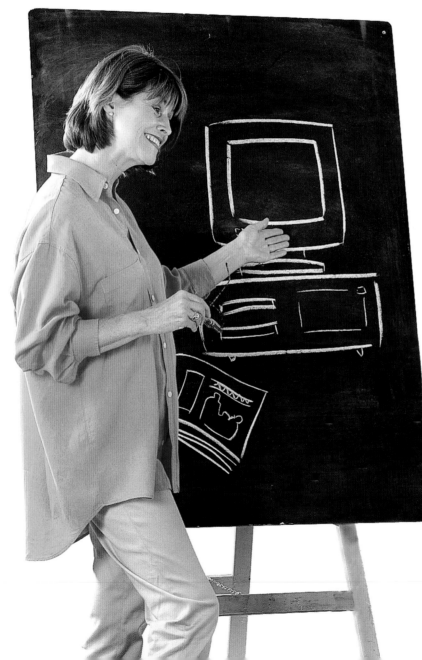

With easy step-by-step tuition, expert advice and inspirational ideas, How To Do Just About Anything On A Computer will help you to put your computer to the best use.

Unlike most other computer books, *How To Do Just About Anything On A Computer* assumes that you are more interested in, say, creating a letterhead than you are in becoming an expert on electronics. For this reason, the book is organised into projects – all the things you are likely to want to do with your PC. These projects are designed to be of real, practical benefit to you and your family.

Learning to use your computer is more fun when approached in this way. You will see why the programs work the way they do, and you can then apply these skills to other tasks.

Each project is broken down into easy-to-follow, step-by-step procedures. The steps are accompanied by pictures that show you what you will see on your screen. This means you will never be left wondering 'Where's the menu they are telling me to click?' because you will get a snapshot that shows exactly where the pointer should be when you click it.

Before you explore the full potential of your PC, you need to set the computer up, learn some housekeeping and get to know Microsoft® Windows®, the ringmaster of your PC's programs. This is covered in the first part of the book: 'You and Your Computer'.

Computers are increasingly reliable, but the 'Troubleshooting' section will help you to solve any glitches. In most cases, you will find what you need to get your PC running smoothly again.

All the rest is down to you: we hope you enjoy the countless tasks you can achieve on your PC.

Getting around the book

How To Do Just About Anything On A Computer contains four sections, taking you from the initial set-up, to connecting to the internet, applying your skills practically and solving problems. Each follows a similar step-by-step format with snapshots of what should be on your screen at each stage of the process.

You and Your Computer

This section guides you through setting up your PC, understanding the roles of hardware and software, and learning the basics of key programs. Find out how to care for your computer and how to maximise its efficiency.

Practical Home Projects

Choose from 37 practical projects that take you through the steps involved in creating a range of documents, including a recipe database, kitchen plan, address labels, home accounts spreadsheet, greetings cards and posters.

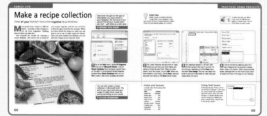

The Internet

Learn how to connect to the internet. Find out how to send and receive electronic mail (email), and access information through the World Wide Web quickly and safely. You can even learn how to create your own blog, use Twitter and sell goods on eBay.

Troubleshooting

Your computer and its related hardware and software can behave unexpectedly at times. If this happens to you, do not panic. This section helps to ease your concerns and offers a wide range of easy-to-follow solutions to common problems.

Special features

The book also offers the opportunity to apply your skills to real-life projects.

Make your PC skills work for you

The book contains larger undertakings that require you to draw on the skills you have developed as you try your hand at individual projects. Use your word-processing skills, your spreadsheet know-how and your graphics experience to take the stress and drudgery out of moving house, running a club or organising a family celebration.

Glossary and Index

Found a word you do not understand? Turn to the back of the book to find clear definitions of the most commonly used terms and phrases. You will also find a comprehensive index to guide you around the book.

Which software?

This book assumes that readers are operating PCs that run Microsoft® Windows® 7 Home Premium. With the exception of a few projects that use specialist software, most projects use either Microsoft® Office® (Home and Business 2010) or Microsoft® Works® 9.0. Any instructions for Microsoft Word (the word-processing program within Office) will also apply to Works Word Processor unless otherwise stated. (If you are using Works Suite 2005 – or later – note that this includes Microsoft Word rather than Works Word Processor.)

And which hardware?

You do not need a top-of-the-range computer to get the most out of this book. The minimum specifications for your PC are a 2GHz processor, 2Gb of memory, a 200Gb hard drive with at least 20Gb of available space, an integrated 512Mb graphics media accelerator and a DVD+/- RW drive. Better still, a 3.1GHz processor with 4Gb of system memory and a 500Gb hard drive with at least 40Gb of available space would make everything work faster. Do not forget music and sound require audio output.

Finding your way around the page

You are guided through every project in this book by means of a series of illustrated steps and a range of visual features. Here are the key features you should look for on the page.

Before you start
Projects begin with a Before You Start box. This outlines points to consider, documentation to collect, and tasks to do before beginning the project.

Extra help
Above and below the steps you will find hints, tips and warnings of common pitfalls.

Step by step
Projects are set out in easy-to-follow steps, from the first mouse click to the last. You get instructions on what keyboard and mouse commands to give, and what programs and folders you need to access to complete the project.

Other programs
This tells you which other programs can be used to complete the project, and how to access them.

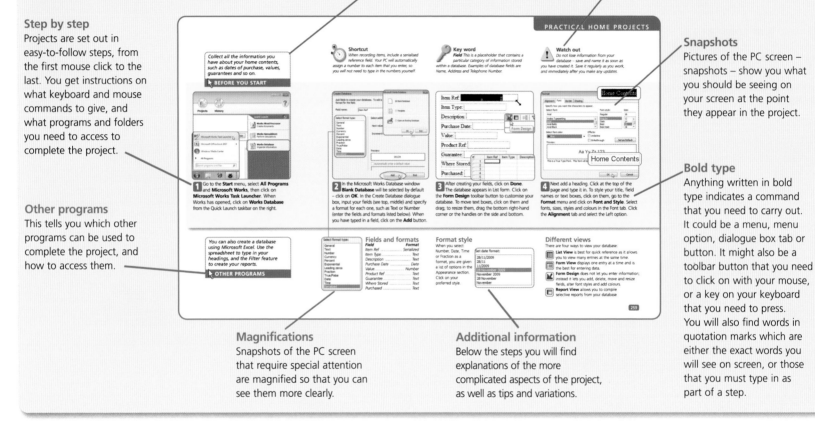

Snapshots
Pictures of the PC screen – snapshots – show you what you should be seeing on your screen at the point they appear in the project.

Bold type
Anything written in bold type indicates a command that you need to carry out. It could be a menu, menu option, dialogue box tab or button. It might also be a toolbar button that you need to click on with your mouse, or a key on your keyboard that you need to press. You will also find words in quotation marks which are either the exact words you will see on screen, or those that you must type in as part of a step.

Magnifications
Snapshots of the PC screen that require special attention are magnified so that you can see them more clearly.

Additional information
Below the steps you will find explanations of the more complicated aspects of the project, as well as tips and variations.

Hints and tips
You will find additional information to help you to complete the task in hand and to improve your understanding of the workings of your PC.

 Shortcut
Look for this symbol for guidance on increasing your efficiency by learning quick and easy ways to complete common tasks.

 Close-up
These offer an insight into the complicated workings of your computer, allowing you to get an idea of what happens 'behind the scenes'.

 Watch out
These warn you about problems that you may encounter, or mistakes you might easily make, as you use your computer.

 Key words
Important words or phrases are defined in order to increase your understanding of the process being addressed on the page.

Bright idea
These are suggestions for variations or additions you can make to a project that can help you adapt it to your specific needs.

Talking to your computer

Your PC is always ready to carry out your orders. You can communicate with it in any of the following ways.

Menus

Some programs, such as Works, have a menu bar sitting across the top of the program window. Clicking on one of the menu options will reveal an extended menu, with many more tasks or functions available. You can then just click on the command you want your PC to perform.

Ribbon

Microsoft Office 2010 has revised the menu format into a 'Ribbon'. This runs across the top of the screen of all

Office programs – including Word and Excel – giving access to commands through different 'tabs'. Clicking on a tab changes the Ribbon to show buttons for a number of associated tasks, collected into 'groups'. Some drop-down menus will still appear where there are a number of options.

Toolbars

Toolbars feature a series of buttons that can be clicked to access frequently used commands. They offer a quick

alternative to using drop-down menus in programs such as Works. The toolbar or toolbars (some programs have several) are located at the top of the program window or on the left-hand side of the screen. To find out what a toolbar button does, place your mouse pointer over it – in most programs a description pops up.

Dialogue boxes

If your computer needs you to make a decision or give it additional information, a box will pop up on your screen asking you to confirm or alter the program's standard settings, or type in some information.

Do so by clicking in the relevant parts of the box, by selecting choices from lists, or by typing in what's required. Some dialogue boxes contain identification tabs, which

you click on to access other, related elements. In Excel's Format Cells dialogue box, there are tabs for Number, Alignment, Font, Border, Fill and Protection. If you click on the Font tab (below) you can select a font, font style, size and colour for your text.

Mouse instructions

You will often be asked to use the buttons on your mouse. These are the terms used:

Click Press and release your left mouse button once.
Double-click Press and release your left mouse button twice in quick succession.
Right-click Press and release your right mouse button once (a pop-up menu will usually appear).
Drag Press your left mouse button and, keeping it pressed down, move your mouse so that your cursor 'drags' across the screen (this is used to highlight text or reshape an object).

Keyboard help

Use your keyboard to take shortcuts to commonly used commands (see page 74 for details). If you are advised to use one of the special 'hot keys' (shown right), you

will often find a picture of the recommended key, such as the one shown left.

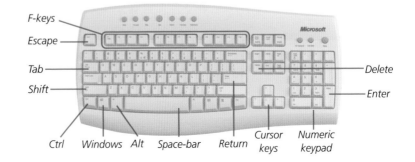

F-keys
Escape
Tab
Shift
Ctrl   Windows   Alt   Space-bar   Return   Cursor keys   Numeric keypad
Delete
Enter

YOU AND YOUR

The better you **understand** your PC, the more you will get out of it. Knowing what each element of the PC does, and how to **set it up** properly, will get you up and running. And good **housekeeping** practices will ensure that your PC functions **efficiently**. Once you master the basics, you will have laid the **foundations** for successful computing.

COMPUTER

Setting up your computer

Your new PC has arrived. Start off on the right foot by setting up your work area properly

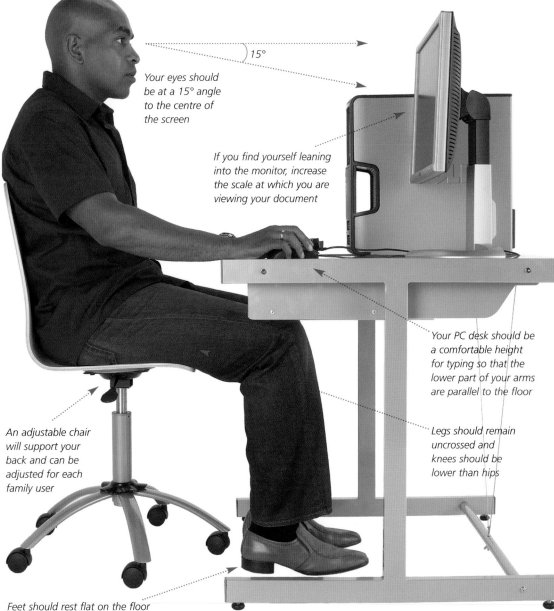

15°

Your eyes should be at a 15° angle to the centre of the screen

If you find yourself leaning into the monitor, increase the scale at which you are viewing your document

Your PC desk should be a comfortable height for typing so that the lower part of your arms are parallel to the floor

An adjustable chair will support your back and can be adjusted for each family user

Legs should remain uncrossed and knees should be lower than hips

Feet should rest flat on the floor

Your computer will be a valuable tool for all the family, so it is worth taking time to plan your computer space and system well, to ensure it is both easy and safe to use.

Ideally, it is best to convert a small room – or a corner of a larger one – into an office so that all the family can use the computer without being disturbed. When selecting an area, check that there is adequate space and several mains sockets, not just for your PC equipment but for a desk lamp too. Unless you have a wireless modem, you will also need to be near a phone socket so that you can connect to the internet.

Set aside some time – 3 to 4 hours – to set up your computer properly. Think carefully about how to arrange your area, as a poorly laid out system will be irritating and may even prevent you from using your computer to the full.

It is a good idea to spend some time reading those manuals, too. You need to know where to plug in the cables!

● *Invest in a proper computer desk. This allows you to alter the height of the monitor and keyboard, and tuck the keyboard away when not in use.*
● *Buy an adjustable chair, which all the family can adjust for good posture and maximum support.*
● *If your feet do not rest comfortably on the ground, buy a footrest.*

COMPUTER FURNITURE

Naming and placing the parts of your computer

Your PC's hardware comprises all the parts that you can actually see and handle. Knowing exactly where to place each of these elements will ensure a safe and efficient work area.

Monitor
This houses the computer screen. Position your monitor to avoid reflections, but do not face a bright window yourself as this may lead to eyestrain.

System unit
This is the part of your computer that connects everything together. Leave space so that you can plug in the cables easily. Do not leave cables trailing.

Mouse
Place the mouse to the left or right of your keyboard to minimise arm movement. Use a mouse mat to create the correct amount of friction for the mouse, and be sure there is room to move the mouse back and forth.

Speakers
Many PCs now have built-in speakers, but if your PC has external speakers you should ensure they are well spaced at desk level or higher, not just pushed under the desk.

Keyboard
Make sure the keyboard is on a stable and level surface within easy reach. Leave enough space in front for hands and wrists. Ensure that the desk is at the correct height.

Printer
Position your printer near the system unit. Make sure there is sufficient space around it for loading the paper trays.

Watch out
Repetitive strain injury *(RSI) is muscle strain due to repeated actions. Home PC users are unlikely to experience problems, but a good posture and typing technique are still essential. When working at your PC, stand up, stretch and move about regularly.*

Hardware and software

Understanding how these operate is key to success

Hardware and software work together to allow you to perform the wide variety of functions possible on your PC.

Hardware is the actual 'body' of the computer system, comprising the system unit and all the elements that you can plug into it, such as the keyboard. Your computer's hardware determines which type of operating system you can use, and so it is not necessarily possible to use one type of system on another computer.

Software is the thinking part, or brain, of your computer, putting all the hardware to work. The most important piece of software on your computer is the operating system. By translating your instructions into a language that the hardware can understand, the operating system lets you communicate with various computer parts and control how

the computer and its accessories work. Microsoft® Windows® is the most popular operating system for PCs. An operating system is so important to the workings of a computer that, without one, you cannot open any files, use a printer or see anything on the screen.

Your computer also needs to use specialised software, called programs, to perform specific functions, such as writing letters, editing a report, playing a computer game or keeping a check on your household spending. There are thousands of programs available, each designed to perform different, sometimes specialised, tasks. These programs enable you to do almost anything, from writing formal letters and compiling spreadsheets, to editing your digital imagery and even making your own films.

Other types of computer

Apple Macintosh computers, or Macs, work in a similar way to PCs in that you access documents through a desktop. Although some programs, such as Microsoft® Word, are available for both Macs and PCs, the two versions are different and cannot be run on the other operating system.

Swapping files between PCs and Macs can sometimes be difficult as older files do not always translate very well.

Introducing your software

Understanding what software does will help you to get the most out of your PC. This introduction describes the operating system and the different types of program available.

The operating system

The most vital piece of software, the operating system allows you to interact with the computer's hardware. It manages the saving of files on the hard disk, translates commands given through the keyboard and mouse, and sends data to the screen or printer. It also interacts with other programs you may be running, allowing them to communicate with the hardware.

Any software packages you use rely on the operating system to provide this basic level of hardware communication. Most new PCs are supplied with Windows 7 as their operating system. Earlier versions include Windows Vista and Windows XP.

Which program?

SPREADSHEET PROGRAM

For making complex budget calculations and carrying out financial analysis you can use a spreadsheet program. This program can also show figures as a chart or graph, making it easier to understand.

WORD-PROCESSING PROGRAM

To write letters, reports or other documents that are mainly text-based, use a word-processing program or the word-processing tool in software suites (see below). Most include a range of fonts and style features and allow you to insert pictures.

GRAPHICS PROGRAM

To work with pictures, use a graphics program. This will help you to create greetings cards, invitations, posters and personal stationery. You can use the graphic galleries available on your PC or from CD-ROM galleries. You can also use your own photographs.

DATABASE PROGRAM

To make address lists, or lists of contact details, use a database program. Software suites often have a database tool, or you can use a separate database program for more complex work.

GAMES PROGRAM

Playing with games is an entertaining way of becoming more adept on the computer. You usually have to buy each game program separately, although some systems come with some simple games included.

OTHER PROGRAMS

Whether you want to access the web and send email, install specialist financial software or edit your digital photos, there are many specialist programs available to suit your needs.

Key words

Software suite *A software suite incorporates the basic aspects of several programs in one package. While their components may not be as powerful or as versatile as individual programs, low-cost suites such as Microsoft Works offer value for money and let you perform many useful tasks.*

Storing software on your hard disk

All software, whether it be the operating system or programs, uses storage space on your hard disk. This space is measured in terms of 'bits' and 'bytes'.

A bit is the smallest unit of computer storage. A combination of eight bits makes up a byte.

A kilobyte (Kb) is 1,024 bytes; a megabyte (Mb) is 1,024 Kb; and a gigabyte (Gb) is 1,024 Mb.

A typical home computer will have about 500Gb of hard disk space. This space is soon used up – the Microsoft Office suite alone can use several hundred megabytes of disk space, while Microsoft Works uses around 60Mb.

Making the most of hardware

Get the most out of your PC **by** understanding **the purpose of** each part

Once you have unpacked your PC and set up the different hardware elements, it is worth taking the time to get to know exactly what each part does.

All PCs contain the same basic elements. Knowing how they fit together and operate as a unit – and understanding where you fit into the picture – will help you and your family to get the most out of home computing. Your computer is simply a tool that, if it is given the correct instructions and data, will make your day-to-day life easier and more enjoyable. You enter instructions and information into the computer via the mouse and keyboard. The results can be seen on your monitor's screen and printed out on your printer. The most important part of the computer – the system unit – links all these elements together.

Whatever make of computer you have, it will have these same key components that allow you to use it. Although most computers look similar, there are variations between models, so always check instructions in the computer manual to make sure you are using your equipment correctly.

The mouse

A mouse is used to select items on screen and move the text cursor (a flashing line that identifies where new text appears). You move the mouse around with your hand and a mouse pointer moves around on the screen, allowing you to select menus and click on commands.

The monitor

Your monitor is home to the computer screen, which shows you what your computer is doing. Monitor screens come in different sizes – in the interests of preventing eyestrain, the bigger the better. LCD (liquid crystal display) flat screens take up less space and can give much sharper pictures than older CRT (cathode ray tube) designs.

The keyboard

A keyboard is used for typing in data and commands, and has the familiar typewriter keys plus a number of extra ones. On the right is a separate numeric keypad, plus navigation keys (with arrows) that help you to move around the screen. There is also a series of function keys along the top that allow you to give special commands.

Watch out

Always use the Shut Down command from the Start menu before turning the power switch off. Never turn the power switch off when Windows is running. Most newer PCs automatically switch off power when shutting down.

Bright idea

If environmental issues are a concern for you, look out for 'green' hardware. Some manufacturers have used plastics and packaging in their computer systems that can be recycled.

The system unit

This is where all the cables plug in. Your system unit will contain disk drives such as a CD-ROM drive. In new PCs, a CD-RW drive and perhaps a DVD-RW drive may be included.

Optical drive
Your PC has a CD-ROM and/or a DVD-ROM drive. Use it to install new software, and play music CDs or DVD movies. You may also have a CD-RW and/or DVD-RW for saving files.

USB (Universal Serial Bus) ports
Ports on the front of a PC make it easier to connect devices.

Integrated sound ports
You can connect a microphone, headphones and speakers to these ports.

Power switch
This is used to turn your PC on. Some much older PCs also use this button to switch off.

Power-in socket
This is used to connect the PC to the mains supply.

Serial ports
Older PCs may have serial ports to connect the mouse, keyboard and an external modem to the PC.

Integrated sound ports
If you have speakers, a microphone or headphones with colour-coded plugs, they can be connected to these colour-coded ports. There may be other ports elsewhere on your PC for this equipment.

USB ports
Use these ports to connect items such as music players, scanners, cameras and joysticks. They are also used to connect a mouse, keyboard and an external modem, if you have one. There may also be convenient extra ports on the front of your PC.

Printer (or parallel) port
On older PCs this provides the connection to the printer, although most now use USB ports.

PC expansion card slots
The ports here let you connect other devices, such as speakers and monitors, to expansion cards fitted inside the PC.

All-in-one devices

If you are buying a printer, you might consider an all-in-one device (AIO). This combines the job of several different hardware devices – a printer, a photocopier, a scanner and a fax machine. Some can also print directly from digital cameras. Not only do AIOs save on space and avoid the messy and confusing jumble of connecting cables, they produce good-quality printouts at relatively fast printing speeds and are easy to set up and use.

Laptop computers

All the components of a laptop computer are in a single unit. The screen is smaller and not as bright as on a desktop computer. The keyboard is smaller and does not have the extra keys. The mouse is built-in, as a tiny joystick or touchpad.

Laptops can be powered from the mains or by a rechargeable battery, but do not expect more than six hours of use from a single charge.

Starting up your computer

You have set it all up – now switch on and begin using your PC

Once your computer's been set up properly, you are ready to get going – so remember to make sure it is switched on at the mains.

Turn on the computer via the power switch on the system unit. You also need to turn on the monitor. The Windows 7 logo then appears above a set of scrolling green lights, showing that the computer is checking itself over. After a few moments you will see the Logon screen. Click on your username (you will need to enter a password if you use one). After a few moments you will see a colour screen that Windows calls the Desktop. Small pictures, or icons, will appear on the Desktop, and you may also see a message asking if you would like to find out about new features.

The Desktop icons

Through the Desktop icons you can access important utilities and all your work. To open an icon place your mouse pointer over the top of it and double-click with the left mouse button.

 In Windows 7, click on the Start button to see the **Start Menu**. This contains links to all of your programs, files, photographs and music, and to system utilities and help text. The programs and files you use most often have their own links. Despite its name, the Start menu is also the place to go if you want to lock your computer, turn it off, or switch to another user. When you first start Windows 7, you will see at least one icon on your Desktop, the Recycle Bin. Your PC manufacturer may have added others.

 Recycle Bin is where files or folders are moved for deletion. The bin can be emptied for permanent deletion or items retrieved if you made a mistake.

 Computer shows you all your computer's disks (hard drive and CD/DVD drive).

Documents leads to a folder that you can use to store any files you create.

 Network allows you to access and view other computers connected to your own.

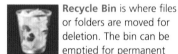

The Windows **Taskbar** is the area that, by default, is located at the bottom of your screen and contains taskbar buttons. It is divided loosely into three areas. On the left is always the Start button followed by the Quick Launch toolbar containing shortcuts to your favourite programs, such as Microsoft Internet Explorer. On the right is the notification area, containing a clock and icons giving access to programs and important status information. As you open new windows, they will appear as buttons in the middle of the Taskbar, so you can always see what is open, even when other windows cover them.

Basic window features

Programs and files are displayed inside a window, and your computer can display several windows at once. This key will help you to find your way around.

Address bar
This shows you where you are, and also allows you access to other files and folders.

Minimise button
This reduces the window to an icon on the Taskbar.

Maximise button
This enlarges the window to fill the screen. Click on it again to return it to its original size.

Title bar
This displays the name of the window. To move the window, click on the Title bar and, with the left mouse button pressed down, move the mouse pointer across the computer screen. This is called 'dragging'.

Close button
This closes the window.

Scroll bars
To view any hidden contents of a window, click on the arrows at the ends of the scroll bar or click on and drag the slide bar up.

Menu bar
This contains drop-down menus through which you issue commands.

Window borders
To resize windows, place the mouse pointer over the window's border. When the pointer changes to a double-headed arrow, hold down the left mouse button and drag the window into the size you require.

Toolbar
Toolbar buttons provide shortcuts to common commands.

Status bar
This gives information about the contents of the window.

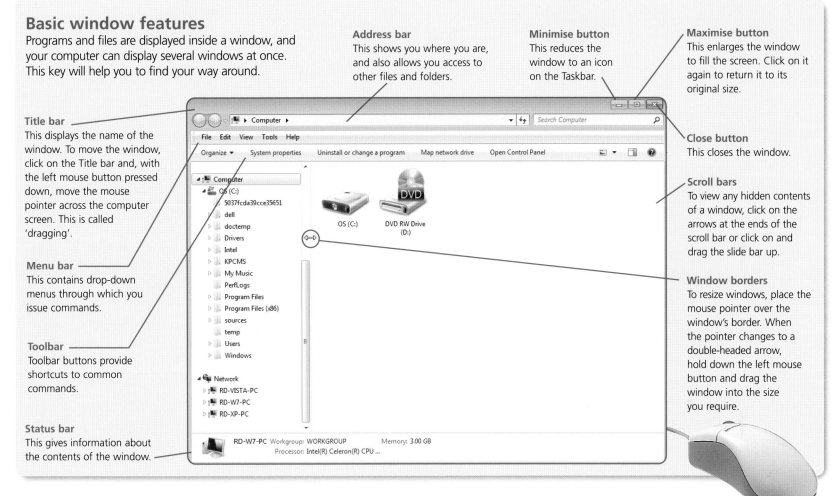

Desktop gadgets

Desktop Gadgets
Add gadgets to the desktop
Get more gadgets online │ Uninstall a gadget
Restore desktop gadgets installed with Windows

Windows 7 has a series of mini-programs, called Desktop Gadgets, that you can add to the Desktop. To view available gadgets go to the **Start** button and click on **Control Panel**, **Appearance and Personalization** and then click on **Desktop Gadgets**. The Desktop Gadget Gallery displays a set of standard gadgets to install. With the gallery open, double-click on a gadget to add it to the Desktop. The gadget will appear on the right-hand side of the desktop but you can reposition it anywhere you like by clicking and dragging on its handle.

Using the mouse

Once your computer is switched on, you can really see how the mouse works. Moving the mouse on your desk moves the mouse pointer on screen.

Place your mouse pointer over an icon and a box will appear telling you what the icon does. When you want to look 'inside' an icon, press the left mouse button twice quickly. This is known as 'double-clicking'. The double-click principle applies to the opening of programs or files.

An introduction to programs

Improve your skills **more** quickly **by getting to** know your PC's programs

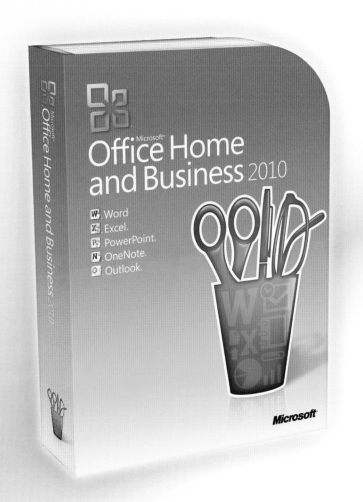

Windows, the operating system, helps to connect each element of your PC together, but cannot perform practical tasks such as letter writing and calculating your bills. For these jobs you need to use additional software – called applications, or programs – which is designed to carry out specific tasks.

Personal computers are often bought with a varied package of programs already installed – known as bundled software or software suites. Two of the most popular packages are Microsoft® Works and Microsoft® Office.

Your package explained

Works, a package of 'mini-programs' grouped together, offers you tools to perform most of the tasks you might want to carry out on a home computer, and it also includes many pre-set documents, known as templates, that you can customise for your own purposes (you are given step-by-step guidance on how to do this).

Works Suite is an expanded version of Works. It uses Word as its word processor, and contains some extra programs, such as an encyclopedia.

Office comprises several individual programs – Word, Outlook®, PowerPoint® and Excel. The more sophisticated capabilities of each of these programs, compared with their equivalent in Works, means that they can be used to produce a wider range of documents. Because they are more advanced, together they use up more of your hard disk space than Works. You will find templates available for both Office and Works.

Understanding your software suite

Knowing what each program in your software package can do will help you to decide which will be the most appropriate for the tasks you want to perform.

Microsoft Office

 Word is an extremely powerful word processor, which is able to produce 'written' documents of all kinds, including letters, memos, newsletters and posters. You have the option to create documents from scratch or, for many types of document, to use one of the program's templates. Templates have a preset layout into which you enter your own text. This is a much quicker and easier way to create new documents.

 Excel is a spreadsheet program, used for organising and calculating numerical data. It is ideal for keeping track of all types of budgets and accounts. Like all spreadsheets, it takes the form of a grid containing 'cells' into which you input figures and formulas to make calculations. Excel allows you to have several spreadsheets, or 'worksheets', within the same document, and enter calculations using figures from each of the worksheets. This is particularly useful when organising, say, a major event that comprises mini-projects. Once data is entered, you can then select, or 'filter', specific information to analyse.

Excel can also produce a range of charts and graphs that can be used to illustrate your spreadsheet figures.

These are particularly useful as they simplify complicated numerical information, presenting it in a clear, easily understandable manner.

 Outlook is an 'information management' program. It contains an address book into which you can enter contact details for friends, family and business associates. It also has a diary and calendar that helps you to keep track of your current schedule and forthcoming appointments. Outlook can also be used to send and receive emails through the internet or through an internal company network (intranet).

 PowerPoint is most often used in business. It enables you to create presentations for conferences, company meetings and marketing projects. It gives you the means to structure information efficiently and incorporate graphics within your text. It even offers animation effects to maximise the impact of your presentation. You can create notes for your own use in addition to handouts for your audience.

As well as being a useful business tool, PowerPoint can also be used at home to make a computerised slideshow for your friends and family.

Microsoft Works

 Word Processor allows you to create a range of word-based documents, and has many templates to help you to design pages. It is similar to Microsoft Word, but slightly less sophisticated – for instance, Word allows you to add colours and borders to text boxes needed to create business cards.

Calendar lets you keep track of appointments, important dates, birthdays and anniversaries. It integrates with the Works **Address Book**, so that you can be reminded automatically about a friend's birthday, for example.

 Spreadsheet allows you to monitor and analyse numerical data. It also offers a number of templates for common documents such as household bills, invoices and accounts, which you can customise and use.

Database is ideal for recording details about related items. For example, you can record details of your household contents. Using its ReportCreator function you can sort and group selected information (say, to update your household insurance), perform calculations and add some explanatory notes.

Accessory programs

Accessories are small programs within Windows that perform specific tasks. Your computer will almost certainly contain a calculator, a drawing program (Paint), simple games and a basic word-processing program (WordPad).

To open an accessory program, click on the **Start** button, then on **All Programs** and then **Accessories**. Click on the program you want to use.

Windows Easy Transfer

This mini-program is used for transferring files, folders and program settings from one computer to another. Use this step-by-step process to move user accounts, internet favourites, email settings, contacts and messages.

To open Windows Easy Transfer, click on the **Start** button, then on **Getting Started**, and then **Transfer your files**.

In the Windows Easy Transfer window, click on **Next**, select a transfer method to use: An Easy Transfer Cable; A Network (wired or wireless); An external hard disk or USB flash drive. Make your selection and follow the on-screen prompts.

Getting around a document

Learn how to open a program and navigate around the screen

Opening a program and creating a new document will be among the first things you do on your computer. The process is similar in most programs. The steps are the same whether you are using a spreadsheet, database or word-processing program.

All programs can be accessed by clicking on the **Start** button on the Taskbar that runs along the bottom of the screen, then clicking on **All Programs** in the menu that pops up. Another menu appears listing all the programs on your system. Click on the program you want to open. The program opens and a blank document appears. You can now start typing.

Before you do this, it is useful to understand the different parts of the window. The window shown below is from the Microsoft Word word-processing program.

Inputting commands

Whichever program you are using, you input commands using your mouse and keyboard. These commands might relate to the look of the document or to the material it contains.

The mouse

Your mouse is the best way to access command options through the 'Ribbon' in Office programs (see opposite) or through menus and toolbars in Works documents or in Windows Explorer. To activate items on screen (a button on the Ribbon, for example), use the mouse to move the cursor over them and press your left mouse button down then release it (a process known as 'clicking').

If you are asked to 'click', press and release the left mouse button once; to 'double-click', press and release the left mouse button twice in quick succession.

If you are asked to 'drag' (you will do this to move items on the screen or to select text), press the left mouse button and, holding it down, move your mouse. As you do so, a section of text will become highlighted, or the on-screen item you clicked on will also move. When the relevant text is selected, or the item has moved to the correct position, release the mouse button.

'Right-clicking' – that is, clicking with the right mouse button – anywhere on screen will activate a pop-up menu offering formatting functions and other options. Click on an option to activate or open it.

The keyboard

Typing in text and data is the most obvious use of the keyboard. But it is also possible to issue commands by using special combinations of keys (these keyboard commands are discussed on page 74).

You can also use the arrow keys at the bottom of your keyboard to move the cursor around within a document. Most people find this more laborious than using the mouse, though.

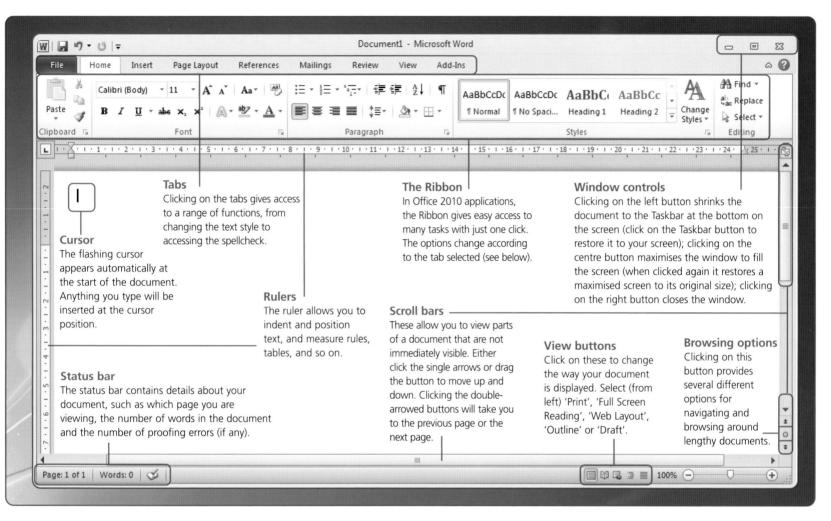

Tabs
Clicking on the tabs gives access to a range of functions, from changing the text style to accessing the spellcheck.

Cursor
The flashing cursor appears automatically at the start of the document. Anything you type will be inserted at the cursor position.

Rulers
The ruler allows you to indent and position text, and measure rules, tables, and so on.

Status bar
The status bar contains details about your document, such as which page you are viewing, the number of words in the document and the number of proofing errors (if any).

The Ribbon
In Office 2010 applications, the Ribbon gives easy access to many tasks with just one click. The options change according to the tab selected (see below).

Scroll bars
These allow you to view parts of a document that are not immediately visible. Either click the single arrows or drag the button to move up and down. Clicking the double-arrowed buttons will take you to the previous page or the next page.

Window controls
Clicking on the left button shrinks the document to the Taskbar at the bottom on the screen (click on the Taskbar button to restore it to your screen); clicking on the centre button maximises the window to fill the screen (when clicked again it restores a maximised screen to its original size); clicking on the right button closes the window.

View buttons
Click on these to change the way your document is displayed. Select (from left) 'Print', 'Full Screen Reading', 'Web Layout', 'Outline' or 'Draft'.

Browsing options
Clicking on this button provides several different options for navigating and browsing around lengthy documents.

Using the Ribbon

Office 2010 no longer uses toolbars and menus to access commands, although these features are still present in Works. The new versions of Office's popular programs, including Word, Excel and Powerpoint, instead feature the 'Ribbon'.

The Ribbon only presents options that relate to the object currently selected. The functions displayed therefore change depending upon the tab chosen – 'Insert' or 'View', for example – and will also change as different items, such as a table or paragraph, are selected.

The buttons on the Ribbon are grouped by similar functions. Click on the buttons to access commands or click on the small arrow at the bottom of a group – called a dialogue box launcher – to see extra options. When you start using Office 2010, the Ribbon's one-click functions will quickly become second nature.

23

The basics of word processing

Learn the essentials of working with text in documents

Once you have opened a new document in Word, Office 2010's word-processing program, you can start typing in text. The great advantage that computers have over typewriters is that they allow you to revise and refine your text as much as you wish. You can also adjust the appearance of your text, its size, shape, colour and position on the page, and the spacing between individual letters, words and lines. You can even add special effects such as shadows. This is known as 'formatting'.

Becoming familiar with the terms used in word processing, and the basics of working with text, will enable you to create and modify documents with ease.

Setting up your document

Before you start typing you should set up the page as you need it. To do this, click on the **Page Layout** tab, then click on **Orientation** and select **Portrait** or **Landscape**. You can then click on **Size** and choose the paper size from the drop-down menu. Finally, click on **Margins** and amend the settings if you need to, then click on **OK**.

Typing in text

> I would like to raise several points:
> • Seventy people have confirmed that they are
> • Twenty people have confirmed that they are
> • Four people have yet to respond

To enter text, just type on the keyboard. As you type, the words will appear at the cursor position on your screen. When you reach the end of a line, the text will automatically flow on to the next line. To start typing on a new line before reaching the end of the current one, press the **Return** key on your keyboard and continue to type.

Highlighting text

To format a section of text, you first need to select, or 'highlight', it. To do this, place your cursor just before the relevant section and

> Maureen Brooks
> 58 Somerfield Close
> Aldershot
> Hampshire

press and release your left mouse button once (this is called 'clicking'). Press the mouse button again and, keeping it pressed down, move the mouse to the right (this is called 'dragging'). As you do this the text appears in a blue bar. Release the mouse button once the relevant text is highlighted.

To highlight all the text in a document, press the **Ctrl** key and, keeping it pressed down, press the '**A**' key.

Formatting the text

Once text is highlighted it is ready to format, or style. Go to the **Home** tab and click on the **Font** dialogue box launcher (see 'Using the Ribbon' below). Many of Word's formatting options can also be quickly accessed on the Office 2010 'Ribbon'.

Fonts

Your word-processing program offers a range of fonts (particular styles of type).

Brush Script

Impact

Perpetua

To view the list of fonts, click on the arrows (this is called 'scrolling'). Click on your choice of font (it becomes highlighted).

Colour

To alter the colour of text, click on the arrow next to the 'Font color' box, scroll through the colours and click on your choice. But

You can choose a whole range of different colours

remember that using too many colours on one page can be overpowering.

Effects

You will be presented with a number of special effects that you can apply to text.

Shadow

Outline

Engrave

To choose one, click in the relevant box (a tick will appear). Click the box again to remove the effect.

Preview

The Preview pane shows you how your choices of font, size and effects will look.

OK

Click on **OK** to apply your formatting changes to the highlighted text.

Font style

Once you have chosen a font, select a font style for it. Typically, you can choose whether your text appears in a regular format, or in italics or bold. To select a font style, click on your choice from the 'Font style' box.

Regular
Italic
Bold

Size

The size of text is measured in 'points' (pts). The greater the point size, the larger the text. Point sizes, though, are not uniform across all fonts, which means that 10pt text in one font may be taller than, say, 12pt text in another font. To alter a point size, scroll through and click on your choice in the 'Size' box. A good rule of thumb is not to use text smaller than 8pt, as it becomes difficult to read.

Underline

You can underline text in a number of ways. Click on the arrow next to the 'Underline style' box, scroll through the options and click on your choice. If you do not want text to be underlined ensure **(none)** is selected.

Dotted
Words only
Wave

Using the Ribbon

Most of the styling options shown above also appear in the 'Font' group that sits under the **Home** tab. The tools within the 'Font' group can be accessed with just one click – often launching a pop-up menu to choose from. If you would like to make a number of changes, it might be quicker to launch the Font dialogue box – click on the small arrow at the bottom right of the 'Font' group.

To style your text, first highlight it and then click on the appropriate button on the Ribbon. (To see what a button does, place your mouse pointer over the button – a small box describing its function pops up.) Buttons for changing text size, alignment and colour can all be found on the Ribbon. You can also change the font – select your text and click on the arrow by the font name. Hover over a font name and your text changes on the page.

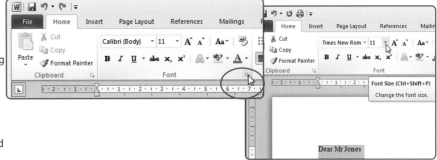

Laying out your document

Word allows you to adjust the structure of your documents, making them easier to read and drawing attention to important information.

Adding borders

To add a border around a section of text to give it definition, highlight the relevant text (here, the company address) then go to the 'Paragraph' group under the **Home** tab and click on the arrow beside the **Border** button. Click on your choice of style.

Paragraph indents

A simple way to distinguish where each new paragraph begins is to indent its first line. Click in the paragraph, then launch the Paragraph dialogue box by clicking on the arrow at the bottom right of the 'Paragraph' group. Click on the arrow beside the 'Special' box and select **First line**. In the 'By' box set the space required then click on **OK**. You can indent entire paragraphs by highlighting them and clicking on the **Increase indent** button within the 'Paragraph' group.

Bullets and numbers

To make lists easier to read, add a bullet point or number before each item. Highlight the list then click on the **Bullets** or **Numbering** button under the 'Paragraph' group. The Numbering button will number points sequentially.

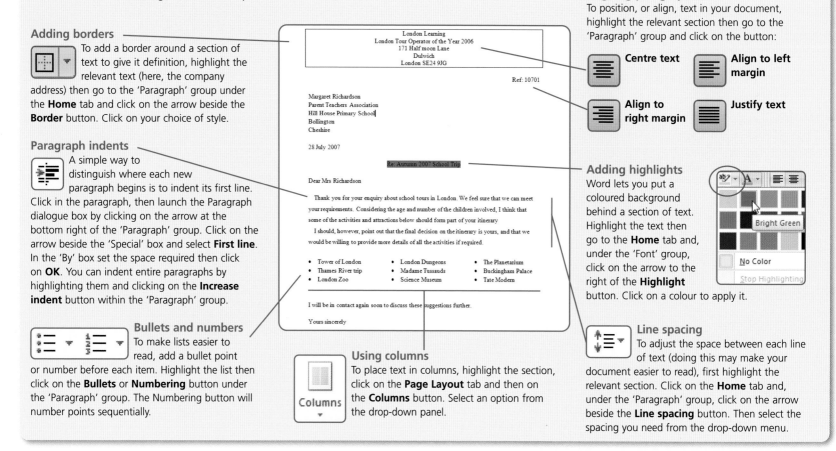

London Learning
London Tour Operator of the Year 2006
171 Half moon Lane
Dulwich
London SE24 9JG

Ref: 10701

Margaret Richardson
Parent Teachers Association
Hill House Primary School
Bollington
Cheshire

28 July 2007

Re: Autumn 2007 School Trip

Dear Mrs Richardson

Thank you for your enquiry about school tours in London. We feel sure that we can meet your requirements. Considering the age and number of the children involved, I think that some of the activities and attractions below should form part of your itinerary

I should, however, point out that the final decision on the itinerary is yours, and that we would be willing to provide more details of all the activities if required.

- Tower of London
- Thames River trip
- London Zoo
- London Dungeons
- Madame Tussauds
- Science Museum
- The Planetarium
- Buckingham Palace
- Tate Modern

I will be in contact again soon to discuss these suggestions further.

Yours sincerely

Aligning paragraphs

To position, or align, text in your document, highlight the relevant section then go to the 'Paragraph' group and click on the button:

Centre text

Align to left margin

Align to right margin

Justify text

Adding highlights

Word lets you put a coloured background behind a section of text. Highlight the text then go to the **Home** tab and, under the 'Font' group, click on the arrow to the right of the **Highlight** button. Click on a colour to apply it.

Bright Green

No Color

Stop Highlighting

Line spacing

To adjust the space between each line of text (doing this may make your document easier to read), first highlight the relevant section. Click on the **Home** tab and, under the 'Paragraph' group, click on the arrow beside the **Line spacing** button. Then select the spacing you need from the drop-down menu.

Using columns

Columns

To place text in columns, highlight the section, click on the **Page Layout** tab and then on the **Columns** button. Select an option from the drop-down panel.

What if I make a mistake?

Undo Typing (Ctrl+Z)

Repeat Typing (Ctrl+Y)

If you make a mistake, click on the **Undo** button on the Quick Access toolbar. You can continue to click on it to undo previous commands. If you undo an action that you then want to redo, click on the **Redo** button. (In Works, you can undo the 100 previous commands. Go to the **Edit** menu and click on **Undo** or **Redo**.)

Moving or copying text

File   Home   Inse

Cut

Copy

Paste

Format Painter

Clipboard

To move a section of text, go to the **Home** tab and use the buttons in the 'Clipboard' group. Highlight your text and click on the **Cut** button. The text will disappear. Position the cursor where you want the text to reappear, click once, then click on the **Paste** button – the text will reappear in your document in its new position.

To copy a section of text so that it appears more than once in a document (you can also copy text from one document to another), highlight it and then click on the **Copy** button. Position the cursor and click where you want the text to appear, then click on the **Paste** button.

Finishing touches

Once you have finished formatting and laying out your document, it is a good idea to check it for spelling and grammatical errors. Also, you can now add extra features, such as headers and footers.

Spelling and grammar check

Vennison Stew with Orange

Preparation Time: 20 mins plus
Cooking time: 1 hour

When you type in text, some words may appear with a wavy red or green line underneath. A red line indicates a possible spelling error; a green line indicates a possible grammatical error. When you have finished typing your document, go to the **Review** tab and click on **Spelling and Grammar**, or press the **F7** key.

Your PC scans your document, selecting the underlined words for you to check and suggesting how to correct the 'error'. If you do not agree with any of the suggested changes, click on **Ignore Once** or **Ignore All**; if you agree, click on the relevant suggestion, then on **Change**.

Thesaurus

The Thesaurus function helps you to find alternatives to repeated words, and suggestions for more suitable words. To do this, highlight the word you would like to find an alternative for, go to the **Review** tab and click on **Thesaurus** (in Works, click directly on **Thesaurus**). Or, press the **Shift** key and, keeping it pressed down, the **F7** key.

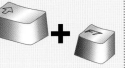

In the column on the right you will see a list of alternatives. Click on the word you want to use, then click on the arrow to the right of it and select **Insert**. In Works, you will see a dialogue box when you click on Thesaurus. Select a replacement word and then click on **Replace**.

Counting your words

If you are writing a long article or essay, it can be useful to know how many words you have written. Go to the **Review** tab and in the 'Proofing' group click on **Word Count**. Word will also count the pages, paragraphs and even characters used. (In Works, you are given a total word count for your document, including footnotes, headers and footers.)

Word Count	
Statistics:	
Pages	6
Words	2,545
Characters (no spaces)	12,398
Characters (with spaces)	14,921
Paragraphs	38
Lines	174

☑ Include textboxes, footnotes and endnotes

Close

Headers and footers

Word-processing documents can include a section at the top and bottom of each page – known as headers and footers, respectively. Text entered into these sections automatically appears on each new page of your document. This is useful if you want to include a title at the top of each page or a date or page number at the bottom. To add a header or footer in Word, click on the **Insert** tab and go to the 'Header and Footer' group. Click on **Header** and/or **Footer** and choose from the pre-formatted templates in the list.

How To Do Just About Anything on a Computer – Windows 7 Edition

Header

Footer

Page 1

In Works, click on **Header and Footer** from the **View** menu. Type your text into the 'Header' box and add any repeating text in the 'Footer' box. Then click **Close**.

Spelling and Grammar: English (U.K.)

Not in Dictionary:

Vennison stew with orange

Ignore Once
Ignore All
Add to Dictionary

Suggestions:

Venison

Change
Change All
AutoCorrect

☑ Check grammar

Options... Undo Cancel

Research

Search for:
happily

Thesaurus: English (U.K.)

Back

▲ Thesaurus: English (U.K.)

▲ luckily (adv.)
luckily
fortunately
thankfully
opportunely
well
favourably
as good luck would have it (Dictionary Form)
sadly (Antonym)

Templates

Office 2010 has built-in and online templates to help you to construct quickly a professional-looking document. Click on the **File** tab and then on **New**. Under 'Available Templates' select an existing template or a category from Office.com. Click on a category to display its options, make your selection, then click on **Download** to use the template.

In Works, click on **Templates** and select a category from the left pane to see options in the right. (If a sub-category appears, make a further selection.) Then click on **Use this style** to finish. You are now ready to create your document from the template.

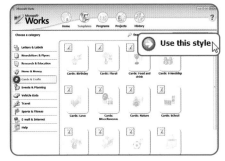

Figuring out spreadsheets

Learn how to use spreadsheets for financial planning and budgeting

Of all the computer functions, spreadsheets are the hardest to get to grips with. But a small investment of time and effort will soon pay dividends, because once you have the hang of them, spreadsheets can perform complex financial calculations. You can, for example, set up a spreadsheet to work out the true cost of running your car, including such invisible outlay as depreciation and wear and tear. All you have to do is 'explain' the task to the program once: it will do all the arithmetic for you, month after month, year on year.

Opening a new spreadsheet

This book deals with the two most widely used spreadsheet programs: Microsoft Excel and the spreadsheet tool in Microsoft Works. To open a document in either program, go to the **Start** button and select **All Programs** then **Microsoft Office Excel 2010** or **Microsoft Works**.

If you open Excel, a new blank document will automatically appear on screen. If you open Works, the Works Task Launcher will open. Click on the **Programs** tab, then on **Works Spreadsheet** button, then on **Start a blank Spreadsheet**.

Using templates

Microsoft Excel provides a number of templates that you can use to create your own spreadsheet. When you open a new document, click on the **Templates** button to see those available. Some will have been supplied within your Office 2010 software, but the majority need to be downloaded for free from the Microsoft Office Online website.

Saving your document

After opening a new document in Excel, click on the **File** tab and select **Save As**. In the Save As dialogue box, select a folder in which to save your document, give it a name and then click on **Save**. In Works, go to the **File** menu and click on **Save As**. The Save As dialogue box appears. Click on the arrow at the side of the 'Save in' box and scroll down to select a folder in which to save your document. Enter a file name, then click on **Save**.

Finding your way around

Identifying the various elements of your spreadsheet document will help you to navigate around it more easily, and so use it more effectively. Most elements are the same for all spreadsheet programs.

Understanding spreadsheets

A spreadsheet is a grid of 'cells'. The columns are like the columns in a ledger – you can use them to make lists of figures and perform calculations. Each column is identified by a letter of the alphabet, and each row by a number. So every cell has its own unique address, comprising the letter of the column and the number of the row it is in (A1, A2 and so on). You can type numbers, text or formulas into these cells. The formulas make it possible to get the program to do all the complicated and laborious arithmetic for you.

Using the Formula bar to input data

When you first open a spreadsheet, cell A1 is automatically selected as the 'active cell' – indicated by a thick black line around the cell – and you can type directly into it. To make entries into other cells, click on them first. As you make entries, they will appear in the Formula bar located below the toolbars. You can view and edit the contents of a cell in the Formula bar.

To the left of the Formula bar are two buttons (marked 'X' and '✔') that only appear after you type something in. If you make a mistake in your entry, click on the **X** button to cancel it; if it is correct, click on the ✔ button to enter it (or press the **Return** or **Tab** keys).

What you can see

Spreadsheets look quite complicated, but once you understand how they work and how to find your way around them, they are easy to use. The documents displayed here are from Microsoft Excel. The main difference between these and Works documents is that there are fewer toolbar options in Works.

When using spreadsheets, the mouse pointer becomes a thick white cross, rather than the normal arrowhead you will see elsewhere.

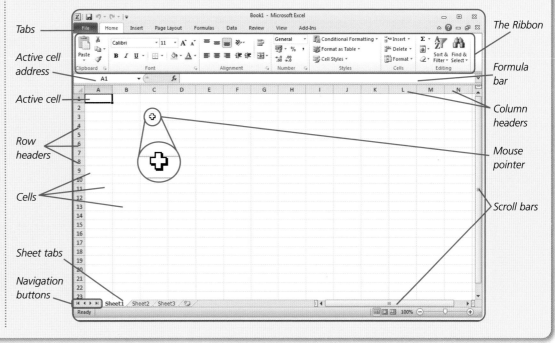

Tabs · Active cell address · Active cell · Row headers · Cells · Sheet tabs · Navigation buttons · The Ribbon · Formula bar · Column headers · Mouse pointer · Scroll bars

=B3*C3

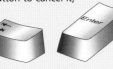

Moving around a spreadsheet

You can move from one cell to the next in several ways. You can either click on the next cell using your mouse, navigate to the cell you want using the four arrow keys on your keyboard, or press the **Tab** key. To move to a previous cell, press the **Shift** key and, keeping it pressed down, the **Tab** key.

In Excel, unless you want to move to a new row, do not press the **Return** key, as this will activate the cell below the one you are currently in.

Selecting cells

You can select cells for styling, cutting and copying in several ways. To select a column or row of cells, click on the blue column or row header. To select cells that are adjacent to each other, click on the first cell and, keeping the left mouse button pressed down, drag the cursor across or down the screen until the entire range of cells is selected, then release the mouse button.

If the cells you want to select are not adjacent, but are dotted throughout the spreadsheet, press the **Ctrl** key on your keyboard and, keeping it pressed down, click on each of the cells in turn.

Tips for using spreadsheets effectively

When you are dealing with numbers, it pays to give some thought to how to lay out the spreadsheet. When you type in information, be as careful as possible.

Adding titles and headings

To make it easier to identify your spreadsheet and navigate around it, it is helpful to enter a title at the top of the sheet, and to give separate headings to columns and rows. To do this, click on a cell and type in your text.

Adjusting column widths

If an entry is too long for its cell, adjust the width of the column. Place your mouse pointer over the right-hand edge of the blue column header. When it becomes a double-headed arrow, press the left mouse button and, keeping it pressed down, drag it to the desired width. Release the mouse button. You can make the column automatically adjust to include the widest entry in any of its cells by placing the mouse pointer in the same position and double-clicking.

Locking row and column headings

Often, column and row headings can disappear off screen when you scroll through large spreadsheets, making it difficult to keep track of which figures relate to what. To keep the headings viewable at all times, drag the small button at the top of the scroll bar down. This splits the worksheet into two independent panes, one to house the headings, one for the rest of the spreadsheet.

Enter identical data in multiple cells

To enter the same data into adjacent cells in a row or column – or common data that has a set sequence, such as the months of the year or days of the week – use the Fill function. Type an entry into the first cell. Place the mouse pointer in the lower right-hand corner of the cell. When it becomes a small black cross, press the left mouse button, keep it pressed and drag it over the cells you'd like filled. Release the mouse. To enter the same number into several columns and rows at once, select the cells and type in the number. Now press the **Ctrl** key and, with it, the **Return** key.

Moving and copying data

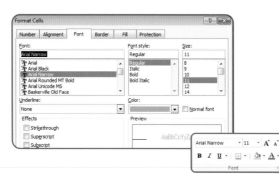

To move data, use the Cut, Copy and Paste commands found under the **Home** tab. Highlight the cells you want to place elsewhere (the source range). To remove the source range, click on the **Cut** button (left). The cells become selected. To leave the source range in its position and copy it, click on the **Copy** button (middle) instead. Now click on the top left-hand cell of the position where you want the moved information to appear (the target range). Click on the **Paste** button (right).

Insert and delete columns and rows

Your spreadsheet design can be edited according to your needs. For example, you can insert a new column or row. To do this in Excel, click on the blue column or row header (these contain either a letter or number) where you would like your new one to be placed. Go to the **Home** tab and in the 'Cells' group click on **Insert**. You can then select **Insert Sheet Rows** or **Insert Sheet Columns** from the drop-down menu. A new row/column appears before the one where your cursor is positioned. To delete a row or column, click on its header, then on the **Delete** button.

In Works, all four commands – **Insert Row**, **Delete Row**, **Insert Column** and **Delete Column** – are found in the **Insert** menu.

Sorting by rows

Spreadsheet entries can easily be sorted, or prioritised. You can, for example, have items appear in order of expense. To do this, select the column(s) to be sorted. In Excel, go to the **Home** tab and in the 'Editing' group click on **Sort & Filter** then on **Sort**. In Works, go to the **Tools** menu and click on **Sort**. Both Excel and Works allow you to choose which column or columns you want to sort. You can choose whether you want to list the results in ascending (A-Z) or descending (Z-A) order. Make your choices, then click on **OK**.

Formatting cells

To change the style of the text or figures in your spreadsheet, first select the cell or cells to be formatted. Next, go to the **Home** tab and in the 'Cells' group click on the **Format** button. Select **Format Cells** at the bottom of the menu. In the Format Cells dialogue box, click on the **Font** tab. Select a font, style, size and colour as desired, then click on **OK**. Alternatively, select the cells, then click on the relevant buttons in the 'Font' group.

Performing calculations

It is the ability of spreadsheets to perform complex calculations that makes them such a powerful tool. It is worth the effort to learn how to use formulas correctly.

Adding figures
In Excel you can add together the contents of columns, rows or any combination of selected cells. Select the cells and their total is displayed on the Status bar at the bottom of the screen.

	10
	10
	10
	10
Sum: 50	10

Using the AutoSum function

Both Excel and Works have an AutoSum toolbar button to calculate figures.

In Excel, to add figures in adjacent cells in a column or a row, select the relevant cells then go to the **Formulas** tab and click on the **AutoSum** button. The total will be displayed in the next cell of the column or row.

In Works, you must click on a blank cell in the column or row you want calculated, then click on the **AutoSum** button. The cell references, or addresses, for the cells will appear in a formula. If they are correct, press **Return**; if not, type in the correct cell references. The total will appear in your selected cell.

`=SUM(C2,D2,D3,` In Excel, to add up figures in cells that are not adjacent to each other, click on an empty cell, then on the **AutoSum** button. The selected cell will display the legend '=SUM()'. Enter the cell references of the cells to be calculated. You can do this manually or by clicking on them, inserting a comma between each one. Each coordinate will be added to the formula automatically. Press the **Return** key.

To add up figures in cells that are not adjacent to each other in Works, click on an empty cell then press the '=' key on your keyboard. Works now knows you want to enter a formula. Enter the cell references of the cells to be calculated, either manually or by clicking on them, inserting a '+' sign between each one. Press **Return**.

To delete a formula in a cell, press the **Delete** key.

Further functions in Excel
There are a number of preset functions in Excel that can take the effort out of spreadsheet calculations. Click on an empty cell to make it active and type in '='. Click on the arrow button between the Active cell address box and the Cancel button near the top of the window. A drop-down menu will appear. Click on an option and a dialogue box will appear, giving a brief description of the function it performs, such as the average value of selected cells, or depreciation of an asset (for example, a car) over a specified time period.

SUM	▼
SUM	
AVERAGE	
IF	
HYPERLINK	
COUNT	
MAX	
SIN	
SUMIF	

Further functions in Works
For other calculation functions in Works, click on the **Easy Calc** button on the toolbar. A dialogue box appears, which lists common calculations and more specialised ones. Click on the **Other** button at the bottom of the box for a scrollable menu of the program's 76 preset functions with more detailed descriptions.

Easy Calc

Click the function you want to use in your formula.

Common functions

Add — Adds together two or more using a formula.
Subtract
Multiply
Divide
Average

Other functions

Other — Displays a complete list of functions

Cancel   < Back

More complex equations in Excel and Works
You are not restricted to simple sums – you can create formulas for any type of calculation. Click on an empty cell and press the '=' key. Then type in the cell references of the cells to be calculated in your formula, separating them by the relevant 'operators' – the symbols for addition (+), subtraction (-), multiplication (*) and division (/). Press the **Return** key.

Item	Units ordered	Price per unit	Total	Disc
Gloss Paint	6	9.99	59.94	
Brushes	4	5.99	=B3*C3	
Sandpaper	3	6.99		

Spreadsheet programs automatically process some operators before others (for example, multiplication and division before addition or subtraction) so, to ensure that one part of the equation is calculated before the rest, enclose it in brackets.

| Final Total | =(D2-E2)*(D3-E3) |

Setting number formats
To help to prevent incorrect calculations in Excel, it is wise to format cells for currency, dates, percentages, times and so on. Select your cell(s) then go to the **Home** tab and in the 'Cells' group click on the **Format** button. Select **Format Cells** from the drop-down menu and in the dialogue box click on the **Number** tab. Choose 'Number' from the menu of options, select the number of decimal places and, if a negative number, a style, then click on **OK**. Works offers fewer options: go to the **Format** menu and choose **Number**.

| Number | Alignment | Font | Border | Fill | Protection |

Category:

General
Number
Currency
Accounting
Date
Time
Percentage
Fraction
Scientific
Text
Special
Custom

Sample

Decimal places: 2

☐ Use 1000 Separator (,)

Negative numbers:

-1234.10
1234.10
-1234.10
-1234.10

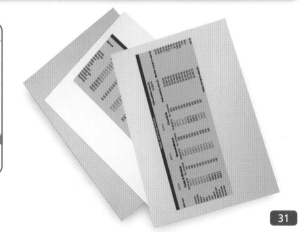

An introduction to databases

Learn **how to use** database programs **to keep records that** you can sort

Databases are used for storing and organising large amounts of data about related topics. For example, you can create a database to catalogue your recipe collection and then search it to find all the lamb dishes or all the dishes using coriander.

A database's ability to organise and prioritise data in different ways also makes it suitable for storing names, addresses and contact details. If you forget someone's surname, you can search the database by first name only, by phone code or by address.

Databases are far more than just deposit boxes for information, however. They can also make useful calculations – for instance, enter the value of each item of your household contents, then add up the total value to provide a guide to how much you should insure your possessions for.

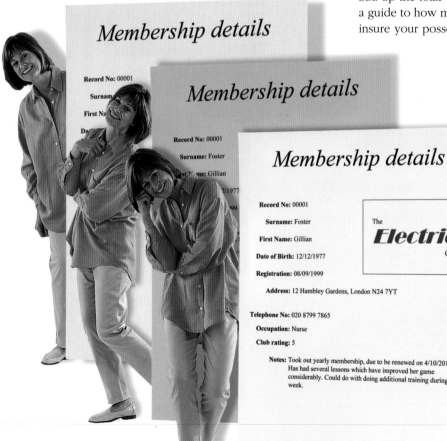

Working with fields

The building blocks of a database are fields. Each field represents a category of information. In an address database, they might be surname, first name, address, telephone number and so on. To build a database, you must first create fields for it.

Membership No.	First Name	Surname	Street Address	To

Creating records

Once the fields have been created you can begin to make your entries – each entry is known as a record. For each record, you fill in the fields. The database allows you to organise the records in a number of ways – for example, you can list them in alphabetical order or by date. You can also browse through the records, search for a particular entry and print out selected aspects.

First Name: Fiona
Surname: Green
Street Address: 11 Westferry Circus
Town or City: London
Postcode: E14 4HE

Opening a new database

From the **Start** button, select **All Programs and** then **Microsoft Works Task Launcher**. From the Quick Launch menu on the right-hand side, click on **Works Database**. When the Microsoft Works Database dialogue box appears, select **Blank Database** and then click on **OK**.

Building a database

When you open a new database, the Create Database dialogue box appears, in which you specify fields. Do not worry if you miss one out, or enter them in the wrong order, as you can edit your database later.

Setting up fields

As you enter field names you are given a chance to format and choose a style for them.

Field name

Type your field name into this box. Field names should not be more than 15 characters long (this includes spaces between words). The more fields you create, the greater the flexibility of your database. It is sensible, for example, to create separate fields for first names and surnames so you can search by either category.

Try to enter field names in the order that you wish them to appear in your database. It is good practice to be as organised as possible at this stage.

Format

You have a choice of formats for your field

names. These relate to the type of information you are entering. The date field, for example, is automatically set up for the day, month and year. Select an option by clicking it. A small black dot indicates that the Format is active.

Choose the following formats for the appropriate information:

General This is the default setting for all field names. Text entries are aligned to the left, and numbers to the right.

Number This lets you specify the way that numbers are displayed. For example, you can select the number of decimal places, or whether negative numbers appear in red.

Date Select this to specify how dates are displayed – by month only, with or without the year, or with the month as text rather than a number.

Time Select either 'AM' or 'PM', and whether to include seconds as well as hours and minutes.

Text Use this to display numbers as text rather than figures, or to include dashes or spaces (useful when entering phone numbers).

Fraction If you want to store fractions – 2¾, for example – choose this format. When entering data, type a space between the whole number (2) and the fraction (3/4) to let Works tell them apart. The decimal equivalent appears in the Entry bar when the cell containing a fraction is selected.

Serialized Choose this format to get Works to automatically add a serial number to each record. This unique number is useful if you need to sort records into the order in which they were entered.

Additional options

You will be given style choices for how you want your number, date, time, fraction and serialised formats to appear. For example, you may want to include decimal values in your numbers, and within dates to have months written out in full. Scroll through the lists and click on your choice.

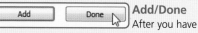

Add/Done After you have created a field and selected a format and appearance for it, click on **Add** to confirm your selection and move to another field. When you have created all your database fields click on **Done**. Your database will appear in List View, with your field names as headings at the top of columns.

✔		Membership No.	First Name	Surname	Stre
☐	1				
☐	2				

Database programs

Microsoft Works includes a database tool. It also contains a selection of database templates – you can open these and use them as they are, or customise for your own needs.

Office 2010 The Standard edition of Microsoft Office does not include a specific database program, but its spreadsheet program, Microsoft Excel, can perform many of the same tasks (see page 35).

Saving your database

When your database appears for the first time in List View, it is called 'Unsaved Database'. You should save it immediately with an appropriate name.

Click on the **Save** toolbar button or go to the **File** menu and click on **Save As**. A dialogue box appears. In the 'File name' box, type in a name for your database. Click on the arrow beside the 'Save in' box to see the destinations to which you can save your file. Select a folder then click on **Save**. For more detailed information on saving documents, see page 36.

Getting around your database

Your new database appears in List View, which looks similar to a spreadsheet. There are three other ways to view your database, too. Become familiar with them before entering any records.

Different points of view

You can view your database in four different ways, each of which lends itself best to a particular use. All the views can be accessed via the **View** menu, or by clicking on the appropriate buttons on the toolbar.

List View

 Immediately after you create your fields, your database is displayed in List View. This view allows you to see a number of records at the same time. It is useful when you simply want to browse your records, move data (copy and paste) from one record to another, or when entering a series of numbers or dates.

You can enter information into your database in List View by first clicking on a cell then typing your entry (it appears as well in the Entry bar at the top of the window). List View is also used to display the results of any searches that you run.

Form View

 Each record can be viewed separately using Form View. Most people prefer to enter information using this view – it means you can see the entries for all the other fields as you enter new data into the database.

> **Record No:** 00001
>
> **Surname:** Foster
>
> **First Name:** Gillian
>
> **Date of Birth:** 12/12/1977
>
> **Registration:** 08/09/1999

Form Design

 In Form Design you structure the look of the Form View. You can rearrange fields and their adjoining field boxes to suit your own needs. You can also style the field labels by using a contrasting font or adding a colour and other elements. Here, for example, we have used colour and a border to give focus to the club name.

To move field names around the page, click on them and drag them into place.

To adjust the size of a field box, first click on the right or bottom edge, or the bottom right-hand corner of the field box, and then, with the left mouse button pressed down, drag it until all the information you want to include fits in the box.

> Town or city: Bristol
>
> DRAG
>
> Surname: Knighton
>
> Street Address: 233 Bedminster Brid▮ ⊡ RESIZE
>
> Town or city: Bristol

Report View

 A good database allows you to extract data. Through Report View you can design and print out a report that organises your information by related subjects. It also lets you perform calculations on fields, such as the total of subscription fees club members have paid to date.

Record No	Surname	Fees Paid/Owed
00001	Foster	£52.50
00002	Ianni	£46.20
00003	Knighton	£37.30
00004	Davidowicz	£62.50
00005	James	£33.72
00006	Adams	£15.04
00007		
		£247.26

Club Database - Money ow

Record No	First Name	Surname	Street Address	
00001	Gillian	Foster	12 Hambley Gardens	
00002	Paulo	Ianni	Flat 4, 7 Frith Street	L
00003	James	Knighton	233 Bedminster Bridg	B
00004	Ursula	Davidowicz	25 Ellesmer Road	B
00005	Peter	James	773 Long Lane	G
00006	Finola	Adams	12 Kings Road	F

Inputting your records

You can enter data into your database in either List View or Form View (see above).

In List View, click on the relevant cell and type into it. To move to the next cell, either click in it using your mouse, or press the **Tab** key on your keyboard. (To return to a previous field, or cell, press **Shift** and **Tab**.) Unlike spreadsheet programs, pressing the Return key will not move your cursor to the next cell or row in a database.

In Form View, click the field box adjoining the field name and type your data. Press the **Tab** key to move to the next field (or the next record when you come to the end of the current one), and the **Shift** and **Tab** keys to return to a previous field, or record.

Navigating through forms

In Form View and Form Design you can view other records by clicking on the appropriate arrows displayed on each side of the current record number at the bottom of the window.

The arrows immediately to the left and right of the current record name take you to the previous and next records respectively. The arrows to the outside of these take you straight to the first and last records.

⏮ ◀ Record 3 ▶ ⏭ Zoom 100%

Finding information and sorting your records

Databases allow you to prioritise and organise your information as you please, and to search for specific entries quickly and easily.

Finding information

A single database in Microsoft Works can store up to 32,000 records. To locate a record quickly, you can initiate a search. In List View go to the **Edit** menu and click on **Find**. The Find and Replace dialogue box appears on screen. In the 'Find what' box type in a key word or words (be as specific as possible), select the **All records** option and click **OK**. Records containing your key word will appear in a list. To return to your full list of records, go to the **Record** menu, select **Show** then **All records**.

You can search in Form View in the same way but the records are displayed one at a time. To move between them, click on the arrows at the foot of the screen.

Sorting records in your database

You can use the Sort function in Works to re-order your database. Go to the **Record** menu and click on **Sort Records**. In the Sort Records dialogue box you can choose to have your records prioritised by up to three fields. For example, by first sorting by 'Date of birth' in ascending order, the oldest person in your database will appear at the top of the list, and the youngest person last. If you then sort by 'Surname' in ascending order, those who share the same date of birth will then be listed alphabetically. Sort a third time by town in ascending order. Now those who share the same birthday and name will be listed alphabetically by town.

Click on the arrows to the right of each Sort box, and scroll through the lists to select your choice of field. You have the option of sorting records in Ascending or Descending order (Ascending lists entries A to Z, or 1, 2, 3 ...; Descending lists entries Z to A, or 10, 9, 8 ...) depending on the field content.

Editing your database

After you have created a database, you can add and delete information, and perform calculations.

Inserting new records

To insert a new record between existing records, click on the row number where you want to insert it in List View. Go to the **Record** menu and select **Insert Record**. To delete a row, click on the row number, go to the **Record** menu and select **Delete Record**.

Adding and moving fields

To add a field, click the field heading where you would like it to appear in List View. Go to the **Record** menu and select **Insert Field**. Choose to insert it before or after the selected one. A dialogue box appears – give the new field a name and click on **OK**. To delete a field, click its heading then go to the **Record** menu and select **Delete Field**.

To move a field, click on the field heading in List View. Move the mouse pointer to the edge of a highlighted cell. When it changes to a 'drag' pointer, drag the field to its new location. To move a record, click on the row heading and do the same. In each case you must be able to see the intended destination in the window.

Calculating data

You can perform calculations on values in two or more fields and display the results in another. If you have fields for 'Price' and 'Deposit', create a third called 'Total Due'. Click its heading and type '=Price-Deposit' in the Entry bar to show the balance.

Microsoft Excel as a database

Microsoft Excel can be used to perform database functions. Instead of entering field names, headings are typed into the spreadsheet, in cells along the same row. Records are entered into the rows below. (Records must be numbered manually, so create a heading for 'Record No.'.)

To look at a subset of your data, use AutoFilter. First, highlight the data to be filtered. Go to the **Data** tab and click on the **Filter** button in the 'Sort & Filter' group. Each column appears with a menu arrow on the right. Click on the arrow on the item

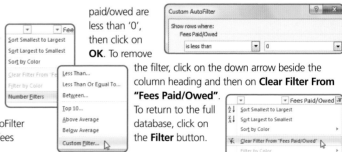

you want to filter (here Fees Paid/Owed). From the drop-down menu select **Number Filters**, then **Custom Filter** from the sub-menu. Now set your criteria. For example, in a 'Fees Paid/Owed' column, you can select records to see only those people who owe money. In the Custom AutoFilter dialogue box, specify records for which the fees

paid/owed are less than '0', then click on **OK**. To remove the filter, click on the down arrow beside the column heading and then on **Clear Filter From "Fees Paid/Owed"**. To return to the full database, click on the **Filter** button.

Saving and printing

Transform your work into printed documents

Your computer stores work in much the same way as a conventional filing system. The documents that you create on your PC are kept in folders. Within the folders are sub-folders that help you to organise the different areas of your work. For example, if you create a folder for office work, you could then create sub-folders for business correspondence and accounts. As with any filing system, it is vital to organise it well right from the start.

Windows 7 helps by automatically creating folders for different types of files. You can easily set up all family members as new users of the computer, each with their own set of files and folders. A well-ordered system makes it easy to save and retrieve your work – far easier, in fact, than with a traditional paper-filled filing cabinet.

Printing is easy

Printing your PC files (these are the documents you create, rather than the folders in which you store them) is one of the most useful skills you can master on your computer. Depending on the type of printer you have, you can print on a variety of paper sizes and weights (thicknesses). You can print out sticky address labels and even print directly onto envelopes.

By using the many font styles, colours and graphics available on your PC, you can produce printed work that looks professional.

As soon as you create a new document, save it. Continue to save it as you work. This way, should your PC crash, your work will not be lost.

SAVING YOUR WORK

1 To save a file, click on the **Save** button on the Quick Access toolbar or click on the **File** tab and choose **Save As**. A dialogue box appears. In the 'File name' box, type in the file's name. At the top of the box you can see the place in which your file would currently be saved.

Page settings

To adjust how your document prints out, click on the **Page Layout** tab and then on the dialogue box launcher in the 'Page Setup' group. Click on the **Margins** tab to choose the space around your page and either 'Portrait' or 'Landscape' orientation. Click on the **Paper** tab to select your paper size. Click **OK**.

*In Works, if a sub-folder is selected but you want to return to the main folder (moving up one level), click on the **Up One Level** button. To return to a main drive, click on the arrow beside the 'Save in' box, scroll through the list that appears and click on the drive.*

Bright idea
*You can set some programs, including Word, to save files automatically – reducing the risk of losing work. Launch Word and then go to the **File** tab and click on **Options** at the foot of the menu. Click on **Save**. Now click next to 'Save AutoRecover information every:' and set a time interval. Finally, click on **OK**.*

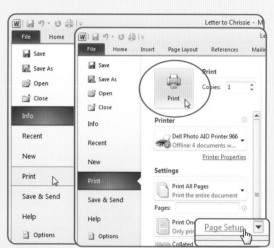

2 To change where your file is saved, use the arrows to the right of the destinations at the top to navigate to the location where you would like to save your new file. If you want to create a new folder, click on the **New folder** button. A new folder will appear, ready for you to type in a name, here 'Letters'.

3 Your new folder automatically becomes the new destination for your file. Click on **Save** to save your document into it. The document name now appears on the document's Title bar, and an icon and the file name for the Word file appear in the new sub-folder.

4 When you are ready to print your document, go to the **File** tab, then click on **Print**. Your current 'Printer' and print 'Settings' are displayed. Click on the down arrow, on the right, to change a setting. Click on **Page Setup** to view a full set of options. Make your selections and click on the **Print** button to finish.

Saving and printing in Works

To save a file, click on the **Save** toolbar button or on **Save As** in the **File** menu. The Save As dialogue box appears. In the 'File name' box, type in the file's name. Click on the arrow to the right of the 'Save in' box to choose where to save

your file. Click on **Save**. To create a sub-folder within, say, your 'Household' folder, click on the **Create New Folder** button. Type in a name for the 'New Folder' that appears and click on **Open**, then on **Save**. To print your file, click on **Print** in the **File** menu, select the options for copies and page range, then click on **OK**.

Print preview

To check how your document looks before printing, click on the **File** tab and choose **Print**. A preview of your file is displayed in the right-hand panel. To return to your document layout, click on the **Home** tab.

How your computer works

Discover what happens inside your PC when you switch it on

When you switch on the system unit of your PC it has to complete several automatic operations before it can process the commands you will subsequently input via your keyboard and mouse.

To ensure that the operating conditions are as they should be, all your hardware components, such as your memory and keyboard, are checked to make sure that they are undamaged and are able to communicate with each other and with your software.

This process is called 'booting up'. It takes only a minute, but it is the most important minute of your PC's working day. If the hardware and software do not communicate properly, nothing else on your PC will work.

Your computer's memory

The basic functions of your computer are governed by different types of 'memory'.

RAM

Random Access Memory (RAM) is the memory used by your computer temporarily to store the files and programs you are working on. It can process your commands extremely quickly. This type of memory only works when the computer is switched on; when it is turned off, anything left in RAM is lost.

ROM

Read Only Memory (ROM) holds basic details about the computer and a small, self-test program that runs every time you switch the computer on. ROM is part of your computer's 'identity', and is retained when your PC is turned off. You cannot change or remove what is stored in the ROM, which is why it is called 'read only'.

CMOS

Complementary Metal Oxide Semiconductor (CMOS) memory stores your computer's settings, such as which type of hard disk it uses. The CMOS also remembers the date and time. It is powered by a small battery that recharges itself when the computer is switched on (switch it on at least once a month for an hour or two).

BIOS

The Basic Input/Output System (BIOS) memory controls your computer hardware. The BIOS tells the operating system which hardware to expect to come into operation and how it is arranged. It is as if your computer were a chef, and the BIOS his assistant, checking he has all the necessary ingredients. The BIOS is stored within the ROM.

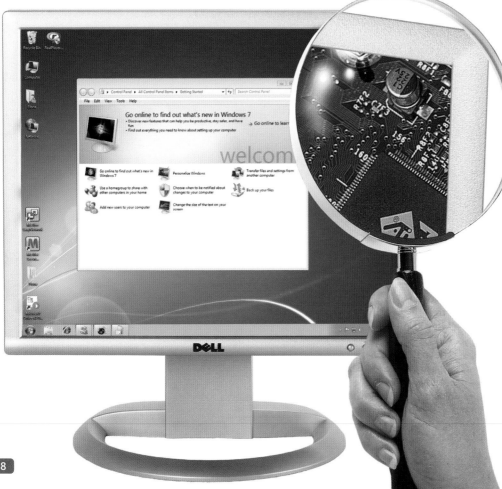

⚠ Watch out

If your PC was not shut down properly the last time you used it, a message will flash up the next time you switch it on. If this happens, allow your PC to boot up, then restart it immediately. This ensures that the shut-down mistake has no lingering after-effects.

🔍 Close-up

In addition to switching on your system unit, you may also have to turn on your monitor, and any other peripheral units, such as a scanner or printer, if they have separate power sources.

When you switch on ...

The first 2 minutes after you switch on are vital to the performance of your computer. Here is what happens after you press the power button.

Start up your computer

The first sound you will hear is the whirr of the fans. These regulate the temperature inside the system unit and operate for as long as the computer is switched on. Be careful not to cover any of the air vents on your PC as this will cause overheating. A modern computer can have as many as three fans blowing air over critical components, such as the graphics card.

Roll call

The first task your computer performs is the POST (Power On Self Test). This checks that the most important components such as the hard disk are present and working correctly. While your PC is going through this test you should see lights flickering on and off as the computer tests the CD drive, hard drive and keyboard. During these initial tests, the computer also checks the CD or DVD drive for a start-up disk – this allows you to make repairs in case of a major problem.

Once the POST is complete, Windows 7 starts to load. You will see a black screen with the Windows 7 logo and a series of green lights scrolling from left to right. These show that Windows is loading all the information it needs to coordinate the various components of your computer system. The tasks it performs at this stage include loading drivers – special programs that enable components like video cards to work – into memory; looking for new devices that may have been added to the computer since it was last switched on; and detecting any network that your computer may be attached to.

When this process is complete you will see the initial Windows 7 screen. Click on your user name (if you use a password, type it in and then press **Return** or click on the coloured arrow). Windows will play a sound and load your personal configuration – your choice of Desktop pattern and icons on it.

A quicker start

If you have used PCs with older versions of Windows, you will notice that Windows 7 starts up more quickly than its predecessors and does not show pages of numbers and letters before it starts to load. One of the reasons for the quicker start is that Windows 7 can stop the computer from doing certain time-consuming tests before starting to load Windows. Also, the operating system loads in a more efficient way, so that it can take only a few seconds before you are ready to use your PC.

The Welcome screen

Once you have logged on as a user, you will see the Welcome screen. If not, click on **Start, Getting Started**. From here you can access many useful tools to get you started with Windows 7. The screen gives you immediate access to information about your PC and some online resources that can help to protect your PC or give you information about new features.

Click on an item in the panel below 'Welcome', then on the corresponding option next to the green arrow button, for in-depth information on that topic. You will need to be online to access some of these options.

The hard disk

This is a series of magnetised metal disk platters. They are read by a small arm that passes over them – a little like an old-style record player. However, the arm never touches the disks – it skims thousandths of a millimetre above the platters, which you can hear spinning.

Clutter-free Desktop

What you see on your Desktop depends on the PC manufacturer. You may have an almost empty Desktop, showing just the Recycle Bin. In this case, to access your Documents, Pictures and Music folders, click on the **Start** button and select the folders from the right-hand pane. You can make these folders appear on your Desktop if you prefer. To do this, click and drag a folder onto the Desktop – this creates a 'Shortcut' icon to the folder.

How software works

Learn how the operating system, programs and your PC's hardware interact

No matter how powerful your PC, it is an inert box of chips and wires until it is told what to do and think. Computers function only when they are given instructions. Software is the electronic 'brain' that gives your PC these instructions. The most fundamental piece of software on your computer is the operating system. The operating system on most PCs is Windows. Just as your brain coordinates your thoughts with your movements, so Windows controls all the actions that you ask your PC to do, from printing a page to closing a window.

From DOS to Windows

Much of the history of PCs has been an exercise in making life easier for users. The original operating system for PCs was DOS (Disk Operating System). To use this system you had to know the language, and you typed in commands one by one. These commands were quite complicated, and meant that DOS was difficult for most beginners.

In Windows 7, the DOS system is still accessible as a program called Command Prompt. If there is a fault with Windows, computer specialists can use this facility to execute text-based DOS commands to control the way the computer works at the most basic level.

Fortunately for most users, working with Windows requires no knowledge of computer languages. It has a Graphical User Interface (GUI – pronounced 'gooey') that allows you to operate your PC by moving your mouse pointer around the screen and clicking on buttons, menus and images. All Windows-compatible programs and additional hardware can be accessed through the Windows system.

Windows gets updated regularly and contains new features and improvements with each upgrade. The most recent version, Windows 7, offers a much updated look and lots of new features. Windows 7 promises to be a more stable and easier-to-use system for home users than previous versions.

Bright idea
Before buying a new program check the packaging to see how much RAM it needs, and make sure that your computer has memory to spare (see below).

The Taskbar that runs along the bottom of your Desktop shows you which programs you have open – each is displayed as a separate button. In this Taskbar, Windows Explorer, Internet Explorer, Microsoft Word, Excel, Outlook and Works Task Launcher are open.

How does Windows work with other programs?
Understanding what happens when you open a program within Windows will help you to operate your computer more effectively.

The role of Windows
Application programs (so-called because they are designed to be 'applied' to a specific task) rely on Windows to communicate at a basic level with the computer's hardware. This 'middleman' role does away with the need to duplicate the same basic features into every application. Programmers are able to concentrate on making sure each program performs its specialist tasks as well as possible.

So, for example, when you save files and the Save As dialogue box appears on screen, this communicates with Windows, as well as the program you are using.

What happens when you switch on your PC?
When you switch on your computer, Windows starts automatically. Its program code is read from the hard disk then loaded into the computer's RAM memory.

If no software other than Windows is loaded, all you can do on your PC is see which files are on your hard disk, adjust your PC's settings and run some very basic programs. For most other tasks, you have to call on application programs.

Even Windows accessories, such as Internet Explorer, Paint and WordPad, are separate programs dedicated to their own jobs of web browsing, painting small pictures, and simple word processing, respectively. (For more information on specific programs you are likely to use, see page 20.)

Opening programs in Windows
When you open programs they too are loaded into the computer's RAM memory. They then draw on Windows' facilities to communicate with your computer's hardware.

Windows allows you to run several programs at once, and to move easily between them. For example, if you wanted to edit and then insert a picture into a Microsoft Word document you were working on, you could open a graphics program, edit the picture, then insert it into the Word document. At the same time, you could be researching the subject of the document on the internet using the Internet Explorer program.

The importance of memory
As each new program is opened it loads up into the computer's RAM memory, alongside the other software already running. This is why it is important that your computer has enough RAM (at least 1Gb, although 2Gb will make your computer run much better). If you do not have enough RAM to run a particular program, your computer stores the excess data on its hard disk. This makes all the programs you have open run much more slowly. (To find out how to add more RAM to your PC, see page 344.)

When you have finished working with a program you should close or exit it. The program then unloads from the RAM, freeing it up for use by other programs. This may also speed up the operation of the other programs that remain open.

Checking your RAM
To find out how much RAM you have on your PC, click on the **Start** button and then select **Control Panel** from the right-hand side.

Click on **System and Security** and then on **System** to see basic information about your computer. This will tell you which version of Windows you are using; information about the processor; and the total amount of RAM installed (1Gb is the minimum required for Windows 7 but 2Gb is preferable).

Storing all your data

How to make space for everything you need

Your computer's hard disk is where all your programs and documents are stored. The more programs and documents you have, the less disk space there is in which to store them. As the hard disk fills up, your computer will slow down. Disposing of unwanted documents in the Recycle Bin, and uninstalling software you no longer use, will help to conserve hard disk space (for more details, see pages 54-55). However, you may eventually need to use extra storage devices.

Your first choices

Your computer will probably have a CD-RW drive built in. This is like an ordinary CD-ROM drive in that it can read music and data CDs. But it can also 'write' information onto special blank CDs. As much as 750Mb (megabytes) of data can be stored on each disc, and Windows 7 makes it simple to store data this way. If you do not have a CD-RW drive, it is easy and cheap to add one.

Most new computers have a combined CD-RW and DVD-RW drive. This enables you to watch DVDs on your PC – films or music videos, for example – and record to DVD. Each DVD can hold more than 9Gb (gigabytes) of data, and can be a great way to hold a large number of digital photos. The downside is that the disks are still relatively expensive.

If you are looking to move files from one PC to another, then a flash drive is a good option. These small devices connect to your PC through a USB port. They are relatively inexpensive, and have a number of memory options.

On older computers you may find a floppy disk drive. Floppy disks can store only up to 1.44Mb of data each, which many users now find too limited.

You should be aware that sharing data on any portable storage device is a common way of spreading viruses, so ensure you have an up-to-date virus checker on your PC.

Connecting a drive

The storage devices described here are separate items that need to be connected to your system unit. Almost all devices of this type will connect to your PC using a USB socket. Most drives use USB 2.0 interfaces, which allow for extremely fast transfers – as long as your PC is similarly equipped.

Close-up
The units for memory and storage on a PC are:
1,024 bytes = 1 kilobyte (Kb)
1,024 kilobytes = 1 megabyte (Mb)
1,024 megabytes = 1 gigabyte (Gb)
1,024 gigabytes = 1 terabyte (Tb)
Generally, the 1,024 is 'rounded' down to 1,000.

Which storage device?

These devices are all suitable for storing large quantities of information. If you need to transfer data to other PCs, make sure each PC has the same type of drive.

Flash drive

Flash drives are small devices that are powered through your PC via one of the USB ports. They are economical to buy and highly portable. There is a range of memory options to choose from – the cheapest carry 64Mb of data and the highest capacity flash drives hold 256Gb.

DVD-RW

Many PCs now have DVD-RW (rewritable) drives, which can read and write to DVD discs as well as ordinary CD-ROMs. These drives offer huge amounts of storage – as much as 9.4Gb per disc – but can be expensive, as are the special discs used for recording.

CD-RW

One of the most cost-effective forms of storage for your PC is a CD-RW (rewritable) drive. This will write to CD-R discs, which cannot be erased, or to CD-RW discs that can be overwritten as many times as you like. CD-RW discs can hold up to 750Mb of data.

External hard drives

If you have a lot of space-hungry programs on your computer, or want an easy way to back up your files, you should consider buying an external hard drive to supplement your existing hard drive. External hard drives from manufacturers such as Iomega, Lacie and Western Digital can offer a capacity up to 4Tb (terabytes) – which is more than enough for most people's needs.

Formatting CDs or DVDs

Before you can copy files to a CD or DVD, the disc must be formatted. Insert a disc into your PC's CD or DVD drive. In the AutoPlay dialogue box, that appears, click on **Burn files to disc**. In the Burn a Disc dialogue box select either 'Like a USB flash drive' which means you can add, edit or delete files at anytime. This is often referred to as 'Live File System'. Or 'With a CD/DVD player' which means files cannot be edited or removed after burning - called 'Mastered'. For more information click on **Which one should I choose?** Click on **Next** to prepare the disc.

Supplementary hardware

Extend your computer's capabilities with added devices

Once your computer knowledge and confidence grows, you will be eager to expand your PC's capabilities. A wide range of devices is available that will make working with your computer even more interesting and enjoyable.

If you like to use images in your work, a scanner is a cost-effective way to get high-resolution images into your computer. Not all images need to be scanned. Digital cameras let you take photos and transfer

them to your PC, without a scanner. You can also buy a small video camera called a webcam to connect to your computer. As well as being fun, it allows you to hold video conferences with colleagues who also have a webcam. Connect a digital camcorder to your PC, and you can start to make home movies.

You can also buy hardware to make the most of today's on-screen entertainments. The latest generation of joysticks, for instance, take game playing to a new dimension.

These extras can be built up over time. You need not buy everything on the same shopping trip.

With added hardware, you can really make the most of your computer, turning it into a complete home office and entertainment centre.

Modems

Almost all home computers have an internal modem that allows you to connect to the internet using a phone line. If your computer does not have an internal modem, you can add an external model. To take advantage of an always-on, broadband internet connection, you will need a cable modem or an ADSL model – either wired or a wireless 'router' (see right). See pages 88-89 for more information on internet connection.

Bright idea
Although most computers now come with a built-in standard modem, they can go wrong and often are not worth the cost of repair. Instead buy a new external modem, which attaches to your computer by a USB cable.

Watch out

While wireless routers are popular, there is an increased security risk. Make sure you always password-protect your router and install a firewall on your PC.

Scanners

A scanner will transform your paper images and photo prints into graphic files that you can then edit and use on your PC. The most versatile kind of scanners are the 'flatbed' variety.

Picture quality is described in terms of resolution, measured in dots per inch (dpi). The more dots that make up an image, the higher the resolution and the better the quality of the image. Buy a scanner with a resolution capability of at least 600 dpi.

Digital cameras

These cameras take photos without using any film. You transfer pictures directly to your computer through a connection lead or digital memory card reader. The price of digital cameras has

Wireless router

Home users are increasingly opting for a wireless router for access to their broadband service. These 'hubs' require a power point and a phone line and then, after the installation of their linked software, will allow more than one computer to have access to the same service, without any trailing wires.

decreased rapidly in recent years, so good-quality images can now be taken with quite low-cost cameras.

When you consider that you have no need to buy film and get it developed, they are very good value.

Joysticks

If you are a fan of computer games, a joystick is essential. These devices plug into a port in your system unit. The best joysticks are those that also provide feedback – recoiling as you fire guns, or shaking as you drive over rocks – but these 'force feedback' devices only work with games software that supports them. You can also buy steering wheels and pedals for driving games.

Webcams

These are small video cameras that connect to your PC. They can be used for video conferencing, but are now popular with home PC users for 'live chats' with friends and family that live far away. For the best sound and picture quality, you will need a powerful PC and a broadband internet connection.

Microphones

A microphone is useful for audio tasks, such as recording a voiceover or a narration.

They come as external devices or are built in. You can also buy microphones with speech-recognition software, so you do not have to type: just speak your thoughts, and the words appear in your document. This software may take a long time before it recognises your voice and gives the best results.

Installing drivers

Additional hardware often needs software called a driver to allow Windows to control the hardware. Many devices now resolve this problem because they are 'plug and play' – this means that the software is automatically installed on your computer when the device is added. In other cases Windows 7 does the work for you. It recognises the hardware as soon as it is added to your PC and connects to the web to find a suitable driver. You may need to run the set-up program provided on a CD with the hardware. When buying a peripheral device, always check that it will work with Windows 7 and that suitable drivers are available.

More software for your PC

Extend the uses of your computer with extra programs

When you bought your PC, a selection of software may have been included. Packages often focus on Microsoft products, including Microsoft® Works Suite and Microsoft® Office. These packages contain a number of programs that allow you to perform a wide range of functions, such as word processing and spreadsheet work. The software packages that come with your computer are known as 'bundled software'.

Although this bundled software allows you to perform many different tasks on your PC, you are bound eventually to want to use more specialised or advanced software. If you have a digital camera, for example, you may want a photo-editing program, such as Photoshop Elements. Or, if you have children, you may want a selection of games to play. You should also use virus-checking software to be sure your computer is kept free from viruses. All such software is readily available, and easy to load onto your PC, but there are a few points you should check.

Checking the requirements

Before you buy a new piece of software, check the information on the packaging to ensure it runs on your version of Windows. You should also find out how much memory (RAM) and hard-disk storage space it requires.

To see how much disk space you have available, go to the **Start** menu, click on **Computer**, then on **System properties** to see detailed information about your PC.

Close-up
When buying goods by mail order through a magazine advertisement, check that the magazine operates the Mail Order Protection Scheme (MOPS). This offers consumers protection if the software does not perform the tasks claimed of it.

Watch out
Copying programs from friends is not obtaining software for free – it is stealing. Unless you have purchased a licence, you are breaking copyright laws and could be prosecuted.

'Free' software
You do not always have to buy new software for your PC. Some of it can be obtained free, if only for a limited period.

Play, buy and sync your music, films and more.

iTunes is a free application for your Mac or PC. It organises and plays your digital music and video on y...

Freeware, shareware and evaluation software
Freeware describes software that is available completely free. Most of the programs have been written by PC enthusiasts and are of good quality.

Shareware and evaluation software are offered free for a limited period (usually 30 days), after which you will not be able to operate the program.

If you want to continue to use a shareware program you must pay a fee (usually much lower than the price of similar, shop-bought packages). To continue using evaluation software, you must purchase a full copy.

Sources of software
Specialist PC stores and electrical shops are good places to start, but the other sources outlined below may save you money.

Downloading programs
You can download shareware, freeware and evaluation software – known as 'beta' software – from the internet. Locate a dedicated website (see below), then follow the on-screen instructions on the site.

Your PC will tell you how long the download will take – a big program can take hours on a dial-up connection. Once it has downloaded, you will need to install the program before running it.

PC magazines
Look out for free, cover-mounted CD-ROMS on PC magazines. Some CDs will hold 'full product' or complete programs, while others will offer demonstration or shareware versions.

Buying mail order
Mail-order or 'direct' software vendors offer competitive pricing over high-street retailers. Look at the adverts in PC magazines to compare prices. Software can be downloaded from the internet or dispatched by post.

Where for wares?
JUMBO! (www.jumbo.com) is a website that lists many of the shareware and freeware programs that are available to download. Here, a version of Sudoku Expert is being downloaded. Always make sure that your download is compatible with Windows 7.

Jumbo > Games > Board / Puzzle

Sudoku Expert

Version: 1.01
Date: Tuesday, February 26, 2008
File Size: 739 KB
Company: CTP Soft - About Sudoku Expert
Platform(s): Windows ALL
License(s): Shareware
Price: $9.50
User Rating: 5.3 (out of 10)

DASHBOARD

Download This File

Sudoku Expert Version: 1.01 - 2/26/2008
Access an unlimited number of high-quality Sudoku puzzles.

Filing your work

Learn how to name and save your files, and to organise your work efficiently

It can be far easier to locate your work in a well-organised filing system on your computer than it is in a normal paper filing system.

Your computer is an electronic filing cabinet. Each piece of work is stored in folders (as are all the programs you use). Folders can be stored in other folders which are like the drawers in the cabinet. It is tempting to keep all your files on your computer Desktop where you can see them but, as with a real desk, it makes life easier if you tidy things away before the clutter gets out of hand.

Filing made easy

Do not worry that you will forget where you put files, because Windows makes it easy to find them. It is like having an efficient personal assistant – or as if your filing cabinet could tell you exactly what is in all its drawers.

You can access your computer's filing system using a handy facility called Windows Explorer. Through it, you can move folders and files around, make new folders and even copy, or duplicate, folders and documents.

There are several ways to create folders. The method you use will depend on how you save your work.

CREATING FOLDERS

1 To create a folder in Windows Explorer, go to the **Start** menu, select **All Programs** then **Accessories** and click on **Windows Explorer**. Alternatively, hold down the **Windows** key and press **E**. In the left pane, click on the drive, library or folder in which you want to create a new folder.

Naming your files

Always name your files logically so that, should you misplace one and not remember its full name, you can still activate a search for it. If several members of the family are using the computer, Windows 7 creates separate folders in which each person can store work. In shared folders, use your name or initials when naming documents so that you do not get confused as to whose files are whose.

Bright idea
*To rename a file or folder, right-click on it and select **Rename**. Type in the new name over the highlighted old name.*

Key word
Library Use the Library function to view and arrange files from different locations. There are four default libraries: Documents, Music, Pictures and Videos. You can also create your own new libraries, see below.

---

2 Click on the **New folder** button on the toolbar at the top of the window. In the right pane a new folder appears, with its name highlighted. The default name, 'New folder', will be replaced as soon as you begin typing in the new name.

You can also create new folders in which to store work as you save your documents. In the Save As dialogue box click on the **New folder** button. A new folder will appear, ready for you to name.

In addition, it is possible to create new folders by using your right mouse button. When you need to create a new folder, click on the right mouse button, select **New** and then **Folder**. The default name on the folder that appears will be replaced as you type in the new name.

Finding lost files

To find lost work, launch Windows Explorer from the Taskbar and click on a Library – **Documents**, for example. Type the keyword or keywords you can remember into the search bar (top right) – any matching folders and files will be listed on the right pane, below the search bar, with your keyword or keywords highlighted in yellow. Click on one to see information about it appear at the foot of the window.

Create a new library

Click on the **Start** button, then on your user name, here 'Fiona'. In the left pane click on **Libraries**, then on the **New library** button. Type in a name – here 'Genealogy' – and press **Enter**. To add, move or copy files to a library, the library must first contain a folder so it knows where to store files. With a library selected in the left pane, click on **Include a folder**. Click on a folder to select it, then on **Include folder**. This folder automatically becomes the default save location.

Copying and moving files

Keep your documents in order

There will be occasions when you need to copy or move files. You may want to make a back-up of a document (a duplicate copy of a file to use in case your other one becomes damaged or lost), or transfer a file to another computer to work on. Perhaps you need to copy work onto a CD or DVD, or would simply like to store a file in a more appropriate folder on your computer. Whatever you want to do, Windows makes it easy.

To copy to a CD or DVD, first insert a writable CD or DVD into the drive.

BEFORE YOU START

1 In the AutoPlay dialogue box that appears, click on **Burn files to disc**. In the Burn a Disc dialogue box give the disc a name to identify what it will store. Then select how you want to use the disc and click on **Next**. A progress bar will be displayed while the disc is formatted ready to receive your data.

2 Now click on **Open folder to view files**. Navigate to the folder containing the items to copy or move. Click and drag them from the right panel to the disc icon in the left panel. A progress bar is displayed while they are copied. Alternatively, click on an item in the right panel and then click on **Burn** on the toolbar.

Formatting options

When you copy files to a CD or DVD, Windows uses the 'Live File System' format by default. This allows you to write to the CD/DVD again and again. If you do not want the content on your CD/DVD to be overwritten, or if you need a disc that will play in PCs with an older version of Windows or in CD/DVD players, choose 'Mastered' instead. To do this, click on **With a CD/DVD player** option in the Burn a Disc dialogue box, and click on **Next**. Copy your files then click on **Burn to Disc**.

Watch out
*Dragging a file from one drive to another will copy the file – the original will remain on the source drive while a copy is placed on the destination drive. If you drag a file to another location on the same drive, the file will simply move to the new location, without a copy being made. To create two copies of a file within a drive, right-click on the file and select **Copy**. Then right-click on the destination and select **Paste**.*

*To copy a file onto your hard disk open **Windows Explorer** from the **Start** menu.*

▶ BEFORE YOU START

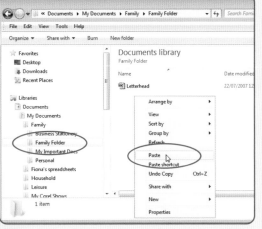

1 In the Windows Explorer window, locate the file or files you wish to copy. Click on the file. (To select several files at once, press the **Ctrl** key on your keyboard and, keeping it pressed down, click on each of the files in turn.) Right-click on the last selected file name and choose **Copy** from the drop-down menu.

2 Now locate the folder into which you wish to copy the selected file or files. Click on it in the left pane, then right-click in the pane on the right and select **Paste** from the drop-down menu. The copied file(s) now appear in this pane, alongside any files that were already in the folder.

3 You can also store a copy of a file within the same folder as the original. Right-click on the relevant file, and from the drop-down menu select **Copy**. Click in the folder space below, right-click again and choose **Paste**. To distinguish the copy from the original, Windows automatically adds '– Copy' after the file name.

Relocating files

Just as with a conventional paper filing system, it will often be necessary to move your files and folders to more suitable locations. Windows Explorer helps you to do this. Click on the file or folder, then, keeping your finger pressed down on the mouse button, drag the file or folder over to its new location. When the destination folder is highlighted, release the mouse button. The file or folder will then move.

Bright idea
*Save time by copying or moving several files at the same time. Press the **Ctrl** key and, keeping it pressed down, click on each of the files or folders. Release the **Ctrl** key and move or copy them as usual.*

Maximising disk space

How to make the most of the space on your computer

Ensuring that your computer works efficiently means organising your folders and files effectively and using the available storage space properly.

As you create files and folders you will use more and more hard-disk space. This will not be a problem initially but, as the hard disk fills up, your computer may slow down as it searches for the correct file or folder, or performs a task. You will also find it more difficult to install new programs.

Deleting out-of-date folders and files, and uninstalling old software, will free up disk space, allowing your PC to run smoothly.

Watch out
If you intend to delete (or restore) a folder from the Recycle Bin, remember that Windows will delete (or restore) the entire contents of the folder, not just the file you are interested in. Be sure you want to do this before proceeding.

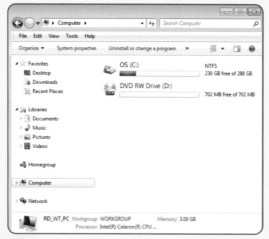

1 To check how much space you have on your hard disk, click on the **Start** button and select **Computer** on the right. In the pane on the right, you will see a list of 'local disks'. Your hard disk is the drive icon marked '(C:)' – here it is 'OS (C:)'.

2 Right-click on **OS (C:)** and select **Properties** from the drop-down list. In the Properties dialogue box click on the **General** tab. Here you can see the amount of Used and Free space, as well as the full hard-disk capacity. A pie chart gives an instant overview. Click on **OK** to close the window.

How much space do I need?

To keep your computer working efficiently, it is important that you keep a minimum of 700Mb of hard-disk space free. If you want to install new software, check how much disk space the software requires.

To do this, insert the software CD, set up the installation and look for the screen that lets you know how much space is required. If you do not have enough space available, quit the installation by following the on-screen instructions.

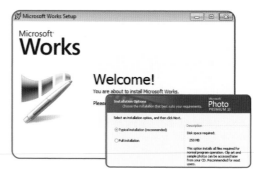

To delete files or folders, go to the **Start** *menu, select* **All Programs,** *then* **Accessories** *and click on* **Windows Explorer.**

DELETING FILES

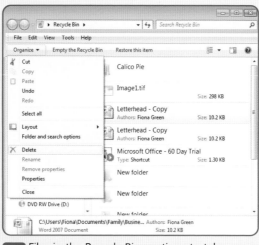

1 Click on the file or folder you wish to delete. Click on the **Organize** button and select **Delete**, or press the **Delete** key. A prompt box asks you to confirm your command. Click on **Yes** to send the files or folders to the Recycle Bin on your Desktop.

2 Files in the Recycle Bin continue to take up space until the bin is emptied. To completely remove an item from your computer, double-click on the **Recycle Bin** Desktop icon. Click on the item, then on the **Organize** button and select **Delete**. You will be asked to confirm your choice.

If you send a file to the Recycle Bin by mistake, Windows allows you to restore it to its original location.

RESTORING FILES

The Recycle Bin has a useful safety net if you make a mistake in deleting an item. To rescue a file from the bin, double-click on the **Recycle Bin** Desktop icon, right-click on the file you want to rescue and then on **Restore**. Your file will now be restored to its original location.

Empty your bin

If you want to empty the Recycle Bin completely, double-click on its Desktop icon. A window will open showing the contents.

Now click on the **Empty the Recycle Bin** button. Confirm the command at the prompt.

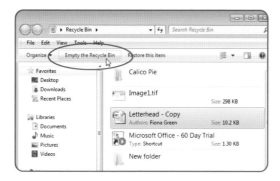

Watch out

To remove program files, use the special Uninstalling function described on page 54. Do not drag them into the Recycle Bin.

Tidying your hard disk

Learn **how to** uninstall **software to** create space **on your PC**

Over time, your PC's hard disk may become clogged up with programs you no longer use. Removing them is often the best way to create space and ensure that your computer continues to run smoothly.

It is essential that programs are removed completely. Simply dropping them into the Recycle Bin is like pulling up a weed and leaving the roots behind.

Get it right

To ensure effective removal, programs may have their own uninstall facilities, to be found in each program's folder. For the many that do not, use the Uninstall a Program function in Windows.

The steps here are a guide only, as each uninstalling process is unique.

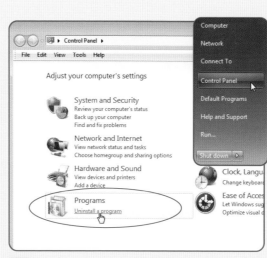

1 Windows 7 has a built-in utility that helps you to remove unwanted programs properly. Go to the **Start** menu, click on **Control Panel**. In the window that appears, click on **Uninstall a program** under 'Programs'.

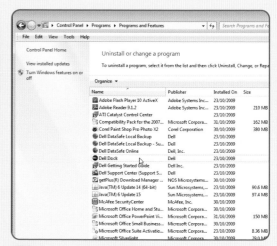

2 The 'Uninstall or change a program' window appears, with a list of all the programs that can be removed using this process. Scroll through and click on the one you want to remove.

Watch out
Before uninstalling any programs, check that no-one else in the family wants to keep them. Then close down all active programs before starting the uninstall process.

Specialist uninstalling software

Some programs do not come with an uninstall option which means Windows will not put them into its 'Uninstall or change a program' list. Other programs may be listed but then throw up problems while you are trying to uninstall them. To deal with these programs, consider buying some of the specialist uninstalling software available. Most of this software is inexpensive and can sometimes be obtained as shareware (software distributed free with magazines for a trial period).

Bright idea
Before you uninstall any software, back up any related data that you wish to keep and ensure that you still have the original installation CDs in case you want to reinstall the program later.

If you have placed a shortcut on your Desktop to the program you have deleted you will need to remove the shortcut separately yourself.

▶ REMOVING SHORTCUTS

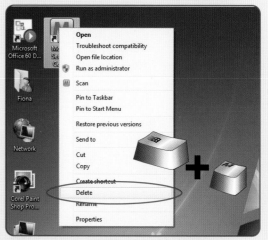

3 Click on the **Uninstall** button (some programs may have a 'Remove' button instead). Your PC will open an uninstalling program designed for the software you have chosen. It will ask you to confirm your decision to uninstall. Check that you have selected the right program, then click on the **Yes** button.

4 Your PC will now uninstall all relevant files. A dialogue box will show you the operation in progress. (If some program files are shared with other programs, you will be asked whether you want to remove them. To be safe, choose **No**.)

5 To remove a shortcut on the Desktop to a program that you have deleted, first minimise all your windows to view your Desktop. You can do this by holding down the **Windows** key and pressing **M** at the same time. Right-click on the shortcut icon that you want to remove and choose **Delete** from the pop-up menu.

Watch out
When uninstalling some programs you may be required to insert the original program CD before you can continue. Make sure that you have the CDs available.

Understanding computer viruses

Take **the right** precautions **to keep your** computer healthy

Vigilance pays when it comes to viruses. Make sure you install an anti-virus program on your computer and run it regularly.

Viruses are computer programs designed to cause harm rather than good. Once inside your PC they can cause all sorts of problems, from making unwanted messages appear on your screen, to causing programs to crash, or your printer to stop working. In rare cases, they can even delete all the data on your hard disk.

There are several ways a virus can infiltrate your computer. When they first appeared, viruses were most-often passed on via floppy disks. Nowadays, the biggest threat comes from the internet. Viruses are most-often 'caught' by downloading infected files attached to seemingly innocent email messages.

Anti-virus software

No matter how your computer catches a virus, you probably will not be aware of it until something goes wrong and damage has been done. However, you can take precautions and limit the risk of catching a virus.

The first step is to buy an anti-virus program, such as McAfee's VirusScan. You should also subscribe to an update service, so that your PC will be protected against new viruses. Lastly, install a firewall, especially if you use an 'always-on' broadband service.

Then it is a matter of using your common sense. Treat all email attachments with caution. Set up a weekly routine where you install any new updates to your anti-virus software and run a full check on your hard disk.

How viruses infect your PC

Identifying the different sorts of viruses, and knowing how they spread from one computer to another, will help you to keep your PC infection-free.

TYPES OF VIRUSES

File virus

A file virus infects program files such as spreadsheets, games or accounting software. Once the affected program is running, it can infect other programs on your hard drive.

Macro virus

A macro virus infects individual documents. It affects files created in programs that use macro programming language, such as Microsoft Office's Word and Excel programs. One way to protect against this family of viruses is to set a high level of Macro Security. Go to the **Office** button and click on **Excel Options** at the bottom of the window. Then click on **Trust Center** and select **Trust Center Settings**. Click on **Macro Settings** in the left pane and choose the level of security you want from the options in the right pane. Click on **OK**.

Boot and partition sector viruses

These viruses infect the system software; that is, the special parts of the hard disk that enable your computer to start, or 'boot up'. These viruses may prevent you getting your computer to work at all. They operate by removing your PC's start-up instructions and replacing them with their own set of instructions. You may need specialist help if your computer catches this type of virus.

THE WAYS VIRUSES ARE SPREAD

Portable storage devices

Always be wary of portable storage devices, such as flash drives, as they are made to move files or programs between computers. The more machines that a portable drive or disk is used on, the greater the chances of it picking up a virus and passing it on.

Email

You should be really cautious about opening a file attached to an email as the file itself may carry a virus. As a general rule, do not open up files attached to unsolicited email. However, some email programs can catch viruses simply by opening an infected email message.

CD-ROM

You are safe with a CD-ROM (except in the unlikely event that it was embedded with a virus during manufacture). 'ROM' stands for Read Only Memory, which means it will not accept viruses – or, indeed, any other kind of information. But, with recordable or rewritable CDs you need to be as careful as with other portable storage devices.

Wksstecd4
(D:)

Internet

Do not download software of dubious origin from the internet. Use a reputable company providing software that you know about, such as Corel, IBM, Microsoft, McAfee or Symantec-Norton.

Watch out

Be careful when buying software on a disc. Ensure it comes from a reputable source and that the packaging has not been tampered with. If the disc has been used there is a chance that it carries a virus. Remember, pirated software is illegal and greatly increases the chances of catching viruses.

Key words

Computer bug *A computer bug is different to a virus in that bugs are accidents or mistakes in programming, rather than programs specifically designed to cause harm.*

Keeping up to date

Update Windows **so it stays** stable and secure

Microsoft Windows 7 is a highly secure operating system and many home users will never experience any problems. However, even a system as stable as Windows 7 occasionally needs minor revisions. These are made available via Windows Update and the easiest way to get them is over the internet (see page 88 for how to get online).

The Microsoft website can check out your system and prompt it to download recommended updates. You can even set up your machine to do the checking automatically, so that it alerts you when a new update has been released.

Windows Update can fix minor problems in the ways that Windows operates – nine times out of ten you will not have even noticed that there was a problem – but most updates are made to improve the security of your computer. Security updates are almost inevitable, as no manufacturer can think of every way that a malicious mind might try to break down their product, and obscure security lapses are only discovered after a product has been released to the general public.

Whenever an update to Windows is released, Microsoft publishes information on its website about what is being updated and the problem that it is correcting. Using this information, you can decide whether or not you need to update your system – often the problems addressed on the website are not relevant to home users.

Microsoft also occasionally releases 'Service Packs' – packages of updates and improvements that can be downloaded from the Microsoft website or ordered on CD-ROM.

Bright idea
Keep up to date – it's free.
Windows updates, and updates to other Microsoft products, will not cost you anything. The only possible charges that may apply are from your phone or internet service provider (see page 88).

You need an internet connection to use Windows Update (see page 88). Make sure your modem is plugged into a phone socket.

▶ BEFORE YOU START

Bright Idea
Office Update works in a similar way to Windows Update to keep Microsoft Office fully up to date.

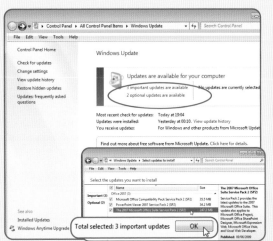

1 Go to the **Start** button, click on **All Programs**, then on **Windows Update**. The Windows Update screen will now be displayed. Click on **Check for updates** from the left-hand pane to start the update process. A progress bar displays while the checking takes place.

2 After the scan is complete, a results window opens stating the number of critical and/or optional updates available. There may be none. Click on **important updates are available** (a number will precede this if relevant), for details. Click to select updates to install – a review is displayed in the right panel. Click on **OK**.

3 Click on **Install updates**. A progress bar will appear during the installation and, when complete, a results window will show a summary of the update. Read and accept any licence agreements and wait while the installation finishes. When this is completed you will be asked to restart your PC.

Auto updating

Your PC can automatically check for updates when you are online. The process can be slow, so a fast internet connection is preferable. To set automatic updates, go to the **Start** menu and click on **Control Panel** in the right-hand pane. Next, click on **System and Security** and under 'Windows Update' click on **Turn automatic updating on or off**. Click on the **Install updates automatically (recommended)** option from the drop-down menu, then set your frequency and time options. Finally, click on **OK** to save this setting.

Defragment and clean up the hard disk

How to help your computer to perform at its best

Taking care of your computer means ensuring that the hard disk is working at its optimum level. Defragmenting and cleaning the hard disk on a regular basis will help it to do this. Defragmenting makes sure large files can be stored in such a way that access to them is as easy and quick as possible. Removing unwanted files from your hard disk will free up space and make your computer work much more efficiently.

Windows 7 has two useful tools – Disk Defragmenter and Disk Cleanup – that carry out these tasks. You should use these tools on a regular basis to maintain the smooth running of your PC.

> *It can take half an hour or more to defragment your hard disk. Do not set the process in motion if you have not got this time to spare.*

DISK DEFRAGMENTING

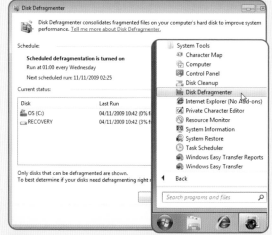

1 To start a manual Disk Defragmentation process, go to the **Start** menu, select **All Programs**, then **Accessories**, click on **System Tools**, then on **Disk Defragmenter**.

Close-up

When you save a large file, your computer will often split it up into fragments and store it in different locations on the hard disk. Your computer can still find the file but it takes longer to do so. Disk Defragmenter rearranges the fragments of a large file so that they are stored next to each other. This makes it easier and quicker for your computer to access files.

Bright idea
If you use your computer to edit your home videos, you will be placing many gigabytes of data onto your hard disk. Even a large disk can fill up quickly and become badly fragmented, so it is a good idea to regularly defragment the disk drive.

Find files you do not need on your hard disk and delete them to free up memory.

DISK CLEANUP

2 In the Disk Defragmenter dialogue box, click on the **Defragment disk** button to start the process. The Windows 'circle' starts spinning, showing that the process is working. If you need to stop the process, click on **Stop operation** and continue at some other time. Click on **Close** to finish.

1 Go to the **Start** menu, select **All Programs**, **Accessories**, then **System Tools**, then click on **Disk Cleanup**. The Disk Cleanup dialogue box displays a progress bar as the amount of space to be freed up is calculated.

2 In the dialogue box that opens, click in the check boxes next to the file or files you wish to delete. Click on **OK** then in the Disk Cleanup dialogue box click on **Delete Files** to confirm the operation.

Set the schedule
You can set the schedule so that your PC runs the defragmentation program overnight once a week. In the Disk Defragmentation dialogue box, click on the **Configure schedule...** button (to the far right of the box), then select how often and at what time you would like it to run. Then click **OK**. Just remember to leave your PC switched on that night.

Caring for your equipment

Cleaning hardware **regularly will** prevent problems **in the future**

Your computer needs simple but regular maintenance to stay in good condition. Problems such as your mouse seizing up, or the keys on your keyboard becoming stuck, can be avoided easily if you clean your equipment regularly. And keeping your work space clean and tidy will create a more pleasant environment for everyone to work in.

Simple measures include making a rule that you do not drink or eat at or near your PC, and that you protect it with a suitable dust cover when not in use. When cleaning, spare a few minutes to check that those 'spaghetti' wires are out of harm's way, too.

Kit yourself out

Have a cleaning routine that you carry out once a month. As with any type of cleaning, ensure that you have the correct materials for the job. Computer stockists offer a variety of cleaning products, but a multi-purpose cleaning kit is probably the best choice for the home user. A typical kit comprises PC wipes, PC buds, cleaning cloths, cleaning fluid and a cleaning card. You should also consider buying a dust spray.

Before you start cleaning, make sure you have turned your equipment off at the wall socket – it is never safe to use fluids with electricity.

Dust and stains on your screen can make it difficult to read.

⚠ Watch out
Never use ordinary household spray polish or liquid spray cleaners on your keyboard. If liquid gets between or under the keys, it can damage the mechanism.

💡 Bright idea
Before cleaning your keyboard, turn it upside down over a bin and shake it gently. Much of the debris that has slipped between and under the keys will fall out.

Cleaning your hardware

A few minutes of light maintenance every month is all that is required to keep your machine running at peak performance and in showroom condition.

The keyboard

Because your keyboard is an exposed component of your computer, dirt will inevitably accumulate between and under its keys. To remove it, wipe the keys with special cleaning buds or use dust spray to blow away dust. If you have them, work cleaning cards dipped in cleaning solution between the keys.

The printer

Check the paper paths of your printer to ensure they are clean and free from ink or toner. Use wipes to remove any spillage, but take care not to get toner on your hands or clothes as it is difficult to remove. Do not touch the printing mechanism itself unless the print manual gives cleaning advice on this. Perform a print test (see your print manual for instructions) to check on the ink or toner level. Replace print cartridges or toner as required.

CD and DVD drives

Keeping your CD and DVD drive clean ensures that programs and files can be accessed smoothly and are less prone to data loss.

Specialist CD/DVD cleaning disks are available from computer stockists. Simply insert the appropriate cleaning disk and follow the on-screen instructions.

The monitor

It is important that you keep your monitor screen in pristine condition. Using a dirty, stained screen leads to unnecessary eyestrain. Use a PC wipe to keep the screen clean, clear and safe – the non-smear varieties are best for the job.

The mouse   Follow this routine to keep your mouse running smoothly.

1 Turn the mouse upside down and wipe the base firmly with a special PC wipe.

2 Twist the mouse-ball cover so that it opens and the ball falls out into your hand.

3 Clean the mouse ball with a lint-free cloth. Dab it with sticky tape to pick up any dust or dirt that has accumulated on it.

4 Using a PC bud, remove dust from inside the socket, focusing on the rollers that make contact with the ball. Finally, put the ball back and replace the cover.

Cleaning an infrared mouse

1 Turn the mouse upside down and then wipe the base.

2 Using tweezers or a PC bud, gently work out any dirt or dust that has built up around the infrared sensor eyehole.

Welcome to the world of Windows

Fast and flexible – your PC's operating system lets you use your PC with confidence

To drive your car you do not need to know the intimate workings of an engine. It helps should you break down, but it is not essential. So it is with Windows. You do not need to know the layers of code that make it run, you just need to know the best way to drive it, while getting the most benefit.

Windows gets its name from the fact that every program – word processor, database, spreadsheet – operates inside its own window on your PC's Desktop.

Keeping your house in order

Windows is an 'operating system' – the set of instructions that make sure your computer runs smoothly. It keeps your files in order, and allows your PC to perform basic jobs, such as printing.

You can personalise Windows to suit your needs by, for example, giving your computer its own background (a picture or pattern that covers your Desktop).

Windows 7 has a choice of dramatic images to decorate your Desktop.

Key words

Start menu *This is where you can quickly access key functions, such as customising Windows controls. Click on the **Start** button and a menu pops up. Select an item by clicking on it.*

Advances in Windows

Since Windows first appeared, it has been updated to keep pace with new technology. Windows 7 is the latest version but Windows XP is still widely used.

Windows 7 contains many familiar features – a Desktop with a Recycle bin, a Start button and Taskbar. Like earlier versions, Windows 7 can only run software that is compliant with Windows.

The Windows Start menu is retained, with dedicated folders for music, pictures and other types of file. Windows 7 also integrates closely with the internet and is more stable than its predecessors.

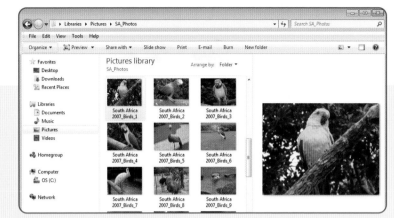

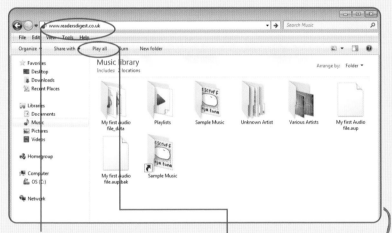

Windows 7 lets you connect to internet sites by typing a web address into the Address box. You have to be connected to do this.

Windows puts buttons on the toolbar that are linked to tasks relevant to the folder being looked at. In 'Music', for example, there is the option to 'Play all'.

Changing face of PCs

In the days of DOS – the PC operating system before Windows – the way to print a file, say, was by typing in intricate commands in computer language (below).

```
Command Prompt
Microsoft Windows [Version 6.1.7600]
Copyright (c) 2009 Microsoft Corporation.

C:\Users\Fiona>
```

The birth of Windows 3.1, then Windows 95 and 98, literally changed the face of PCs. The visual nature of Windows lets you see exactly what you are doing on your PC's Desktop.

The mouse became the new steering wheel. It allows you to move

and organise files by picking them up and dropping them into the folders that you have created and named.

The Start button and Taskbar introduced in Windows 95 meant that you could find files, open programs and use Windows' many tools in just a few moves of the mouse. Windows 7 has streamlined many features and added some extras – such as 'see through' windows (see page 82) and a way of arranging windows in a three-dimensional stack.

Bright idea

*Help is always at hand. Click on the **Start** button and select **Help and Support** from the right-hand menu. Alternatively, simply press the **F1** key on your keyboard to get assistance relevant to the program you are using.*

Getting to grips with Windows

Organise **your Desktop for** maximum efficiency **and** ease of use

Your computer's Desktop is much like a conventional desk in that it holds files, folders, documents and tools. These are all represented on your PC by icons.

By double-clicking on any icon you will open it. The opened icon – whatever it represents – will appear as a separate window on your Desktop, and its size, shape and position can all be set by you.

Having several windows open on your Desktop at once can be just as confusing as having a pile of papers scattered all over your desk. But there are ways to keep your work area tidy and boost your efficiency.

Managing the size of a window
The buttons in the top right-hand corner of a window control its appearance.

The Minimise button
Click on the **Minimise** button to shrink the window to a button on the Taskbar. Clicking on the Taskbar button will restore the window to the Desktop.

The Maximise button
Click on the **Maximise** button to expand the window to fill the whole screen. When a window is maximised, the button changes to a Restore button. Click on this to restore the window to its original size.

The Close button
Click on the **Close** button to close a window or program.

Scroll bars
Often, you will not be able to see all the contents of a window. When this happens, scroll bars appear to the right of, and/or bottom of, the window.

To view the window's contents, click on the arrows at each end of the scroll bar, or click on the slider itself and, keeping your finger pressed down on the mouse button, drag it along.

Resizing a window
To adjust the height or width of a window, click on any of the window's edges (the mouse pointer will change to a double-headed arrow when you are in position). Keeping your finger pressed down on the mouse button, drag the window in or out.

To resize the width and height at the same time, click on the window's corner and drag it diagonally.

Shortcut
*You may find it easier and quicker to maximise windows by double-clicking on the **Title** bar that runs across the top of them.*

Close-up
*To see what is behind a maximised window, press the **Alt** key and then the **Tab** key (with **Alt** still pressed). Open windows appear as icons in a blue panel. Press the **Tab** key to move along the icons and when the one you want is selected, release the **Alt** key to open it up.*

Bright idea
*If several windows are open and you need to see your Desktop, right-click on the **Taskbar** and click on **Show the Desktop** in the pop-up menu. To restore the windows to your screen, click on **Show Open Windows**.*

Arranging windows on your Desktop

Windows is extremely flexible when it comes to organising open folders and documents.

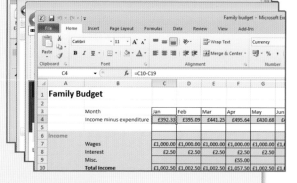

Stacking your windows

You can arrange your windows so that you can see the contents of each one at the same time. Individual windows can be 'stacked' in a neat arrangement across your screen so that every open window is visible on the Desktop.

Right-click on the **Taskbar** and select **Show Windows Stacked**. This arranges all your folders and open programs into a tile-like layout. To revert back to your former screen, right-click on the **Taskbar** and select **Undo Show Stacked**.

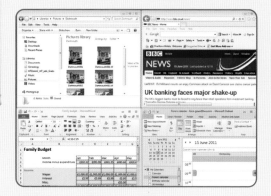

Working with a number of windows

Ideally, it is best to have just one or two windows open on your screen at any one time. This not only keeps your Desktop tidy, but also makes it less likely that you will file documents in the wrong place.

Cascading windows

Another handy option is Cascade Windows, which arranges windows so that each one overlaps the one before, diagonally, from the top left-hand corner of your screen. This is useful if you have several windows open, as you will still be able to see the name of each one filed behind the other. Clicking on a cascaded window will bring it to the front of your stack.

To operate this function, right-click on the **Taskbar** then click on **Cascade Windows** from the pop-up menu. To revert back to your former screen, right-click on the **Taskbar** and select **Undo Cascade**.

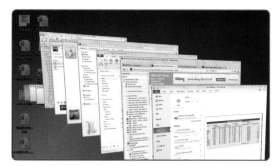

Exploring Windows 7

Windows 7 offers some alternative ways of managing open windows. Here are three display features that employ the latest 'user interface' technology. Flip 3D (shown left) can be opened by pressing the **Windows** key and the **Tab** key at the same time. This will show you all open windows in a 3D display. Hold the **Windows** key down and press the **Tab** key to move through them. Windows Flip (top right) displays all your open windows on a blue bar in the centre of your screen. Press **Alt + Tab** to open it, and tab through them. You can also see a 'thumbnail' image of an open document (bottom right) if you hover the mouse over an item on the Taskbar.

Personalising your Desktop

Decorate your PC to make it feel like part of the furniture

We all like to add individual touches to our houses. The colour that we paint our front door and the layout of our front gardens make us feel that our home truly belongs to us. It is just as easy to put a personal stamp on Windows.

If, for instance, you do not particularly like the background colour or pattern of your Desktop you can change it by selecting a different background from Windows' library. The options include landscapes, flowers, shapes and animals. You can change your Desktop background again easily if you get bored with it.

Background design

To change the background on your Desktop, right-click anywhere on the Desktop and select **Personalize** from the pop-up menu. In the box that appears, click on the **Desktop Background** option. You can then choose from a list of pictures that are grouped under headings such as 'Architecture' and 'Characters'. Alternatively, you can click on **Browse** to find and use one of your own images.

Click on an image to temporarily change your Desktop to your selection. Under 'Picture Position' choose from the drop-down list of options. Experiment to see which you like best – Fill, Fit, Stretch, Tile or Center. Click on more than one image and choose an option under 'Change picture every:'. When you have selected your new background and positioning option, click on **Save changes**.

Key word

Properties *Nearly everything you see in Windows has its own 'Properties', which gives valuable information about your PC's resources and allows you to vary its settings. To see an item's properties, right-click on the object and select* **Properties** *from the pop-up menu.*

Bright idea

To remind yourself of an important or amusing message or slogan, select the **3D Text** *screen saver. Type in your text and select a font, colour and style for it, along with the speed at which you wish it to travel across your screen.*

While you were away …

Screensavers appear when your PC is on but not in use. They can be fun and also protect work from prying eyes. To select a screensaver, right-click anywhere on the Desktop and select **Personalize** from the pop-up menu. Click on the **Screen Saver** option. Scroll through and select an option in the 'Screen saver' box. It then appears in the preview window. (You can choose **Photos** to display the images in your Pictures folder as your screensaver.) Set the length of time your PC waits before activating the screensaver in the 'Wait' box, then click on **OK**.

On some PCs the Screen Saver tab has an energy-saving option that reduces the amount of power to your monitor and/or hard disk after a set period of inactivity. Click on **Change power settings** *(left) and select appropriate timescales from the list.*

More than just a Desktop

Themes allow you to change your background, window colour, sounds and screen saver all at once. To apply a theme, right-click on the Desktop and then on **Personalize**. In the 'Change the visuals and sounds on your computer' panel, select a theme from the various categories that are standard with Windows 7.

Setting passwords for users

If your PC has more than one user, each can have their own personalised version of Windows 7. They can access the PC without interfering with other users' settings. Each has their own background, folders and Start menu items.

Users with administrator rights can set up accounts. Go to the **Start** menu, click on **Control Panel** then click on **Add or remove user accounts** under 'User Accounts and Family Safety'. Beneath the main pane in the box that appears, click on **Create a new account**. Enter a user name and select an account type, then click on **Create Account**. The account appears in the User Accounts window. Click on it and select **Create a password**.

Customising Windows controls

Tailor **your** computer's settings **to make it work the way** you want

When you are using your PC it is helpful to know that you can tailor Windows controls to suit your needs. For example, you can change the speed at which your mouse double-clicks, alter the size and shape of the mouse pointer, and change the appearance of your screen. Left-handed users can even swap the role of the mouse buttons.

If you are visually impaired, changing the shape and size of your mouse pointer will help you to see it more clearly on screen.

Mouse settings

To customise your mouse settings, go to the **Start** menu, click on **Control Panel**, **Hardware and Sound** then on **Mouse** under 'Devices and Printers'. There are five tabs at the top of the Mouse Properties dialogue box – Buttons, Pointers, Pointer Options, Wheel and Hardware.

Buttons allows left-handed users to swap the role of the mouse buttons; Pointers lets you choose a 'scheme' for your on-screen pointer; in Pointer Options you can alter the speed at which your mouse pointer moves; and in Wheel you can adjust how far your mouse wheel scrolls down the page.

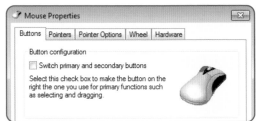

Bright idea
*Windows is aware of British Summer Time and can change the clock in spring and autumn. In the Date and Time dialogue box, you can request a reminder. Tick the box by **Notify me when the clock changes** and then click on **OK**.*

Date and time

The current date and time are displayed on the right-hand side of the Taskbar.

To set the date or time, click on the Taskbar Clock. A calendar pops up. Click on **Change date and time settings** beneath the calendar. Under the Date and Time tab, click on **Change date and time**. You can then click on the arrows to change the time, or click on the calendar to amend the date. Click on **OK**.

*To prevent pressing the Caps Lock key accidentally and typing in capital letters, use Toggle Keys, which will alert you with a warning sound. In the Ease of Access Center, click on **Make the keyboard easier to use**. Then click in the box next to **Turn on Toggle Keys** and click on **OK**.*

Disability options in Windows

Windows offers help to users with disabilities. Go to the **Start** menu, select **Control Panel**, then **Ease of Access**. These are some of the options available within the Ease of Access Center:
● If you are hard of hearing, set your PC to send out visual warnings. Click on the **Replace sounds with visual cues** option. Choose your visual warning notifications. Click on **Apply**, then on **OK**.
● If you have trouble moving your mouse, click on **Make the mouse easier to use**. Turn on Mouse Keys to use the numeric keypad on the right-hand side of your keyboard to move your mouse pointer.

● If you are visually impaired, click on **Optimize visual display** and select the high-contrast viewing mode. You can also have text and descriptions read aloud by clicking in the box next to **Turn on Narrator**. Click on **Apply**, then on **OK** to keep your settings.
● Users with slight visual impairments can also use the Magnifier. At the foot of the 'Optimize visual display' box, click in the box next to **Turn on Magnifier**. This will create a separate window at the top of the screen that displays a magnified portion of the screen.

Setting sounds

If your PC has a sound card you can configure Windows to play a number of built-in sounds. Go to the **Start** menu, select **Control Panel**, then **Hardware and Sound**, then click on **Change system sounds** under the 'Sound' category.

In the Sounds tab, scroll down and click on an event in the 'Program' box. Now click on the arrow under the 'Sounds' box, scroll through and click on your preferred sound (or **None** for no sound). Click **OK**. To preview sounds, select a sound from the list and click on **Test** to hear it.

Close-up
*Windows 7 lets you decide how you open folders on your Desktop (with one click or two), and whether folders open within the same window or separate windows. Go to the **Start** menu, click on **Control Panel** and then on **Appearance and Personalization**. Under 'Folder Options', click on **Specify single or double-click to open**. In the General tab of the dialogue box, click beside the setting you want and then click on **OK**.*

Create your own shortcuts

Fine-tune **the way you work on** your PC, **and** save **yourself** time and energy

O nce you are familiar with the basic workings of Windows and you have a reasonable understanding of which programs and commands you use most often, you can begin using shortcuts to help you to launch or activate them quickly.

You can create simple shortcuts to folders, documents and to almost anything else, including a printer, program and a drive. These can then be activated directly from the Desktop or Start button. You can also arrange for programs to launch when you start up Windows.

The Start menu

The Start menu in Windows 7 watches how you use your computer and changes its contents accordingly. For example, the lower part of the left-hand column will gradually fill up with a list of programs that you use most often – there is no need to tell Windows to do this.

Like most things in Windows 7, the Start menu is fully customisable. You can choose how many programs it displays and whether it shows a list of the ten documents that you most recently worked on. If you choose, you can also customise the Start menu to show links to the documents you have opened most frequently.

You do not have to rely on Windows 7 to put programs in the Start menu for you. You can also choose to 'pin' a program to the menu so that it is always quickly available for you to start up. Click on the **Start** button to open the Start menu, click on **All Programs** and choose the program you wish to add. Right-click on it, and choose **Pin to Start Menu**. The program's icon will now appear in the upper left-hand part of your Start menu.

Close-up
Windows 7 allows each user of a computer to set up the Start menu, Taskbar and Desktop to suit their preferences. When you log in to the computer, your Desktop and menus will appear just the way you like them.

Bright idea
Users of earlier versions of Windows will now find the Show Desktop button has been moved to the far right of the task bar, where you can temporarily view or peek at the Desktop by using the mouse to point at the button. Open windows will fade to reveal the Desktop. Move the mouse away to make them reappear. Alternatively, click on the button to minimise all open windows. Click again to restore them.

Customise the Start menu to suit the way you work

You can change the Start menu to suit how you use your computer. Choose whether you want to view items in new windows or as further menus – you're the boss.

Viewing folders as menus

It can sometimes be quicker to view commonly used items, such as the Control Panel, as a menu attached to the side of the Start menu, rather than cluttering up the screen with a new window.

To view the Control Panel as a sub-menu, right-click anywhere on the Taskbar at the bottom of the screen. In the pop-up menu select **Properties** then click on the **Start Menu** tab. Click on **Customize**. Under the 'Control Panel' section, click on the **Display as a menu** option. Click on **OK**, then on **Apply**, and on **OK** again to close the Taskbar and Start Menu Properties dialogue box.

Now when you open the Start menu and move your mouse pointer over Control Panel on the right pane, a list of all your Control Panel items will open to the right. You can use the same procedure for other Start menu items – you might add the Computer, Pictures and Music folders, for example.

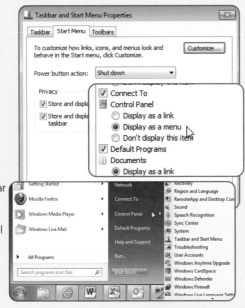

Show on Desktop

It often helps to be able to reach your most commonly used items from the Desktop.

To place an icon for Documents on the Desktop, click on **Start** to open the Start menu. Right-click on **Documents**, and choose **Send To** from the drop-down menu, then **Desktop (create shortcut)** from the sub-menu of options that appears. Every time you start up your PC now, a shortcut for Documents will appear. Double-click on the icon to access all the files within the folder.

Windows 7 will allow you to place as many shortcuts and/or files and folders on the Desktop as you like. Try to avoid too much clutter though.

The ultimate time-saver ...

You can arrange for a frequently used program to launch whenever Windows starts. Go to the **Start** menu, click on **All Programs** and navigate through the pop-up menus to find the program you want. Right-click on it and choose **Copy**. Click on **Start** and then **All Programs** again and double-click on **Startup**. The Startup items folder will open. Right-click in it and choose **Paste Shortcut**. A Shortcut icon for the program you have chosen will now appear in the Startup items folder. When you next restart your computer and log in, your chosen program will start automatically.

Quick keyboard commands

Save yourself **time by using** 'hot-keys' **instead of your** mouse

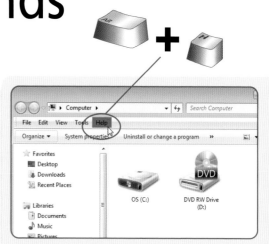

Nearly all the actions or commands you perform with your mouse can also be done by pressing 'hot-keys' – single keys or a combination of keys on your keyboard. For example, in Microsoft Word you can access the spelling and grammar facility by pressing one of the 'F', or function, keys at the top of your keyboard, or print by pressing the Ctrl and 'P' keys at the same time.

Using the hot-keys is quicker than using your mouse, especially if you do a lot of work from the keyboard, such as word processing.

Taking control with shortcuts

There are a number of keyboard options that can help you to quickly perform everyday tasks on your PC. Once you have a program running, you can hold down the **Ctrl** key and press **N** to open a new file or window from that program. To close a file – in any program – hold down **Ctrl** and then press **W**. Cut, copy and paste functions can also be easily accessed with keyboard combinations. Hold down the **Ctrl** key and press **X** to cut, **Ctrl** + **C** to copy and **Ctrl** + **V** to paste.

Some options in menus allow you to use the keyboard to choose them. For an example, launch Word, go to the Office button and look at the 'Exit Word' button. The 'x' is underlined, indicating that you can press **X** to select it. Look out for similar, underlined shortcuts.

Shortcut
*Most keyboards have a Windows key – found between the Ctrl and Alt keys. Press it to open the Start menu and use the cursor keys to move around the menu items. Press the **Return** key to open a highlighted option or program.*

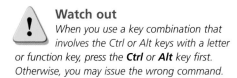

Watch out

*When you use a key combination that involves the Ctrl or Alt keys with a letter or function key, press the **Ctrl** or **Alt** key first. Otherwise, you may issue the wrong command.*

Key words

***Keyboard shortcut** This describes a key combination that replaces a mouse command. It can take the form of pressing just one key, such as a function key, or several keys, such as **Ctrl** + **F4**.*

Accessing the Quick Access bar

The Quick Access toolbar present in the Microsoft Office 2007 programs – including Word, Excel and PowerPoint – allows you to use many of the most common functions with just one click. Initially, it will include only the Save, Undo and Redo commands, but you can choose to add others.

To customise the Quick Access bar, click on the down arrow to the right of the bar. A menu appears, showing all the functions that can be added. Click on one to select it – a tick appears on its left, and an icon will be added to the toolbar.

Using the function keys

The function keys along the top of your keyboard perform pre-assigned duties, or functions.

Press **F1** to access a program's Help facility. This helps you to solve software problems.

From the Window's Desktop, press **F3** to access the Find: All Files dialogue box (above). This lets you search your hard disk to find a file.

You can use function keys in combination with other keys. To close a window or program, for example, press the **Alt** key and the **F4** key at the same time.

Moving around the Desktop

You can use keyboard shortcuts to move around your Desktop. For example, click on the **Computer** icon then press the arrow keys to move around your various Desktop items. They become highlighted when selected. (Against the default Windows 7 Desktop this is very subtle in appearance.) Press **Return** to open a selected icon – try this on your Documents folder.

The same principle applies inside the folders. In Documents, use the arrow keys to move around the folder's contents. Press **Return** to open a file or folder.

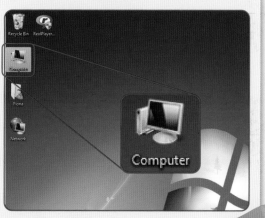

Important command keys

F-keys

Escape

Tab

Shift

Ctrl Windows Alt Space-bar Return Cursor keys Numeric keypad

Delete

Return

Becoming a dab hand

If you have more than one window open, you can bring each one to the front of your Desktop using the **Alt** + **Tab** keys. Press (and hold) **Alt** then **Tab** and a bar will appear with icons showing all the windows you have open. The uppermost window's icon will have an outline around it. To move to the next and subsequent icons, press the **Tab** key while still holding down **Alt**. Release on the window you want to view.

Windows built-in programs

Learn about these mini-applications and they will soon become indispensable

Windows comes with a number of programs, known as Accessories. These are really useful and – even better – they do not cost a penny extra.

If you need to open a text document created in a program you do not have, you can use the Notepad text editor. You can play music on your computer and create compilation CDs using Windows Media Player. Once you familiarise yourself with Windows' accessory programs, you will be surprised how often you use them.

Where to find accessory programs

To find Windows' accessory programs, go to the **Start** menu, select **All Programs** then **Accessories**. A menu with the accessory programs will drop down.

These include a Calculator, Paint for image editing and Notepad for very basic word processing.

The Accessories menu contains other useful system tools to keep your computer up to date. For example, under System Tools, Disk Cleanup will remove unwanted files and Character Map will help you to find those accented characters that are always hard to locate.

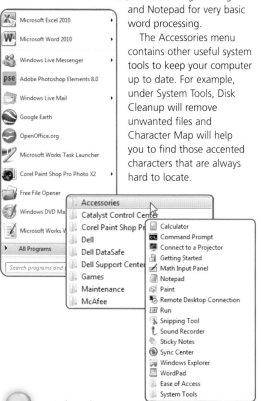

Bright idea

Windows Media Player can 'rip', or extract, music data from your CDs and store it on your hard drive. To save hard disk space, the music is stored in a special read-only format called WMA, which stands for Windows Media Audio. See also 'Create a party CD' on page 236.

Close-up
*Notepad will only let you work in one font and font size per document. Go to the **Edit** menu and click on **Set Font**. Select a font and size. These will then be applied to the whole document.*

Everything you need from a word processor

WordPad is an effective word processor that has many features in common with Word. It includes a toolbar that lets you do tasks quickly, has a good selection of fonts and font sizes and even lets you format text. The only important function it lacks is a spellchecker.

Notepad is far more basic. Referred to as a text editor, rather than word processor, it creates only plain text files – that is, files that lack formatting, such as bullet points or a mixture of fonts. Notepad is the program to use if you need your document to be readable on any type of computer.

For your entertainment

Windows Media Player allows you to play many different kinds of audio and video files, as well as extract audio from CDs to store and play back from your hard drive (see below left). Using Media Player, you can create your own playlist and burn personalised CDs. You can also have psychedelic images swirling on screen while your songs play, and choose from a number of offbeat 'skins' that change the complete look of the program – from ultra-modern to plain surreal!

Special characters

Character Map lets you view the characters that are available in a selected font, but do not have a dedicated key on the keyboard – accented letters, for example. To use them, copy individual characters or a group of characters to the Clipboard. From there, you can then paste them into your document.

Working with images

Paint is a simple drawing package that lets you do some basic photo editing. You can also, with practice, create your own artwork. It can be a useful tool, but if you plan to take a lot of digital photography, it might be worth buying a full photo-editing program.

Making all your sums add up

Calculator carries out basic addition, subtraction, multiplication and division.

To use it, click on **Calculator** in the Accessories menu. Then, either click the on-screen calculator keys using your mouse, or use the numeric keypad on the right-hand side of your keyboard.

The Copy and Paste options in the Edit menu let you transfer numbers to other programs. If you want advanced functions, go to the **View** menu and click on **Scientific**. Choose **Standard** to return to the basic form.

Make the right connection

Speed **costs** – how **fast** do you want **to go?**

Computers today are designed to communicate with each other, and the wider world, using the internet. This is your gateway to a mind-boggling wealth of entertainment and information. You can chat with friends and family, check email, surf the web, and access everything from music to movies and software.

Windows 7 makes it a simple job to connect to your internet service provider (ISP) and get online – see pages 88-89. Until the fairly recent past, this would have involved connecting through a dial-up modem built into your computer. Such, often frustratingly slow, 'narrowband' connections are still available, but now most people take advantage of much faster 'broadband' options.

Broadband connection

You can surf the web with cheap, high-speed internet access, known as 'broadband', using either ADSL or cable technologies (see page 89).

Broadband is available almost everywhere, and gives you access to the internet at many times the speed of a dial-up link. The connection is 'always on', so you do not have to wait for a modem to dial up and log on before you get started. It makes a big difference.

To download a 5-minute song would take around 12 minutes on a dial-up modem. On broadband, it varies from a few seconds with the slower connections to virtually instantaneous with the highest-speed broadband.

For most broadband packages you pay a flat monthly fee – so no unexpectedly high phone bills. What price you pay depends on the speed of your connection – that is how quickly you can download files. The figure given by ISPs is the maximum possible, so in practice the speed is likely to be less.

In addition, some broadband providers limit how much you can download each month – also called a usage allowance. The limits typically range from 10 to 30 gigabytes (Gb). For light internet use 10Gb should be enough. It allows you to download around 2,500 music files, 14 videos or stream 25 hours of TV a month. If you think you might want to download more, it is best to look for a broadband package that offers unlimited monthly usage.

Picking a broadband connection

A broadband service can be provided in a number of ways and at different speeds. Costs have plummeted in recent years, but before you sign up and commit to a particular scheme you should consider what your exact requirements are.

ADSL

With an ADSL modem (see page 89) connected to your computer, a huge amount of data can be squeezed down an ordinary phone line.

A new generation of superfast broadband – known as ADSL2+ or ADSL Max – is becoming increasingly available. This offers speeds up to 24 megabites (Mb) per second and higher, and is ideal if you have several computers at home sharing the same connection and want to take advantage of newer online services like TV and film on demand.

Cable

If you live in an area where cable TV is available, you can get high-speed internet access through the same fibre-optic cabling. A cable connection can offer broadband speeds up to 50Mb, roughly nine times the speed of the average ADSL connection. Using the full bandwidth available you could download a music album in as little as 11 seconds or an hour-long TV show in just over a minute. Consequently, it is a good choice for people who do a lot of downloading, or homes where several of the family are regularly online at the same time. As with ADSL you need a special modem to connect your PC to the internet.

Satellite

If you live too far away from the nearest phone exchange for ADSL and cable is not available you can still get a broadband internet connection – via satellite. All that is needed is a box and a small satellite dish, connected to your PC, to send and receive signals. With download speeds up to 3.6Mb it is comparable to some ADSL packages, but is generally more expensive. Satellite broadband is widely available and works well in all but the worst weather.

Wireless broadband

For the ultimate freedom to surf the internet wherever you are in the house – or even garden – you can access a broadband connection wirelessly (see page 89). All you need is a router, which combines a modem – ADSL or cable – with a wireless (often referred to as WiFi) access point, called a hotspot. Your PC, video game console or even mobile phone, if they are WiFi enabled, can use this access point to link to your broadband connection.

To get the most from your home wireless network, though, there are a few steps you should take.
• Make sure you secure your network, with a hard-to-guess password. If not, neighbours – or even hackers – can 'piggyback' your internet connection and use it for free.
• If the internet appears slow it may be because there are lots of obstacles, like walls, between you and the router. Try moving location to see if that makes a difference.
• Your router should be as close as possible to the point where the broadband line enters the house.

Mobile broadband

Many mobile phones let you surf the web, wherever you can get a signal. The same mobile coverage is also available for your laptop computer. All you need is a modem, called a dongle, which plugs into a USB port on your PC. Then you can connect to the internet, virtually wherever you are, using the mobile phone networks.

Where possible these devices use the high-speed 3G (third generation) phone networks that should eventually cover most areas. They offer download speeds of up to 7.2Mb.

With mobile broadband you can check your emails, watch a video or just surf the web wherever you are. But watch the cost. Each mobile broadband provider has different pricing schemes and download allowances (expressed in gigabytes – Gb) for their packages. As a rule of thumb, with a monthly 1Gb data allowance you could send 1,000 emails, surf the web for 10 hours or download five 4-minute videos.

There are also other ways to connect to the internet when you are on the move. If your phone or laptop has a wireless card you can use WiFi hotspots in places like coffee shops – just like those on a home wireless network.

Broadband speeds

The speed of your broadband connection, whether ADSL or cable, is affected by the contention ratio – the number of users who share the same connection. Typically, the ratio for ADSL is 50:1 for home users and 20:1 for premium services. This means that you could be competing with up to 49 others for a share of the available bandwidth. In practice, it is rare for everyone to be online at the same time, but connection performance may be worse at busy periods, such as the evening or on a Sunday.

Watch out

One major limitation with ADSL connections is distance. You need to be within approximately three miles of a phone exchange to have an ADSL link. The further you are from the exchange the slower your connection is likely to be. Consequently, it is not worth paying for higher-speed broadband if your line cannot support it.

Making the most of broadband

Connect **your whole** family **with a** home network

Many households these days have more than one computer, each in a different room. It can make sense to join these computers up in a home network, so that they can all share a single printer or scanner. And, with the rapid adoption of broadband internet connections, it also makes sense to allow all the computers in a household to share fast internet access.

There are many different ways to join PCs together in a network, both wireless and wired. However, if there are more than two computers in the house, or if you are likely to be moving computers around (most likely if you have a laptop computer), a wireless network is probably the best solution. This sort of network uses a hub, a device that communicates via radio waves with terminals fitted to all the PCs around the home. The terminals can be cards fitted inside computers or devices attached to the PC by a USB connector. Such a setup can cost surprisingly little, and does not involve any messy wiring and installation of sockets.

Wireless networks most often use a standard called 802.11, often known as the much friendlier 'WiFi'. With a WiFi network you will be able to surf the web in bed or in the garden, and add new computers to your set-up quickly and easily. Although the standard range from network hub to PC is around 25 metres, some enthusiasts have extended this to many miles, using aerials made from old tin cans!

Your WiFi network connects to a broadband internet connection using a separate device called a router. As well as directing internet traffic to the different computers on the network, most routers also work as firewalls, protecting your network from unwanted intrusions via the internet.

⚠ Watch out

The WiFi standard should guarantee that products from different manufacturers will function together perfectly, but this is not always the case. For best results, ensure all your WiFi components come from the same supplier. Many retailers offer 'bundles' for just this purpose.

Building a wireless network

Connect computers and share fast internet access without any messy drilling.

The hardware set-up

The heart of your network is a combined router, firewall and wireless hub. These unobtrusive boxes are best mounted on a wall for maximum range, and will need to be located as near to the centre of your home as possible, to ensure that the signal is strong throughout your property.

Detailed instructions for the set-up and configuration of your router will depend on the particular model and manufacturer you choose. However, networks like this are becoming increasingly popular, so suppliers produce extremely user-friendly devices. They are generally configured using set-up 'wizards' just like those used to set up other hardware in Windows.

Security issues

A wireless network lets you surf the net from your garden. But it will also let anyone else in the vicinity of your house do the same unless you choose the best security options your set-up wizard suggests. At the very least, ensure that all users log-in with a password; better still, use additional security built-in to the WiFi standard, such as Wired Equivalent Privacy (below left). This will prevent any passing hackers or mischievous neighbours from using your network and internet connection or reading your files.

The physical side of things is simple – there are just two cables to plug in to the box: a power lead, and the connection to your ADSL line.

The final touches

Once the router is connected and working, you will need to attach USB terminals to each of your desktop computers, together with the appropriate drivers for each device (older laptops may also need cards to be added). All the software you need will come with the hardware, and this is a simple task that you will carry out only once. Next configure your network on one of your computers. In the **Start** menu, click on **Control Panel**, then **Network and Internet**, **Network and Sharing Center**, and then click on **Set up a new connection or network**. Select **Set up a new network**, and click on **Next**.

The 'Set Up a Network' wizard will then take you through the steps necessary, adding other computers and devices to your network. At each stage, make your selections and then click on **Next**. When finished test your network to ensure that all computers and other devices are connected and working properly. Click on the **Start** button then on your user name. In the left pane of the next window click on **Network**. You should see an icon for your computer and icons for all other computers and devices on the network.

Wireless and safe

All WiFi standard equipment should be able to broadcast and receive using something called Wired Equivalent Privacy (WEP). This is a method of encrypting the data that passes between PCs and the hub so that it cannot be intercepted by a hacker. There are stronger forms of protection available if your data is particularly sensitive, but the standard version is quite safe enough for most home users.

Discover new features

Getting the most out of Windows 7 and Microsoft Office 2010

The latest version of any software package will give the PC user some new features to try out. In this case, the latest software from both Microsoft Windows and Microsoft Office is – in some areas – a greatly revised version of the previous release. The new 'look and feel', as well as the new features, may initially be disconcerting for PC users accustomed to an older version, but it does not take long to adapt and discover that the changes really can make the software more user friendly.

Here we give you a quick run through of some of the most useful features in Windows 7 and Office 2010. It should be helpful both to new PC users, and to those who have upgraded from previous versions.

Windows 7
When you first start your PC in Windows 7, click on the **Start** button and then **Getting Started** to display a set of links to various features to help you to set up your PC. Double-click on **Go online to find out what's new in Windows 7**. This will explain some of the important features of Windows 7.

Searching
Every Windows folder contains a Search box in the top right corner. When you type in the Search box, Windows immediately searches the current folder and sub-folders

Jump Lists
This feature displays a list of recently accessed items associated with a program. To open a Jump List, right-click on a program icon on the taskbar. What is displayed depends on the program – Microsoft Word, for instance, shows recently opened documents (above); Internet Explorer shows frequently viewed websites, while Windows Media Player lists commonly played tunes.

Bright idea
*You can also use the Jump List feature from the Start menu. Click on the **Start** button and move the mouse pointer over the right-pointing arrow to the right of a program and select from the drop-down list.*

'Contextual' tabs appear only when necessary, to aid you with the current task. If, for example, you are inserting a picture into an Office document, you will see 'Picture Tools' displayed in the bar above the additional contextual tab 'Format', giving you an extra Ribbon of commands related to that task.

for file names and any other details that match your search text. Windows then displays its Search Results in the right-hand panel, below the menu bar, with matches to your search text highlighted in yellow. If no items are found, click in the search box again and enter further search criteria, such as Date, Size and Authors.

Alternatively, you can use the Search box on the Start

menu. Click on the **Start** button and type a word, or part of a word, into the box. As you type, items that match your text will be displayed on the Start menu above.

Windows Media Center
You can enjoy live or recorded TV, movies, music and pictures with the Windows Media Center. Click on the **Start** button and select **All Programs**, then **Windows Media Center**. The first time you do this, you will be presented with a Welcome screen inviting you to choose a 'Setup' option – Express or Custom. Make your selection and click on **OK**.

Windows Aero
This special feature gives a translucent glass frame style to your windows, letting you view whatever is underneath. Move your mouse pointer over an item on the Taskbar to view a thumbnail

of the contents of the window. This feature incorporates Windows Flip 3D. Hold down the **Windows** key and press **Tab** to preview your open windows in a three-dimensional stack. With the Windows key held down, continue to press **Tab** until the window you want appears at the front, then release.

Power off
Click on the **Start** button, then on **Shut Down** to start shutting down Windows. To the right of Shut Down is a triangular button – click on this to reveal other options. Click on **Sleep** to put your PC into a low power mode, or **Lock** to lock your PC – you will need to enter a password to unlock it.

Microsoft Office 2010
The Ribbon
This toolbar gives easy access to many tasks with just one click. The tools change according to the tab selected. (See page 23 for more information on the Ribbon.)

Dialogue box launcher

Click on the small diagonal arrow next to a group name on the Ribbon to access the related dialogue box.

Customise the Quick Access Toolbar
To add a command to the toolbar, click on the **Customize Quick Access Toolbar** button. Choose a command from the drop-down list, or select **More Commands** to view more categories. Select one, click on **Add**, then on **OK**.

Viewing and zooming
Click on the viewing percentage at the bottom right of your window to access the Zoom dialogue box, which will allow you to zoom in or out of your document. Alternatively, drag the slider bar.

Control Panel
Windows 7, by default, displays the items of the Control Panel in 'Category' view – showing items grouped together under a common heading. If you have used earlier versions of Windows, you might find that viewing the Control Panel options as icons is easier – this shows items as icons in alphabetical order. Open the Control Panel by clicking on the **Start** button, then on **Control Panel**. To change the view, click on **Category** next to 'View by:' and select either **Large icons** or **Small icons** from the drop-down list.

CONNECTING TO

The **internet** and the **World Wide Web** (the collection of websites created by businesses, societies and individuals) are expanding at a staggering rate. Users can now find **information** quickly on almost any subject. The internet also allows people to send messages in the form of **email** (electronic mail) to every corner of the world. Find out how to **connect** to the internet, then go and **explore** this vast storehouse of knowledge.

THE INTERNET

Welcome to the internet

A meeting place, shopping centre, travel agent and library in one

The internet is made up of a network of millions of computers throughout the world that allow people to access a wide range of information and services. It comprises the World Wide Web, through which people access this information, and facilities such as electronic mail (email), chat areas, forums and newsgroups.

Email is a major part of the internet. Messages are typed into a computer then sent via the internet to other email users tens or thousands of miles away – all for no more than the cost of a local phone call. If you have a particular interest, forums and newsgroups provide an opportunity to exchange opinions and ideas. Many internet service providers (ISPs – the companies that provide connection to the internet) set up discussion areas in which you can comment on issues that interest you.

A spider's web of information

The World Wide Web (WWW or web) is the public face of the internet. It is a vast conglomeration of websites, made up of web pages. The text and images you see on the internet are part of a web page.

Web pages are written in a computer language called HTML, or hypertext markup language, that allows pages to be linked together. A collection of linked pages forms a website, which in turn can be linked to other sites around the world, forming a global spider's web of connected sites.

All websites have unique addresses. These act like phone numbers, connecting your computer to the computer that holds the web page you want to view.

To find your way around the huge tangle of websites – or 'surf the net' – you need a web browser. This is a program that allows you to view pages and move around the web. The most popular web browser is Microsoft Internet Explorer, which is usually installed with Windows 7 and is free of charge. Other web browsers include Mozilla Firefox and Safari.

Once you are online, the web is your oyster. You can use it to buy goods – including books, music, food and clothes – to book holidays, to research any subject, to keep in touch with family and friends, and even to play computer games. For key areas you can explore on the web, see opposite.

All you need to connect to the internet is a modem and an account with an internet service provider (ISP).

The world at your fingertips

Once connected to the internet, you are ready to explore the potential of the World Wide Web. This is made up of a collection of websites that promote a multitude of subjects and interests.

NEWS CHANNEL

Updated at 15:35 GMT, Wednesday

Banker Neil Ellerbeck jailed

UK send to Afgh:

Gordon Bro to send 5 personne cond

The media

The web allows you to access the latest news from newspapers, magazines and broadcasting companies. Many of these services are free. With the correct software you can watch live television broadcasts from the other side of the world. You can even get news of events before they reach the TV news bulletins or the papers.

Travel

Use the web to access travel guides, check the latest weather reports, book flights and accommodation, view exchange rates, and find out what other visitors thought of a destination.

Shopping

You can buy virtually anything on the internet – from new shirts to a new home. The internet also has online shopping malls designed to bring together websites for shoppers in one place. (To find out how to shop on the internet, see page 112.)

Research

Whether you are studying for a qualification or pursuing a personal interest, there are websites to help you. You will even find online encyclopedias. (See pages 126, 130 and 136 for research projects on the internet.)

Health and medicine

The web is an invaluable resource when it comes to health matters (but it is not a substitute for going to the doctor). You can find out about medical conditions, research treatment options and even get online advice – but not a diagnosis – from doctors and other health experts.

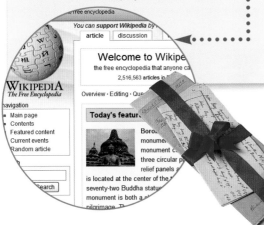

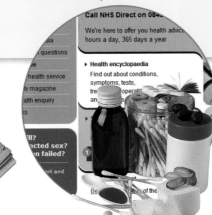

What you need to get online

To surf the internet you must have a PC, a modem and an internet service provider

Getting connected to the internet is easy and relatively inexpensive. To begin with, you need a modem or other connecting device (see opposite). This provides your link to the internet. Then you need to arrange an account with an internet service provider (ISP). The ISP you choose is your gateway to the internet. It allows you to browse the World Wide Web and to send and receive email. Your ISP is also the place where any web pages you have created are stored. It makes them available to other users of the internet.

An ISP could be a large organisation, such as BT, Virgin Media and AOL, or a small, independent operation that might only serve the area in which you live. Finding an ISP to suit your needs is the most important aspect of getting online.

Types of internet service provider

The term ISP is used to describe all the companies that provide you with access to the internet. However, these companies offer differing levels of service.

● Internet access providers (IAPs) offer a basic package. These companies give you a connection and web browsing software, such as Internet Explorer, and an email program, and provide technical help over the phone. An example of an IAP is UKU (below).

● Online service providers (OSPs), like IAPs, provide a gateway to the internet and email handling. They then offer an extra level of service – or 'content' – including special news, information and entertainment channels, shopping services, chat rooms and topic-based newsgroups or forums. OSPs often have a home page designed to make using the internet accessible to newcomers. AOL is one of the best-known OSPs (below).

Key words

Web browser *This is a piece of software that acts as your window on the internet. Your ISP will provide you with this in its start-up pack. There are a number of browsers, with Microsoft Internet Explorer and Firefox the most popular.*

Questions to ask about ISPs

There are many ways to go online. You can connect via a dial-up account using a phone and a modem, though most opt for broadband – a fast, always-on connection, which is particularly good if you use the internet a lot.

Ways to pay

Dial-up connections are either flat rate or pay-as-you-go. With flat rate you pay a monthly charge that gives you 'unlimited' time on the internet (although round the clock usage is usually discouraged).

Pay-as-you-go means that you pay no monthly fee, but pay the cost of each phone call your modem makes to your ISP. The longer you spend online, the more you pay. For a light internet user, pay-as-you-go services offer

the best value. Broadband connections are available with various options depending on the provider. For a small monthly fee, you gain access to the internet with a low downloading capacity and limited speed of download. For a higher monthly fee, you may receive an unlimited download capacity and a faster download speed.

Do you get any added extras?

If you want added content, in the form of business pages, chat rooms, shopping services and so on, make sure that the content you get suits your needs.

Find out how many email addresses you can have on one account. Having more than one means that each family member can have their own address and send and receive email from the same computer. Or, if you work from home, you could have one email address for personal mail and another for business use.

Find out whether you are allocated any web space on which to set up your own website. If so, how much space do you get and is it free?

Ask whether your phone calls to the support helpline are free or charged at the local call rate. Some ISPs that offer 'free' services charge premium rates for support calls, while other ISPs offer 24-hour-a-day support. Above all, ask if technical support is available when you are most likely to need it – the first time you connect up to the internet. You should also check on the ISP's reliability:

will you get through on your first try or will the line stay engaged?

Get a real feel with a free trial

Many ISPs offer a free trial of their services, in some cases up to 90 days. If you take up a trial offer make sure that all sections of the service are user-friendly.

Are you impressed with the standard of content? Also, how easy is it to send and receive email through the ISP? (See page 90 for more details on sending and receiving email.)

Dial-up, ADSL or cable?

Most users of the internet prefer an always-on, broadband connection, via either **ADSL** or **cable**. ADSL stands for Asynchronous Digital Subscriber Line, and is a technology that allows very fast connections to be made using ordinary phone lines. The availability of the service depends on your phone provider and your distance from the local exchange. ADSL subscribers generally pay an installation charge on top of a monthly fee.

Cable TV companies also offer fast internet services, through the same cable as the TV signal. Both ADSL and cable connections require special modems, or routers, normally provided as part of the package by the ISP.

A modem and dial-up connection is another way of accessing the internet from home. A modem sends information to, and receives information from, the internet. But dial-up modems work slowly – connecting at a maximum of 56 Kbps (kilobits per second).

Wired or wireless?

Modems and modem/routers come in two main types: wired and wireless. In a wired system, a cable links your computer directly to a phone socket or to a modem/router which is in turn connected via another cable to a phone socket or TV cable. A wireless system, as the name suggests, means your computer has no cable connection to the router but can, in theory, pick up an internet signal via the router from anywhere in the home.

Send and receive email

Using your PC to revolutionise the way you keep in touch

In addition to the World Wide Web and all its resources, the internet also provides electronic mail, or email. For many people email is the single most useful feature of the internet.

Email functions at a staggering speed. A message can reach a computer on the other side of the world in minutes, and at a fraction of the cost of more traditional forms of communication. And because you do it all from your Desktop, it is extremely convenient, too.

Every email program has its own look, but all operate in a similar way. Here, we take Microsoft Live Mail as an example.

Close-up
Email addresses take the form of name@somewhere.com. 'Name' refers to the sender's name, and 'somewhere.com' refers to the host computer where mail is stored until it is collected by the recipient. Your ISP will provide you with an email address.

1 Click on **Start**, **All Programs**, **Windows Live**, then on **Windows Live Mail**. The Windows Live Mail sign-in dialogue box will appear inviting you to sign in with your Windows Live ID. Enter your User Name and Password and click on **OK**. If you do not have an ID it is easy to sign up (see below).

Need a Windows Live ID?
Windows Live ID is a single sign-in service developed by Microsoft to provide users access to Windows Live Messenger, MSN Hotmail, MSN Music and other sites and services. If you do not already have a Windows Live ID, you can sign up using your existing email address or by creating a new Windows Live address. Go to https://signup.live.com, click on **Sign Up**, and fill in your details.

Email safety

Windows Live Mail has built-in features that help to keep your identity safe. Launch Windows Live Mail and click on the **Backstage view** tab (top left of the window), then click on **Options**, **Safety Options**. Click on the **Options** tab to set a level of Junk email protection. Click on the **Safe Senders** and **Blocked Senders** tabs to create lists for filtering incoming emails. Click on the **Phishing** tab to set options against potential phishing attacks. Click on **Security** to set options for Virus Protection, Download Images and Secure Mail.

Key word

Phishing *Sending an email that falsley claims to be legitimate in an attempt to get a person to surrender private information that will then be used for identity theft.*

2 To write an email message, with the 'Home' tab selected, click on **Email message** from the 'New' group. A blank message appears. Type your recipient's email address in the 'To' box, a title for your message in the 'Subject' box and the message itself in the main panel.

3 You can style your message by using tools from the Ribbon above the message content. You can make text bold, italic or underlined, add emoticons (see page 104) and more. When finished, click on **Send**. Your email program may ask whether you want to connect to the internet. If so, click on **Connect** and send your message.

4 To collect email from your ISP, click on the **Send/Receive** button from the 'Tools' group. For all options click on the down arrow and select from the drop-down list. To reply to an email, click on **Inbox** in the left pane and then on an email message to select it. Now click on **Reply** from the 'Respond' group. Enter your message and click **Send/Receive**.

Sending attachments

You can send pictures and other documents with emails. To add an attachment to a message in Windows Live Mail, click on **Attach file** from the 'Insert' group and navigate to the file to attach. Click once on the file to select it, then on the **Open** button. The file will be added to the message.

Address books

Windows Live stores your contacts' details in its Address Book. To send a message to someone in your address book, click on the **To** button to the left of the address box, then on a contact name, then on **To ->** at the bottom of the box. Alternatively, click on **Contacts**, in the bottom of the left pane, select a contact name, and then click on **Send email** from the pop-up options.

Starting out online

Set up your web browser and you are ready to surf the internet

Many people are daunted by the idea of venturing onto the internet. But, in fact, going online for the first time is a simple matter. It is no more difficult than installing a new piece of software. To connect to the internet you will need an internet service provider (ISP) and a modem or ADSL – see pages 88 and 89 respectively. You also need a web browser. This is a piece of software that opens the door through which you enter the web. Once your browser is set up, you can explore the vast and fascinating world beyond.

Understanding web browsers

A web browser allows you to access websites and navigate between them. All web browsers are the same in principle. They contain an address box, in which you type a web address, and an area in which web pages are displayed.

The most popular browser is Microsoft Internet Explorer, which will almost certainly have come preinstalled on your system, and will also be added if you install Microsoft Works, Works Suite or Office. It is a good idea to keep your web browser up to date so that you are able to view new types of content on the internet.

Whether or not your PC came with its own browser, your ISP may also provide you with one in its start-up kit. This could be Microsoft Internet Explorer, but some ISPs, such as AOL, provide you with their own specially designed web browser. You can have more than one web browser, just as you can have more than one word processor or spreadsheet program.

When your ISP software first loads, look for a button that says 'Internet', 'Browse the internet', 'Explore' or something similar. Clicking on this will start up the browser.

Many ISPs offer CD-ROMs that make it simple to set up an internet connection. You can also set one up using the New Connection Wizard in Windows 7.

GETTING ONLINE

Get to know your way around your web browser

Your browser gives the internet a face and allows you to view all its resources. Learning to use it effectively will make surfing the internet more enjoyable and rewarding.

Use the **Back** and **Forward** buttons to navigate backwards or forwards through downloaded pages. Some browsers clearly label them Back and Forward.

Most browsers have a main menu bar containing drop-down menus. Using these menus you can print web pages, configure your ISP settings and access help facilities.

Most browsers include some form of search facility to help you to find information. Type a key word or words into the search box then click on the magnifying glass icon (or press the **Return** key).

Many sites list their content in a 'navigation panel'. Blue text, sometimes underlined, indicates a link – click on it to see the relevant page.

The Address box is where you type web addresses. Press the **Return** key to download the web page.

When you have a number of web pages open, each one is displayed on a separate tab. Just click on the tabs to switch between web pages.

This is the main viewing area, into which web pages are downloaded and displayed.

Use the scroll buttons to see all the information on a long web page. A mouse with a scroll wheel makes this easy.

Web addresses explained

Every web address is unique, in just the same way as your phone number. In fact, it can be helpful to think of a web address as a phone number, whereby you 'dial' the website's address to view it.

The 'www' in a web address tells you that the site belongs to the World Wide Web. After the 'www' you are told the domain name (this 'points' to the computer that holds the website) and where that computer is located

('.uk', for the UK; '.au' for Australia; and so on). Addresses do not always end in the country of origin. If you see '.com' at the end, for example, this indicates that the site is commercial. If you see '.gov', the website is a government agency.

For many pages, extra text appears after the domain name. This shows the location of the pages within the website.

http://www.readersdigest.co.uk/

How to find information

Exploring **the** internet **is easy** once **you know where to** start

O nce your internet connection is up and running you are ready to explore the World Wide Web. The quickest way to find information is to type the web address of a site you want to visit into your browser's address box and press the Return key on your keyboard. The site's first page (known as the home page) will appear on screen. You can move around the site by clicking on links.

If you do not know the address of a website, you can find information using a search engine. This will search for key words or categories that you select, then present you with a list of sites to visit. Click on the links to view the sites. The key to effective use of the internet is narrowing your searches by using more specific key words so that the number of sites yielded is manageable.

Be as specific as you can in your search and tell the search engine exactly what you are looking for. You can get tips on better searching from the engines themselves.

USING A SEARCH ENGINE

1 Connect to the internet. In your web browser's address box type the address of a search engine, here **Yahoo!** (http://uk.yahoo.com), and press **Return**. The site's home page will now appear. Type your key words into the search box, suggestions are offered to you as you type, and click on **Web search** or press the **Return** key.

Which search engine?

The website at www.searchenginewatch.com explains how the main search engines work and how efficient they are. Here are the addresses of some popular search engines (prefix with http://).

- www.google.co.uk
- uk.altavista.com
- www.freeserve.co.uk
- www.ask.co.uk
- www.yell.co.uk
- uk.yahoo.com

Your internet service provider might also have its own search facility (see pages 88-89).

Most text within a site that appears in a uniform contrasting colour and is underlined, or becomes underlined when you hover your mouse over it, is a link to another part of the same site or to a new site. Click on the coloured underlined text to activate the link.

Watch out

Do not type a web address into a word search box as you may not be taken to the website. Type only key words for your search.

2 A list of related websites will appear. (Some engines tell you how many sites have been found.) Use the scroll bar to the right of the page to view the list. To view a site, click on the coloured title, which may also be underlined. Use your browser's **Back** button to return to previous pages.

3 Most search engines, including Yahoo! (http://everything.yahoo.com/uk/), allow you to search by category. Click on a category from the panel on the left and you will be presented with subdivisions to narrow your search. Click on **More Yahoo! Sites** to display additional categories grouped alphabetically.

4 To find information on motorcycle racing, for example, click on **Sport** on the Yahoo! home page. Then click on the **Motorsport** tab, and finally **Moto GP**. This reveals a list of sites, standings, resources and chat areas. Click on a link to open it.

Search by batch

Most search engines present their list of sites in batches (usually of ten). When you reach the bottom of the first batch in Google, click on **2** for the next batch, and so on.

Information collected for you

Some websites hold databases of information that make searching easy. For example, Bigfoot (http://search.bigfoot.com/en/index.jsp) lists individual email addresses, and Google groups (www.groups.google.com) holds discussion group conversation archives.

Google groups has its own search engine that will find topics of discussion for you. Type, say, 'apple pie recipe' into the search box and click on **Search Groups** or press **Return**. The search results will list messages from discussion groups about your search topic.

Your PC can use more than one search engine at a time. Copernic is a program that collects results from many search engines. Download it free of charge from the internet.

SERIOUS SEARCHING

Watch out
Make sure your internet connection is running before you double-click on the Copernic icon. Otherwise, you will not be able to use it.

1 Type 'www.copernic.com' into your browser's address box and press the **Return** key. From the main panel of the home page, click on **Free Download**. On the next page click on **Download Copernic Agent Personal v6.20 – English**, and follow the prompts to install the software.

2 Launch the program, and in the 'Search' panel on the left, click to select a category, here 'The Web'. Type key words into the 'Search' box above and press **Return**. The number of search engines being used, per category, is displayed as the search progresses.

3 Copernic searches through a variety of search engines, collates the findings and displays them in the right-hand panel. Your search key words are highlighted in yellow with the score percentage for each site on the right, ranked by most relevant. Click on a link to open a site in your web browser.

Bookmarking web pages

Browsers allow you to record the addresses of favourite websites you have visited. This saves you having to remember the addresses and means you do not have to spend time online searching for the sites again. As long as you are connected to the internet, a click on a bookmarked address will open up the site.

The process of bookmarking websites is similar in all browsers (look out for a facility called 'Bookmarks', 'Favorites' or 'Favorite

Places' on your browser's toolbar). To bookmark a site when you are on the internet, first open the site, then go to the **Favorites** menu and click on **Add to favorites**. The Add Favorite dialogue box appears with the address of the site you are visiting. Click on **OK**.

To access this site again, click on the **Favorites** icon on the toolbar. A list of your bookmarked addresses will appear in a column on the left. Click on the relevant address to load the site.

Key Word
Metasearch engine *Metasearch engines gather information from several search engines simultaneously, displaying the results in a single list.*

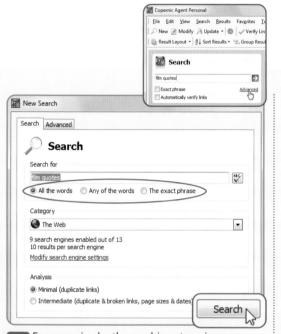

Other collective (metasearch) search engines are also free but don't require downloading.

MORE SERIOUS SEARCHING

4 For more in-depth searching, type in your keyword or words and click on **Advanced**, under the search box. Here you can check your spelling, select options for 'All the words', 'Any of the words' or 'The exact phrase'. Make your selection then click on **Search**.

1 An example of a metasearch engine is infospace. Open your browser and type 'www.infospace.com' into the address bar and press the **Return** key. Infospace gathers results from leading search engines Google, Yahoo!, Bing and real time updates from Twitter feeds. Type a word into the search box and click on **search**.

2 Another alternative metasearch engine is Dogpile. Type 'www.dogpile.co.uk' into your address bar and press the **Return** key. Then from the home page type in your key word or words into the search box and click on **Go Fetch**.

Close-up
Do not forget to use links to track down information. Links are a key part of the World Wide Web. They appear as underlined text on a web page and let you jump directly from one page or site to another. Most websites have links to other similar sites, so you may find the information you want browsing from one to the next.

Security on the internet

How to ensure users of your PC are protected when online

Internet newcomers are naturally concerned about security. They worry about whether it is safe to send credit card details over the internet, or whether children will come across undesirable material. Many people also have concerns over the privacy of email and the unauthorised issue of their email addresses, as well as the threat of computer viruses.

All these concerns are valid, but there are measures you can take to guarantee the integrity of the sites your family visits, and the confidentiality of your personal details.

Keeping it safe and sound

Whether shopping, browsing or emailing, there are ways to guarantee your security on the internet.

Shopping and security

If a shopping website states that it uses 'encryption' technology to transfer credit card details (a complex, almost unbreakable, scrambling system), there should be no security problem. Secure sites display a padlock symbol on your browser's address bar to the right of the web address – older versions of web browsers display the symbol at the bottom. Also look for the VeriSign or thawte logos, both of which indicate a trustworthy website.

Children and the internet

The best way to protect children from coming across undesirable material on the internet is to use special software. Programs such as Cyber Patrol and Net Nanny block access to sites known to have unsavoury content.

You can also get software that creates a log of all the sites that have been visited from your PC, and so keep a check on what your children have seen. You can use the History button on your web browser to do a similar job (see below right).

In Windows 7 you can set up a 'Content Advisor' ratings system to control how much of the internet a person can view according to levels of language, nudity, sex and violence. To do this, click on the **Start** button, then **Control Panel**. Click on **Network and Internet**, then on **Internet Options**. Click on the **Content** tab

and then on the **Enable** button. In the Content Advisor dialogue box, select the **Ratings** tab and click on each category, then adjust the slider to set a rating level. Setting all categories at 'Level 1' effectively bars all access to the web, apart from the most child-friendly sites. Click on **OK** when you have finished and you will be prompted to set a supervisor password. You must type it in every time you change the Content Advisor settings, so do not lose it.

Watch out

It is possible, but very unlikely, that your email could be intercepted as it is sent across the internet. But anyone who uses your PC could read your incoming email once it has been received, which is a good reason for being discreet in what you write.

Viruses and the internet

Computer viruses can seriously damage your PC. The best way to avoid getting a virus from the internet, or from any other source, is to use an anti-virus utility.

There is also a risk of infection from 'macro viruses' that enter your PC via email attachments. You can set a high level of Macro Virus protection in any Microsoft Office program (Word, Excel, Powerpoint or Outlook). Click on the **Office** button, then on **Word Options** (substitute Excel, PowerPoint or Outlook, depending on the program). Click on **Trust Center** in the left panel, then on **Trust Center Settings...** in the right panel. Choose a level of Macro security and click on **OK**.

A computer on an 'always-on' broadband connection to the internet can be open to malicious attack. To protect against this, Windows 7 includes a 'firewall' – software that prevents unauthorised access to your machine. Click on **Start**, **Control Panel**, **System and Security** and then on **Action Center**. Click on **Security** to view firewall, virus protection and spyware protection settings.

Safeguard your email address

Sometimes, your email address can be obtained by companies or individuals who send you junk email, known as 'spam'. Try to avoid this by omitting your email address from forms that you fill in by hand or on the internet.

Only give your email address to individuals of your choice. Good internet trading companies should give you the option of withholding your address, even to reputable, third-party vendors. Never reply to an unsolicited email, as this confirms yours is an active address.

History button

A simple way to keep an eye on the websites that have been visited from your PC is to use the History button that comes with Internet Explorer. When you press it, a log of all sites that have been accessed will appear to the left of the Explorer window.

You can set the number of days that the History button monitors in Internet Explorer. Go to the **Tools** menu and click on **Internet Options**. With the **General** tab selected, go to the 'Days to keep pages in history' box and input the number of days that suits you. You can also choose to clear the History folder.

Explore the world of multimedia

Watch video and animations, play games and listen to the radio on your PC

The term 'multimedia' describes the ability of modern computers to deliver many different kinds of information at once: the elements of multimedia are generally pictures, text, animations, sounds and video. For example, you might find a short clip to accompany a film review, or a live radio feed at a news site. The quality of what you experience depends on the speed of your internet connection: if you have a fast, broadband internet connection, you will able to download and view long video pieces and animations, take part in interactive games and listen to high-quality music files.

Sights and sounds on the internet
In order to enjoy the extra dimension of multimedia, you may need to add extra features to your browser.

Bring your web browser up to speed
Microsoft Internet Explorer and almost all other web browsers can handle basic forms of multimedia. However, to view video clips and animation on some sites you need mini-programs called 'plug-ins'. These vary in sophistication, but the best of them can play animations, video and interactive games.

The most popular plug-ins are Flash™ and Shockwave®, both from Macromedia, Inc., and RealPlayer® from RealNetworks®. Flash uses ingenious programming to pack complicated animations, games and interfaces into small files that download quickly. Shockwave allows more complicated games and interactivity to be displayed within your browser, even including video images.

RealPlayer is one of the most popular plug-ins for 'streaming' audio or video content to your PC. Streaming means that you can start listening to or watching a file before it is completely downloaded – the file plays while the download continues in the background, saving you a long wait. The quality of the streamed sound and pictures depends on the speed of your connection: the faster the better.

Key word

Plug-in *This is a piece of software that adds new features to your web browser. After a plug-in has been installed, your browser will use it automatically whenever necessary.*

Watch out

If you have a pay-as-you-go dial-up connection, listening to internet radio stations can become expensive. But if you have a flat-fee connection, or a broadband contract, you can listen for as long as you like.

Downloading a plug-in

This section tells you how to download the RealPlayer plug-in from RealNetworks. The procedure for downloading other plug-ins is similar.

Connect to the internet and launch your browser. In the address bar, type http://uk.real.com/realplayer/ and press the **Return** key.

Click on the **Download Free RealPlayer SP** button (or similar – the website changes

http://uk.real.com/realplayer/

often). Now click on **Free Download**. If a 'File Download – Security Warning' dialogue box is displayed click on **Save**. In the Save As dialogue box

select your Downloads folder and click on **Save**. Double-click on **RealPlayerSPGold** and the Welcome screen displays the License agreement. Read it and click on **Accept** to continue with the installation process.

Install the plug-in

In the next screen select a location for RealPlayer to be installed and whether you want a Desktop shortcut added, then click on **Next**. Now choose your **RealPlayer Setup** from the options displayed. Basic RealPlayer is free while the other options incur a fee. Make your choice and click on **Continue**. Finally, fill in the Product Registration form and click on **Continue**.

RealPlayer will launch automatically to complete the set-up process. The RealPlayer home page shows links to a variety of different types of audio and video content.

Using the plug-in

You will probably use the player for RealMedia clips on other websites. Here we show examples of audio and video material on the BBC website (www.bbc.co.uk).

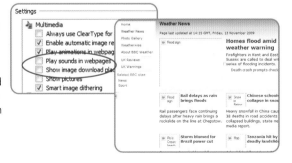

Turn off to speed up

Multimedia files can often be very large, which means that a web page with lots of multimedia elements, such as sound and animation, can take a long time to open. If you would rather not have these elements present when you are using the web, you can instruct your browser not to download them. Go to the **Start** menu and right-click on **Internet**. Click on

Internet Properties then on the **Advanced** tab. In the Multimedia section you will see that some items have ticked boxes beside them. Choose the features you want to keep and those you want to disable. If you want to disable sounds and images, for example, click in the boxes to remove the ticks. Click on **Apply**, then on **OK**. Next time you access a web page, it will appear without sound or images.

Chat to others online

Use the World Wide Web to make new friends and contacts

One of the most exciting things about the internet is that it brings people together. People who share similar interests can keep in touch via email and by subscribing to mailing lists; others who want to chat in 'real time' (messages appear on the other person's computer screen as you type) can use instant messenger programs to 'talk'. A growing section of the internet, called Usenet, is made up of thousands of discussion groups. Here, people post messages that can be replied to, and so start a discussion. You can get a list of the main discussion groups from your internet service provider (ISP).

Find out which of your friends are regularly online and use Windows Live Messenger. Gather their email addresses ready to add to your Messenger contacts.

BEFORE YOU START

1 Go to the **Start** menu, select **All Programs**, then **Windows Live Messenger**. If you do not have a Windows Live ID, click on the **Sign up for a Windows Live ID** link at the bottom of the window, and follow the step-by-step instructions. When you next open Windows Live Messenger, click on **Sign in** to begin chatting.

There are other instant messenger programs available, such as Yahoo Messenger and AOL Messenger. You can also search the internet for sites such as www.tucows.com, from which you can download messenger software that is compatible with MSN, Yahoo and AOL.

OTHER PROGRAMS

Bright idea

Windows Live Messenger can automatically update your address book whenever your contacts change their details. Just subscribe to Windows Live Contacts to make sure that you never lose touch!

2 Once Messenger is set up, your Messenger window appears on screen. To close the window, make it larger or minimise it, use the buttons on the top right-hand corner. To open the window, double-click on the Messenger icon in the task bar at the bottom right of your screen.

3 To add a Messenger contact, select **Add a contact** from the **Contacts** menu. Enter your contact's details in the 'Instant messaging address' box along with their mobile number. Click on **Next**. Type an invitation message and then click on **Send invitation**. Your contact will receive a message and, if they accept, you will be connected.

4 To send a message, double-click on your contact. A conversation window opens. Type your message in the bottom section and press **Enter**. Leave the window open and the reply appears under your message. Close the window and the reply pops up at the bottom right of your computer screen – click on it to continue your chat.

Sign up to Messenger

To sign up to Messenger, you may first need to install the program. Type **Windows Live Messenger** into your web browser, and then select a link from the MSN sites displayed. Once you are on the Windows Live Essentials page, click on **Download**, then in the next window select where to save the program and click on **Save** to download the Windows Live suite of software to your PC. A progress bar displays while the download takes place. Once the download is complete, click to add a tick next to the programs you want to install. Click on **Install** to complete the installation.

Key word

Emoticons These are small pictures or icons, which can be added into messages to show emotions, such as laughter. In the conversation window, click on **Emoticons** and then click on an emoticon in the drop-down menu.

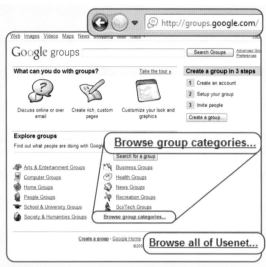

5 To have a three-way conversation, go to the Actions menu and click on **Invite a contact to join this conversation**. Choose and click on a contact in the next dialogue box, then click on **OK**. When you finish chatting, simply close the window, and when you want to chat again just click on the Messenger icon on your Taskbar.

6 Discussion groups – unlike chat – do not operate in 'real time'. You post a message and check back to see if anyone posts a response. To find a group, type http://groups.google.com into your web browser's address box and press **Return**. Click on **Browse group categories** to start, then on **Browse all of Usenet**.

7 To find UK groups, scroll down the list of options and click on **uk**, and select a category from the list of UK groups (here **uk.d-i-y**). A list of 'thread' subjects is now listed. To start a new discussion, click on the **+ New post** button at the bottom.

Sharing files by Messenger

With Windows Live Messenger you can share files on your PC with others, which can be a good alternative to sending big files by email. Start an instant message conversation and click on **Files** then **Publish files online** from the drop-down menu. In the 'Create a folder' window that appears give the folder a name, select options for sharing and when finished click on **Next**. In the 'Add files to' window either drag files into the large box or click on **Select files from your computer**, and navigate to the folder containing the files to share. Click on a file to select it and then on **Open**. When you have finished adding files, click on **Upload**. A progress bar displays while the files are uploaded. Finally click on **Let people know**, to inform your contacts of the shared folder. Click on **Send**.

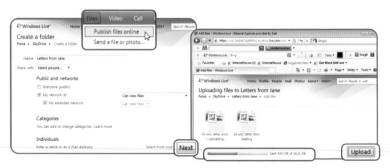

8 You will then be required to register. Click on **Create an account now**, and fill in your email address and a password, and read the terms and conditions. If you are happy to go ahead, click on **I accept**. **Create my account**. An email will be sent to you. Click on the link in the email to verify your email address and account.

9 Return to 'uk.d-i-y' and click on **+ new post**. Type a subject and message in the panels that appear. When you have finished, click on **Post message** and then on **Return to uk.d-i-y**. You may have to wait a short time before it appears on the site. Keep checking back to see when your message and replies to it appear.

10 To reply to a posting, click on it. In the next window, all the replies from other users are displayed. Click on them to read them and then, if you like, add your own message by clicking on **Reply to author**. You must have logged in before you can post your own reply. Type in your reply and click on **Send**.

Bright idea
You can also share photos in Messenger during an instant message conversation. Click on **Photos** *and navigate to the folder containing the photos to share. Click to select an image and then on* **Open**. *To select multiple images from the same folder hold the* **Ctrl** *key down as you select the images.*

Join the online party

Track **what your** friends **and** family **are up to with** Facebook

Facebook is a phenomenon. Originally launched in 2004 as a way for students to keep in touch, it has quickly become the most popular social networking site on the internet. It is a place where, whatever your age, you can share in what friends, family and colleagues are doing and in turn let them know about your activities. You can also make new friends and join groups with people who share your interests – anything from fan clubs and protest campaigns to games and business ideas. Once you are logged on to Facebook, you can share photos, music and videos, and organise and invite people to parties and events – and you can make it as public or private as you want.

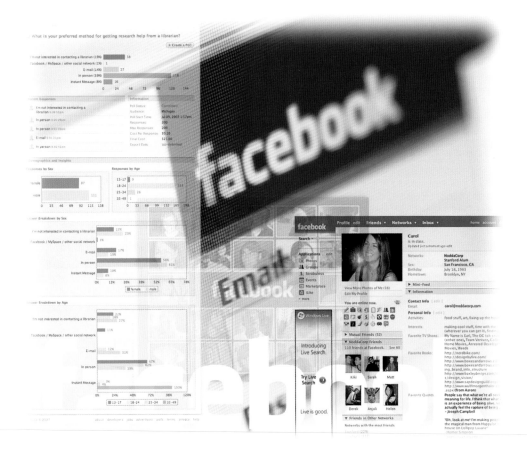

Ask your friends to see who is on Facebook and, if they are, find out their username or email address. Then you can build your network as soon as you are registered.

BEFORE YOU START

1 Joining Facebook is free. Connect to the internet, then in your web browser's address bar type **www.facebook.com** and then press **Return**. Enter your details – first name, last name and so on – and click **Sign Up**. To finish the sign-up procedure, including a security check, see below.

Completing the sign-up process

When prompted, under 'Security check' type the two words you see into the text box and click on **Sign Up**. A confirmation email is sent to the email address you entered in step 1, above. Click on the link in the email to activate your account.

Close-up
You may find that Facebook can only access some of the major email hosts like Googlemail, Hotmail and Yahoo. If it cannot access your account it will tell you and suggest alternative ways of adding your contacts.

Bright idea
When you create your Facebook account, do not worry if you have no time to complete the steps 'Find friends', 'Profile information' and 'Profile picture' (see below). This information can be added or edited later. Click on **Profile** or **Find friends** on the blue bar at the top of any Facebook page to fill in the details.

Close-up
Use your real name when signing up for Facebook. Unlike some social networks where you can use an alias, Facebook is built on the premise that the quickest and best way to build your social network of friends and family is to be yourself.

2 Facebook then helps you to find friends who may already be on the site. It does this by checking the list of addresses in your email account to see if there are any matches with existing Facebook users. To do so, fill in your email address and password and click **Find friends**. Alternatively, click on **Skip this step** to go to the next step.

3 Now create your profile – the information about you that is most often made public. Add your secondary school, college or university in the boxes provided. Type in the name of the company where you work, if appropriate. Facebook prompts you with selections as you type – click on one to use it. Click on **Save & continue**.

4 Based on the information in the previous step, people with matching information in one of their profile boxes are displayed. Click on **Add as a friend** to send them an email. Their status will change to 'Friend requested'. If they accept, they are added to your list of friends. Click on **Save & continue**. To add a profile picture, see below.

Picture yourself on Facebook

Adding a picture of yourself makes it easier for friends to find you – when they search they can be sure they have got the right Janet Smith or John Brown. Or use a photo of one of your hobbies or interests, such as a football or a political rosette. If no picture is loaded, Facebook adds an icon of a silhouetted head and shoulders. You can change your profile picture whenever you like. Click on **Profile** in the blue 'facebook' bar at the top of any page, then on **Upload a photo**. In the 'Upload your Profile picture' box that appears, click on **Browse**. Then in the 'Choose File to Upload' box, select a suitable picture and click on **Open**.

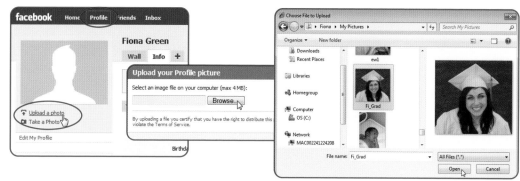

Close-up
*Your profile information is grouped into four sections. **Basic Information** covers details like your birthday, relationship status and political views. **Likes and Interests** deals with your activities and favourite entertainments. **Contact Information** lets you give out your address or phone number. **Education and Work** allows you to include the schools you attended and places where you have worked.*

Bright idea
*You may want friends to send birthday greetings without having to reveal exactly how old you are. You can do this by not showing your full birth date in your profile section. In the 'Basic Information' category, click the drop-down menu below 'Birthday' and select **Show only day and month in my Profile**.*

5 On the 'Welcome' page you can edit and add information you may have skipped when setting up your account. Click on **Edit profile**, then, on the next page, with the **Info** tab selected, click on one of the four section headings to display its contents (see 'Close-up', above). Click on the **Wall** tab to post a message (see below).

6 Facebook is always helping you to find new friends. The easiest way to start is to click on **Find friends** on the top menu bar. On the 'Friends' page you can search for people you know by name or email address. Facebook will also make 'Suggestions'. Click on **Add as a friend** if you want to make contact.

7 To let people know how you are feeling at any particular moment you can update your 'status'. Click on **Home** on the bar at the top of any page or click on **News Feed** in the pane on the left. Type in your status message in the Publisher panel (see below) under News Feed and then click on **Share**.

Have your say
The 'Wall' is the main message board for your site, where you and your friends can exchange comments and see what is happening in your lives. At the top of your Wall is a text box that says, 'What's on your mind?'. This is where you can let people know what is happening in your life. When you click on the box, the default prompt text disappears as you write your own message – a casual thought, the latest family news or simply what you are doing at the moment. Here we have just announced our arrival on Facebook. Click on the **Share** button to finish. This area is also called your 'Publisher'. You can use it to post content to your Wall and use the icons next to 'Attach': to add photos, video, details of an event or links to websites.

Photo albums

To create a photo album, click on **Profile** at the top, then, with the **Photos** tab selected, click on the **+ Create a Photo Album** button. Type in an album name, location and description, and select a privacy option from the drop-down list. Click on **Create Album**. Follow the on-screen instructions, and, if prompted, install the Facebook plug-in for easy photo uploading. Navigate to the folder containing the photos to upload. Select which photos to add, then click on **Upload**.

Close-up

*There are three different types of events. Anyone can attend an **Open** event – a festival, concert or other big show. If you create a **Closed** event, only those you invite can attend, but others can read about it. With a **Secret** event only those you invite will know about it.*

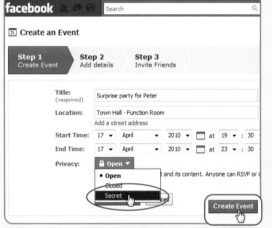

8 Scroll down through the News Feed page to see what is happening with friends and family. To add your thoughts to a posting click the **Comment** link below the posting, write your reply and click on the **Comment** button. To show your appreciation of someone else's views click on the **Like** link.

9 To set up your own event, click the **Events** icon in the panel on the left. In Step 1 enter a title, location and times. Select from the Privacy drop-down options – **Open**, **Closed** or **Secret** event. Click on **Create Event**. In Step 2 add more details. Click on **Save and Continue**. In Step 3 add attendees and click on **Send invitations**.

10 The invitation is now added to your friends' events. Check back to the Events page and you will see details of your event. In the column on the right click **Edit event** if you want to change details. Any replies will be indicated by a red square containing a number at the top of the page. Click on the number to view the replies.

Profile privacy

While it can be good to make new friends you may not want your profile to be viewed by everyone. In Facebook you can decide exactly how secure you want your profile to be. Click on **Account** at the top right of the navigation bar and then on **Privacy Settings** from the drop-down menu. For each section you can then control exactly who can see your details by selecting an option from a drop-down menu: 'Everyone', 'Friends of friends', 'Only friends' or a customised selection made up of specific people you choose, or just yourself.

Eventful browsing

Although virtual networking can be fun, it is even better to get together in person. Through Facebook you can see what public events are on near you – or arrange your own party for selected friends. To see what might be going on, click the **Events** calendar icon in the panel on the left to reveal options for 'Friends' events', 'Birthdays' and 'Past events'. Click on a sub-category to view its contents.

Be a social networker

Share the highs and lows of life, moment by moment, on Twitter

If you want to know what the people who interest you are doing right now – from celebrities to politicians, or simply like-minded contacts – tune into Twitter. The social networking site lets you see what is happening around the world at any given moment. You can share the thoughts of well-known figures like Stephen Fry or Jamie Oliver, discover what major events are preoccupying people or let your own personal network know what you are up to.

What makes Twitter different from other online contact sites is that each posting, known as a 'tweet', can be no more that 140 characters, including spaces. It leaves no room for waffle. Each tweet is posted on Twitter at http://twitter.com. When you send out a tweet, your followers – those people in your network – can see it instantly. That makes it great when a quick response is needed, such as when you find a hero of yours is just about to be interviewed on the radio.

Think of a username for yourself. Keep it short and simple (preferably under 10 characters) as your name counts towards the maximum of 140 characters per tweet.

BEFORE YOU START

1 Connect to the internet. In your browser's address bar type **www.twitter.com** then press **Return**. On the Twitter home page you will see a list of the most popular topics right now, over the last day and in the past week. Click **Sign up now**. Enter a user name, password and your email address, and click **Create my account**.

Who are you?
It is worth taking some time to complete your Twitter profile, which can include a one-line biography of up to 160 characters. As you are introducing yourself, make it interesting, fun and eye-catching, with an attention-grabbing photo or icon. This will attract more followers and help you to build your network.

Finding friends

In step 2, 'friends', you can find friends to add to your home timeline using email. Twitter will compare your contacts with its own email directories to find any friends who are twitterers. Enter your email address and password and then click on **Find friends** – or click on **Next step: others** to skip this step. In step 3, 'anyone', enter a username, first name or last name to search for. Click on **Next step: You're done!** to finish.

Close-up
When you write a message in the 'What's happening?' box, the number of characters you have left is displayed above. The number automatically decreases as you type.

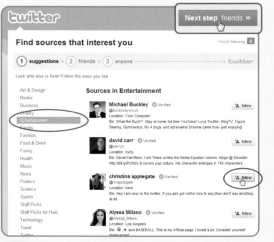

2 The 'Find sources that interest you' section is divided into steps. In step 1, 'suggestions', click on a topic from the list on the left, here **Entertainment**, scroll down and select a twitterer, here 'christina applegate', and click on **follow**, then click on **Next step: friends**. To continue with steps 2 and 3, see 'Finding friends', above.

3 To complete your profile, click **Settings**. Add your location and real name, so others can easily recognise you. To add your photo, click on **Picture**, then on **Browse**. Navigate to the picture to use, click on it, then on **Open**, then **Save**. Click the **Protect my tweets** box to only let people you approve follow your postings. Click **Save** to finish.

4 To send a tweet, go to the Twitter home page and click **Sign in**, top right. Enter your login details and click on the **Sign in** button. Write a message in the 'What's happening?' box – see above. Click **update** to finish. When you read a tweet, add it to your favourites by clicking the 'star', or **Reply** by clicking the link bottom right.

Learning the Twitter language

Because of the short space available for postings Twitter has developed its own shortcuts. If you see 'Retweet' or 'RT' it means that someone is copying a tweet from another user. On your home page click **@yourusername** to see any tweets that mention you. Under the Trending Topics section you can see the current hot topics – some start with the # symbol, or hashtag. This is used to group tweets together by topic, so they appear under one clickable link. For example, click on **#nowplaying** to go to a list of tweets from people saying what they are listening to or viewing.

Bright idea
*As Twitter is all about immediacy, use your mobile phone to keep tweeting on the move. At the bottom of your home page, click on **Turn on your mobile phone**. Text **START** to a mobile provider listed, to begin texting your tweets. The latest generation of smart phones, like Apple's iPhone and the BlackBerry, offer applications that allow complete access to your Twitter account.*

Shopping on the internet

Buying **what you want is** just **a question of** point and click

Online shopping is now an everyday activity. Users have access to a far wider range of goods than can be bought in local shops. Many people prefer online shopping because of the convenience – no parking or queues, the 'shops' are open 24 hours a day, seven days a week, and goods are delivered to the door.

The prices of goods offered over the internet are extremely competitive. Even after paying for delivery they can work out cheaper than shopping by conventional means.

In this project we show you how to buy a book and a piece of computer hardware. Use the steps as a general guide to buying any goods online.

Have a good idea of what you want to buy before you go online – it is easy to get distracted and buy things you do not need.

BEFORE YOU START

1 Connect to the internet. In your web browser's address box type in the address of an internet shopping website (in this case, www.amazon.co.uk). Press **Return** and then wait for the site's home page to appear on screen.

Popular shopping sites

Addresses for popular shopping sites include:
- www.amazon.co.uk (books and music)
- www.itunes.com (music)
- www.pcworld.co.uk (computer equipment)
- www.interflora.com (flowers)
- www.lastminute.com (tickets and travel)
- www.tesco.com (supermarket)

Bright idea

When you buy over the internet make a note of information such as the date of purchase, item, cost, contact phone number or email address. This makes follow-up queries easy.

*When you click on the **Add to Shopping Basket** button you are not committed to buy at this point. You are simply collecting items.*

2 Navigate through to the type of product you are looking for. For example, if you want to buy a book, click on **Books** in the navigation panel on the left of Amazon's home page. Then use the fly-out menu to narrow your search. Alternatively, click on **Books** from the fly-out menu and select a category from the 'Browse Books' panel.

3 The most popular titles and types of book appear at the top of the list of entries for each category. Shakespeare, like other major authors, brings up hundreds of available titles – these are grouped together into sub-categories to make searching easier.

4 For information on any book, such as reviews or its price, click on the title. If you want to purchase a book, click on the title then on the **Add to Shopping Basket** button. To make the purchase, click on **Proceed to Checkout** or carry on shopping to look for further items.

Making a quick search

On the Amazon home page you will see a search box near the top of the page. If you are searching for a book, type in the author, title or subject of the book and, in the box to the left, click on the arrow and select 'Books' from the drop-down menu. Then click on **Go!**. A list of relevant books appears, which you can browse through before choosing whether you would like to buy any.

Shopping Basket

You can see the items in your Shopping Basket by clicking on the **Basket** icon at the top of the Amazon site. This page lists all the items you have selected to buy. If you decide not to buy something in your basket, click on the **Delete** button next to the item. If you would like to continue browsing, click on the browser's **Back** button.

Bright idea
If you are reluctant to send financial details over the internet, look for an option to fax, phone or post your order.

Using the internet to buy computer hardware can save you money. We used the Lycos search engine, at www.lycos.co.uk.

► COMPUTER HARDWARE

5 Enter your email address and select either 'I am a new customer' or 'I am a returning customer' option, as appropriate. Then click on **Sign in using our secure server**. Fill in your details and follow the on-screen instructions to complete your purchase. You can cancel the transaction up to the last minute.

6 Type www.lycos.co.uk in your web browser's address box, then press **Return**. When the home page appears, click on **pages from the UK**, and on the **Shopping** button at the top right. Once the Shopping page appears, enter a description of the item you would like in the 'Search' box at the top and press **Return**.

7 Lycos lists all the products that match your description, displaying the lowest price for each product and the number of sellers. Find the product you want and click on **COMPARE PRICES** for details of vendors, availability and prices or **BUY DIRECT** to buy from the manufacturer. Make your choice and click on **BUY NOW**.

Secure shopping

Never give out your credit or debit card details on the internet unless the seller uses a secure server for payments. In Internet Explorer 8, the way to tell this is to look for the padlock icon displayed in the Security Status Bar, located at the right of your web browser's address box. The Security Status Bar is not normally displayed unless you are about to enter a site where special security issues exist. Click on the padlock icon to view a security report for the site you are about to enter. The background colour of the address box may also change to indicate potential security issues:

White (default) – no information is available.
White (with padlock icon) – communication is encrypted and is therefore secure.
Green – the site has been checked and its identity approved.
Yellow – proceed with caution as this site appears to be misrepresenting its identity.
Red – do not use this site. Red indicates a known problem, such as expired or revoked encryption. These sites have been reported to Microsoft.
    In all cases, avoid entering sensitive data until you are sure that the website is the one you intended to visit.

Watch out

The internet makes it easy to buy things from overseas. However, while some goods can seem cheaper, they may not be suitable – for example, US mains voltage is different to that in Europe. Also, duties and delivery charges can eat away any apparent savings.

Shopping Basket

Items in Basket:	1
Total:	**£205.30**
Delivery:	Free
Your Saving:	£61.40
Checkout	

[Security Info]

This site is secure and utilises the latest 128bit encryption and with a (SSL) certificate from VeriSign you can shop with confidence

caboodle
for all your office needs

Login / Register | My Account | Business A...

Home | Office Supplies | Ink Cartridges & Laser Toners | Postal Supplies | Technology | Facilities | Eco Office | Brand Stores

Enter Search Term... | Search | 0844 371 9466

Browse
Office Supplies
Accountancy
Business Books
Business Cases
Desktop Accessories
Desktop Stationery
Diaries + Calendars
Ergonomics
Filing + Archive
Labels
Limited Offers
Notebooks + Pads
Paper
Presentation
Writing + Correction
Ink + Laser Supplies

Add to Favourites | Save My Printer

EPSON STYLUS WIFI PHOTO PRINTER PX800FW

Epson Stylus PX800FW WIFI Photo Printer
C11CA29301

EPSON

Product Code	485-8767
Stock	80
Delivery	Next Day
Was	£266.70 exc.VAT

£236.10 inc.VAT

Only: **£205.30** exc.VAT   Qty 1   Add +

Click here to enlarge image

Alternative Products | Specification | Overview

Should you need help choosing the right product for you click here to email us.

Epson Stylus PX800FW WIFI Photo Printer C11CA29...

Qty **1** **Add +**

Name: *	Fiona
Surname: *	Green
Username: *	FiGreen
Password: *	••••••••••
Confirm Password: *	••••••••••
Email Address: *	fiona-green@hotmail.co.uk
Contact Number: *	020 7715 8000

Where?

Address Quickfind!   **Find Address**

Address Details

Address Line 1: *	11 Westferry Circus
Address Line 2:	
Address Line 3:	

Proceed

Place Order
Please complete the information below and click 'Continue'. If you wish to amend your order or add items to it please click 'Edit Basket'.

Payment

Type of Card:	MasterCard/Eurocard ▾
Name on Card:	F Green
Card Number:	1234 3456 5678 7890
Expiry Date (mm/yy):	01 / 10
Security Code:	555

Billing / Card Holder Details

Company:	
F.A.O.	Fiona Green
Address Line 1:	11 Westferry Circus
Line 2:	
Line 3:	
Town:	Canary Wharf
County:	London
Post Code:	E14 4HE
Country:	United Kingdom

Find Address

Promotions
Enter Promotion Code:

Edit Basket

Delivery Address

Company	
F.A.O.	Fiona Green
Address Line 1	11 Westferry Circus
Line 2	
Line 3	
Town	Canary Wharf
County	London
Post Code	E14 4HE

Find Address

Continue

VeriSign Secured
VERIFY
About SSL Certificates

8 Check the details and specifications carefully to make sure that the product is the one you want. If everything seems right, click on the **Add +** button (some websites have Buy Now or Add to Basket buttons instead).

9 Once you have added everything to your shopping basket, click on **Checkout** (this button may be called 'Order' or 'Buy' depending on the site). If prompted, follow the instructions to create a customer account, clicking on **Proceed** and **Submit** as you progress through the registration, delivery and payment processes.

10 The final step is to enter your card details. Check for a padlock or the VeriSign Secured symbol to ensure that the vendor is using encryption (see page 114), and click on the **Continue** button. You will normally receive confirmation via email. Then simply wait for your goods to be delivered.

Compare prices

There is no need to visit lots of websites to be sure that you are getting good value. Comparison shopping sites, such as ShopGenie.co.uk, do the legwork for you, checking the price of an item at many different online shops. The best ones include tax and shipping costs, so you know you are seeing a true comparison.

ShopGenie.co.uk
where to buy online

Computers & Software | Electronics | Mobiles, Phones & Faxes | H...
Games, Consoles & Toys | Travel

epson printer px710w   Search

ShopGenie : Where to buy online

COMPARE PRICES

Overview	Designation	Merchant	Price	
	Epson Photo printer PX710w Category: Printers	very	£202.50 price details Availability: Availability: In stock	GO ›
	Epson Photo printer PX710w Category: Printers	marshall ward	£202.50 price details Availability: Availability: In stock	GO ›
	Epson Photo printer PX710w Category: Printers	additions DIRECT	£202.50 price details Availability: Availability: In stock	GO ›

Computers & Software
Laptops - Desktop Computers - GPS - Graphics

Sell and earn online

Use the power of eBay to auction household items

The world's largest and most frequently used internet auction site, eBay is the perfect place for anyone wanting to sell unwanted or surplus possessions and turn them into extra cash. There is virtually no limit to what you can sell. Whether it is a collection of old records, a sofa you no longer need, an outgrown bicycle or a car that you want to replace, you will find a ready marketplace of eager buyers. And rather than dragging your goods to car boot sales or local fêtes you can run your online 'shop' from the comfort of home. It is a simple, easy and safe way to start selling on the internet.

Assemble key information about what you want to sell. In particular measure and weigh the items to estimate delivery costs, and take some photos.

► BEFORE YOU START

1 To create your eBay account, connect to the internet. In your web browser's address box type **www.ebay.co.uk** and press **Return**. On the home page, click the **register** link and fill in your details. When you have completed this, eBay will send you a confirmation email with a link and instructions on how to confirm your registration.

Registering

When you register, you will need to give details of a credit or debit card, and your bank account, so have the information handy. You will not be charged – the information is used simply to verify your identity. You can use the details, though, to pay eBay's listing fees for your sales items.

Close-up
There are three basic types of fee that eBay charges sellers. The 'Insertion Fee' allows you to have a listing on eBay. It is based on your starting price and you pay this whether or not your item sells. 'Listing Extras' are charges for the extras you can add to help your listing to stand out – such as additional photos or bold lettering in search results. 'Final Value Fees' are percentage-based charges on the value of the item, if it sells.

Bright idea
Read the listings for the products closest to your own and take note of the information – or photos – that they have included. This also helps you to choose the best category for selling your item.

2 To get an idea of what your item is worth, search eBay to see what similar products have sold for. Click the **Advanced Search** link at the top of any eBay page. Type in the key words that describe your item – here, 'Crystal decanter'. In the 'Search including' section click on **Completed listings** and then click **Search**.

3 To place your listing, click on **Sell** (top right of page). In the 'List your item for sale' box enter a title for the listing, ideally 3-5 words. Try to include what the item is, its brand name, size, colour, model and age. Select **Quick Sell**, which has the most popular options to get your item listed quickly, then click on **Start selling**.

4 The 'Create your listing' page is divided into six sections. Section 1 displays the title you entered on the previous page. To change this, click in the box and edit – a character count shows how many letters you have left. In section 2 select a category for your item. If unsure, click on **Browse categories** to see the full range of categories.

Create your user ID

When you choose a user ID, it cannot be your email address or a name taken by another eBay user. Type a user name of your choice into the box and click on **Check availability**, to see if it is taken. If it is, the message 'Sorry, that user ID is not available' will be displayed and alternative IDs will be listed under 'Our suggestions'. Click on one to select it, then on **Next** and follow the prompts. Alternatively, keep trying different IDs of your choice. When choosing your user ID, select a name that gives the right image – not too silly or easily misconstrued.

Selling vehicles

The 'Quick Sell' option is not suitable for selling vehicles. Click instead on **Sell a car or motorbike**. In the 'Select a category' page, 'Cars, Motorcycles & Vehicles' will be selected in the first panel. Click on a subcategory in the second and third panels, then on **Continue**.

Close-up
The first photo is free. It is added as your Gallery Picture, which will display in search results. Additional photos can be added, for which you pay a small fee.

Bright idea
Choosing your price demands careful research. When you search eBay for items like yours, you need to look at the number of items that are currently for sale and how many of them have actual bids. Are there just a couple that people seem to be fighting over? Consider what makes them different from the rest. With some idea of what price your item might reach, you need to decide what the minimum is that you would accept.

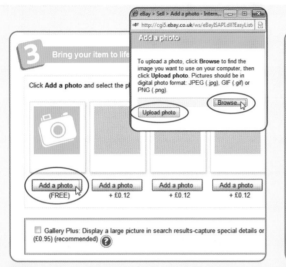

5 To add a photo, click on **Add a photo** in section 3. In the pop-up window that opens click on **Browse**, and navigate to the folder containing your photo. Click on it to select it and then click **Open**. Click **Upload photo** to finish. Add any additional pictures – such as the decanter's box – in the same way.

6 In section 4 select the item condition from the drop-down list and type in a description of the item in the panel below. Click on **Add important details about your item** to extend automatically the form to include additional options related to your item. Here, they are type of glassware, era and country of origin.

7 In section 5 enter your starting price (the default is set to '£0.99') and select the number of days for the auction from the 'lasting for' drop-down list. Add delivery charges – click on **P&P Calculator** if you need help to work this out. Select the size of your parcel, its weight and its destination – then click on **Get estimate**.

Your sales pitch

After the title (see step 3), the description is your chance to really sell your item. Repeat the title information as potential buyers may have skimmed over this. Also explain why you are selling. Buyers may be happier to make a bid if they know it is a duplicate present or you have a newer model. And give full details of the item's size, condition and special features – and history, if it is rare or collectable. If the item is unused, you can genuinely list it as new. If you have only used it a couple of times, say that rather than simply list it as second hand or used.

Keep in touch with your buyers

During the auction you will probably get questions from potential buyers. The questions will be emailed to you and delivered to your message centre on 'My eBay'. To access them, click the **My eBay** button at the top of the page and then on the **Messages** tab. When replying through the message centre, you can tick a box under a reply to add it to the bottom of the auction page so all potential bidders see it.

Shortcut
As much of the bidding is done at the last minute, time your auction to end when most people are able to take part – typically in the evening or on a Sunday.

Close-up
For items that are too big and heavy to post, you can stipulate that buyers have to collect, either in person or by courier. To work out your postage, weigh your item and the packaging and go online to www.royalmail.com for the latest prices. You can also add a small charge for handling.

When the auction has finished

You will be sent an email telling you whether your item has sold and how much for. The email will contain a link to a section of eBay where you can send out an invoice and receive payment for your sold item.

8 Scroll down to section 6 to select how you want to be paid. PayPal is the best option – eBay insists that new sellers offer it. To sign up, see below. Once you are registered, enter the email address linked to your PayPal account in the box beside 'Accept payment with PayPal'. Click **Save and preview** to see how your listing will appear.

9 First you can view the listing fees you will pay. Then scroll down to preview how your listing will look. Check that all is correct. As the listing is bigger than the window available you will need to scroll around to see everything. If you want to change any details, click **Edit listing**. When ready click on **Place listing**.

10 A 'Congratulations!' message appears. To see what is happening to your sale click the **My eBay** tab, top of any page, and, with the 'Activity' tab selected, scroll down to the Active Selling section. You can see if bids have been made, the price and the number of 'watchers' – people who have clicked the 'Watch this item' button.

Making payments safe online

Like many other online retailers, eBay uses PayPal as the safest and fastest way to send and receive money, backed up by fraud protection measures. Having lodged their payment details with PayPal, the buyer can pay you instantly and securely using a credit card or from a bank account. PayPal processes the funds and sends them to your PayPal account. From there, you can transfer the money to where you like. To set up a PayPal account, open your browser, type **www.paypal.co.uk** into the address bar and click on **Sign Up**. In the 'PayPal for you' panel click on **Sign up now**. Enter your details in the next window and click on **Agree and Create Account** to end.

World wide diary

Share your thoughts and experiences with the world via a weblog

If you would like to get creative, share your thoughts on issues you care about, make new friends, and perhaps even earn a little money, then a weblog could be for you. A weblog – or 'blog' – is essentially an online diary or journal, on a hobby or any topic that interests you. It is fun, free and does not need any technical expertise.

All you need to do is come up with an idea for your blog – you can aim to be entertaining, light-hearted or authoritative, it is up to you. Once you have your intentions clear in your mind, you can just follow the steps in this project and, before long, you will have joined the millions of people already in the blogging world.

Plan out the theme of your blog, and work out what would be appropriate to include. You should always be careful in choosing your content.

BEFORE YOU START

Google blogs   endangered species   Search B

Blog results

Browse Top Stories

Published
Last hour
Last 12 hours
Last day
Past week
Past month
Anytime
Choose Dates

Subscribe:
Blogs Alerts
Atom | RSS

Related Blogs ARKive - a unique collection of thousands of video
http://www.arkive.org/
World Wildlife Fund - Wildlife Conservation, Enda
http://www.worldwildlife.org/
U.S. Fish and Wildlife Service Home - http://www.
Defenders of Wildlife - Protection of endangered
http://www.defenders.org/

The IUCN Red List of Threatened **Species**
5 Nov 2009
... update of the IUCN Red List of Threatened **Species**™ shows th
47677 assessed **species** are threatened with... more · Arabian Le
nimr) 2008 IUCN Red List Status: Critically **Endangered**. ...
HKS Library New Resources - http://www.hks.harvard.edu/library/

Lay of the Land: Brown Pelican Removed From **Endan**
2 hours ago by Matt Kirby
Yesterday, the Department of the Interior announced that the brow
recovered and that it will soon be removed from the list of threatene
species. This is a huge win and acts as a powerful testimony ...

1 Explore the blog world for advice on how to start. Search for blog topics that interest you at Google (http://blogsearch.google.com) and Blog Catalog (www.blogcatalog.com) or explore lists of popular blogs on the blog tracker blo.gs (http://blo.gs/most-watched.php).

Blogging for free

Dedicated 'blog hosting' websites provide a home for your online diary where visitors can read your musings, browse photos, watch videos and even contribute their own thoughts. There are many blogging sites where you can sign up for free (see 'Choosing where to blog', right), and most offer simple ways for you to update the content of your blog – by email, for example – while travelling. Blogs are indexed, too, so potential visitors with similar interests can find your blog more easily.

Bright idea
Choosing the right name for your blog can be important in attracting readers. Think about who you want to appeal to – whether your blog will be humorous or business-like, for example – and try to create a name that reflects this.

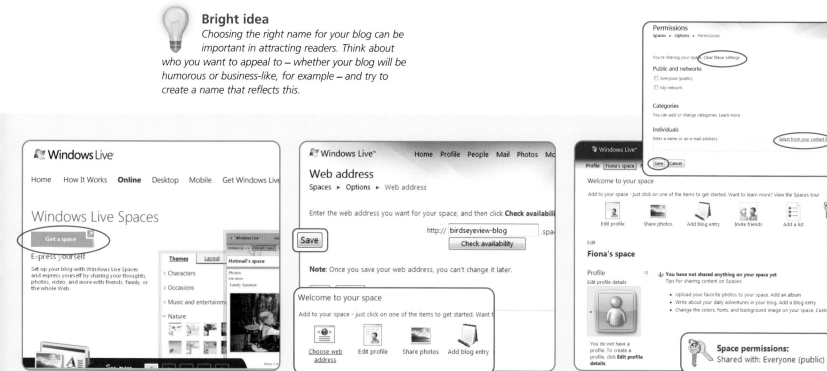

2 Setting up and running a blog can be tricky so, as a first-time 'blogger', use a service such as Windows Live Spaces. Go to http://www. windowslive.com/Online/Spaces and click on **Get a space**. Complete the registration form and choose a login password (or you can use your existing Windows Live ID password, if you have one).

3 Click on **Choose web address** and type in a name for your blog. Pick an imaginative name rather than a more predictable one. The blog here is about wildlife, so it is called 'Bird's Eye View'. Pick a variation for your web address and click on **Check availability** to make sure no one else is using it. If all is fine, click on **Save**.

4 You are now ready to customise your Space. Initially your blog can be viewed by everyone, but if you want to be selective about who views your blog, click on the **Everyone (public)** link. Click on **Clear these settings** then on **Select from your contact list** to add contacts of your choice. Click on **Save** to finish.

Choosing where to blog

Windows Live Spaces is used in this project to build a blog, but there are plenty of free alternatives if you would like to experiment. Blogger (right), www.blogger.com, is a well-established Spaces competitor and Bloglegion (left), www.bloglegion.com, lets you add photo albums, podcasting and friends lists to your blog pages.

! Watch out

Visitors to internet sites have little patience – you only have a few seconds to grab their attention. Try breaking up your text with headings and a few different fonts to help readers to scan your blog entries.

✓ Publish entry 📄 Save as draft 📄 Preview en...

Date/time: 13 November 19:20

Title (required): Welcome to my blog!

Category: None   ▼ Add a category

✂ 📋 📋 Font style ▼ Font size ▼ Paragraph size ▼ **B** *I* U ...

😊 Hello, visitor, and welcome to my first blog entry! 😊

It's taken a while, but finally I've found the time to get started on a blog at W Spaces, As you probably know, I'm fascinated by natural history and wildlife stories on:

- my discoveries when walking the local hills,
- birds I've spotted at the lakes,
- what's going on with the local wildlife club, and
- as many digital photos as I can possibly squeeze in

Feel free to join in and add your own comments and experiences

Add blog entry

Insert Line

5 In the pane at the top click on **Add blog entry**. Enter a title and type your first story in the box: a simple welcome message and details about your blog. Use the toolbar to style your entry like on a word processor and add emoticons (facial expression icons – see page 104) and more. Hover your cursor over a button to see what it does.

📄 Preview entry

Fiona's space

Profile ⚙   Blog
Edit profile details   Add | Summary
14 November
Welcome to my blog!

😊 **Hello, visitor, and welcome to my first blog entry!** 😊

It's taken a while, but finally I've found the time to get started on a blog at W Spaces, As you probably know, I'm fascinated by natural history and wildlife stories on:

You do not have a profile. To create a profile, click **Edit profile details**.

- my discoveries when walking the local hills,
- birds I've spotted at the lakes,
- what's going on with the local wildlife club, and
- as many digital photos as I can possibly squeeze in

View profile details

Network ⚙   **Feel free to join in and add your own co**

Your friends say a lot about who you are - add them to your profile.

11:28 | Add a comment | Permalink | Blog i...

✓ *Publish entry*

Share photos

6 Click on **Preview entry** to see how your blog will look then on **Publish entry**. This is a good start, but adding some digital photos would help to give the blog more colour. To create a photo album that can be accessed from the main blog page, click on **Share photos**. On the next screen click on **Create album**.

🪟 Windows Live™   Home Profile People Mail Photos More▼ MSN▼   Search P

Add photos to My SA adventure
Fiona ▸ Photos ▸ My SA adventure ▸ Add photos

50 items ready to upload (Total size: ~15.98 MB)

Remove from upload list

South Africa 2007_...   South Africa 2007_...   South Africa 2007_...   South Africa 2007_...   South Africa 2007
~293.44 KB   ~301.07 KB   ~315.89 KB   ~302.52 KB   ~297.42 KB

South Africa 2007_...   South Africa 2007_...   South Africa 2007_...   South Africa 2007_...   South Africa 2007
~341.59 KB   ~353.46 KB   ~332.63 KB   ~357.07 KB   ~342.10 KB

Upload   Drop more photos here, and click **Upload** whe

7 Enter an album title and click on **Next**. You can then browse images on your hard drive. Click on **Select photos from your computer**. Click on individual photos and then on **Open** to add them or press **Ctrl + a** to select a complete folder and click on **Open**. To remove a photo click on the **x** above it. Click on **Upload**.

Get paid to blog

Blogging is about fun, not profit, but some successful blogs can make at least a little cash by including adverts. If you are interested in using adverts, you can try an advertising scheme such as Google AdSense (right), at www.google.com/adsense, supported directly by the blog-creation site Blogger (www.blogger.com).

Google AdSense

English (UK) ▼   H

Earn money from relevant ads on your website
Google AdSense matches ads to your site's content and you earn money whenever your visitors click on them.

Green Garden Tips
Spring *into summer*

Roses, Daisies and more
Local florists. Same day delivery
Freshest flowers from £10.99
www.seedsandsaplings.co.uk

Gardening Tips

Sign up now »

Sign in to Google AdSense with your
Google Account

Email:
Password:

Sign in

I cannot access my account

Place ads on your site

Quality over quantity

It is important to update your blog at least weekly, ideally every one or two days, to prevent your audience losing interest and moving elsewhere. But frequency is not the whole story and it is really important to concentrate on the quality of your content. If you write interesting and informative pieces then readers will stick around, even if they only visit every couple of weeks or so.

8 It may take a little while for your photos to upload. You can reorder them by selecting **Arrange photos...** from the 'Sort by:' drop-down list of options. Click on **Save** to finish. Your photo album appears as a small slideshow whenever people view your blog.

9 To use images in blog entries, click on **Home**, **Profile**, **Space**, **Add blog entry** and then **Add Photos**. Choose 'Select photos from your computer' or here **Add from existing album**. Click on the album and select photos to upload, tick your selections, then click **Done**. Click on **Preview entry** to view, then **Publish entry**.

10 Windows Live Spaces lets you create 'Lists' on anything you choose, such as favourite books, films or holiday destinations. Go to your space and click on **Add a list**, select a style from the 'List type' panel. Add a title, here 'Favourite places' and a description then click on **Save**. Add items to your list and click **Next** to view your list.

Bright idea
There is nothing more annoying than writing your entry, only for the upload to fail. Try writing each entry in a Word file – where you can save it as you go – then copy and paste it into your blog program.

Finding readers

Once you have great content, you need to find people to read it. Start by telling your friends and online contacts about the blog. Include the 'URL' (the web address) in your emails, and spread the word in web forums. You can also submit your web address to online blog directories, such as www.blogcatalog.com, www.dmegs.com and www.bloghub.com.

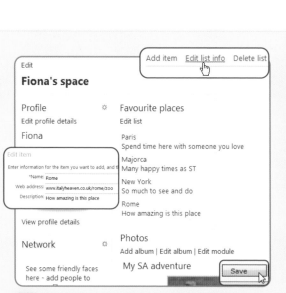

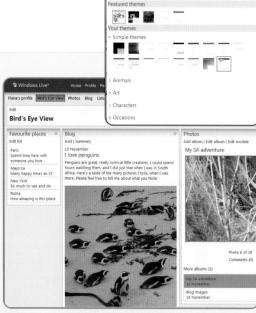

11 By adding links to associated sites, lists can be useful for your readers. Use www.google.com to find suitable websites. Add each item by clicking on **Edit** and entering the web address. When you have finished, click on **Edit list info** and change the name from 'Custom List'. Click **Save**, then on 'your space' to view the finished list.

12 To give your site a more individual look, click on **Customize**. Select **Change the theme** to choose a new colour scheme and **Change the module** to remove features you do not want or to reorganise others by dragging and dropping. Try out other options and click on **Close** when you have finished. Click on **Save** to record your changes.

13 Spaces blogs can be updated via email, so you can also post entries from a mobile phone that has email. Click on **Options**, **E-mail publishing** then tick **Turn on e-mail publishing**. Type in your email address in step 1, create a secret word in step 2, then decide what options you want to set in the remaining steps. Click **Save** to finish.

Encourage feedback

It is easy to get visitors to a blog, at least once, but if they are going to stick around then you need to make them feel involved. Do this by posting questions to your readers, asking them for their own thoughts, ideas or experiences. Let them use the Spaces Comments feature to discuss the blog with you and other readers – you will create a community spirit that keeps people coming back.

Stay out of trouble

Blogs are all about free speech but you still need to be careful what you write. If you disagree with someone, by all means say why, but do not libel them by making accusations that you could not back up in court. Do not copy text or graphics from other sites and pass them off as your own. Also be aware of any other restrictions imposed by your blogging service (see http://spaces.live.com/coc.aspx for the Spaces Code of Conduct) or click on the link at the bottom of the Options page.

Watch out

If you publish your email address on your blog, you will receive spam – unwanted junk email. Try to beat the automatic email readers by breaking it over two lines – a human will work it out, an automatic reader might not!

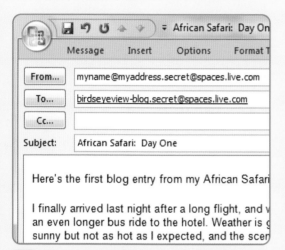

14 Spaces now displays an email address for updating your blog. Add this to the address book on your mobile phone. Any emails sent from your nominated email account to that address will go straight to the blog. This is handy, but be aware that anyone who discovers the email address will have update access to your blog, too.

15 By now you have a great-looking blog, so the next step is to attract visitors. Try to find blogs you like on the same topic as yours in a directory such as DMEGS, www.dmegs.com, then link to them (see Step 11) or write a blog entry about them. Send an email to the author, who may then link back to you, so sending some visitors your way.

16 Now that you have seen how to set up and run your own blog, you can pick up advanced tips on blogging by visiting the Hack MSN Spaces blog, http://d3vmax.spaces.live.com/. For more general advice on blogging, you could take a look at www.bloggerforum.com, www.bloggertips.com and www.bloggingpro.com.

Advertise your updates

To alert your audience to blog updates as you upload them, try out Real Simple Syndication (RSS). To turn this on in Windows Live Spaces, check your blog is set to 'Everyone (public)' by going to **Options** and then **Permissions**. Click on **Options** again and then on **General**. Tick the **Syndicate this space** box and then on **Save**. To explore the Live Alerts system further, visit http://alerts.live.com.

Research on the internet

Use today's technology to learn about our yesterdays

The World Wide Web is a great tool for historical research. Whatever your field of interest, there are bound to be sites, discussion groups and library resources dedicated to that topic.

If, for example, you are interested in the First World War, you will find thousands of resources on the web. Some will be pages produced by amateur historians, some will be educational sites aimed at children and some will be highly academic.

The first step is to do a search. Here we use the search engine Yahoo!, but you can use any one you like and pick your own path through the wealth of information on the Great War.

Make a note of which direction you want your search to take. Be as specific as possible to limit the number of 'hits'. For example, search for 'Somme' rather than 'battles'.

▶ BEFORE YOU START

1 Connect to the internet as usual. In your web browser's address box type in the address of a search engine, here http://uk.yahoo.com/, and press **Enter**. The search engine's home page will appear. Type a key word or words into the search box, suggestions are offered to you as you type (see p127), and click on the **Web search** button.

Popular history sites

Sites with information on war history include:
- www.historychannel.com (general history site)
- www.encyclopedia.com (free online encyclopedia)
- www.worldwar1.com (reference works and discussions)
- www.bbc.co.uk/history/war (numerous war articles)

Remember to use your web browser's Back and Forward buttons to revisit websites and pages you have opened since going online.

Key words
Home page *This is the opening page for any website. It will tell you what the site includes and provide links to the various parts of the site.*

World War 1 Trench Warfare
World War 1 Trench Warfare. The Western Front during **World War 1** ... **World War 1** Weapons. The German Army (The Axis) In 1914 at the Outbreak of **World War 1**, ...
hubpages.com/hub/World_War_1_Trench_Warfare

Trench warfare - Wikipedia, the free encyclopedia
Overview | **World War I...** | **World War I...** | **World War I...**
In **World War I**, both sides constructed elaborate **trench** and dugout systems opposing each other along a front, protected from assault by barbed wire. ...
en.wikipedia.org/wiki/Trench_warfare - 229k

World War I: Trenches on the Web
Online history of **World War I** featuring a range of reference materials as well as images, discussion forum, and links.
www.worldwar1.com

World War 1 Trenches - Image Results

BBC - History - **World** Wars: Life in The **Trenches** Virtual Tour
Take a virtual tour of a typical day in the **trenches**. The soldiers are cleaning their

2 A list of websites will appear. A search for 'World War I' yields millions of sites, including eye-witness accounts, picture archives and sites selling memorabilia. Scroll down and click on **World War I: Trenches on the Web**.

World War I
Trenches on the Web

An Internet History of The Great War

GOOD STARTING POINTS

REFERENCE LIBRARY *New visitors should report here. Now includes Site-Map.*

SELECTED TOURS OF THIS WEB SITE
Theme based guided tours for new visitors in a hurry to get started

1914-1918 SUPER SEARCH FACILITY
Access the Very Best First World War Sites & Resources on the ...

WWI DISCUSSION FORUM
Stop by and put in your two cents (francs, pfennigs, tuppence, etc...)
Forum Now Hosted By the Western Front Association, U.S. Br...

3 When the site opens, use the scroll bar on the right-hand side of your window to move down the home page some considerable way. You will find a list with the heading 'Good Starting Points'. Click on **Reference Library**. This is a good place to begin your research.

Trenches on the Web
LIBRARY

When | Who | What | Where | >Back | Maps

Biographies: Index

General Erich Ludendorff

4 Through the Reference Library you can access huge amounts of data, including biographies, maps, artwork and even sound recordings of the period. Click on one of the buttons to access an area of your choice.

Let Search Assist help

When using Yahoo! you can set Search Preferences to help you get to the websites you want quicker. By default, search suggestions are displayed as you type into the search box. To change these preferences, type a word into the search box, click on **Settings** found top right of the drop-down panel. Click on one of the three options displayed and then on **Save**.

http://uk.yahoo.com/

Yahoo! UK
File Edit View Favorites Tools Help
Suggested Sites ▾ Get More Add-ons ▾

YAHOO!
UK

My Yahoo! | Preview email with the Yahoo!

YAHOO! SITES ⚙ Edit
✉ Mail

Web | Images | Video | News

world war 1
world war 1 records
world war 1 trenches
world war 1 medals
world war 1 pictures
world war 1 facts
world war 11

Settings

YAHOO! SEARCH
UK & IRELAND

Welcome, fionagreen39 Sign Out -Yahoo! - Search Home - Help

Search Preferences

Search Assist

Save | Cancel

Select how often Search Assist suggestions are shown:
○ Always - Show Search Assist whenever suggestions are available
● Default - Display search suggestions only when I need assistance
○ Never - Do not automatically display search suggestions

Bright idea

When you come across interesting sites, bookmark them (see page 96). This way you can revisit them quickly, without having to search for them again or remember their address.

5 To find other sites of interest, click on your web browser's **Back** button to return to the Yahoo! website. Click on another site such as **World War 1 Pictures** to view a wide selection of images from this period.

6 For a search on a more detailed aspect of the Great War, return to the Yahoo! website. Enter a more specific search term and select a page from the results returned. Below the title of each page is an excerpt from that page, which will give you an idea of its contents.

7 Once you have read the page you have selected, you can click through the links on the site to access more pages, where you can find other information. When you have finished, you can use your browser's **Back** button to return to your original search results.

Saving pictures

To save an image onto your hard disk, right-click on the image and select **Save Picture As** from the pop-up menu that appears. Click on the arrow beside the 'Save in' box, scroll through and select a folder in which you want to save the image. Give the image a name in the 'File name' box then click on **Save**.

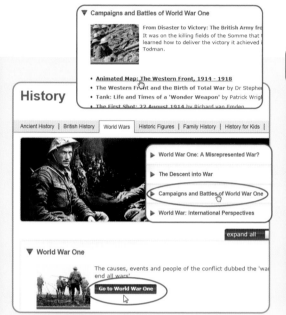

8 For impressive resources on WW1 history, go to www.bbc.co.uk/history/worldwars. The website contains a detailed timeline of the war's events and fascinating features. Click on **World War One**, then **Go to World War One** then **Campaigns and Battles of World War One**. Finally click on the 'Animated Map' link.

9 Click on **Launch the animation** to start. The map uses the Flash plug-in – you will be asked if you would like to install it if you have not already done so. Once the map has downloaded, click on **Play** to follow the evolution of the trenches, with animations showing the key battles. Click on **Next** to view each battle in sequence.

10 The BBC site also covers the human side of the war, with stories about individuals from the major fighting powers. The options under **The Human Experience of War** allow you to choose different ways to browse through the site's extensive contents, by topic, time or people.

Printing a web page

To print out a web page for future reference, go to the **File** menu on your browser's menu bar at the top of the screen and click on **Print**. In the Options tab of the Print dialogue box you can choose how to print out web pages with frames (separate elements that may not all print out at the same time).

File	Edit	View	Favorites	Tools	Help
New Tab					Ctrl+T
Duplicate Tab					Ctrl+K
New Window					Ctrl+N
New Session					
Open...					Ctrl+O
Edit with Microsoft Office Word					
Save					Ctrl+S
Save As...					
Close Tab					Ctrl+W
Page Setup...					
Print...					Ctrl+P

Primary school learning

Help children to expand **their** knowledge **through the** internet

The World Wide Web is, among many other things, a learning resource. It is full of material that can enhance children's understanding of their school subjects and of the world around them. There are thousands of educational sites, along with related sites that both parents and children will find useful. This project shows you a selection – some are bright and breezy interactive sites, others contain details of the National Curriculum.

Using the internet for education is fun, and it equips primary-age children with learning skills they are likely to use throughout their school years, and beyond.

Make a daily study plan so you can work out exactly which subjects to study and when, to make more efficient use of your time online.

► BEFORE YOU START

1 Connect to the internet. In the browser's address box type in a search engine address – here, http://kids.yahoo.com, an engine specially designed for children. Press the **Return** key. When the home page loads, type a key word into the search box and click on **Search**.

Searching by category

In addition to a search box, some search engines let you search by category. You narrow your search by clicking on subdivisions that have been made already. This is useful for children who might misspell key words.

Close-up
Keep a record of a website's address by adding it to your web browser's Favorites file (see page 96). Once entered, all you need do to view the site is click on the entry in the list instead of typing in the web address every time.

Key Word
Add-on *Also referred to as Plug-in, an add-on can be a new time-saving toolbar button, a shortcut to speed up searching, a themed look or software that enhances other programs. Add-ons cannot normally be run independently.*

*Click on the **Back** button to revisit websites and pages already viewed since you have been online.*

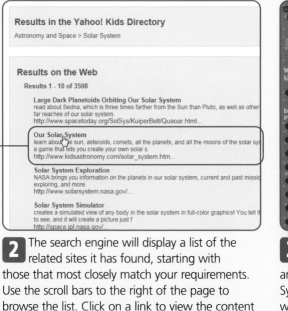

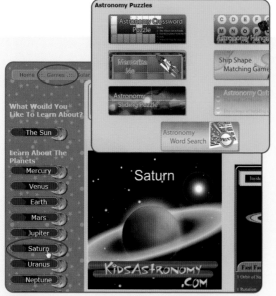

2 The search engine will display a list of the related sites it has found, starting with those that most closely match your requirements. Use the scroll bars to the right of the page to browse the list. Click on a link to view the content of a website – here **Our Solar System**.

Most search engines provide a brief description of the contents of a website. This helps you to decide whether the site is likely to be useful or not.

3 The home page of that site will then appear. KidsAstronomy.com is a site that uses exciting animations and graphics to explain how the Solar System works. To view some of the features you will need the Flash plug-in, an add-on to your browser. Click on the button and follow the prompts to install it if necessary.

4 Click on a button or link (indicated by different coloured text and underlining) to explore the site. Click on **Games**, at the top of the web page, to reveal many educational games to improve your child's knowledge of astronomy. To return to the list of other sites, click on your browser's **Back** button.

Useful educational sites
You may find these websites particularly useful for children under 11:
- www.bbc.co.uk/education (contains a dedicated section to primary school learning)
- www.quia.com/web (fun and games for all ages)
- www.nationalgeographic.com/world/index.html

Bright idea
*If you have a dial-up connection you can teach children how to read long web pages offline to keep your phone bill down. If you are using Internet Explorer, go to the **File** menu and click on **Work Offline**.*

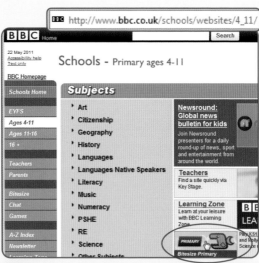

5 For more serious learning, click on **FREE Online Class** at the top of the home page to enter the Student Center. Here are two courses for different age ranges, 7-11 and 13-18. Pick your Astronomy Packet to download and follow the prompts.

1 Reading and spelling are key parts of primary school learning. BBC Schools – Primary ages 4-11 site (www.bbc.co.uk/schools/websites/4_11/) is packed with links to interactive learning pages, Games, chat sites and aids for Teachers and Parents. For spelling fun click on **Bitesize Primary**.

2 This area is organised into two columns: KS1 and KS2. From the left-hand column, KS1, click on **Literacy – Pirate Spelling**. A screen will display as the software loads. You will need to have your speakers turned on to use this page (see below).

*When you find a page that contains useful information, you may want to print it. Click on the text first, then go to the **File** menu and click on **Print**.*

Sounds right

Many interactive learning websites require sound. To ensure your sound is set up correctly, click on the **Start** button then on **Control Panel**, **Sound**. In the Sound dialogue box check that your speakers have a green tick next to them, if not, click on **Configure** and follow the on screen prompts.

Key Word
Download This means to permanently receive data to a local system (your PC) from a remote system (a website or email server).

Well-organised websites, such as MaMaMedia in step 5 below, will give you a guarantee that their own pages and the sites they link to are child-friendly and safe.

For Grown-Ups | Web Safety Center | PRIVACY POLICY
Legal Terms and Conditions | Sponsorship Information | Tech Help

3 Click on a button to choose a level of spelling, here, **Medium**. You will be prompted to either write in or choose the correct letters to complete the word. When the page has finished loading, click on **Play** to start the spelling game.

4 Listen to the word given and click on an option to complete the word. If you mishear the word, click on **Listen again**. If you get the answer incorrect you are prompted to click on **Try again**. Add the correct option to automatically move to the next step. When completed, you can replay or move to another level.

5 Learning is easier when it is fun. The MaMaMedia site (www.mamamedia.com) contains lots of animation, colour and energy. This is a site your children are sure to enjoy, perhaps as a break from homework.

Acrobat reader

This free software and browser plug-in is used for viewing specially formatted documents. To install the software, launch your web browser and type **www.adobe.com/acrobat** into the address bar. On the Adobe home page click on **Download Reader** and follow the on-screen prompts to download the software to your computer.

Download:
📄 Download Reader

For extra learning material click on the **Worksheet** button at the bottom of the page. Click on **File** then **Print**, or on the **Print** button, to create a fun worksheet to colour and fill in.

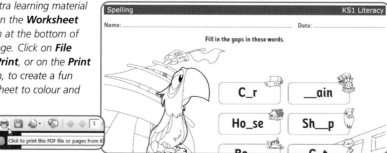

Key word
Email Electronic mail (email) is a form of
high-speed communication that is supported by
the internet. Messages can be sent down phone lines to
people on the other side of the world in seconds.

Close-up
Links to other web pages and sites usually
appear underlined and in a different colour
from the main body of text on a page. A mouse pointer
will always change to a pointing hand when it passes
over a link. Just click once on a link to open it.

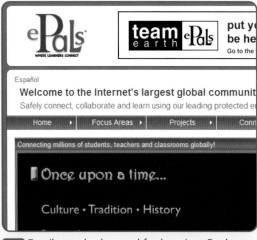

6 Another search engine geared towards
children is Ask Kids (www.askkids.com).
A child can type in a question and click on **Search**,
or click on a topic button to help to narrow their
search. Answers to questions will be displayed, plus
a list of websites that contain relevant information.

7 Email can also be used for learning. Epals
(www.epals.com) is an internet-based
organisation that links schoolchildren from
around the world via email. It can bring together
pupils of a similar age who are studying similar
types of subject.

8 There is plenty of information on schools
available on the web, which can be useful
when choosing a primary or secondary school. The
Ofsted site (www.ofsted.gov.uk) is a good place to
start as it contains basic information and the latest
school inspection reports.

Navigating between windows

Sometimes, when you click on a link to another site,
a new window opens in front of the original
window. If you want to return to the original site,
you have to make the original window 'active'.

To make the original window active, minimise or
close the new window and then click on the original
window (clicking on the **Back** button in the new
window will not work).

Watch out
To prevent children accessing unsuitable material on the internet, consider buying a web-screening program, such as Net Nanny or Cyber Patrol (see page 99).

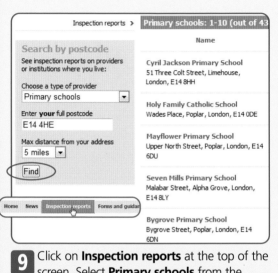

9 Click on **Inspection reports** at the top of the screen. Select **Primary schools** from the 'Choose a type of provider' drop-down menu, select a register type from the drop-down menu and enter your postcode in the box below. Click on **Find** and a list of local primary schools will appear. Click on the name of a school to find out more.

10 Websites can provide a great source of facts and information to help with homework. Learning Alive (www.learningalive.co.uk) has sections for both primary and secondary school pupils.

11 Finally, combine learning with fun. Take a look at The Yuckiest Site on the Internet (http://yucky.discovery.com), a child-friendly interactive science site that provides education and entertainment.

Secondary school learning

Gather material to help you to study for your examinations

The internet is a valuable aid to learning and study. In addition to helping with research for everyday school work, students can find lots of useful material that relates to GCSE and A-level syllabuses.

Certain sites offer the chance to browse past examination papers, take part in question-and-answer sessions, and chat with other students online. And when it comes to preparing for exams, students can get help setting up revision timetables.

But not all web-based learning is geared towards specific exams. Language students can hone their skills by reading online foreign-language magazines, and you should be able to find resources for all areas of study.

First make a list of the subject areas you wish to study, then make a note of appropriate key words and phrases to search by.

BEFORE YOU START

1 Connect to the internet. In your web browser's address box, type the address of a search engine (here, www.google.co.uk), then press the **Return** key. After a few seconds the home page will load and appear on screen.

Close-up
Although the full address of a website includes either 'http://' or 'ftp://' before the 'www...', you do not necessarily need to type this into the address box. For most websites, you can simply start the address with 'www'.

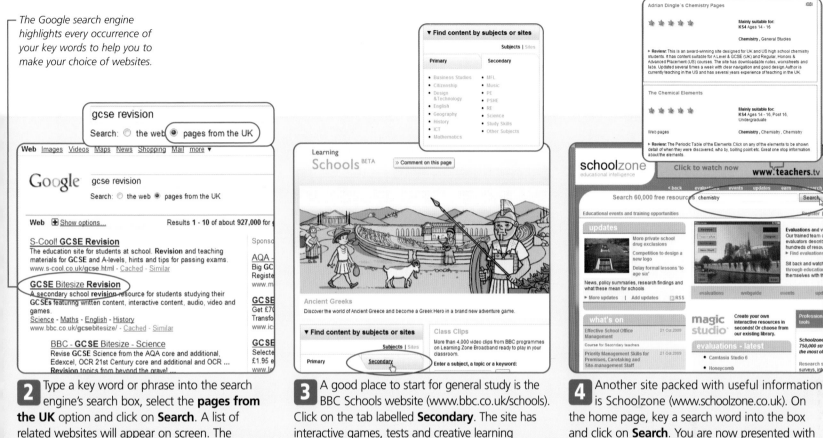

The Google search engine highlights every occurrence of your key words to help you to make your choice of websites.

2 Type a key word or phrase into the search engine's search box, select the **pages from the UK** option and click on **Search**. A list of related websites will appear on screen. The number of sites found is listed at the top of the page. To open a particular site, click on its address.

3 A good place to start for general study is the BBC Schools website (www.bbc.co.uk/schools). Click on the tab labelled **Secondary**. The site has interactive games, tests and creative learning modules to help with National Curriculum subjects.

4 Another site packed with useful information is Schoolzone (www.schoolzone.co.uk). On the home page, key a search word into the box and click on **Search**. You are now presented with a list of research material, that is star-rated and reviewed by teachers.

Keep yourself posted

It is not just links to other websites that are in a contrasting colour and often underlined on web pages – links to email addresses are as well. Look out for free subscriptions to educational newsletters that you can receive via email.

⚠ Watch out

When you do a word search, be as specific as you can. A search for, say, 'GCSE exams', might yield unsuitable results, such as personal CVs listing GCSE passes. See page 94 for advice on searches.

5 PlanIT Plus (www.planitplus.net) is a site designed for students in Scotland. It offers a mass of information on learning, schools, courses and careers, categorised into zones. Click on the tabs at the top of the page to access the various zones.

6 A great site for finding out the workings of just about anything is How Stuff Works (www.howstuffworks.com). It covers a range of subjects, from car engines to tornadoes, and offers an extensive question-and-answer section.

7 Search engines will help you to find sites offering other exam-related information and advice. For example, type 'exam techniques' into your search engine and look through some of the sites it comes up with. Here, 'Know-it-All' provides advice on planning revision, stress management and exam techniques.

Attention parents!

Chatting online can be addictive. If you allow your children to chat to other students on the web, it is sensible to limit the time they spend doing so, just as you would do when they are on the phone.

There are online timer programs that help you to keep tabs on time spent chatting and the cost (if you have a dial-up connection). You can set an alarm to go off when your chosen time has been reached. Try Computer Time by Software Time (www.softwaretime.com).

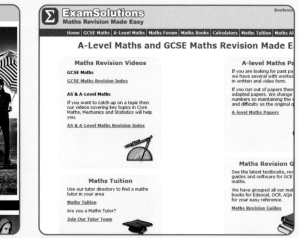

8 For help on researching and writing an essay, visit the Internet Public Library at www.ipl.org/div/teen/aplus. This site gives practical step-by-step information on planning, researching and writing an essay or project, and also offers help with creating a revision timetable.

9 Arts students can view key museum and gallery exhibits at first hand with virtual guided tours. Visit the Museum of Modern Art in New York (www.moma.org) or the National Portrait Gallery, London (www.npg.org.uk), for example, for important works of art.

10 There are lots of maths sites on the web. ExamSolutions (www.examsolutions.co.uk) offers a number of options to help students. Maths tuition, a forum, revision papers, video tutorials and a lot more are available online to help to solve tricky problems.

Keep your focus

It is easy to become sidetracked when going through search results. Be disciplined about assessing each page quickly and deciding whether a site is likely to contain useful information about the subject you are researching. If it does, save the site as a bookmark or a favourite (see page 96). Then click on the **Back** button to return to the results page.

Useful educational sites

You may find these websites particularly useful for children aged 11-16:
- www.dictionary.com (online spelling and grammar guide)
- www.learnthings.co.uk (online lessons)
- www.studysphere.com (general educational resource)
- www.dcsf.gov.uk (further education advice)

11 S-cool (www.s-cool.co.uk) has plenty of information for students revising for their GCSEs or A-levels and much more. First click on a subject from either the **GCSE** or **A-level** panels that you would like help with. This takes you to a list of topics where you can focus your revision on specific areas.

12 Prospective schoolleavers can seek advice on writing their curriculum vitae. Click on **Articles** at the top of the screen, then scroll down the page and click on **CV writing**. Here you will find help on how to structure your CV. Remember this is the initial impression a company will get of you. Scroll down for examples of CV styles.

13 Further down the 'Articles' page click on **Interview skills**. Here you will find information on how to prepare, what to do the night before and how to tackle the big day. There is also advice on how to make a good impression and what not to do during the interview.

Search a site

Many websites have their own search engines to help you to locate a specific topic within the site. Type in a key word for the subject area you would like more information on and click on **Search**. Click on a topic to display its content.

Search results

S-Cool Revision Summary
... the character in the scene? What might **Shakespeare** have intended? Always show an awareness of ... or speak to each other? How does **Shakespeare** build up the tension during the extract.? Are ...

Remember It - Anonymous - 09/06/2010 - 17:31 - 0 comments - 0 attachments

Effect of the Extract on the Audience
... use asides, or speak to each other? How does **Shakespeare** build up the tension during the extract? Are there problems ... to overcome them within the modern theatre? Does **Shakespeare** use descriptive language to describe events that would be difficult ...

Revise It - Anonymous - 09/22/2010 - 08:48 - 0 comments - 0 attachments

Preparing for the Exam
... Many English students lose sight of the fact that **Shakespeare** wrote plays to be performed, not novels just to be read. In the **Shakespeare** extract exam you are expected to analyse closely a specific extract ...

Revise It - Anonymous - 09/22/2010 - 08:47 - 0 comments - 0 attachments

Bright idea

For further information and suggestions on how to write and design an eye-catching curriculum vitae, turn to page 160.

Watch out

Students using the internet to study and revise should always check with their teachers to make sure that what they are looking at is relevant to their particular course.

If you find educational CD-ROMs expensive to buy, remember that you can borrow them from public libraries.

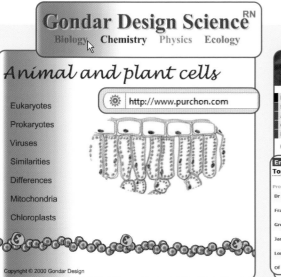

14 Search engines can also help you to find sites that are written by academics or teachers but are not necessarily linked to larger sites. For example, www.purchon.com is a site run by a teacher for pupils at his school, but is useful for anyone studying biology, chemistry, physics or ecology.

15 The schools section of the BBC website has an area devoted to GCSE revision. Go to www.bbc.co.uk/schools and click on **GCSE** from the Bitesize panel at the bottom of the page. In the Subjects panel click on a subject to browse a list of topics. You can test yourself, answer sample questions and take a mock exam.

16 You can also use the internet to find and buy additional educational resources. For example, BrightMinds (www.brightminds.co.uk) sells educational CD-ROMs online. Use any search engine to locate other suppliers.

Losing a link

Websites come and go on the internet all the time. You might sometimes click on a link and get a message saying that the page either no longer exists or that 'A connection with the server cannot be established' (this often means the page no longer exists). So be prepared for the occasional disappointment.

Work offline

If you have a dial-up connection and find you are becoming engrossed in a single detailed web page, remember that you can work offline and so save the cost of your call. With Internet Explorer, for example, go to the **File** menu and click on **Work Offline**.

Games on the internet

You will never lack a playing partner when you are online

The internet is an unrivalled source of entertainment as well as information. In fact, when it comes to computer games, the internet is in a league of its own, as it not only provides the games, but the players too.

Many online games are adventure or action-based, but there are plenty of gaming sites catering to more diverse tastes. There are, for example, a large number of chess-related services, some of which allow you to play against opponents from around the world in 'real time' – that is, live over the internet. If, however, you do not want to spend money connected to the internet while you play, you can opt to play games by email. You can also download games to play at your leisure.

For security reasons, when playing against others online, it is advisable not to divulge any personal details such as phone numbers.

 PLAYING GAMES BY EMAIL

1 There are plenty of websites offering free access to online games. If you like playing Sudoku, then go to www.sudokuonline.co.uk. There are thousands of grids to choose from, links to other sites, books and toys to purchase and much more. If you need help to get started click on **Sudoku Tutorial** from the left panel.

💡 **Bright idea**
Online advertisements can be an irritation. However, it is easy to resize the window and block them out. Just click on the bottom right-hand corner of your browser window and drag the corner up and in until the advert has been hidden.

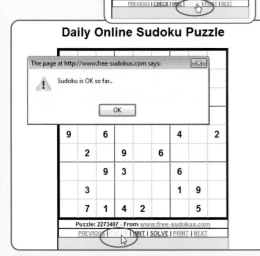

Daily Online Sudoku Puzzle

The page at http://www.free-sudokus.com says:

⚠ Sudoku is OK so far..

[OK]

Puzzle: 2273407 - From www.free-sudokus.com

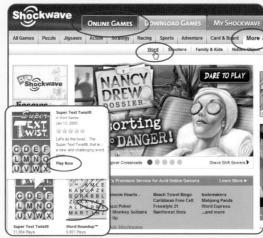

Watch out

When downloading from some sites, do not click on any 'Warning' boxes that say you have won a prize. A new window will open, taking you to a different site. It is very unlikely that a prize will be waiting for you.

2 Enter your answers by clicking on an empty square and typing in a number. Your numbers appear in blue. Click on **CHECK** at any time and a pop-up window shows your progress. Click on **OK** to close it. If the game is too hard, click on **SOLVE** to complete it. When you have finished playing, click on **NEXT** to play another game.

3 For a wide choice of online games, try www.shockwave.com. For an example of a word game, with **Online games** tab selected at the top of the screen click on **More**, and then on **Word** from the drop-down options. Scroll down the screen and click on **Super Text Twist** and then on **Play Now**.

4 A new window will open and the game will load. Once the game has loaded, click on **CLICK TO START!**. Then click on the lettered balls to form a word and click on **Enter**. If the word matches with the dictionary it will appear in the grid on the left. Repeat the process until the time runs out.

Game playing preparation

A good way to prepare for an online game is to click on the various information links or tabs in the game's main window. For information about Text Twist, for example, click on the tabs to read the rules, pick up useful tricks and tips, read reviews and learn about how to share the game.

Super Text Twist®

☆☆☆☆☆ Avg. Rating · ✦ Share This Game ▾ · Game Instructions ▲

Click on the balls to form a word, then press the Enter. If the word is in the dictionary for the game, it will show up on the left-hand side of the game. Use the TWIST button when you get stuck to help you see other words. You may also use the keyboard to enter words.

See in-game help for detailed instructions.

How many words can you spell from a jumbled group of letters before time runs out? That's the task in Super Text Twist®, a deceptively challenging word game.

Go on and do the Twist!
Want more text twisting F-U-N? Play TextTwist® 2!

*Many game sites require regular users to sign up. To sign up to Shockwave, click on **Join: FREE**, fill in your account details, then click on **Sign Up**.*

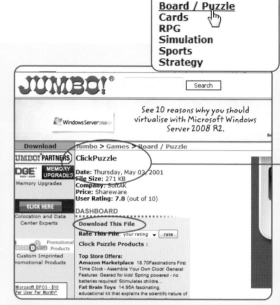

Watch out

Using a high-speed broadband connection can make online gaming faster and more fun. But make sure you protect your system with a 'firewall' – software or hardware that stops other internet users accessing files on your PC.

5 On the internet you can also access strategy and fantasy games that work by sending your moves to your opponent(s) by email. To find one of these, go to www.excite.com and type **games by email** in the 'Search the Web' box. Select a site from the search results listed.

6 The Jumbo! site has a vast selection of programs – some of which are games – that users can download. In your web browser's address box type in 'www.jumbo.com', then press **Return**. Now click on **Games** at the top of the right-hand panel to see the games available.

7 Click on **Board/Puzzle** in the 'Games Subcategories' panel, then scroll down and click on a game that interests you – here ClickPuzzle. A screen will appear with information about the game and an option to download it. Click on **Download This File**.

Software for free

● **Shareware** is software distributed free for a limited period. When the licence expires you should buy the program if you want to continue using it.

● **Freeware**, as the name suggests, is software that is distributed free of charge and can be used indefinitely. However, it often comes without any user support.

● **Demo/Sample software** is a reduced version of a commercial program. You use it to decide whether you want to buy the complete program.

File sizes

When you download a game file from the internet you will usually be told the size of the file. A file of a couple of hundred kilobytes should take just seconds to download, but a file of several megabytes could take considerably longer depending on your connection speed. Games that contain lots of sophisticated graphics take the longest to download.

Watch out
*Some games are free to download but may still come with some restrictions. Read any licensing agreements before you play. Tick the 'I agree with …' box and then click on **Next** each time you are prompted, to continue with your install.*

Bright idea
Avoid deleting downloaded files after the programs have been installed. If possible, back them up onto a separate storage device, such as a flash drive or rewritable CD (for more on storage devices, see page 43). The installation programs may be needed again at a later date.

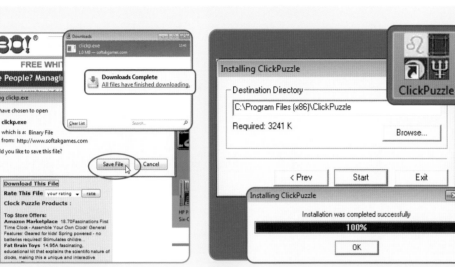
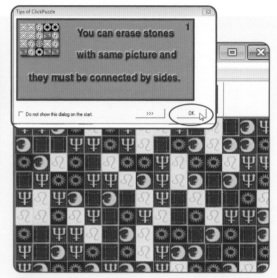

8 In the Opening clickp.exe dialogue box that appears, click on **Save File** to download the game. When the Downloads dialogue box appears, double-click on **clickp.exe** (a security warning box may appear – if you agree with it, click on **Yes**). Next the Installing ClickPuzzle dialogue box appears, see 'Watch out' above).

9 In the Installing ClickPuzzle dialogue box that appears, select the destination directory for the installed game to be stored and then click on the **Start** button. Click on **OK** when the installation is complete. A shortcut button to the game will be added to your Desktop.

10 Double-click on the shortcut icon on your Desktop to start a game. A 'Tips of ClickPuzzle' box will appear that gives you help with playing the game. To view more information, click on the chevron button. Click on **OK** to close the tip box and play the game.

Keeping secure
On some PCs a File Download – Security Warning dialogue box appears, warning the user that the action they are about to perform may be dangerous. If you are not confident that the file you are downloading is from a safe and reputable source, click on **Cancel** to abort the process.

Remove a game
To delete a game from your computer, click on the **Start** button and select **Control Panel**, then **Uninstall a program**. Highlight the program you wish to delete – here 'ClickPuzzle' – and click on **Uninstall/Change**. Then just follow the prompts.

Chess is a popular game on the web. You play against a computer or a person in real time. If you have a dial-up connection, set a time limit on moves to keep costs down.

► PLAYING CHESS ON-LINE

Bright idea
Before you begin playing a game of chess, print out and study a copy of the game rules and any tips you are given for online chess etiquette.

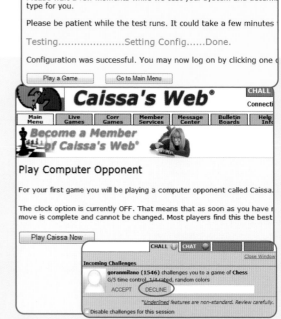

11 A good site for playing chess online is www.caissa.com. Type this in your browser's address box and press **Return**. When the home page loads, new players need to sign up for their free membership. To do this, click on **play online chess now!** and this will take you to a page where you can sign up for an account.

12 Fill in your personal details. Type in a 'handle' (the name by which you will be known when playing), and click on **check for availability**. If that name is available, fill in the rest of your details and click **CONTINUE**. Make sure your password is easy to remember, as you will need it to log on to the site in future.

13 You should now see a splash screen as your account is configured, and the message 'Account verified!' when completed. Click on **Play a Game**. Your first game is automatically set to play against the computer, so click on **Play Cassia Now** to proceed. If an online challenge message appears, click on **DECLINE** for now.

Try before you buy

Some web-based chess services are free – ChessManiac for example – but others, including Caissa's site (above), are membership services for which you have to pay a fee. Free trials help you to decide whether or not it is worth paying for these services.

Added insight

If you prefer to learn how the system works before you play a game, watch one first. Click on the **Live Games** tab, then on **Watch Games**. Click to select a game from the list.

White	Black	Game	Speed			
united00	salonikios	Chess	G/2			...18
docsebba	Caissa	Chess	G/30			...04
christos	Caissa	Chess	G/30			...d
Pemaquid	pelotudo	Chess	30/15	17:02:19	16. Nxf4	17:07:31
konbul1453	nala	Chess	30/15	17:06:25	22... Bd8	17:18:49
constructorul	Caissa	Chess	G/30	17:07:43	40... h5	17:21:13
goranmilano	Ratman	Chess	G/5	17:10:06	52. Kd6	17:17:50
albell	Sunaco	Chess	30/15	17:10:31	18... Be7	17:20:47
Sonny52	Tatomas	Chess	30/15	17:13:22	16... Qxd5	17:20:32
ONFIRE	niaz1	Chess	30/15	17:13:42	9... Nf6	17:21:12

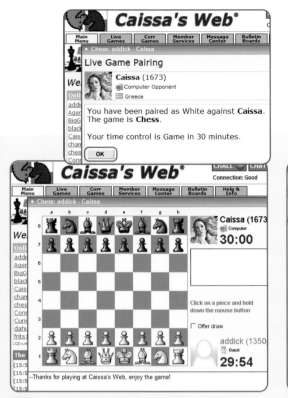

14 In the next window, Live Game Pairing, you will see that you have been paired as white against Caissa, and your time control has been set to 30 minutes. When you are ready to play, click on **OK**. As white always starts, click and drag a pawn to move it and start the game.

15 Caissa (black) will then respond with a move. After each of your moves, you will see Caissa make a move. Moves are listed in the panel on the right. If you are clearly beaten, click on **Resign** to finish the game. Click on **Main Menu**, and online players appear in the 'Online Players' panel, with you listed at the top.

16 When you are ready to play a person, go to the Live Game Room (click on your browser's **Back** button), and in the Play a LIVE Game panel click on a player – here 'krieger4'. The Live Game Pairing window will confirm your challenge. Click on **OK** to start the game.

Online etiquette

When playing games online remember that you are often playing against other people – not a computer – and so the usual rules of social etiquette apply.

For example, you should not leave your computer without a mutual agreement to stop playing. One of the Caissa site's particular rules is that you should never prolong a game that you are clearly going to lose.

PRACTICAL HOME

This section will guide you, **step by step**, through **37 practical projects** over a range of subjects. Each task is self-contained – you require **no prior experience** of the program used. Suggestions are also made of ways you can bring the projects together to undertake more **ambitious events**, such as organising a reunion.

PROJECTS

Design a letterhead

Create **your** personal stationery **with an** individual **look**

I n the age of email and internet chat, the importance of letters is often overlooked. However, we all still need to send letters from time to time – whether they are formal instructions to solicitors or insurers or a chatty letter giving an old friend your latest news. Whoever you are writing to, a well-designed letterhead giving your name and contact details will save you time in starting your letters as, once you have created your letterhead, you can save it as a template. This means that you can use it each time you write a letter and if any of your details change, you can easily alter them on the template.

Decide what you are going to use your letterhead for. If it is for letters to family and friends, you can be creative with your choice of fonts.

BEFORE YOU START

1 Go to the **Start** button, click on **All Programs** and select **Microsoft Word 2010**. Now click on the **Page Layout** tab from the Ribbon and then on the Page Setup dialogue box launcher, bottom right of the Page Setup group.

*To create a letterhead in Microsoft Works, go to the **Start** menu, click on **Microsoft Works** and then click on **Works Word Processor** from the 'Quick launch' menu on the right.*

OTHER PROGRAMS

Bright idea
If you have an email address or website, remember to include them in your letterhead.

Susannah Matthews
Designer
104 Chamberlain Avenue
Maidstone, Kent ME16 4LR
Telephone: 01622 442 7272

Header

[Type text]

Susannah Matthews
Designer
104 Chamberlain Avenue
Maidstone, Kent ME16 4LR
Telephone: 01622 442 7272

Susannah Matthews

2 In the Page Setup dialogue box with the **Margins** tab selected, set the Top, Bottom, Left and Right margins. In the Headers and Footers section of the **Layout** tab, set the 'From edge' distance between the header and the top of the page. Click on **OK**. Now click on the **Home** tab.

3 You are going to create your letterhead within the Header section of your document. Go to the **Insert** tab and, from the 'Header and Footer' group, click on **Header** and then select **Blank** from the drop-down list of styles. Type your name, address and phone number in the '[Type text]' prompt area.

4 Now highlight your name, click on the **Home** tab, then on the Font dialogue box launcher and select a font, style and size, hovering the mouse pointer over these to view them in the Preview window. Then click on **OK**. Style your address using the same method.

Using Word's templates

Word 2010 has lots of templates that you can use to create personalised letterheads. Click on the **File** tab and select **New**. Scroll down the list under Office.com Templates and select **Stationery and specialty paper**, then **Seasonal and holiday stationery**. Choose a style from the selection of thumbnail images, here Holiday stationery (with snow scene), and click on **Download**. Highlight the text and type in your details.

Works templates

Microsoft Works also has a templates feature. Open up Microsoft Works and click on the **Templates** button and then, from the list on the left, choose **Letters & Labels**. Next, click on the **Letters** icon and choose a template style, then click on **Use this style**. Type in your details as you follow the on-screen instructions.

To save your letterhead as a template, go to the **File** menu and select **Save As**. In the dialogue box click on the **Template** button in the bottom right-hand corner. Then type in a name for your template and click **OK**.

WORDPOWER

Handles *The term describes the four round and four square symbols that appear on the corners and sides of an object when selected (see step 6). Click and drag outwards or inwards to resize an object.*

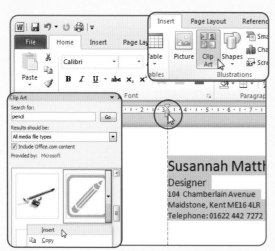

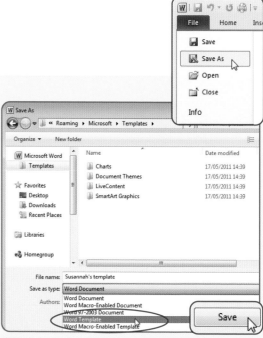

5 To add a clip art image to your letterhead, highlight your letterhead text, click and drag the left indent marker on the ruler to the right. Click on the Insert tab then on **Clip Art** from the 'Illustrations' group. Type a keyword in the 'Search for' box in the Clip Art pane and click on **Go**. Click on an image and select **Insert** in the pop-up menu.

6 Go to the 'Arrange' group and click on **Wrap Text**, then select **Square**. Click on the image and drag it to reposition it to the left of the text. Resize the image by clicking and dragging on one of the corner handles. Click on **Close Header and Footer** on the far right of the Ribbon.

7 When you are happy with your design, save it as a template that you can use again and again. Click on the **File** tab and select **Save As**, then choose **Templates** from the left panel. Give the template a name, select **Word Template** from the 'Save as type' drop-down options, and click on **Save**.

Use your toolbar

The toolbar buttons at the top of the screen help you to style your text quickly. Highlight the text and then click on the relevant button to make it bold, to italicise it or to underline it. You can change your text's position by clicking on the left, centre or right alignment buttons.

Change your picture or clip art

If you would like to change the artwork you originally chose for your letterhead, first open the template. Then double-click on the picture or clip art image. Next, go to the 'Adjust' group and click on the **Format** tab and select **Change Picture**. You can now browse pictures or clip art and select the new image. Click on **Insert** and, if necessary, click and drag on the handles to resize it (see step 6, above).

Bright idea
*Save yourself time by using automatic dating for your letters. Click where you want the date to appear in your document, go to the **Insert** tab and click on **Date and Time**. In the dialogue box click on your preferred style and then click on **OK**.*

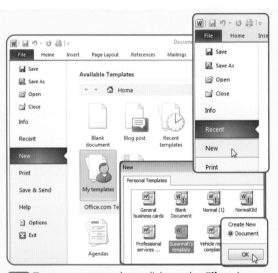

8 To use your template, click on the **File** tab and select **New**. Under Available Templates click on **My templates**. The New dialogue box appears. Look for your new template, here 'Susannah's template'. Click on it and then on **OK** to create a new document.

9 The cursor will flash below your letterhead. Use the **Return** key to create a few blank lines and then type your letter. To save it, click on the **File** tab and select **Save As**. By default your document will have a temporary name Doc1 or similar so you need to create a permanent name.

10 In the Save As dialogue box, click on **Libraries** then **Documents** on the left. At this point you can select a sub-folder or create a new folder if you wish. Type in a name for your document and click on **Save**. This letter will now be saved, and your letterhead template can be used again.

Changing your template
In Word, click on the **File** tab and select **Open**. Under 'Microsoft Word' on the left, select **Templates** and then, in the right-hand pane, double-click on your template. Make your changes and click on **Save**.

In Works, choose **Works Word Processor** from the Quick launch taskbar. Click on your letterhead in the list of templates, make your changes, go to the **File** menu and select **Save As**. Double-click on the old file in the Templates folder to replace it with the new one. Click on **Yes** in the dialogue box to confirm your choice.

*To see line spaces and other 'hidden' elements, go to the Home tab and click on the **Show/Hide** button.*

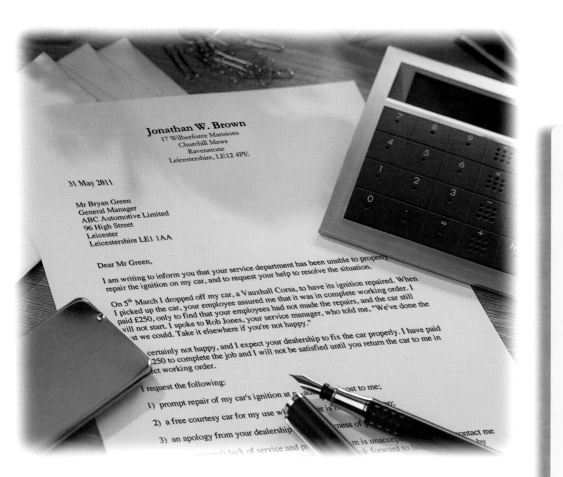

Assemble all relevant documents and make a quick note of the points you wish to make. Check that you are writing to the appropriate person to deal with your letter.

▶ BEFORE YOU START

Microsoft Office Home and Business (E
- 🅇 Microsoft Excel 2010
- 🄽 Microsoft OneNote 2010
- 🄾 Microsoft Outlook 2010
- 🄿 Microsoft PowerPoint 2010
- 🅆 Microsoft Word 2010
- Microsoft Office 2010 Tools

Microsoft Silverlight

Microsoft Works

◀ Back

Search programs and files

File   Home   In
- 💾 Save
- 💾 Save As
- 📂 Open
- 🗁 Close

Info

Recent

New

Print

1 Go to the **Start** button, click on **All Programs** and select **Microsoft Word 2010**. Click on the **File** tab on the far left of the Ribbon, at the top of your screen. Now scroll down the list of options and click on **New**.

Send a formal letter

Give your business correspondence a professional look

Writing a formal letter can sometimes seem quite daunting, but Word 2010 includes many ready-made templates that make it straightforward. Simply pick a template design, type in your details and relevant information and re-style the document as appropriate.

It is usual to include the name, company position and address of the person you are writing to. It is also a good idea to include an official reference. For example, if you are writing to your bank, you could give your account number. When replying to a letter, look out for a reference, and repeat that.

You can also create a letterhead in Microsoft Works. Open Works then click on the Programs button. Choose Works Word Processor from the Quick Launch menu on the right.

▶ OTHER PROGRAMS

Watch out
Some templates have American formatting. To change these elements to an English format, see example in the panel, right.

To change the format of a date field for example, highlight it, right click and select **Edit Field**. In the Field dialogue box, select a format under Field properties, Date formats and click on **OK**.

Close-up
To save time and keep the document accurate, Microsoft Word 2010 automatically inserts the date into templates, if appropriate.

2 Under 'Available Templates', icons are organised into two groups: 'Home' – those already installed with Word or previously downloaded; and 'Office.com Templates' – those available online to download. Click on a category to select a template to use, here **My templates**.

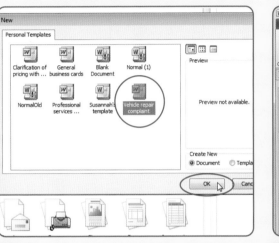

3 The 'Personal Templates' folder contains any templates already downloaded. Click on a template to select it, here **Vehicle repair complaint**, then click on **OK**. This template was previously downloaded using the method described below.

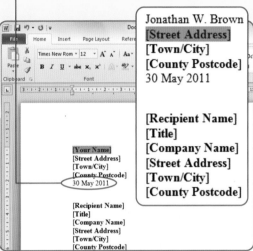

4 The downloaded letter will have bracketed bold 'prompt' areas within it. Click inside the square brackets to highlight the prompt, and type your own details. Other areas of the letter will also need to be modified, highlight these as you go through and add your own details.

Accessing Office 2010 UK templates

Microsoft Office 2010 templates accessed from 'Office.com' are generally styled for the US audience. To access UK formatted templates, launch your internet browser and type **http://office.microsoft.com/en-gb/templates** into the address bar and press **Return**. Here you will find hundreds of Office 2010 compatible templates grouped in categories. Click on a category to view its options, make your

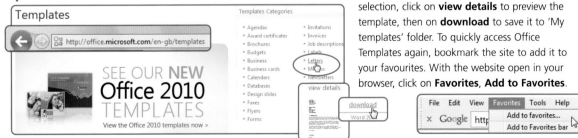

selection, click on **view details** to preview the template, then on **download** to save it to 'My templates' folder. To quickly access Office Templates again, bookmark the site to add it to your favourites. With the website open in your browser, click on **Favorites**, **Add to Favorites**.

Watch out
You are in danger of losing your work if you do not save it frequently. Make a habit of saving your letter every few minutes.

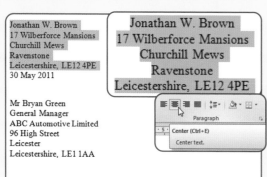

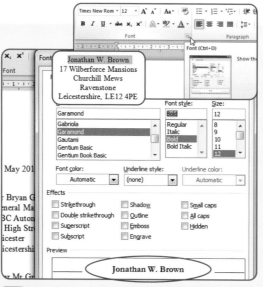

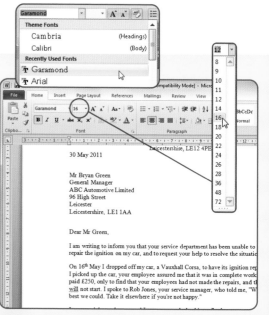

5 You can personalise your letter by positioning your own details in the centre of the page. Highlight your name and address, then go to the **Home** tab at the top left of your screen, and click on the **Center** button, from the Paragraph group.

6 To style your letter, first highlight your name at the top. Next, click on the **Home** tab and click on the Font dialogue box launcher. Select a font, style and size – you can see how it looks by clicking on a style and then viewing it in the Preview window at the bottom of the box. Make your selection and then click on **OK**.

7 Continue to style the remainder of your text, using the tools outlined in step 6. You can apply different styles to paragraphs, sentences or even individual words – just highlight the area you would like to style. For speed, you can use the font and font size shortcuts on the Ribbon as shown.

Select a font

If you know the name of the font you want to use, type its first letter into the Font box. All the fonts beginning with that letter will then appear at the top of the Font window. This saves you scrolling through all the fonts on your PC.

Change the scale

If you would like to magnify your document to see it in more detail, you can do so without adjusting the type size. The scale can easily be changed by clicking on the '+' or '-' zoom buttons found on the status bar at the bottom of your window. Alternatively, click on the **View** tab at the top of the window, then click on **Zoom**, select one of the options, then click on **OK**.

Bright idea
It is often easier to spot mistakes on a printed page than on screen, so after printing your letter read it through carefully to check for errors.

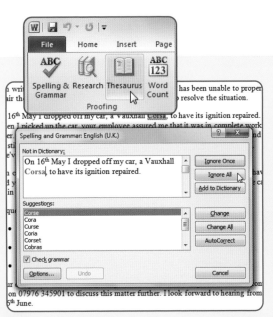

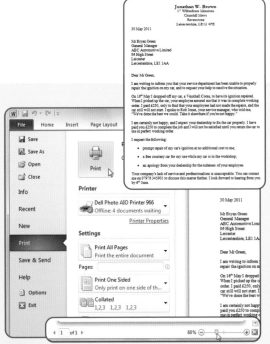

8 To check for any spelling mistakes, click on the **Review** tab, go to the 'Proofing' group and click on the **Spelling & Grammar** button. If you only want to check a section of the document, highlight the relevant text before clicking on the button.

9 If Word questions a spelling, click on **Ignore** or **Change** depending whether the word is misspelt. If you cannot think of the exact word you want, you could use the Thesaurus. Click on the **Review** tab and, in the 'Proofing' group, click on **Thesaurus** to find words with similar meanings.

10 To see how your letter will look, click on the **File** tab, then on **Print**. Here you can preview your letter using the zoom slider and page change buttons. If you need to make a change, click on the **Home** tab to return to your letter. To print, select your printer and click on the **Print** button.

Make your point

If you are making a number of important points in your letter and wish to emphasise them, type each one on a new line. Highlight the whole section, click on the Paragraph dialogue box launcher and choose an option to increase the line spacing. Finally, click on the **Bullets** button to pick out each of your points.

- prompt repair of my car's ignition a
- a free courtesy car for my use whil
- an apology from your dealership fo

Improve your service as

If you are the chief organiser of a tennis club, bridge club or amateur operatics society, your PC can make light work of the daily administration

At the heart of all successful clubs is a well-organised and unflappable secretary. It is the kind of job that requires attention to detail, an ability to prioritise a large number of tasks, and a head for figures.

The simplicity and flexibility of today's computer software makes such duties both enjoyable and much easier to manage.

A sensible starting point for any club secretary would be to set up a database containing members' personal details: addresses, contact phone numbers, relevant abilities and so on. It is also a good idea

Project planner

Create a folder named after your club. Add sub-folders for each area of administration.

- Club administration
  - Members
  - Money
  - Minutes
  - Communications
  - Publicity
  - Results & events

a club secretary

to create a standard membership form that can be stored on your computer and then printed out for any prospective club members to complete. Once you have a database set up, it is a simple task to produce address labels for your club correspondence.

Using a second database, the secretary of a sports club can produce tables to show fixtures, results and club rankings.

Keeping club accounts and tracking membership fees are simple tasks once you set up a spreadsheet. You can then use it for recruitment-based fiscal planning.

For communications with other organisations, create your own club stationery. You could design a club logo using Paint or another graphics program. The logo could then be used on club newsletters or, with the help of an outside supplier, on merchandise such as club ties and keyrings.

You might like to consider compiling a pictorial club history on your computer. Somebody could write a short account that can be published for members' interest.

And do not forget that many members will be online. If you compile an email address book, you can send information on rankings, fixtures and social events to everyone at once.

With the wide availability of online banking, monitoring your club accounts could not be simpler. And, provided there is the right software compatibility, you can usually download information straight from your bank to your spreadsheets and pay bills online.

Ideas and inspirations

Customise the following projects and ideas to suit the needs of your club. That way, you will spend less time on administration, and far more time enjoying the club's benefits. Once you have set up the basic documents you need, maintaining them should be a quick and easy matter.

172 Membership database
Compile a handy reference document to keep a record of all your members' details.

276 Club accounts
Keep track of income and outgoings, and budget for projects, such as buying new equipment.

176 Produce address labels
Print off address labels for all your club members to make correspondence quick and easy.

196 Create a greetings card
Send your members (or prospective members) cards for Christmas or to publicise a club event.

230 Design your own poster
Design your own logo or artwork for stationery, club posters or internet use.

Start the ball rolling

- Compile and collect all membership details and transfer them to your database
- Transfer a copy of the club's accounts to a spreadsheet on your computer
- Set up an online bank account
- Produce a club logo for all communications
- Arrange for all league or club information to be sent via email to online members

Write an eye-catching CV

Make the most of your experience and achievements

Your CV, or curriculum vitae, is intended to make a favourable impression on potential employers. As well as giving details of all the companies you have worked for and how long you were employed by them, it explains what your responsibilities were and what skills you have developed.

Keep your CV brief and to the point. If possible, try to fit it on a single page. Select a clear, easy-to-read font and do not be tempted to make the font size too small in an effort to squeeze everything in. Also, keep your CV's design simple, with well-defined sections that make it easy to extract information.

To make sure all your dates of employment are correct, collect your old P45 forms and refer to them as you type in your details.

► BEFORE YOU START

1 Go to the **Start** button, click on **All Programs** and select **Microsoft Word 2010**. Click on the **File** tab on the far left of the Ribbon at the top of your screen. Now scroll down the list of options and click on **New**.

*You can also create your CV in Microsoft Works. Open Works then click on the **Templates** button. Choose **Letters & Labels** from the list on the left, then click on **Resume (CV)**.*

► OTHER PROGRAMS

Bright idea
When you write your accompanying letter of application, use the same fonts as in your CV. Not only will your letter and CV complement each other, but they will also have a professional appearance. A potential employer may well form the impression that you pay attention to detail.

2 Under 'Available Templates', icons are organised into two groups: 'Home' – those already installed with Word or previously downloaded; and 'Office.com Templates' – those available online to download. Click on a category to select a template to use, here **My templates**.

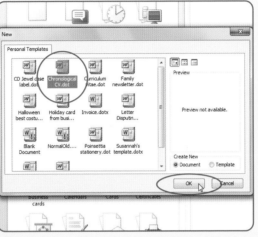

3 The 'Personal Templates' folder contains any templates already downloaded. Click on a template to select it, here **Chronological CV**, then click on **OK**. This template was previously downloaded using the method described below.

4 Your downloaded CV will have bracketed bold [Prompt] areas within it. Click inside the brackets to highlight the prompt, and type your details as appropriate. Use the 'Tab' key to move to the next area of the CV and add your own information.

Accessing Office 2010 UK templates

Microsoft Office 2010 templates accessed from 'Office.com' are generally styled for the US audience. To access UK formatted templates, launch your internet browser and type **http://office.microsoft.com/en-gb/templates** into the address bar and press **Return**. Here you will find hundreds of Office 2010 compatible templates grouped in categories. Click on a category – here **Resumes** – to view its options,

make your selection, click on **view details** to preview the template, then on **download** to save it to 'My templates' folder. To quickly access Office Templates again, bookmark the site to add it to your favourites. With the website open in your browser, click on **Favorites**, **Add to Favorites**.

Bright idea

Be prepared! Update your CV on a regular basis, remembering to add details of any training courses, new interests and areas of responsibility.

Watch out

You are in danger of losing your work if you do not save it frequently. Make a habit of saving the changes to your CV every few minutes.

5 Press the **Tab** key to move down to the next section – 'Experience' – or click inside the prompt with the mouse. Type in your job details, starting with information on your latest position. If the template gives more options than you need, simply highlight them and press the **Delete** key.

6 It is a good idea to style your CV a little in case other people have used the same template. Highlight the first date line, then click on the **Font** dialogue box launcher. Select a slightly larger font size and make it italic. Click on **OK**. Repeat for the other 'date' lines.

7 You can customise your CV further by changing the default headings. Here we have changed 'Experience' to 'Employment'. Highlight the heading 'Experience' and type **Employment** in its place.

Quick Access Toolbar

This is a customisable toolbar that contains, by default, three commands – Save, Undo and Redo. To the right of these is the Customize Quick Access Toolbar button, showing a downward-pointing arrow. If you wish to add further commands to the toolbar, click on this button and select a command from the list or click on **More Commands**. Click on

Add and then on **OK** to finish. Alternatively, right-click on a command on the Ribbon then click **Add to Quick Access Toolbar**. If you would prefer to have the Quick Access Toolbar nearer to your work, you can move it below the Ribbon. Click on the **Customize** button and select **Show Below the Ribbon**.

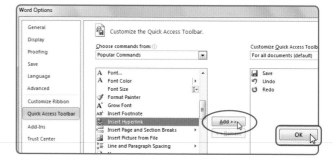

To set columns, go to the **Page Layout** group and click on **Columns**. Select **Two** from the drop-down menu of options.

If you cannot see your Return symbols click on the **Show/Hide** toolbar button in the Paragraph group. (In Microsoft Works, go to the **View** menu and click on **All Characters**.)

2 Go to the **Insert** tab and click on **Table**, then on **Insert Table**. Set the columns and rows to **1** and set the width to **11.5 cm**. Click on **OK**. Next, right-click inside the table and select **Table Properties**. Click on the **Row** tab and set the height to **400 pt** and **At least**. Click on **OK**.

3 Type your text into the table, adding a line space between the details of each course. Highlight the text and click on the **Center** button from the 'Paragraph' group. Next, click on the **Font** dialogue box launcher and choose a font, style and size for your text and then click on **OK**.

4 To adjust the spacing between the details of each course, highlight the first Return symbol (see above) and click on the **Paragraph** dialogue box launcher. On the Indents and Spacing tab, click on the arrows to the right of the 'Before' and 'After' boxes until you are happy with the result. Click on **OK**, and then repeat with the other blank lines.

Checking your spelling

Any words that your computer does not recognise will appear on the screen with a wavy red line underneath. To check the spelling of these words, click on the **Review** tab and then the **Spelling & Grammar** button in the 'Proofing' group. However, just because a computer fails to recognise a word, it does not mean it does not exist. Double-check in a dictionary.

Dinner Menu

Mushroom and herb terrine

Veal escalopes with ham and Marsala

Julienne of root vegetables

Champagne sorbet with wild strawberries

Cheese and biscuits

Using Works templates

Microsoft Works includes templates for several types of menu, with a variety of eye-catching styles to choose from.

To use a template, open the Works Task Launcher, click on **Templates** then, on the left, **Home & Money**. Choose **Menus** from the list of tasks and select a style, then click on **Use this style** to open the template. Choose your design and follow the on-screen instructions.

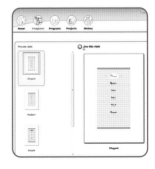

Bright idea
Instead of creating your own border through Word or Works, experiment with the more decorative borders and frames in the Microsoft Clip Art gallery.

For uniformity, design your place cards using the same clip art and fonts that you used in the menu.

▶ DESIGNING PLACE CARDS

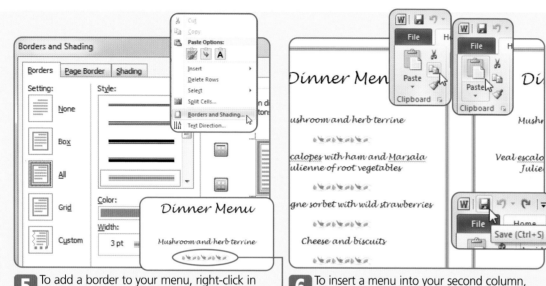

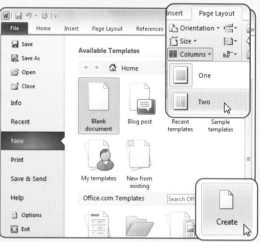

5 To add a border to your menu, right-click in your table and choose **Borders and Shading** from the options. Click on the **Borders** tab and select a setting, style, colour and width. Then click on **OK**.

6 To insert a menu into your second column, press the **Ctrl** key and the letter '**A**' together to select the table. Click on the **Copy** button in the 'Clipboard' group and then click below the table and press **Return**. Next, click on the **Paste** button. Click on the **Save** button in the Quick Access Toolbar to name and save your menu file.

7 To create place cards, click on the **File** tab and click on **New**, then **Blank Document**, then on **Create**. Next, go to the **Page Layout** tab and click on **Columns** and select **Two.** Now save and name your new file using the same method as in step 6.

Adding clip art

Use clip art to enliven your menu. Click in the document, go to the **Insert** tab and select **Clip Art**. The 'Clip Organizer' column appears on the right of the screen. Find an image by typing in a search term, here 'borders', then click **Go**. The results will be displayed in the column. Hover the cursor over

your selected image and click on the bar that then appears at the side. Select **Insert** from the pop-up menu. The image will then appear in your document. To learn how to size and position the clip art, see page 193.

Now copy and paste the clip art between each course using the **Copy** and **Paste** toolbar buttons.

When you set the width of your columns, the spacing between the columns adjusts automatically.

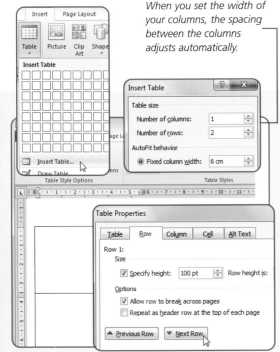

Close-up
*Your place cards may not all fit on a single sheet of A4. To add another page to your document press the **Return** key at the end of the first page – a second page will be created automatically.*

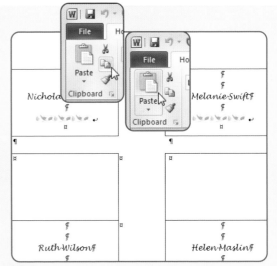

8 Go to the **Insert** tab and click on **Table**, then **Insert Table**. Set columns to **1**, rows to **2** and width to **6 cm**, then click on **OK**. Right-click in the table and select **Table Properties**. In the Table Properties dialogue box, click on the **Row** tab and set the height to **100 pt** and **At least**. Click on the **Next Row** button and repeat the value. Click on **OK**.

9 Click in the lower of the two cells (the top will be the back once the card is folded). Press the **Return** key twice and then type in a guest's name. Highlight it, click on the **Font** dialogue box launcher and select a font, size and style. Click on **OK**. Finally, click on the **Center** button. Then add a clip art image as before (see step 5).

10 To duplicate your card, press **Ctrl** and the letter '**A**' together to select the table. Click on the **Copy** button. Click below the table and press **Return** twice. Click on the **Paste** button. Replace the first guest's name by highlighting it and typing in the next guest's name. Repeat for other cards.

Bright idea
It is worth buying a small guillotine to cut your place cards after you have printed them out. Cutting with a guillotine rather than scissors will ensure the edges of your cards are neat and precise.

To help you to organise the menu for your dinner party, why not set up a database of recipes? Turn to page 294 to find out more.

OTHER IDEAS TO TRY

Create a family newsletter

Keep in touch with distant friends and relatives

A regular newsletter is a great way to keep family members in touch with each other. The first step is to ask your relatives whether they would like to contribute any news, such as a new job or a recently passed exam. They may even like to send in favourite recipes or poems they have written. Set a deadline and suggest they send their contributions to you by email – this will save you typing in their text.

Once all the material has arrived, write your own stories to incorporate them. Finally, decide what you are going to call the family newsletter. It is tempting to use your surname in the heading, but remember that not all family members share the same name.

Prioritise your contributions. If there is not enough space for all your news in the current edition of the newsletter, save some for the next.

▶ BEFORE YOU START

Microsoft Office
Microsoft Office Home and Business (E...
- X Microsoft Excel 2010
- N Microsoft OneNote 2010
- O Microsoft Outlook 2010
- P Microsoft PowerPoint 2010
- W Microsoft Word 2010
- Microsoft Office 2010 Tools
- Microsoft Silverlight
- Microsoft Works
◀ Back

Search programs and files

File Home In
- Save
- Save As
- Open
- Close
- Info
- Recent
- New
- Print

1 Go to the **Start** button, click on **All Programs** and select **Microsoft Word 2010**. Click on the **File** tab on the far left of the Ribbon at the top of your screen. Now scroll down the list of options and click on **New**.

*To create a newsletter in Microsoft Works, go to the **Start** menu, click on **Microsoft Works** and then click on **Works Word Processor** from the 'Quick launch' menu on the right.*

▶ OTHER PROGRAMS

Watch your language

Word templates downloaded from Microsoft's online resource may well have been generated in the United States. To change the language setting to English (United Kingdom), click on the **Review** tab and then on **Language** from the 'Language' group. Click on **Set Proofing Language** and in the 'Language' dialogue box that appears, click on **English (U.K.)**, then on **OK**.

2 Under 'Available Templates', icons are organised into two groups, 'Home' those already installed with Word or previously downloaded and 'Office.com Templates' those available online to download. Scroll down the list to find a category, here 'Newsletters'. Click on **Newsletters**.

3 In the middle panel you will now see a selection of thumbnail images of different types of pre-formed newsletter templates. Click on an image to preview a larger version in the panel on the right. Select a style, here 'Family newsletter', and click on **Download** at the bottom right of the window.

4 Your downloaded newsletter template will appear with text and pictures positioned for you to replace with your own. This template style is already pre-formatted into two columns, containing text and picture boxes ready for you to start creating your newsletter.

Using Works templates

Open Microsoft Works and click on the **Templates** button. From the list on the left, choose **Newsletters & Flyers**. Click on the **Newsletters** icon and choose a template style, then click on **Use this style**. Type in your own details as you follow the on-screen instructions.

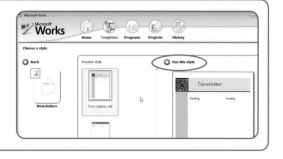

Close-up
To see your text laid out in columns, go to the **View** tab and click on the **Print Layout** button from the 'Document Views group.

Close-up
To see your text laid out in columns, go to the **View** tab and click on the **Print Layout** button from the 'Document Views group.

Bright idea
For a professional look, style all your headings using the same font, font style and font size. Use colour only in the headings as coloured text can be difficult to read.

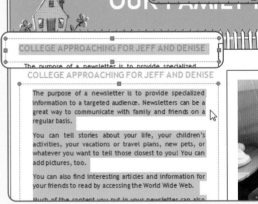

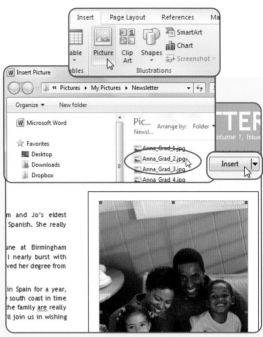

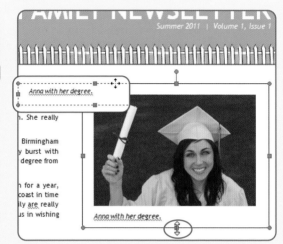

Anna with her degree.

5 Highlight the prompt 'Newsletter Date' and type in a date or season. Now highlight the heading of the first article and type in your own. You can then highlight all the text in the first article and type in your story. Do not worry if it is shorter or longer than the original article as you can adjust the text box later (see page 171).

6 Replace the default photograph with one of your own that goes with your article. Click on the photograph in column two of your newsletter to select it. Click on the **Insert** tab and then on **Picture** from the 'Illustrations' group. Navigate to the folder containing your photos and click on one to select it. Click on **Insert**.

7 Next, highlight and replace the caption text and then click inside the caption text box. When the mouse pointer changes to a 'cross', click and drag the caption box to the required position. Click on the ruled box around the picture and caption to select it, then click and drag on one of the 'square' blue handles to resize it.

Using images

To import photographs or clip art, position your cursor at the top of the document. Click on the **Insert** tab and, in the 'Illustrations' group, click on **Clip Art**. Type a key word into the 'Search for' box on the right and click on **Go**. Click on an image, and select **Insert** from the drop-down menu.

To import photos, you can scan them in or download them from a digital camera and save them on your PC. Click on the **Insert** tab and, in the 'Illustrations' group, click on **Picture**. Find your photograph and then click on **Insert**.

For more details on using clip art, see page 192.

Columns in Works

To set columns in Microsoft Works, go to the **Format** menu and click on **Columns**. Set the 'Number of columns' and the 'Space between' them. Click in the 'Line between columns' box, then click on **OK**. All the text in your newsletter will then reflow into columns.

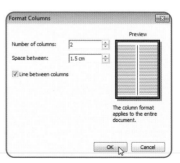

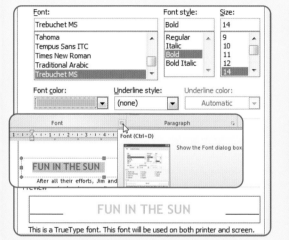

OUR FAMILY NEWSLETTER

TOP MARKS FOR ANNA!

If you want to produce a regular newsletter, save your first one as a template that can be opened and altered for each edition.

CREATE A TEMPLATE

8 Highlight the heading of one of your articles, and click on the **Font** dialogue box launcher. Select a font, font style and size. If you would like to add some colour, click on the arrow next to the Font color box, scroll through and make a choice. Click on **OK**. Repeat for the other headings.

9 To check how your newsletter looks, click on the **File** tab, then on **Print** from the options on the left. Here you can preview your newsletter using the zoom slider and page change buttons. If you need to make a change, click on the **Home** tab to return to your newsletter. When ready, check the options under 'Settings' then click on **Print**.

10 To save your newsletter as a template, click on the **File** tab, then on **Save As.** Click on **Templates** in the left-hand pane of the Save As dialogue box and select **Word Template (*.dotx)** from the 'Save as type' drop-down options. Name your template and click on **Save**.

Adjusting text boxes

All text boxes have eight handles – a round handle on each corner and a square handle on each side.

To adjust the size of a text box, simply hold your mouse pointer over one of the square handles until it changes to a double-headed arrow. Click and drag on the handle and a dotted line will show the new size – release the mouse to keep those dimensions.

Finishing touch

Do not forget to add your name and contact details at the end of the newsletter, and explain how to submit news for future editions.

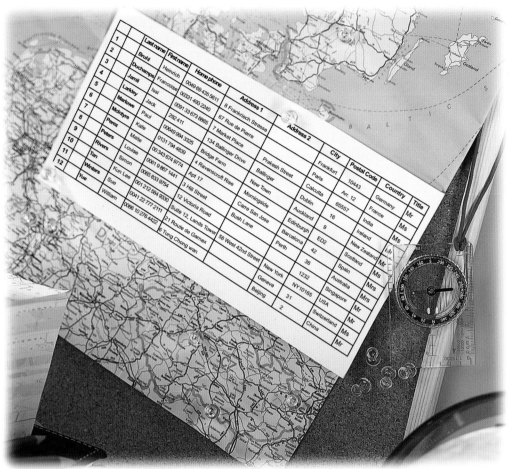

Make an address list

It can be easy to keep in touch with friends and contacts

One of the most useful things you can do with a database is make an address list. And there are many advantages to doing this on your PC. You can easily update it when people move house or change their name; you can sort addresses; you can even create group email lists so that you can send all your friends the same emails at once. You can also search your database for individual words (if, say, you can remember that someone was called Jim but you have forgotten his surname). And you can always print it out if you need to.

Spare yourself having to make amendments later by making sure the details you are going to enter into your database are up to date.

► BEFORE YOU START

1 Go to the **Start** menu, select **All Programs** and then click on **Microsoft Works Task Launcher**. When Works has loaded, click on the Home button on the navigation bar at the top and then click on the **Contacts** tab.

*You can also create an address list in Outlook. Open Outlook and click on the **Contacts** icon in the left pane of the window. Press **Ctrl** and 'N' at the same time to open a new data entry form.*

► OTHER PROGRAMS

Key word

Field *This is a category of information in a database – for example, 'Name', 'Street Address' and 'Phone' are all individual fields.*

Multiple email addresses

If a contact has more than one email address – one for work and one personal, say – type each address into the 'E-mail:' field and then click on **Add**. You can set which is the preferred address by selecting it in the box below and then clicking on **Set Preferred**.

2 You will now be presented with your Contacts folder. If this is the first time you have added a contact, it will be empty except for an entry for you. This is known as 'My Contact' and is automatically set by the software.

3 Make sure your Contacts folder is highlighted and then click on the **New Contact** button. With the 'Name and E-mail tab' selected, type in your contact's first and last names – these then automatically appear in the Full Name field – and add their email address in the relevant box. Click on **Add**.

4 There are several other tabs where further information can be added. Click on each tab and fill in as much information as you want to record. Click on **OK** when you have finished. With your Contacts folder displayed in the address bar at the top, your new entry appears in the list in the right-hand panel below.

Close-up

When using Windows Live Mail, if you cannot see the menu bar, click on the **Menus** *button in the upper-right corner of the window and then on* **Show menu bar** *from the drop-down list.*

Adding email addresses

Make sure you include email addresses, wherever possible, as they can be used in Windows Live Mail. You can set up Windows Live Mail to automatically add addresses to your Contacts list whenever you reply to an email. To do this, launch Windows Live Mail. In the **Tools** menu, click on **Options**, and then on the **Send** tab. Check the box **Automatically put people I reply to in my address book after the third reply**. Click **OK**.

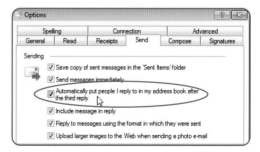

To delete a contact, click on it in your contacts list to highlight it. Click on the **Delete** button on the toolbar. Then click on **Yes** in the Delete File dialogue box to move it to the Recycle Bin, where it can be permanently deleted.

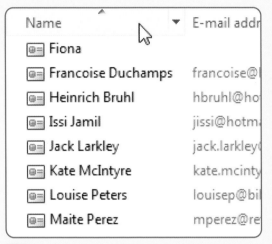

5 Your contacts can be organised in several ways. To sort by name, click on the **Name** column header. The list can be displayed in ascending or descending order of either first or last name – click repeatedly on the **Name** tab to change the display. You can also sort by email and phone numbers.

6 To create a 'group' of contacts, click on **New Contact Group** and fill in the Contact Name box. Contact groups can be used with Windows Mail to send a group email – simply type the group name into the 'To' box. To add contacts to the group, click on the **Add to Contact Group** button.

7 The Add Members to Contact Group dialogue box appears displaying all your contacts. Scroll through your contact list and click on the contact you would like in the group, then click on **Add**. To add more contacts, click on **Add to Contact Group** and repeat the process.

To change the order of the columns in your contacts list, move your mouse pointer over a column and then drag it to the left or right until it is located where you want it.

Searching for contacts

To find a contact, click in the search box in your contacts folder and type the name, or part of the name. As you type, the contacts will be sorted to reflect the letters you have typed. Matches to your search criteria will appear in the panel below, highlighted in yellow.

Now that you have completed your contacts list, why not use it to print out address labels? See page 176 to find out how.

OTHER IDEAS TO TRY

Shortcut
*To print all your contacts, click **Print** on the toolbar. In the Print dialogue box, choose **All Contacts** under 'Print range'. Click on **Print**.*

8 When all of the group members have been added, click on **OK**. Your contacts list will now have an additional entry – in this case, 'Fun pals'. The icon to the left of the name shows that it is a group and not a single contact.

9 To change a contact's details, double-click on the entry in the contacts list. The contact opens in the Name and E-mail tab. To make a change, click on the appropriate tab, amend the details and then click on **OK**. You can click on the **Summary** tab to see some of the information already entered.

10 To print from your address list, click on the contact you need and then click on **Print** from the toolbar. In the Print dialogue box, choose your print range, print style and number of copies required before clicking on **Print**.

Selective printing

You may want to print the details of more than one contact, but not all of them. If so, from your contacts list hold down the **Ctrl** key and click on as many contacts as you wish. Now click on **Print** on the toolbar and in the Print dialogue box click on **Selected Contacts** under 'Print range'. Select a Print Style and finally click on **Print**.

Make address labels

Save time and effort by printing your own labels

Computers come into their own when there are repetitive or time-consuming tasks to be done. Writing addresses on envelopes – at Christmas or for a charity mailshot – is one such task. Why not use your PC to create and print stylish address labels?

It will spare you the tedium of writing them out by hand, and give your envelopes a truly professional look.

You can create labels with a wide variety of designs, text styles and sizes, and you can save them to use over and over again.

You must have the addresses you want to print compiled on a database. To do this, see Make an address list on page 172. You also need to buy sheets of sticky labels.

► BEFORE YOU START

1 Go to the **Start** menu, select **All Programs** and then click on **Microsoft Works Task Launcher**. When it has launched, click on **Works Word Processor** from the 'Quick Launch' taskbar on the right, which will open a blank Word Processor document.

*You can also create address labels in Microsoft Word. Go to the **Mailings** tab and click on the **Start Mail Merge** button and follow the prompts.*

► OTHER PROGRAMS

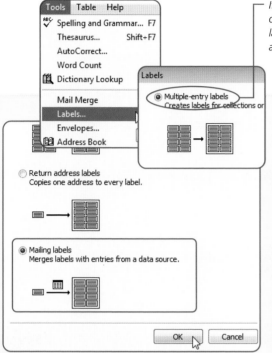

*If you do not have an address book database and just want to print single labels, click on **Multiple-entry labels** and follow the on-screen instructions.*

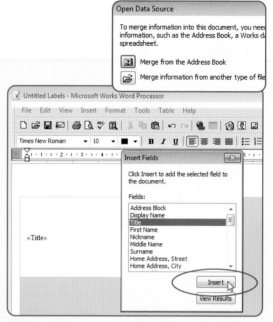

2 Go to the **Tools** menu at the top of the screen and click on **Labels**. The Labels dialogue box appears, where you can select **Mailing labels**. This enables you to merge the addresses you have stored in your Address Book into your labels document. Click on **OK**.

3 In the Label Settings dialogue box, click on the arrow at the side of the 'Label products' box and select the brand and type of your labels. Then, scroll through the Product Number menu and click on the product reference from your labels' box. Next, click on **New Document**.

4 In the Open Data Source dialogue box, click on **Merge from the Address Book**. The Insert Fields dialogue box appears. Click on the first field you would like to use – here **Title** – and then click on **Insert**.

Close-up

Address labels come in a variety of sizes, each with their own reference number. You can buy labels that fill the whole of an A4 page, for example, or specialist labels to put on CDs, DVDs or videos. One of the most common address labels is the L7163, with 14 labels to an A4 page.

Searching for a database

The Open Data Source dialogue box also gives you the option of merging information from other databases you have created.

Click on **Merge information from another type of file** to locate a different data source. Next, scroll down the 'Look in' window to locate your file. You should also scroll down the 'Files of type' window to make sure that your file type is displayed. Finally, click on **Open**.

Watch out
*If you skip the Select Names step, the
addresses of all the contacts in your
Address Book will merge into your labels document.*

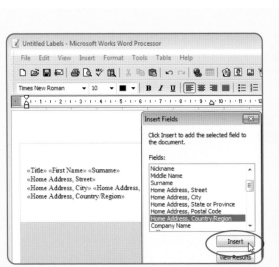

5 Continue to add all the required fields in order. To ensure correct spacing on your labels, press the **Space bar** between fields that appear on the same line. Press **Return** to place fields on different lines. The fields are displayed in the top left-hand label of your document.

6 To choose your addresses, go to the **Tools** menu and select **Mail Merge**, then click on **Select Names**. In the Select Names dialogue box, scroll down the folders menu to select an Address Book folder. Once you have chosen a folder, all the contacts from that folder appear on the left.

7 To select an address, click on it and then click on **Select**. The recipient's name will appear in the 'Merge Recipients' window. Once you have selected all those that will require a printed label, click on **OK**.

Using your block

If you are using addresses from your contacts list, you can click on **Address Block** in the Insert Fields dialogue box to insert the names and addresses of your contacts in a single step. The advantage of this is that any empty fields in a contact's details are not included, so the address reads correctly.

*To select more than one recipient at a time, click on your first contact and hold down the **Ctrl key** while clicking on the rest in turn. Click on **Select** and all the names you have highlighted will then appear in the 'Merge Recipients' window.*

Bright idea
If you design a label that you think you might use again, remember to save it. You will be prompted to do so before you close the document.

Watch out
Do not waste your sticky labels. Before printing, do a test on a sheet of paper and then overlay the paper on your sheet of labels to check the fit. If necessary, add or remove line spaces to improve the layout.

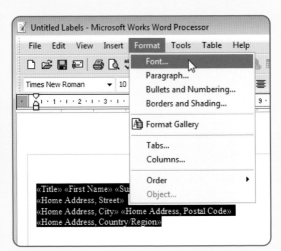

8 To style your addresses, highlight the fields and go to the **Format** menu. Select **Font** and then choose a font style and size. The style you select for this entry will apply to all the addresses in your document.

9 In the Insert Fields dialogue box, click on **View Results**. The first entry in your database appears in the top left-hand corner of your document. Click on the right single arrow button to scroll through all your entries – check each in turn to ensure the details are correct.

10 To view the whole page of labels, click on the Print Preview icon in the toolbar. To print your labels, click on **Print** in the Print Preview window.

Selecting fonts

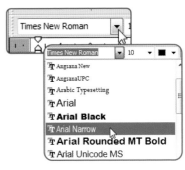

With your text selected in your document, you can also change the font by using the drop-down menu in the Font window of the formatting toolbar. Click on the arrow at the side of the window and scroll down.

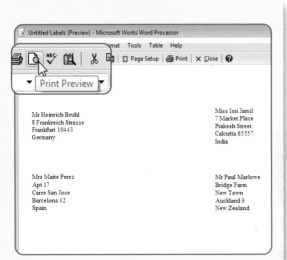

Make a home

Let your computer take care of the

Project planner

Create a folder named after your business. Add sub-folders for each of its various aspects.

- Business
  - Clients
  - Suppliers
  - Finance
  - Product development
  - Publicity

Millions of people around the world have seized the opportunity to start their own business. There is a real thrill to be had from making a go of your own idea, from being your own boss and taking your financial destiny into your own hands.

But with this opportunity come new responsibilities: for accounting, correspondence and publicity; for dealing with suppliers, your bank manager and the tax man, and – perhaps most importantly – for finding your next client. In fact, most of your time could easily be taken up with anything other

business work

details while you take care of the profits

than realising your original business idea.

Your PC can reduce the time spent on many of these tasks. It can even help you to research your business idea before you invest heavily in it.

For correspondence and publicity you could design a logo based on clip art or use a drawing program. It is often easiest to design your stationery and produce correspondence from a template, and keep a record of all your communications either on your computer's hard disk or backed-up on CDs or DVDs.

You can use your PC's database program to create a client database and, from that, customer name and address labels.

Ensure you never miss an appointment by running your business diary from your Desktop. If you use a car for work, you can work out your running costs to claim them as business expenses. And your spreadsheet program will make dealing with your accounts less of a headache.

With your PC you can design your own business cards, or you can reach a much wider audience by advertising it on your blog.

You can also use the internet to correspond by email, compare competitors' prices and services, and surf the web for trade leads – some companies even post supply requirements on Government sites set up to encourage trade.

Before long, your computer will establish itself as your most productive and versatile employee, leaving you more time to enjoy your work.

Ideas and inspirations

Below are some suggestions for limiting the time you spend taking care of your business and maximising its efficiency. The projects can be adapted depending on your own circumstances. If you have business partners, you may wish to divide the tasks between yourselves.

254 Do your own accounts
Organise your income, outgoings and overheads; project future expenditure and profit.

182 Create a business card
Increase the profile of your business and ensure customers have your contact details.

172 Compile a client database
Make sure you do not lose track of anyone by storing their details in an updatable record.

186 Set up a business diary
Keep track of your appointments and timetable a variety of tasks in an on-screen diary.

Also worth considering …

Use pictures as well as words to sell your product to get the message home to potential clients.

298 Create a press pack
With the same techniques used to produce a baby book you could design a mailshot or brochure.

Design a business card

Make a **good impression** on **colleagues, associates** and friends

A well-designed business card can make a huge impact on potential clients and on your business. It reflects on your professionalism and its design can capture key aspects of your business. For example, a cake decorator who uses a picture of a traditional wedding cake and traditional fonts on their business card is likely to attract a different clientele than one who uses a picture of a more unusual cake and modern fonts.

A business card can easily be created using Word, and you can personalise it with your choice of text style and graphics. If you do not run your own business, you might be able to help by designing a card for an association or society with which you are involved.

Think carefully about the sort of information you need to include – try not to overload your card with unnecessary details.

► BEFORE YOU START

1 Go to the **Start** button, click on **All Programs** and select **Microsoft Word 2010**. Go to the **Page Layout** tab, click on the **Margins** button and then **Custom Margins**. With the Margins tab selected, type in '1' for the Left and Right margins – this is so that two cards will fit side by side on an A4 sheet. Click on **OK**.

It is possible to style text and import clip art in Works' word-processing program. You can also size your card accurately in Works, making it a suitable alternative to Word for this task.

► OTHER PROGRAMS

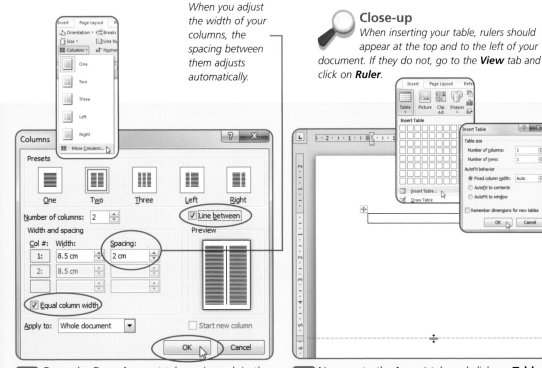

When you adjust the width of your columns, the spacing between them adjusts automatically.

Close-up
*When inserting your table, rulers should appear at the top and to the left of your document. If they do not, go to the **View** tab and click on **Ruler**.*

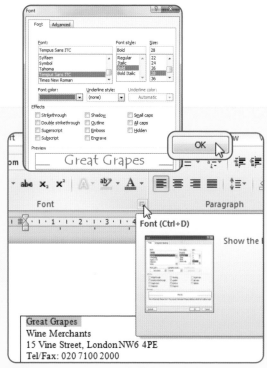

2 Go to the **Page Layout** tab again and, in the 'Page Setup' group, click on **Columns**, then **More Columns**. In the 'Presets' panel, click on **Two**. In the 'Width and spacing' panel make the Width **8.5 cm**. Ensure the 'Equal column width' and the 'Line between' boxes are ticked (to tick, click in them). Click on **OK**.

3 Now go to the **Insert** tab and click on **Table**, then on **Insert Table**. Set the columns and rows to **1**. Click on **OK**. A box will appear – move the mouse pointer over the bottom line and, when it becomes a double-headed arrow, drag the line down to the 5.5 cm mark on the left ruler.

4 Click inside the table and type in your text. To style the text, highlight it and go to the 'Font' group under the **Home** tab. Click on the **Font** dialogue box launcher and select a font, size, style and colour, checking your styling changes in the Preview window. Click on **OK**.

Save your document
Soon after opening your new Word document, remember to save it. Click on the **File** tab and select **Save As** then **Word Document**. Save your business cards into a suitable folder.

Watch out
It may be tempting to use an unusual font for fun, but make sure your text is legible. If your card cannot be read easily, there is little purpose in having one in the first place.

Watch out

Position your clip art image so that there is an equal amount of space around it. This will look balanced and more professional.

5 Add a clip art graphic. Highlight the text and click and drag the **Left Indent** marker on the ruler to create space for the image. Go to the **Insert** tab and, in the Illustrations group, click on **Clip Art**. Type a key word in the 'Search for' box on the right and click on **Go**. Choose an image and select **Insert** from the drop-down menu.

6 To resize the image, click on one of the 'round' corner handles and drag it to the desired size. Do not use the 'square' side handles as this will distort the original shape. Now go to the **Format** tab and click on **Wrap Text**. Select **In Front of Text** from the menu of options.

7 The image is now sitting in front of the text. To reposition the image to the left of the text, click on the image and drag it into the correct position and release the mouse button.

Change clip art colour

If you decide that you want to change the colour of the image you have selected, click on the image to select it, then click on **Color** from the 'Adjust' group. In the Recolor section of the drop-down your original colour is selected. Click on a different colour to change your image.

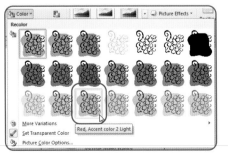

Undoing changes

If you have experimented with spacing and formatting, but find you do not like the results, the quickest way to remove the changes is to click on the **Undo** button on the Word Quick Access Toolbar.

Each click you make takes you back a stage in the development of your document.

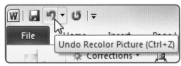

Bright idea
To get the best results, print your cards on card that is 250gsm or thicker. Most home printers only handle card up to 160gsm thick – check the manual – so consider having the file printed at a print shop.

Close-up
To remove a card, right-click on it and, from the drop-down menu that appears, select **Delete Rows***.*

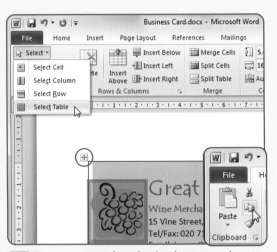

8 To create several cards, simply copy and paste the original. Click on the 'cross' top left of the table to highlight it. Next, go to the **Home** tab and, from the Clipboard group, select **Copy**. A copy of your business card is now stored in your PC's Clipboard, ready for pasting.

9 Click below the original table, go to the 'Clipboard' group and select **Paste Options**. Hover your mouse over the third option **Entire Cell (E)**. The image and text will appear, then click on the button. Repeat to fill the page. When you reach the end of the first column, Word automatically moves onto the second one.

10 Once you are happy with the design of your cards, click on the **File** tab and select **Print**. Here you can preview your cards using the zoom slider and page change buttons. Under 'Settings' choose the page range and number of copies you want, then click on the **Print** button.

Professional results
If you want to print the card at a print shop, save it onto your hard disk and also onto a CD (compact disc) or DVD (digital versatile disc).

Place a formatted disc in the CD/DVD drive and, with your document open, click on the **File** tab and select **Save As**. In the Save As dialogue box select **Computer** and then click on **DVD RW Drive (D:)** (or another destination for saving your document), before clicking on **Save.**

Bright idea
Even if you intend to take the file to a print shop, it is a good idea to print it first at home to check you are happy with your new cards.

Create your own diary

Organise your life – use a computer to help you to plan

Many people have such pressurised schedules that it is easy to lose track of everything that needs to be done. By creating a diary using the Microsoft Office program Outlook, you can keep on top of your hectic schedule and ensure you never miss an appointment again.

With Outlook, you can enter appointments, events, meetings and tasks into your diary and view them by the day, week or month. It allows you to print out a schedule for your day, attach important documents to relevant entries in your diary, and it will even remind you of your appointments.

> *Ask your family or work colleagues if there are any events, tasks or appointments that you should add to your diary immediately.*

▶ BEFORE YOU START

1 Go to the **Start** button, select **All Programs** and then click on **Microsoft Outlook 2010**. Click on **Calendar** from the panel on the left. A blank schedule for the month appears. It includes sections for each hour of the day, a view of the month and a blank list of tasks in the TaskPad on the far right.

> *The calendar in Microsoft Works looks similar to the one in Microsoft Outlook. Open Works, then click on the **Open Calendar** button to launch the program.*

▶ OTHER PROGRAMS

Bright idea
The small arrows beside the name of each month in the daily or weekly view enable you to move quickly to the previous or following month.

Shortcut
To add a new appointment when you are displaying your daily calendar, double-click at the new appointment time and enter the details.

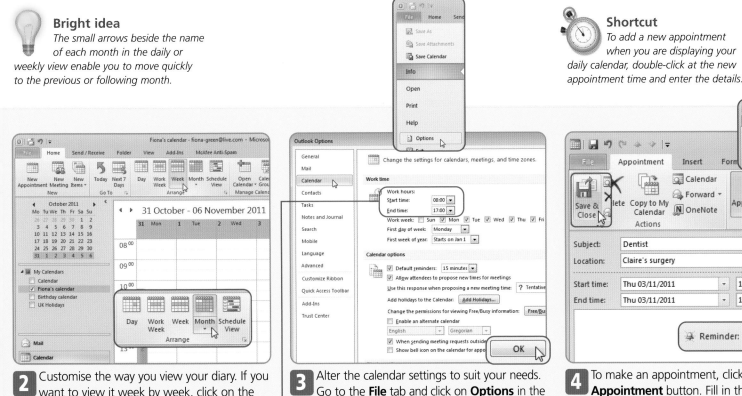

2 Customise the way you view your diary. If you want to view it week by week, click on the **Week** button. To view a whole month at a time, click on the **Month** button. Or, to return to the day-by-day view, click on the **Day** button.

3 Alter the calendar settings to suit your needs. Go to the **File** tab and click on **Options** in the left pane. Now click on the **Calendar** from the left pane. Amend settings by clicking on the arrows beside each box and scrolling through the options. When you have finished, click on **OK**.

4 To make an appointment, click on the **New Appointment** button. Fill in the boxes and add any notes to the panel at the bottom. To set an alert before the meeting, go to the 'Options' group and click on the arrow in the box next to the alarm icon to select how far in advance you want the warning to happen. Click on **Save & Close**.

Terms used in Outlook

Outlook allows you to make four types of Calendar entry, using **New Items** in the 'New' group:
● An **appointment** is an activity that you reserve time for, but which does not involve other people.
● A **meeting** is an appointment to which you are inviting other people.
● An **event** is an activity that lasts at least 24 hours. It appears as a banner at the start of each relevant day.
● A **task** is a duty that you can check off on completion.

Working hours

When you set your 'Calendar working hours', Outlook displays them with a pale background, and your leisure hours are displayed with a tinted background. Clicking on an hour highlights it with a dark background.

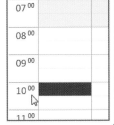

For your alarm to work, Outlook must be running. As part of your daily routine, open the program and minimise it, so that it appears as a button on the Taskbar.

Shortcut

*If you want to delete an appointment in your diary or a task in your TaskPad, click on the item and then click on the right mouse button. Select **Delete** from the pop-up menu.*

5 To view your entry, scroll through the relevant day's calendar. If you need to move an entry to a new time, click on the appointment and drag it to the new time, releasing the mouse button to put it in place.

6 To add a task, first select **Tasks** from the panel on the left. Then click on **Click here to add a new Task** and type in the details. Select a date, if required, by clicking on the arrow on the right of the second column. When you complete the task, click on the box beside it.

7 To add an event, first click on **Calendar** in the panel on the left. Next, click on **New Items** from the 'New' group, and then on **All Day Event**. Enter the details in the window that appears. Click on **Save & Close**. The event will then appear as a banner at the top of the relevant day or days.

Altering entries

To change an entry's duration, first click on it. Place your cursor over the top or bottom edge of the appointment box. When the cursor becomes a double-headed arrow, click and drag the edge of the box up or down.

Different views

You can view your diary in a number of ways. Click on the **View** tab, then on **Change View** from the 'Current View' group and then click on one of the options available.

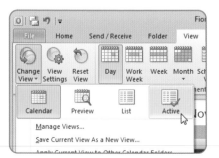

Close-up
You do not need to save your diary as you would any other document – it will save itself when you close it. When you open Outlook again, it will appear automatically.

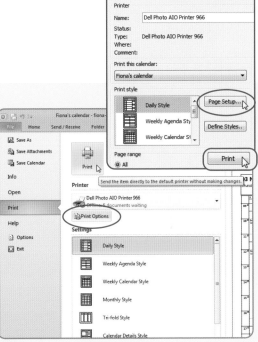

8 To set up a regular appointment, click on **New Appointment**, from the 'New' group. Fill in your information then click on **Recurrence** from the 'Options' group. In the Appointment Recurrence dialogue box, select your recurring pattern from the various options, and click on **OK**.

9 If you have a document that relates to one of your appointments, you can attach a copy to the diary entry. Click on the **Start** button, select **Documents** and locate your file. Right-click on it and select **Copy**. Next, right-click in the relevant appointment window and select **Paste**. Click on **Save & Close** to finish.

10 To print out a daily schedule, click on the **File** tab, and select **Print**. To print using the default settings (Daily Style), click on the **Print** button. Alternatively, click on **Print Options**, then on **Page Setup** (see below left). In the Print dialogue box, check your options and click on **Print**.

Setting print options
In the Page Setup dialogue box you can set options for how you want your diary to print. These include printing the day over one or two pages, adding your list of tasks, choosing which hours of the day to cover and which fonts to use.

Finishing touch
Add a title and date to your diary. In the Page Setup dialogue box click on the **Header/Footer** tab. Type your title in the Header section, and the date on which you printed the diary in the Footer section (you can also add a page number and your name). Click on the **Font** button and choose a font and size in the dialogue box.

Form a pressure group to

Whether you are campaigning to save the rain forest or your local

Project planner

Create a folder named after your group. Add sub-folders to it for each mini-project.

📁 Pressure group
- 📁 Research
- 📁 Contacts
- 📁 Communication
- 📁 Membership
- 📁 Publicity
- 📁 Money

A cross a huge range of concerns – from the global movement to preserve the rain forest through to local campaigns petitioning for traffic-calming measures – the number of people involved in lobbying official bodies has never been greater.

Whether you are starting a new group or opening a local branch of an existing one, it is important to recruit and organise committed members, accrue campaign donations and maintain momentum. Many pressure groups are run by volunteers on slender resources. Your computer can help to make the best use of both.

Increasingly, pressure groups are turning to the internet to formulate and publicise their campaigns. Researching topics online is an obvious starting point. Many educational facilities and research centres release reports via the internet, and the introduction of

make a difference

park, your PC can get the message across

more 'open government' in some countries has led to the publication on the web of a vast quantity of official statistics and information that can aid a campaign.

Newsgroups also offer fertile ground for pressure groups. There are issue-specific noticeboards and forums, where information is traded and debates instigated by interested parties, such as members of other groups and contributors with expert knowledge. Any pressure group would do well to post its details and aims on suitable sites, both to attract members and donations and to collect new information.

A blog is a cheap and effective way to publicise a cause, and is a medium with a truly global reach. The real cost of maintaining a blog is minimal once it has been set up.

Beyond research and publicity, your computer can be used to manage your organisation or branch. You can set up a membership database in Microsoft Works, use a spreadsheet package to manage the group accounts, and produce newsletters and press releases using a word-processing program. You can also create a mailing list or an email list, and print address labels. Consider producing questionnaires or petitions using your database's Form Design feature, and lobby local politicians via email.

Form your plan of action

- Arrange venue/date/agenda for launching group
- Publicise launch meeting
- Arrange a visiting speaker
- Appoint officers and detail responsibilities
- Organise street publicity, collect shoppers' signatures and recruit new members
- Plan local demonstrations/publicity campaign
- Design and produce publicity material and flyers

Ideas and inspirations

Adapt the following projects and ideas to enhance your pressure group's profile, attract new members and make the most of your existing members' time and your group's resources. You may even think of other ways to apply your new skills and your computer's capabilities.

94 Internet research
Find the facts to formulate your argument, or simply keep up to date with affiliated groups.

172 Make an address list
Create a handy, easy-to-manage reference file for all your membership and contact details.

168 Create a newsletter
Keep your members updated about ongoing developments with a brief publication.

120 Create a web blog
Use a blog to publicise your cause and gain the support of others across the world.

276 Accounts
Set up a spreadsheet to keep a close track of membership fees, donations and outgoings.

Also worth considering …

Once your pressure group is up and running, make regular mailshots easy to manage.

176 Make address labels
Use your membership database as the basis for time-saving printed stationery.

Teddy Bear Exhibition
Church Hall
London Lane
Ravenswood
April 20th
2.30–5.30 pm

Using clip art images

Give a touch of creativity to your work by adding illustrations

Clip art illustrations are predesigned graphic images or pictures that you can incorporate into any document to give it a professional look. A gallery of such images is included free with Word and Works.

You can search the image gallery by typing in key words such as 'Christmas', 'Children' or 'Travel'. The illustrations can be used as logos,

borders, dividers or decorative devices. You can also alter the look of an image – cropping it, framing it and colouring it as you want.

It is not always easy to get the best results at the first try, so do not be afraid to experiment with clip art. Before long, you will be making your own greetings cards, wrapping paper, invitations and address labels.

Watch out
Keep your program CDs handy. The clip art gallery contains thumbnails to many thousands of images. The full-sized version may be on an extra CD-ROM, which you will be asked to insert when you place the image in your document.

1 To insert clip art into a Word document, place the cursor where you want the image to go. Next, go to the **Insert** tab and, in the 'Illustrations' group, click on **Clip Art**. A column appears down the right-hand side of the screen with a clip art search facility at the top.

A clip art gallery comes as standard with Word and Works. You can also buy clip art on CD-ROM, download it from the internet or scan in your own designs to use as clip art.

OTHER SOURCES

Key word

Handle *Images have four round and four square handles that appear on the corners and sides. Click and drag inwards or outwards on a round handle to resize both sides. Click and drag inwards or outwards on a square handle to resize one side only.*

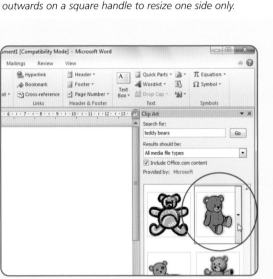

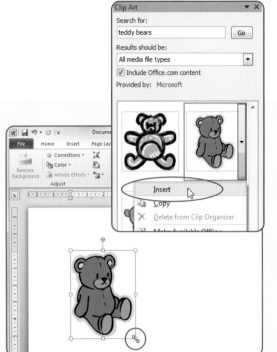

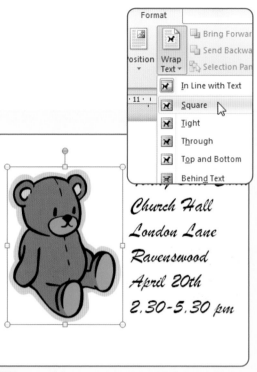

2 To find an image, type a key word into the 'Search for' box then click on **Go**. Any images matching your criteria will then be displayed. When you hover the cursor over an image that interests you, a toolbar appears. Click on the toolbar and a pop-up menu is displayed.

3 To insert the image into your document, click on the **Insert** option in the pop-up menu. To resize it (while keeping it in proportion), click on one of the round corner handles and drag it inwards or outwards to the required size.

4 Next, click on your image and then on the **Format** tab. Click on **Wrap Text** in the 'Arrange' group and then select 'Square'. Any text you type into your document will now appear to the right of the image. To move the image, click on it and drag it to the correct position.

Clip art online

To download online clip art, go to the **Insert** tab and, in the 'Illustrations' group, click on **Clip Art**. Next, click on **Find more at Office.com** at the bottom of the column on the right-hand side of the screen. A browser window will be launched where you can search for images. If you like one, click on it, then click on the **download** link below it (see right).

Positioning text in Works

Microsoft Works offers you three options when positioning text around an image. With the image selected, go to the **Format** menu, choose **Object** and select the **Wrapping** tab. **In line with text** places the bottom of the image in line with the text it precedes. The **Square** option makes text wrap in a straight-sided box around the image. **Tight** makes the lines of text follow the shape of the image.

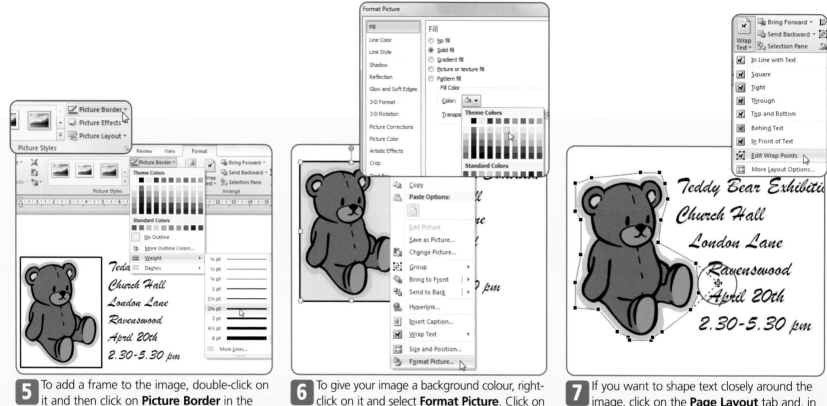

5 To add a frame to the image, double-click on it and then click on **Picture Border** in the 'Picture Styles' group. Click on **Weight** and select a line width. You can also give your line a dashed effect by clicking on **Dashes** and choosing a style. Do not be afraid to experiment – you can keep changing styles until you find one you like.

6 To give your image a background colour, right-click on it and select **Format Picture**. Click on **Fill**, then on **Solid fill**. Click on the **Color** selector and choose a colour. Then move the Transparency slider to lighten or darken the colour. To remove your background colour and frame, select **Fill**, **No Fill** and **Line Color**, **No Line**.

7 If you want to shape text closely around the image, click on the **Page Layout** tab and, in the 'Arrange' group, click on **Wrap Text** and then on **Tight**. To adjust the wrap, click on **Edit Wrap Points** from the same menu. Click on the points that appear and drag them in or out.

Using images with text

If you want to use text with clip art on a page of typescript, you need to decide how to position the text and images together. Double-click on the image and, from the **Format** tab, click on **Wrap Text**. The drop-down menu displays a number of options. Experiment with your layout by clicking on each in turn and seeing how this affects the position of your text and picture on the screen. At the bottom of the menu, click on **More Layout Options** to open the Layout dialogue box. Here you can make changes to Position, Text Wrapping and Size by clicking on the tabs at the top. Make your changes and click on **OK** to finish.

Teddy Bear Exhibitio
Church Hall
London Lane
Ravenswood
April 20th
2.30-5.30 pm

8 You can crop your image – that is, remove part of it. With the image selected, click on the **Format** tab, then on the **Crop** button in the 'Size' group. Drag a handle into the image to crop out the areas you do not want, then click on the **Crop** button again. To restore the image, just click on the **Crop** button and pull the handle back out.

9 If you select **Behind Text** from the Wrap Text options, the text will appear on top of the image. This can look messy but you can make the text stand out by reducing the vibrancy of the image. Double-click on the image and then, in the 'Adjust' group, click on **Color** and then on **Washout**.

10 To centre your text on top of the image, highlight the text and click on the **Center** button in the 'Paragraph' group. Finally, drag the image to sit behind the text.

Teddy Bear Exhibition
Church Hall
London Lane
Ravenswood
April 20th
2.30-5.30 pm

Changing the image

You can alter the way your clip art looks by clicking on the **Color** button in the 'Adjust' group. Hover your cursor over the options in the first row to see the effects for Grayscale, Sepia, Washout and Black and White. The second row gives options for dark colours and the third row gives light colour options. Click on **Picture Color Options** to access additional options for changing background texture, adding shadow, reflection and much more. Click on **Reset Picture** in the 'Adjust' group to discard all of the changes you have made to your image.

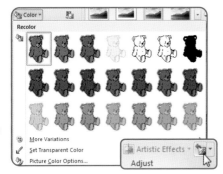

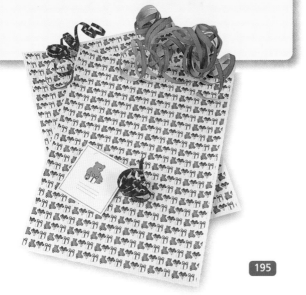

195

Design a greetings card

Send a personal message with your own special occasion cards

Making your own greetings cards allows you to combine a personal message with the image of your choice, and ensures that you always have the right card for any occasion.

On a Christmas card, for example, you could insert a series of photos showing things that you and your family have done over the past year. And for birthday cards you could scan in and use pictures your children have painted (see page 200).

Anyone who receives personalised cards such as these will really appreciate all the thought and effort that have gone into them.

Look at your printer manual to find out the maximum thickness, or weight, of paper your printer can take. Consider mounting thinner paper onto card to give it strength.

► BEFORE YOU START

1 Go to the **Start** button, click on **All Programs** and select **Microsoft Word 2010**. To name and save your document click on the **File** tab and select **Save As**. Select a suitable location, type in a file name, here Christmas Card, then click on **Save**.

*To create greetings cards in Microsoft Works, go to the **Start** menu, click on **Microsoft Works** and then click on **Works Word Processor** from the 'Quick launch' menu on the right.*

► OTHER PROGRAMS

*To view your entire page, first go to the **View** tab and click on **Zoom**. When the Zoom dialogue box appears select **Whole page** and click on **OK**.*

*If the ruler does not appear in your document, go to the **View** tab and click on **Ruler**.*

Bright idea
*To help with accurate positioning go to the **View** tab and click on **Gridlines**.*

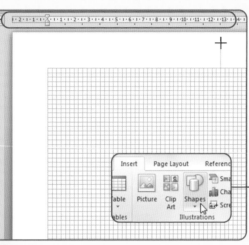

2 Click on the **Page Layout** tab and then on the **Page Setup** dialogue box launcher. Under the **Margins** tab, click on the **Landscape** icon. Under the **Paper** tab choose **A4** from the 'Paper size' menu. Click on **OK**. To create separate pages for the inside and outside of the card, click on **Breaks** and then, under 'Page Breaks', select **Page**.

3 Scroll up to the first page and create a fold line. Go to the **Insert** tab and click on **Shapes** in the 'Illustrations' group. Select the first option **Line** in the 'Lines' section. Using your top ruler as a guide, click and drag to create a vertical line that splits the page in half. The area on the right of the line will be the front of your card.

4 Now select an image. Go to the **Insert** tab, and, in the 'Illustrations' group, click on **Clip Art**. A panel appears on the right of your screen with a search facility at the top. Type in some key search words and click on **Go**. To use an image, hover your cursor over it, click on the bar and then click on **Insert**. See page 192 for more on clip art.

Mounting your design

If your printer cannot cope with card, mount your paper printouts onto coloured card. Choose a colour that matches one of the colours in your image. Cut the card (ideally using a guillotine for a smooth edge) slightly larger than your image, or trim the image to leave a border. Finally, ensure that you have envelopes large enough to hold your cards.

*Click on **Shapes** to reveal a menu of drawing lines, rectangles, shapes, arrows, stars and banner options.*

Repositioning clip art

To drag and drop your clip art around your document, first click on your clip art image. Go to the **Format** tab and from the 'Arrange' group click **Wrap Text**, and then **In Front of Text**. When inserting WordArt (see step 7), click on your WordArt and follow the same procedure as above.

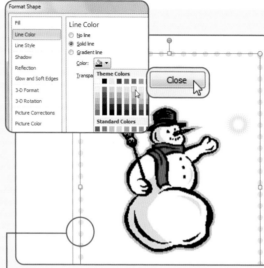

Key word

WordArt This describes the Microsoft library of text formats that you can customise. All you need to do is select a form of WordArt then type in your text. You can colour the text and style it however you wish.

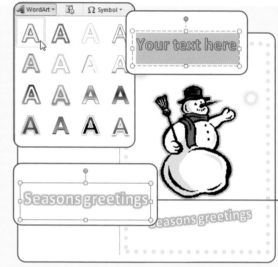

Click and drag your WordArt into position. To resize it, click and drag on one of its corner handles.

5 If you would like to add snowflakes, go to the **Insert** tab, click on the **Shapes** button in the 'Illustrations' group. Under 'Stars and Banners' click on the shape you like, then click and drag to draw it on the page. You can resize the shape with the blue handles, or alter its shape with the yellow one. To rotate the image, use the green handle.

6 To add colour to your snowflakes, right-click on one of the flakes and select **Format Shape** from the pop-up menu. In the dialogue box, click on **Line Color** from the panel on the left. Click on the arrow beside the 'Color' box and choose a colour. Click on **Close**. Repeat to colour the other snowflakes.

7 Now add a message to the front of the card. Go to the **Insert** tab and select **WordArt** from the 'Text' group. In the WordArt gallery, click on a style. A WordArt text box appears, inviting you to type 'Your text here'. Type your message, then highlight the text, right-click on it and select **Font**. Style your text and click on **OK**.

Create a frame

It is easy to create a border that runs around the front of your card. Go to the **Insert** tab and click on the **Shapes** button. Then, in the 'Rectangles' section, click on **Rectangle**. Click and drag on the document to create a frame of the appropriate size.

Right-click in the box and select **Format Shape**. Click on **Fill** in the left hand panel and click on **No fill**. Click on **Line Color** and choose a colour. Click on **Line Style** and choose a width, type of line and dash type. Click on **Close** to finish.

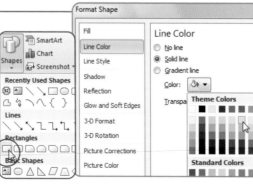

Colouring WordArt

To change the colour of WordArt, select it and then click on the WordArt Styles dialogue box launcher. Next, select **Format WordArt**. In the 'Format Text Effects' box, click on **Text Fill** and choose a colour from the 'Fill Color' drop-down. Next click on **Text Outline** and choose a colour in the same way. Click on **Close**.

Use the alignment buttons to position text within your text box.

*Before you print, remove the fold lines you have used as guides. Click on each of them and press the **Delete** key.*

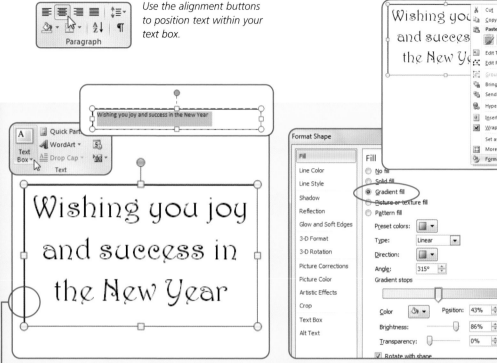

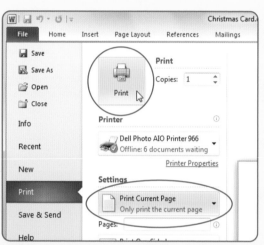

8 Scroll down to the second page and draw a fold line as in step 3. Go to the **Insert** tab, select **Text Box**, then **Simple Text Box** from the drop-down options. Click and drag to draw a box on the right-hand page. Type in your text, highlight it, click on the **Home** tab and select a font and size from the 'Font' group.

9 To give the text box a background colour, right-click on the edge of the box and select **Format Shape** from the drop-down options. Click on **Fill** in the left panel, then on **Gradient fill** in the right panel. Select the colour, type, direction and other options that best suit your image. Click on **Close**.

10 Now click on the **File** tab and select **Print**. In the right panel under 'Settings' select **Print Current Page** and click on the **Print** button. Once printed, place the paper or card back in the printer (you will need to experiment with orientation) and print page 2 on the reverse.

*If you give your text box a background colour (see step 9), remove the border around it before you print. Right-click on the edge of the box and select **Format Shape**. Click on **Line Color** in the left panel, then on **No Line** in the right panel. Click on **Close** to finish.*

Add your own images

Scan **in your** favourite photographs **to** liven up your documents

There is no limit to the variety of images you can use in your documents. If you have a scanner, you can transfer photos, or pictures from newspapers or books, to your own computer.

A scanner takes a digital copy of an image that you can manipulate in any way you wish before placing it in a newsletter, invitation or card (but remember that the use of printed material is covered by copyright laws).

You can scan images with Windows 7 using more than one method. In this project, we will show you two ways of achieving similar results – choose whichever works the best for you and then fine-tune the scanned image to use however you wish.

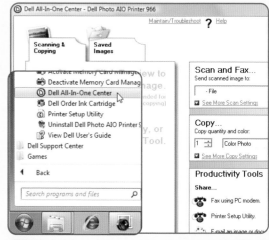

The following steps apply to one type of scanner. As products vary, some screens may look different when using other hardware.

► BEFORE YOU START

1 To begin using your scanner go to the **Start** menu and select your scanning software (here Dell All-In-One Center). When the software has launched, click on the **Scanning & Copying** tab to access the scanning functions.

 Watch out

Most printed material is covered by copyright laws. Unless you are copying it purely for your own use and not for distribution, it is not available for you to use freely. As a general rule, if you are designing a newsletter or poster, you will be breaching copyright laws if you use images from published sources without the copyright owner's permission.

Key word
AIO stands for 'all in one' – this is one machine that incorporates a printer, scanner, copier and fax. They are ideal for use at home.

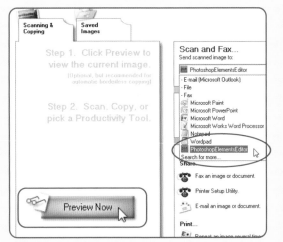

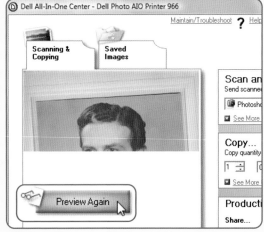

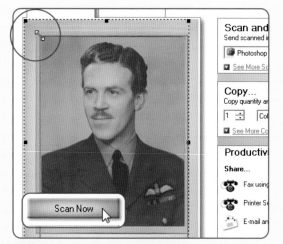

2 If this is the first time you have used the scanning facility of your AIO (see above top), click on the drop-down menu and select an application to edit your images (here Photoshop Elements). Place the image to be scanned on the bed of the scanner and click on **Preview Now**.

3 The scanner now peforms a quick, low-resolution pass over your image so you can decide how you would like to crop it. As the scanner passes over your image it gradually displays on screen. If the image is crooked, do not worry, just reposition it and click on **Preview Again**.

4 When the scan has finished, your image will have a dotted border around it with square black handles in each corner and on each side. Click and drag on these – the mouse pointer changes to a white double-headed arrow – to 'crop' out any areas you do not want to include in the final scanned image. Click on **Scan Now**.

Push-button scanning

Many modern printer/scanners have buttons that you can press to launch an automatic scan of a picture. This Dell AIO device has a set of button options, including one that will scan a document at a resolution suitable for sending in an email message. Other button options launch processes such as scanning an image for a website or sending a scanned image direct to a printer. The exact way these work depends on your hardware and software.

For more control over your scanned image, some models come with software, called a TWAIN driver, that works within an image-editing program such as Photoshop Elements 8.0.

ADVANCED SCANNING

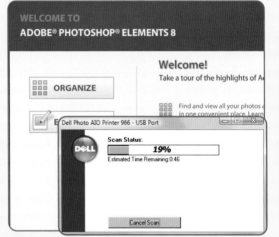

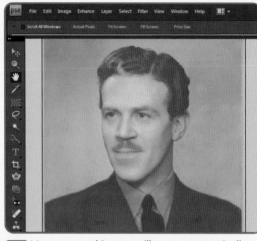

5 The scanner will now make the scan and a 'Scan Status' window will appear to display the progress. When it has finished, your pre-selected image-editing software (see step 2) will automatically launch. (For more on Photoshop Elements, see pages 206-215.)

6 Your scanned image will now automatically open in your editing software. From here you can make adjustments to the image using the toolbar on the left, add a caption or simply save the image to your computer's hard drive. For more on using your images, see page 206.

1 Open your scanner's image-editing program (here Photoshop Elements) and choose **EDIT** from the Welcome screen. Then, in the **File** menu, click on **Import** then on **TWAIN-Dell Photo AIO Printer 966...** from the drop-down list of options. The TWAIN utility will launch.

Scanning a printed image

If you are scanning an image from a newspaper, you may find the scan appears slightly distorted. This arises from the hexagonal pattern of ink dots that printing produces.

You may find a 'de-screen' setting within your scanning controls that contains different settings in 'lpi' (lines per inch). For glossy, printed material select 133-200 lpi; for newspapers select 65-120 lpi. If you do not have these settings try to improve the scan by reducing the sharpness setting (see step 4 on page 203 for how to access Advanced Scan Settings).

Bright idea
Experiment with different settings until you get the look you want. You can greatly increase the image's impact by editing it to suit your own material – it does not have to look like the original.

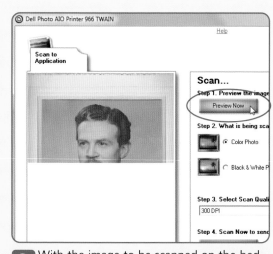

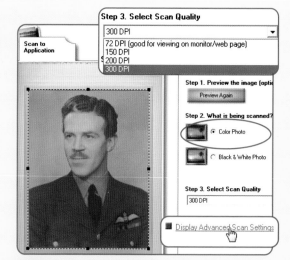

2 With the image to be scanned on the bed of the scanner, click on **Preview Now**. The scanner now peforms a quick, low-resolution pass over your image so you can decide how you wish to crop it. As the scanner passes over your image it gradually displays on screen, in the 'Scan to Application' panel.

3 When the preview finishes, your image will have a dotted border around it with square black handles in each corner and on each side. Click and drag on these – the mouse pointer changes to a white double-headed arrow – to 'crop' out any areas you do not want to include in the final scanned image.

4 In the 'What is being scanned?' panel select the type of image to be scanned (here Color Photo). In the 'Select Scan Quality' panel choose one of the four presets in the drop-down menu. For a greater selection of definitions click on the **Display Advanced Scan Settings** link at the bottom of the 'Scan' panel.

What is TWAIN?

Although it looks like yet another computer acronym, TWAIN does not in fact stand for anything. The name was coined at a time when it was difficult to get scanners and computers to communicate with each other and is taken from the line '... and never the twain shall meet ...' in *The Ballad of East and West* by Rudyard Kipling.

Conserving space

The amount of space your file uses relates both to the resolution at which the image has been scanned and to its dimensions (height and width). By increasing the resolution of this scan from 72dpi to 300dpi, the amount of memory it uses increases by more than ten times.

Ensure the bitmap (.bmp) file format is selected in the File Format box. This means the scanned file can be imported into Word, Works and Paint, the Windows accessory program.

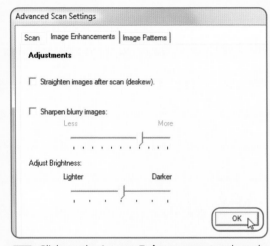

5 Click on the **Image Enhancements** tab and use the slider to adjust the brightness if your original image is under or over-exposed. You can also adjust the sharpness or straighten a wonky image. Click on **OK** and then click on the **Scan Now** button.

6 You will hear the scanning head passing across your image, more slowly than it did when you previewed the image. You will also see a progress bar showing how much of the scan has been completed. When finished, your image will be shown in your image-editing software. To stop this process at any time, click on **Cancel Scan**.

7 Now save your scan. Select **Save As** from the **File** menu and choose a name and location for your scanned image. To use or edit it in other programs, save it as a Windows bitmap (shown by a .bmp at the end of the file name). Click on **Save**. The BMP Options dialogue box will appear. To use the default settings, click on **OK**.

Create a background

You can use a scanned photo as the background picture on your Desktop if you save it as a .gif or .jpg file. Open the folder containing the image, right-click on it and select **Set as Desktop Background**. To adjust the Desktop appearance right-click on it and choose **Personalize** then click on **Desktop background**. You can then select one of the presets to alter the look.

*To crop the image, click on the **Crop** tool in the 'Size' group, then click and drag on one of the black 'line' handles. The mouse pointer changes to a small black cross. To resize the image, click on it, then on one of the white 'round' or 'square' handles, the mouse pointer changes to a white double-headed arrow. Now drag the handle to a new position.*

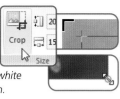

Now try placing your scan into a document to make, say, a card, a mini-magazine or a newsletter.

▶ NEW PROGRAM

8 To place your scan in a Word document, first open the document. Place the cursor where you want the image to appear, go to the **Insert** tab and click on **Picture** in the 'Illustrations' group. Locate the folder containing your scan, click on the scan and then click on **Insert**.

9 To move your image, right-click on it and click on **Text Wrapping** and then on **In Front of Text**. You should now be able to move the image around the page by clicking and dragging it. If you need to resize and crop the image, see above.

The 'Real' Great Escape...

In the second world war of 1939-1945, out of about fifteen thousand British Air Force prisoners who were in permanent camps in Germany, more than three thousand prisoners made an escape: less than thirty ever reached Great Britain or neutral territory, most being recaptured.

In the summer of 1943, RAF prisoners who were NCOs and held at Barth, Stalag Luft 1, on the Baltic coast, were sent to a new camp at Hydekrug, Stalag Luft VI, on the Memel Peninsula. This camp was so near to both the Lithuanian frontier and the Baltic coast, that there was the double chance of anyone who got away from the camp, of either crossing by ship to Sweden, or being

10 To add text, go to the **Insert** tab and select **Text Box** from the 'Text' group. The cursor will change to a large cross. Draw two boxes – one for the heading and one for a caption. Size them in the same way you did for the picture. Now click on the boxes and type in your text.

Using photos in Works

Inserting a photograph in Works is similar to the procedure in Word. Go to the **Insert** menu, click on **Picture**, then on **From File**. Navigate to the folder containing your photograph, click on it and then on **Insert**. The picture will appear in the document. You can resize the picture by clicking and dragging on one of the handles at the corners and the sides of the image. To keep the photograph in proportion, hold down the shift key as you drag a corner handle. Unlike Word, though, you cannot crop or adjust the colours of pictures in Works.

Work with digital images

Put your photos on your PC and start sharing straight away

The benefits of digital photography are now well known – and most people have experienced the ease of using a digital camera. The days of waiting until a roll of film has been finished and then taking it to be developed have gone. While some may miss the surprise of finding what was on the film, there are many advantages to the immediacy offered by digital photography.

The best thing is that you can see quickly and easily whether your photo has come out well. If not, there is nothing to lose by having a second attempt at the perfect shot. Next, by downloading it onto your PC you can print it straight away – a dedicated photo-printer can give great results. You can also email the image file around the world, sharing photos with friends and relatives at amazing speed.

Install Adobe Photoshop Elements 8.0. It is a straightforward process – just follow the on-screen instructions and you will soon be ready to go.

BEFORE YOU START

1 Switch on your camera and connect it to your computer using the USB cable that came with the camera. Adobe Photoshop Elements 8.0 should launch automatically, in which case go to step 5. If not, go to the **Start** menu, click on **All Programs** and select **Adobe Photoshop Elements 8.0**.

Your camera may have been supplied with bespoke software from the manufacturer – this should allow you to perform all the basic print and edit functions.

OTHER PROGRAMS

*You can return to the welcome screen at any time, by clicking on the **Home** button on the menu bar at the top of the screen.*

Watch out

To download from your camera, it must be switched on and in 'view' mode. If it is switched off or in 'camera' mode, it will not appear in Photoshop Element's list of available devices.

2 From the Photoshop Elements welcome screen, click on **Organize**. The program will then load fully, displaying a catalogue of your previously imported pictures. Go to the **File** menu and click on **Get Photos and Videos**, then click on **From Camera or Card Reader**.

3 Before downloading, you can amend some of the 'import settings', such as naming the folder the images will be stored in. Click on the Create Subfolder(s) drop-down menu and select **Custom Name**, and then type the name of your new folder into the box below. To start the image download process, click on **Get Photos**.

4 The Photo Downloader will launch and start copying your photos to the folder you created in step 3. A dialogue box will appear, showing you the progress of the download. If you want to end the process for any reason, click on **Stop**.

Understanding digital film

With a traditional camera, your pictures are stored on a roll of film. A digital camera stores images on electronic memory cards. These come in a range of shapes, sizes and storage capacities, depending on the make and model of camera.

The most common format in compact cameras is Secure Digital (SD), while professional cameras often use Compact Flash cards. Sony products use a proprietary type of card called Memory Stick. Mobile phone cameras often use tiny cards known as Mini-SD. It makes little difference what card your camera uses, but you can only insert the correct type.

All these cards are based on a technology called 'flash memory' that keeps images stored even when the camera is turned off. So, having filled up the card, you can take it out and leave it to one side while you take more pictures using another card, then transfer the pictures to your PC when you are ready.

You could keep all your photos stored on cards, but it is best to copy them to your PC and then store them on recordable CDs or DVDs. You can then re-use your memory card or cards.

Advanced import options

Before you import your photos, click on the **Advanced Dialog** button at the bottom left of the Photo Downloader dialogue box. In the 'Advanced Options' panel you can set the software to 'Automatically Fix Red Eyes', for example, in all your photos.

5 When the files have been copied to the folder you chose, the 'Files Successfully Copied' box will appear. Click on **Yes**. Photoshop Elements will then fix any pictures with red eye (see above). When this process has finished, these images will be ready for editing in Photoshop Elements' Editor mode (see page 210).

6 You can choose the size of the images shown on your screen by using the slider at the top of the screen or by clicking on the four small squares to the left of the slider to see thumbnails of every image. Use the icon to the right of the slider to view single images.

7 The ability to print your photos straight away is a great advantage of digital cameras. Click on **File** and then on **Print** to launch the Prints dialogue box.

Send photos by email

Photoshop Elements allows you to select and attach images to an email. Click on the image or images you would like to send, then click on the **SHARE** button at the top right of the screen and then on **Photo Mail**. If you are using Photo Mail for the first time you will be asked to confirm your preferred email client and then click **Continue**. Click on **Next** at the bottom of the Photo Mail panel. Here you can add the recipient if their details are in your email contacts list (see page 91) and enter any message you would like to send (a default message is provided). Click on **Next**, and in the Stationery & Layouts Wizard screens you can add a caption and amend the design by clicking on the options in the left-hand panels. Click on **Next Step** and when you are happy with the look, click on **Next**. Finally, an email box will appear – check that all the details are correct, and then click on **Send**.

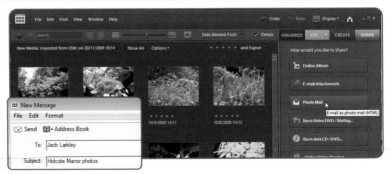

8 The Prints dialogue box shows a thumbnail list of photos and a print preview. Check and amend the settings on the right, 1 Select Printer, 2 Printer Settings, 3 Select Paper Size, 4 Select Type of Print and 5 Print Size. To amend the orientation, click on **Page Setup**. To include more pictures to your 'set', click on **Add**.

9 In the 'Add Media' dialogue box, scroll through the thumbnail images and click on any pictures you would like to include. Click on **Done** when you have finished. If you change your mind about a picture, click on it in the left-hand pane and then click on **Remove**.

10 Photoshop Elements will automatically place the images on the page, rotating images and running onto extra pages, if necessary. Click on the right arrow at the bottom to see additional pages. When you are happy with your layouts, click on **Print** to get immediate copies of your pictures.

Size matters

When emailing photos you should first save them in a compressed format such as JPEG. To do this, ensure you are in Edit mode and choose **Save As** from the **File** menu, rename the image and from the 'Format' drop-down menu choose **JPEG**. Then click on **Save**. In the JPEG Options dialogue box select from one of the four image options to determine the size and quality of the image. Then click on **OK**.

Letting the experts do it

You do not have to print out your artwork yourself. There are lots of companies that offer photo printing services, including high street shops such as Boots and Jessops. You can take your digital camera's memory card into a shop and pick up the prints later. Or you can upload pictures to the internet and get quality prints on photographic paper through the post. You can even order enlargements or special items such as mugs or T-shirts with your pictures on them.

Editing digital images

Make your pictures perfect with just a few tweaks

Using an image-editing program, you can make almost any imaginable alteration to a photo. First of all, you need to have the picture stored as a digital file. It could come from your digital camera, or the picture may have been taken on traditional film – you can have your photos put on CD when you have your film processed, or use a scanner to copy prints onto your PC (see page 200).

Once you have opened an image file in your editing program, you can alter it in a variety of ways. For example, you can turn the photo around or 'crop' it, cutting out parts of the picture you do not want. In this feature, we will show you how to correct 'red eye' and restore a healthy tone to the subjects of your photos – you will be amazed at how quickly you can create great pictures.

Download the images you would like to edit from your camera (see page 206), or scan a printed photo to create a digital file (see page 200).

BEFORE YOU START

1 Automatic flash often causes 'red eye' and spoils pictures. To remove it, first go to the **Start** menu, click on **All Programs** and select **Adobe Photoshop Elements 8.0**. From the Photoshop Elements' welcome screen, click on the second option on the left, **EDIT**.

Other image-editing programs will perform the same tasks – options include Corel Paint Shop Pro, Microsoft Digital Image Suite and the full version of Adobe Photoshop.

OTHER PROGRAMS

Key words

Red eye *When you photograph a person using the flash, light reflected from the back of the eye glows red, known as 'red eye'. Many cameras have an option to reduce red eye but it is also quickly remedied in image-editing software.*

Shortcut

*If you would like a closer look at an image, double-click on the thumbnail. To return to the screen displaying all images, click on **Back**.*

2 Next, go to the **File** menu, click on **Open** and locate the photo you want to edit. When the image appears, click on the **Zoom Tool** in the toolbox on the left, and then click and drag around the eyes. This part of the image will then enlarge so that you can focus on the area with red eye you want to correct.

3 Click on the **Red Eye Removal Tool** in the toolbox on the left. The options at the top of the screen change so that you can alter the size of the pupil and the amount by which you would like to darken it. If you are not sure, leave these settings on the program's automatic set-up.

4 Next, click on an area of red eye in the picture, or click and drag over the affected area. Photoshop Elements will automatically correct the problem. Repeat this process until you are satisfied with the result.

Finding your stored photos

If you are not sure where an image is stored, click on **Organize** from the Photoshop Elements' welcome screen. When the program has fully launched, click

on the **Display** button at the top of the screen and select **Thumbnail View** from the drop-down menu of options, to see all the files that have been downloaded into Photoshop Elements. Scroll through the thumbnails to find the image you would like to edit and click on it. Next, click on the **Editor** button at the top of the screen and select **Full Edit** from the drop-down menu of options. The Editor mode will then launch, with your selected image on screen, ready for you to start work.

Bright idea
*If you want to experiment without losing your original image, use **Save As** from the File menu to create a new file – you just need to choose a slightly different name to store it under.*

5 Click on **File** and then **Save** to save your amended image. If this is the first time you have saved this image, you will be asked to rename the file and you can choose where to store it – click on the **Save in** drop-down menu at the top of the dialogue box and find an appropriate folder. Click on **Save**.

6 Digital photos can sometimes make the subject look quite washed out. You can adjust the tones in Photoshop Elements to restore a healthier look. First, open the photo in Photoshop Elements' Editor mode.

7 Click on **Enhance** from the menu bar at the top of the screen, and select **Adjust Color** and then **Adjust Color for Skin Tone**.

Size matters

The resolution of an image is usually given in 'dots per inch' (dpi). The term '300dpi' means 300 dots across and down each inch. 'Dots' here means pixels. Do not confuse these with the dpi ratings of printers, which refer to the dozens of ink dots needed to print each pixel. Digital cameras are rated in megapixels, referring to the total number of pixels in millions. For a photo to print at 8x6in and a resolution of 300dpi, you need 8x300x6x300 = 4,320,000 pixels – just over 4 megapixels.

Storing a 'true colour' digital picture requires 24 bits multiplied by the number of pixels – this uses up a lot of space. To save space, you can reduce the number of pixels by setting your digital camera to a lower resolution or by changing the file format to a format such as JPEG, where the data is compressed but some colour information is discarded. Essentially, you must balance image quality against file size – but remember that once data is lost, you cannot get it back.

Watch out

It is easy to overdo the changes when adjusting skin tone. If you do, click on the Reset button in the Adjust Color for Skin Tone dialogue box to return to the original image and start again.

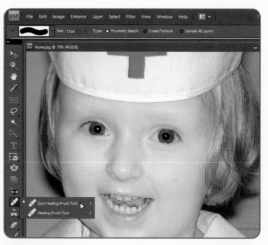

8 Move the mouse over to the face on the image (you may need to click on and drag the Adjust Color for Skin Tone dialogue box out of the way). Once the mouse is in the right area, an eyedropper icon will appear. Click once and Photoshop Elements will automatically adjust skin tone.

9 If you would like to adjust the tones further, drag the sliders for **Tan** and **Blush** along to change the skin (see below), and drag the **Ambient Light** slider to amend the light in the image. When you are happy with the result, click on **OK** and then save the amended image as in step 5.

10 Great photos can sometimes be spoilt by an unfortunate skin blemish. You can quickly remedy these complaints with Photoshop Elements. Open an image that needs correcting in the Editor mode, and click and hold on the **Healing Brush Tool** icon in the toolbox on the left. Select **Spot Healing Brush Tool** from the fly-out menu.

Adjusting skin tones

The Adjust Color for Skin Tone command will automatically alter the colours used in a photo to make the best of natural skin tones. To use this tool in Photoshop Elements, you just need to select it from the toolbar and then click on an area of skin. If you wish, you can manually adjust the brown (tan) and red (blush) colours separately to achieve the final colour you want. When you are finished, click on **OK**. To cancel your changes and start again, click on **Reset**.

Bright idea
If you choose a brush size larger than the blemish, you will be able to correct the skin with just one brush stroke.

Watch out
When using the Spot Healing Brush, the on-screen tool display changes according to the size of brush chosen. Smaller brushes will be displayed as five small dots, so you may need to look closely.

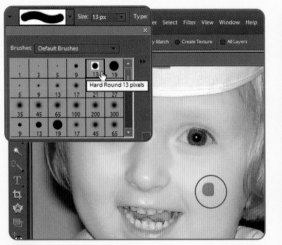

11 You can alter the size of the brush at the top of the screen by clicking on the arrow to the right of the brushstroke. The pixel (px) size will alter automatically. Next, click and drag over the area you would like to amend.

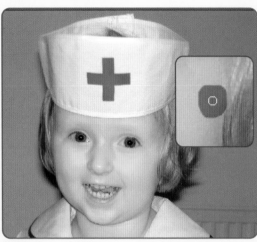

12 You may need to click several times on different areas if you have chosen a small brush size. When you are happy with the result, save the amended image as in step 5.

13 You can easily 'crop' an image to cut out unnecessary background, or focus on a face. First, open the image in Photoshop Element's Editor mode and then click on the **Crop Tool** icon in the toolbox on the left.

Crop images to fit your photo frame

The Crop tool's Options bar allows you to choose a pre-set crop size that will ensure the final image fits a certain size. For example, if you would like your photo to fit a 7 x 5in photo frame, you can choose this setting and your cropped image will fit perfectly.

First, open the image you would like to crop in Photoshop Element's Editor mode. Click on the **Crop** tool from the left-hand toolbox. Next, click on the **Aspect Ratio** drop-down menu in the Options bar that runs across the top of your open image and select **5 x 7 in**. However you choose to crop your photo, these proportions will be maintained.

14 The cursor changes to the shape of the crop tool. Click and drag over the area you would like to keep. When you let go, the unselected area will be partially greyed. To confirm the crop, click on the tick at the bottom right of your selection. Save the image to retain your changes.

15 If you have an image that you would like to turn around, this can quickly be achieved in Photoshop Elements. Open the image in Editor mode, select **Image** and then **Rotate** from the menu bar at the top of the screen. Choose one of the options from the list – rotating 90° left or right, or rotating 180°, can be achieved in one click.

16 Once you are happy with the result, click on the **File** menu and then **Save** to keep your changes.

Finding ready-made images

If you want a particular image, you can find thousands of free photos online at www.google.com/images – type in the subject you want and click on **Search**. You can only use these images, though, in private projects, unless you get the permission of the owner. For 'royalty free' pictures, which come with the legal rights to use them as you wish, you could pay a small fee per picture from www.istockphoto.com or subscribe to a service such as www.clipart.com. Clip-art discs such as Greenstreet's 10,000 Photos (www.greenstreetsoftware.co.uk) are also good value.

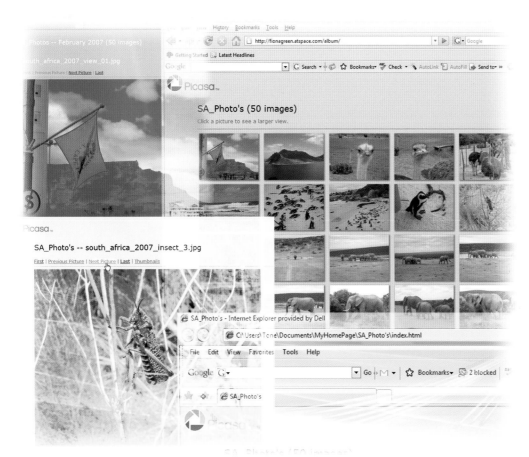

Build an online album

It is easy to create a photo album on the web using Picasa

Many of us have large stores of photos that never make it into an album. With friends and family living far away, sharing these pictures can often be difficult. But the arrival of digital photography has changed all that. Now it is possible to build an online album, where you upload your images to the web for everyone to see. Google provides a free photo-management program called Picasa, where you can assemble a photo album from any collection of images. It can then be used as a stand-alone web page, which can be placed in any web space to which you have access. Once there, everyone can admire your photos using their internet browser.

To create a photo album your pictures need to be digital images. Scan them yourself (see page 200) or download them from a digital camera (see page 206).

BEFORE YOU START

1 Click on the **Start** button, then on **All Programs** and select **Picasa 3**. Browse to the folder that contains the photos you want to use, here 'SA_Photos'. If you cannot see the folder, click on the **File** menu and choose **Add Folder to Picasa**. In the Folder Manager dialogue box, click on your folder, tick **Scan Once**, then click on **OK**.

You can use web editors such as Frontpage or Dreamweaver to build great websites. It is also possible to rent web space from hundreds of providers around the world.

OTHER PROGRAMS

Close-up
*If you do not already have Picasa on your PC,
go to http://picasa.google.co.uk/ and click on
Download Picasa 3.5. The software will download and
be stored with other applications on your hard drive.*

Bright idea
*Cropping your pictures so that the main
subject of the photo is at the centre of the
image makes for a more eye-catching display.*

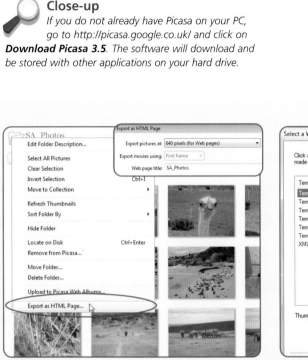

2 Scroll down the thumbnail images to find your photos. Right-click on the folder icon and select **Export as HTML page** from the drop-down menu. In the dialogue box '640 pixels (for Web pages)' next to 'Export pictures at:' will already be pre-selected, as will 'Web page title:', here 'SA_Photos', the folder name.

3 In the Browse For Folder dialogue box, click on the 'MyHomePage' folder in 'Documents'. If it is not there, click on **My Documents**, then on **Make New Folder**, type 'MyHomePage' and click on **OK**. Choose a template from the panel on the left. Click on **Export**. An 'Export as HTML Page' bar displays the progress.

4 Your web browser loads to display the album, so you can see how it will look when it is on the web. Thumbnail images of the photos are displayed – you can click on a thumbnail to see the image at its full size (in this case, 640 pixels wide). In full-size view, you can use the navigation links at the top to move around the images.

Connecting a digital camera

Windows 7 makes it easy to get pictures from a digital camera. Most cameras sold include a USB cable. Connect this to a vacant USB socket on your computer, switch the camera on and it should be recognised and configured automatically. You will see a dialogue box asking what you want to do each time you connect. You can choose whether to print all of the pictures in the camera's memory, view them as an on-screen slide show or copy them across to a folder on your computer.

Album template options

Picasa offers two main types of template (see step 3), with background colour variations in each. The first displays all the thumbnail images in a grid across the page. Click one and the thumbnails are replaced with the photo, shown full screen. The second option (right) creates a frames-based display, where thumbnails are in a narrow scrollable frame on the left, with the currently selected photo filling a large frame on the right. Either type will integrate within the frames of your home page.

Order prints online

Windows 7 lets you order high-quality prints of your pictures online. To do so, connect to the Internet, then click on the **Start** button, **All Programs** and select **Windows Photo Gallery**. Click on the picture you want printed, or hold down the **Ctrl** key to select multiple pictures. Click on the **Print** button and select **Order prints**. Follow the steps on screen to select which printing company to use, and then click on **Send Pictures**. Finally, follow the instructions provided by the printing company to complete your order.

5 Your album is now ready on your PC's hard disk. To make it accessible to others you need 'web space' to store it in, and a program to transfer files to it. Your ISP may offer space, but there are cheap alternatives. Type **www.atspace.com** into your web browser and press **Return**. On the home page, click on **Sign Up for our Free Hosting Plan**.

6 On the next page, select the type of account that you want, and click on **Sign Up**. In the Sign Up window fill in your details, type in the displayed verification code then click on **Sign Up**. In a short while you should receive a confirmation email. To complete your registration with ATSPACE, see the instructions below.

7 You need to download and install SmartFTP (see page 219) to transfer your files. Connect to the internet, then start SmartFTP. In the Address box at the top, type your URL (do not use the http://), for example 'yourname.atspace.com'. Add your user name to the Login box and give your password (see below), then press **Return**.

Registering with ATSPACE

Check your email at the address you gave in step 6. Your confirmation email from ATSPACE will confirm your user name and password. You now need to sign up at http://atspace.com/login-free.html. Once that is done, click on the **Login: Free Users** button, enter your user name and password and click **Login**. On the Control Panel page, click on **Hosting**.

Select the plan that suits you and then click on **Order** at the bottom of the screen. In the 'Get Domain Name' box you can type in your name, for example. This, added to .com, will be what people need to type in order to get to your website. The web address is therefore http://yourname.com. Click on **Continue**. Add your personal details, and click on **Continue** again. Complete the registration and click on **Log Off**.

Bright idea
*If you only want to share one image, then email it instead. Open your image in a program like Paint, go to the **File** menu and click on **Save As**. Select JPEG or GIF in the 'Save as type' box. Now attach the small file to your email and send it on.*

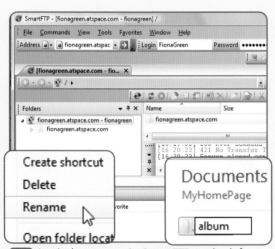

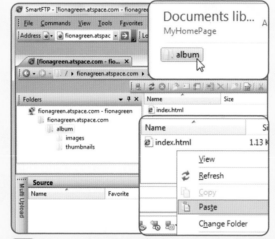

8 A window opens in SmartFTP. In the left pane are folders for the web space name(s) you created; click on one to select it. Next, click on the **Start** button, **Documents** and double-click on **MyHomePage**. You will see a folder with your album title. Right-click on the folder and choose **Rename** from the pop-up menu. Type **album** and press **Return**.

9 Click on the **album** folder and press **Ctrl+C** to copy it. Switch back to SmartFTP and, in the left pane, click on your web space folder. On the right, one file called **index.html** is already shown. Right-click in the right pane and choose **Paste** from the pop-up menu. After a while, your album folder and its files will upload.

10 Launch your web browser. In the address box, type 'yourname.atspace.com/album' (where 'yourname' is the name you gave). You will see your album exactly as it was displayed in step 4, but the images are coming from the web, not from your PC. You can now give your friends the address of your online album.

Download and install SmartFTP

To copy files to the web, you need a FTP (File Transfer Protocol) program such as SmartFTP. This is free for a trial 14 day period, after which you have to purchase it. Open your web browser and type 'www.smartftp.com', then press **Return**. When the page loads, click on **Download SmartFTP**. On the download page, click on **Download SmartFTP Client (64-bit)**. In the next box click on **Save file**, then, if prompted, click on **Save** again. When the file has downloaded, go to your Downloads folder and double-click its icon. Follow the on-screen instructions, clicking on **Next** at each prompt during the install. Click on **OK** to start the trial version or **Buy Now** to purchase.

Create your own calendar

Make a personal calendar with a new photo for every month

With the widespread use of digital cameras, it is now incredibly easy to produce your own, personalised calendar. You do not even need to be creative – Microsoft Office Online supplies a number of templates that, using Excel, you can adapt to make a calendar that is exclusive to you and means a lot to your friends and family.

Most of the work is already done within the template. You just need to select 12 of your favourite images – anything from picturesque landscapes to snapshots of family or friends will work well. It is then up to you to choose any other personal touches you might like to add before printing and binding your own special record for the year.

September 2011

Renew TV licence!

OFF TO SPAIN!

Lunch with Jim

28 Visit to Emma's

Look through your photos and try to choose relevant images – one idea is to show family members with a birthday in the featured month.

> ◤ **BEFORE YOU START**

1 Go to the **Start** button, select **All Programs** and click on **Microsoft Office Home and Business** and then on **Microsoft Excel 2010**. Click on the **File** tab then on **New**. Make sure you are connected to the internet and click on **Calendars** under Office.com Templates (see page 221) in the left panel.

To create a more professional-looking calendar, try using the templates on websites such as www.kodakgallery.co.uk or www.snapfish.co.uk.

> ◤ **OTHER PROGRAMS**

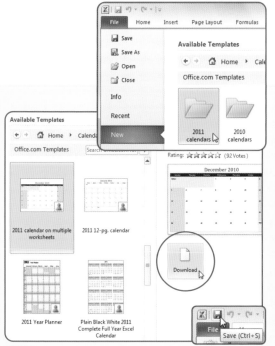

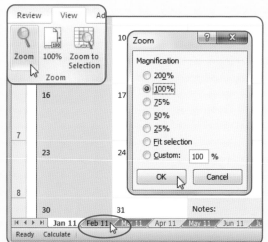

*This template starts on the last month of the previous year. If you don't want this, right click on the **Dec 10** tab and select **Delete** from the pop-up options.*

Many buttons displayed on the Ribbon have an arrow below or next to the command. Make sure that you click on the arrow to view all the options associated with that command.

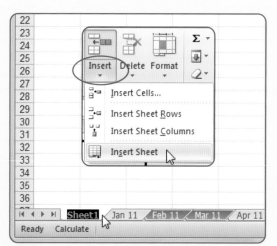

2 In the list that appears, click on the link for **2011 calendars** (or a later year, if needed). Scroll down and select **2011 calendar on multiple worksheets**. Then click on **Download**; the file will automatically open in Excel. Click on the **Save** button on the Quick Access toolbar to save the new document.

3 Each month in this calendar template is on a separate worksheet. To view a particular month, just click on its tab at the bottom of the screen. If you cannot see the whole page, go to the **View** tab and click on **Zoom** to choose a different magnification. Click on **OK**.

4 Now make a photo page. You should already be on the Jan 11 worksheet – if not, click on its tab. From the **Home** tab, go to the 'Cells' group and click on **Insert**, then choose **Insert Sheet** to add a new worksheet for your photo. Double-click on the **Sheet1** tab and rename it 'Jan Photo', and press **Return**.

Accessing Office 2010 UK templates

Microsoft Office 2010 templates accessed from 'Office.com' are generally styled for the US audience. To access UK formatted templates, launch your internet browser and type **http://office.microsoft.com/en-gb/templates** into the address bar and press **Return**. Here you will find hundreds of Office 2010 compatible templates, new and old, grouped in categories. Click on a category to view its options, make

your selection, click on **view details** to preview the template and then on **download** to save it to the 'My Templates' folder. To quickly access Office Templates again, bookmark the site to add it to your favourites. With the website open in your browser, click on **Favorites**, **Add to Favorites**.

Bright idea
Try to use the same colour for the month name throughout your calendar, or pick a predominant colour from each photo to create a stylish and uniform design.

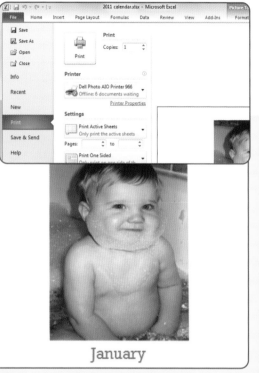

5 Click on **Insert** and then on **Picture** in the 'Illustrations' group. Browse your hard drive to find a photo to use and click on it, then on **Insert**. Resize the image if you need to (see below). Now name the month by clicking in the first available cell in the A column below the photo and type in 'January'.

6 Go to the 'Font' group and select a font from the drop-down menu at the top, set the size to 36pt and choose a colour. Now click in the 'January' cell, go to the 'Alignment' group and click on **Align Center**. Click and drag to resize the 'A' column to the photo width.

7 Go to the **File** tab and click on **Print** to see how the calendar will appear on the printed page. The page is previewed on the right-hand side of the print screen. If you cannot fit both the photo and month name on the page, click on the **Home** tab to go back and adjust the picture.

Resize your images

If the photo is too big, you may only be able to see part of it. Right-click on it and choose **Size and Properties** from the pop-up menu. In the **Size** tab, the 'Lock aspect ratio' box should be ticked – this means the image dimensions are kept if you make a change (that is, if you amend the height, the width will also change).

Landscape-format photos will work best with the calendar template. To fit an A4 landscape page, resize the image to no more than 26cm wide and 15cm high. Using the default cell sizes, it should fit within columns A to O and rows 0 to 35.

If you would like to crop an image, go to the 'Size' group and click on **Crop**. Click and drag on the corners or on the bars – wait for the cursor to become a black bar – on the side of the image to crop out areas you do not need to show.

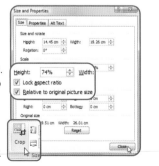

Check your setup

Make sure your page is set up correctly for printing. Go to **Print Preview** (see step 7) and click on **Page Setup**. Under the **Page** tab, make sure the Orientation is set to **Landscape** and the paper size is **A4**. You can also check the margins by clicking on the **Margins** tab. They should be set at 0.75cm – check that your printer will print this close to the edge of the page. Click on **OK** to see how any changes you have made affect the layout – you need to fit both the photo and the month name on the page.

Watch out
Make sure you always tick the 'Create a copy' box when copying Excel worksheets, or you will just move one month's picture sheet to another month.

Bright idea
Use plastic sleeve binders from a stationers to bind your calendar in a durable, inexpensive fashion.

8 Now create the other photo pages. Right-click on the **Jan Photo** tab and select **Move or Copy** from the menu. Select **Feb 11** from the 'Before sheet' list and tick the **Create a copy** box. Click on **OK**. The new sheet appears before the Feb11 page, called 'Jan Photo (2)'. Double-click on the tab and rename it **Feb Photo**.

9 Right-click on the photo and select **Change Picture**. Select a new photo, as in Step 5, and resize it to fit. Overwrite the 'January' text with 'February'. Now repeat the process, copying the worksheets, replacing the photos and changing the text so that you have a photo page for every month of the year.

10 Now print your calendar. Click on the **File** tab and select **Print**. In the Print dialogue box, under 'Settings' select **Print Entire Workbook**. Click on the **Print** button. Staple the printed pages together along the top edge, or take it to a print shop for a more professional binding.

Add photos to special days

To illustrate events such as birthdays or special events, you might like to add photos to the main calendar pages. You can resize large photos in Excel, but it is easier to resize them first in Photoshop Elements (see page 210). Make them no bigger than a few inches or 600 pixels wide. Return to Excel, click in the date cell you would like to add the photo to, click on **Insert** and then **Picture**. Browse your hard drive to choose an image and then click on **Insert**.

If you need to resize the photo to make it fit within the date cell, click and drag on a corner handle and then pull the image in to reduce the size. (Only use the corner handles as this will retain the proportions of the original image.) You can also add a quirky angle by rotating the photo – click and drag on the green handle above the top of the photo to spin it around. A couple of these smaller images each month will really add colour to your calendar.

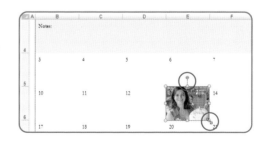

Create an invitation

Make a special occasion even better with your own design

Making your own invitation allows you to create a design that reflects the type of event you are organising – and the type of person you are arranging it for. If it is going to be a lively party, use bright colours and fun fonts. If it is for a more sober dinner party, choose more subtle colours and traditional fonts.

Before designing your invitation, make a note of the relevant information guests will need, including the date, time, location of the event – and any dress requirements.

Decide what size you want your invitation to be. For convenience, it is a good idea to print two or four per sheet of A4 paper.

▶ BEFORE YOU START

1 Go to the **Start** menu, select **All Programs** and click on **Microsoft Word 2010**. A new document appears. Save it by going to the **File** tab and clicking on **Save As**. In the 'Save As' dialogue box select a location, type in a file name, then click on **Save**.

*To create an invitation in Microsoft Works, go to the **Start** menu, click on **Microsoft Works** and then click on **Works Word Processor** from the 'Quick launch' menu on the right.*

▶ OTHER PROGRAMS

Close-up

If you want to design a classic, traditional invitation, choose from the following fonts: Book Antiqua, Copperplate Gothic Light, Garamond, Monotype Corsiva or Palatino Linotype. For a more fun look, try Comic Sans MS, Curlz MT, Kristen ITC or Bradley Hand ITC.

Bright idea

If the event that you are creating your invitation for has a theme – a summer flower show, for example – use colours and clip art to reflect that and impress your guests.

2 Go to the **Page Layout** tab and click on the Page Setup dialogue box launcher. Click on the **Paper** tab and make sure that A4 is selected in the 'Paper size' box. Click on the **Margins** tab and set the Top and Bottom margins to 0 cm. Click on **OK**. A warning box pops up, click on **Fix** then **OK**.

3 Type in your text. To style it, highlight the first part, click on the Font dialogue box launcher and under the **Font** tab, select a font, style, size, colour and effect, then click on **OK**. Continue to style the rest of your text in a similar way.

4 Highlight all of your text and click on the **Center** button, found in the 'Paragraph' group. To add space between the lines of your invitation, press the **Enter** key. Press the **Enter** key repeatedly to add a greater amount of space.

Using Word templates

Microsoft Office Online has a collection of templates that can help you to get started with creating your invitation. Go to the **Start** button, select **All Programs** and click on **Microsoft Word 2010**. Click on the **File** tab then on **New**, scroll down the list of templates under 'Office.com Templates' and click on **Invitations**. In the middle panel, click on a category, here 'Party invitations'. Under each template is a description – click on one to preview it in the panel on the right. Make your choice and click on the **Download** button.

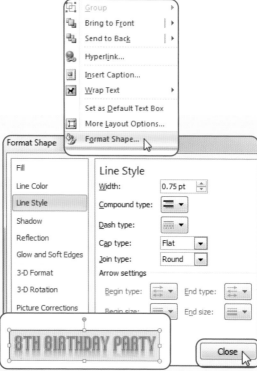

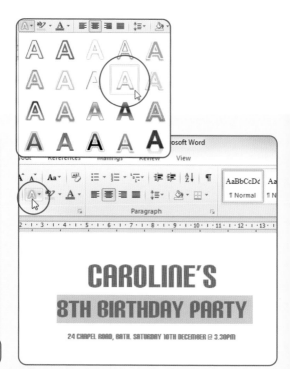

5 To replace a piece of text with WordArt, first highlight the text and press **Enter**. This will remove the text leaving space to be occupied later. Click on the **Insert** tab, then on **WordArt** in the 'Text' group. Select an effect from the drop-down menu. Now type into the box that appears to replace the default 'YOUR TEXT HERE'.

6 WordArt text is held within a box making it easily moveable (see below). To add a fill or line colour, right-click on the frame and then on **Format Shape** from the drop-down. In the 'Format Shape' dialogue box, click on options in the left panel and choose colours, line weights and styles in the right. Click on **Close** to finish.

7 Alternatively, you can easily emphasise any piece of text by adding an effect. Highlight a line of text and click on **Text Effects** in the 'Font' group. A gallery of preset effects is displayed. As you move the mouse pointer over each one, your highlighted text changes to reflect that effect. Click on an effect to select it.

Boxing clever in WordArt

A WordArt box has four round and four square handles that appear on the corners and sides. Click and drag inwards or outwards on a round handle to resize both sides. Click and drag inwards or outwards on a square handle to resize one side only. Click and drag the frame to reposition your WordArt text box. Above the square handle at the top of a box is a round green handle. Click and drag this handle to rotate the box, left to rotate anticlockwise, right clockwise, then release.

Bright idea
For a professional look, print your invitations on card. Not all printers can handle card, so you may need to store the document on a CD/DVD and take it to a print shop.

8 Using the options at the bottom of the text effects panel you can further customise your text by changing the outline colour, adding a shadow, reflection or glow. Experiment with all the options to achieve your desired effect. Here we've used Red, 18 pt glow, Accent color 2.

9 If you wish, you can add a photo to your invitation. Position your cursor at the top of your page. Go to the **Insert** tab and click on **Picture** in the 'Insert' group. In the dialogue box, navigate to your picture, click on it, then on **Insert**. Your text will automatically move down to create space for the new image.

10 Now go to the 'Arrange' group and click on **Wrap Text** and then on **Behind Text**. Your text will then automatically move back onto the first page and sit neatly in front of your picture. To print out the invitation, go to the **File** tab and select **Print** from the left pane. Check options under 'Settings' and click on **Print**.

Adding clip art

If you wish, you can add a clip art image to your invitation instead. Place the cursor where you want the clip art to appear, go to the **Insert** tab and click on the **Clip Art** button in the 'Illustrations' group. The clip art panel appears on the right-hand side of the screen. Type in a search term and click on **Go**. Scroll down the images and click on your choice, then click on **Insert** on the pop-up toolbar. To manipulate your image, see page 192.

Plan the perfect party for

Use your computer to help to organise your celebratio

Project planner

Create a folder called 'Party'. Add sub-folders to it for each mini-project.

- Party
  - Guest list
  - Invitations
  - Letters to suppliers
  - Budget
  - Menus
  - Reminders

An informal get-together at home is one thing, but it is quite a different matter to arrange the kind of special party your friends and relations talk about for years after.

Silver weddings, landmark birthdays, marriages and christenings – these occasions do not come around very often, but when they do you want to be sure it all goes right. The preparations can take months and the planning will have to be meticulous. Venue, catering, entertainment, guests and accommodation – if people are coming a long way – must be booked and confirmed well in advance. You also need to plan the cost of it all.

One of the main areas where your computer can help is in the compiling of a guest list. The Microsoft Works database will store the contact details of guests and of key suppliers, such as caterers. Use your PC's design capabilities to produce invitations, then address them instantly by making labels from your guest

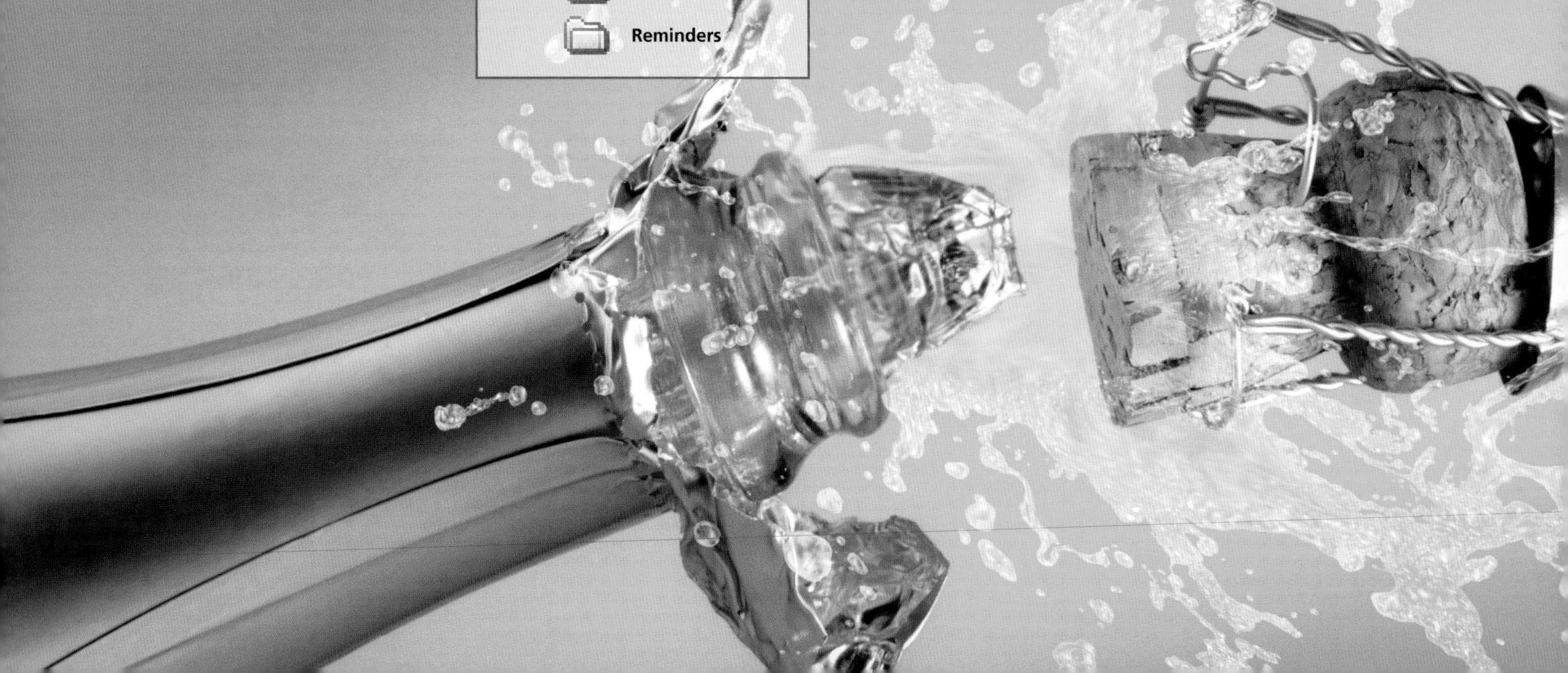

a special occasion

and ensure you have a day to remember

database. As people reply, input the information into the database for a record of confirmed numbers.

Using a database means you will only have to compile the list once, and you can then use it to note additional details: the number of people in each group; who has small children; who is a vegetarian and so on. Now you can estimate the number of people attending, and use a spreadsheet to prepare a budget. Allocate a sum for the cost of the venue and entertainment, and an amount per head for food.

If you need to contact and select caterers, DJs and so on, send out letters written in your word-processing program giving your requirements and requesting quotes. Use the word-processing program to create menus and place cards, too.

Now set up a planning spreadsheet in the form of a 'Celebration countdown'. Use it to schedule remaining tasks.

Once everything is in place, you can relax and start looking forward to the big day.

Pay attention to detail

- Compile guest list
- Book venue
- Organise caterer
- Design and send out invitations
- Book DJ and master of ceremonies
- Compile 'Celebration countdown'
- Write and send reminders/directions

Ideas and inspirations

These suggestions will get you started on organising your event. All the projects can be adapted depending on the nature of your occasion. For example, on your invitation you could include your email address so guests can respond by computer.

172 Guest list and address labels
Set up a guest list to keep track of who you invite and use labels to mail your invitations.

224 Create an invitation
A little imagination – and the versatility of Word and Works – will ensure a good response.

154 Send a formal letter
Use Word to produce business-like letters to suppliers to check availability and prices.

276 Project-based budgeting
Compile a spreadsheet to help to keep track of all your party's expenses.

316 Celebration countdown
In the same way you plan a holiday, create a spreadsheet to organise last-minute tasks.

Also worth considering ...

Whether you have a caterer or are doing the food yourself, guests might like to see the menu.

164 Dinner party menu
If your party involves catering, you could save money by asking guests to select their choice in advance.

Design your own poster

Use graphics and text imaginatively to get your event noticed

When it comes to advertising an event, a colourful, eye-catching poster can really pull in the crowds. It is easy to make a poster for almost any event – from a company dinner to a jumble sale. And with a computer you do not even need to be artistic to design an effective poster.

When designing your poster, you should think about grabbing the attention of passers-by. You also need to make sure that all the essential details of the event – the date, time, place and entry cost – are clearly stated in an easily readable font and size. Soon everyone will know what is going on!

Check that all the information you want on your poster is correct, and think about which type of image will make the greatest impact.

▶ BEFORE YOU START

1 Go to the **Start** menu, select **All Programs** and click on **Microsoft Word 2010**. To create your page, go to the **Page Layout** tab and click on the **Page Setup** dialogue box launcher. In the Page Setup dialogue box, type in measurements for the Top, Bottom, Left and Right margins (at least 1 cm). Click on **OK**.

*You can also use Microsoft Works to design a poster. Open Works, click on the **Templates** button and select **Newsletters & Flyers** in the categories menu on the left. Click on the **Event flyers** icon on the right, choose a style, then click on **Use this style**.*

▶ OTHER PROGRAMS

Bright idea
There are certain fonts specifically designed for headlines – for example: Arial Black, Britannic Bold, Copperplate Gothic Bold and Impact. Try out any that have Black, Bold or Ultra in their name.

2 To create WordArt, type in your first line of text. Highlight the word or words you want to style, go to the **Insert** tab and click on **WordArt** in the 'Text' group. You will be presented with a gallery of styles. Click on a style to select it. Your heading will now appear as WordArt.

3 Now click on the **Home** tab and then on the font drop-down arrow. Font names are displayed in their actual font to help with selection. As you hover the mouse pointer over a font name your text displays in that font. Click on a font, here **Impact**, to change your WordArt. For more on fonts, see above.

4 Now style the remainder of your text. Highlight each section in turn, click on the **Font** dialogue box launcher, in the 'Font' group, and make your choice of fonts, sizes, styles and colours. Make sure you do not get carried away – a good poster should be clear and easy to read.

Making the most of WordArt

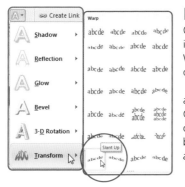

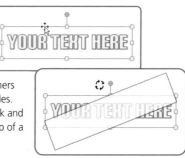

Once you have created WordArt, you can format it further. Select your WordArt image then go to the **Format** tab and click on the **Text Effects** button in the WordArt Styles group. Scroll down and click on **Transform**, then select from one of the many options, here **Slant Up**, in the 'Warp' section (see left).

WordArt boxes have four round and four square handles that appear on the corners and sides. Click and drag inwards or outwards on a round handle to resize both sides. Click and drag inwards or outwards on a square handle to resize one side only. Click and drag the frame to reposition your WordArt text box. Above the square handle at the top of a box is a round green handle. Click and drag this handle to rotate the box, left to rotate anticlockwise, right clockwise, then release.

Watch out
If a clip art image is too large to fit where you want it, the image will drop onto the next page. Reduce its size by clicking and dragging its picture handles and then move it to your desired location.

5 To add space between text, place your cursor at the end of each section and press the **Return** key. For finer adjustments, place your cursor in the line above where you want to add extra space and click on the **Paragraph** dialogue box launcher. In the Spacing section, click on the top arrow beside After to increase the space.

6 To add a clip art image, place your cursor where you want it to appear, go to the **Insert** tab and click on **Clip Art** in the 'Illustrations' group. Type in the subject of your poster in the 'Search for' box in the right-hand column and click on **Go**. Choose an image, click on it and then on **Insert** in the pop-up menu.

7 You can now move and resize your image as necessary, and add more images if you like. To make sure text flows around an image, double-click on it, go to the **Format** tab and click on **Wrap Text** in the 'Arrange' group. Choose **Tight** from the drop-down menu.

Using Word templates

Microsoft Office Online has a collection of templates that might help you with your poster. If you choose to use one, make sure that the paper size and orientation are right for your printer – go to the **Page Layout** tab and click on the **Page Setup** dialogue box launcher and click on the **Paper** tab. Click on the arrow to the right of the 'Paper size' box, scroll through and select your preferred size. To check or change the orientation, go to the **Margins** tab and select Portrait or Landscape.

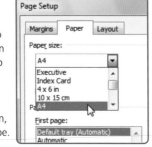

Bright idea
If you have an A4 printer and want to produce a larger poster, copy your file to a memory stick or CD and take it to a print shop. Ask them to print your poster on A3 paper at 141%.

8 The 'Tight' option keeps the text close to your image. 'Square' allows you to position text neatly above, below and at either side of your image. With 'Edit Wrap Points' you define the exact path the text takes around the picture by moving the wrap points. For more choices, select 'More Layout Options'.

9 To add a border, go to the **Page Layout** tab and click on **Page Borders** in the 'Page Background' group. Choose a style, colour, width and setting. (If necessary, click on **Options** and, under Margin, set the size of the gap between the border and the edge of the page, and click on **OK**. Click on **OK** to finish.

10 To view your poster, click on the **File** tab and choose **Print**. Your poster will be previewed in the panel on the right. If you need to make any alterations, click on the **Home** tab and edit as necessary. To print your poster, check the options under 'Settings', then click on the **Print** button.

Importing images

If you want to use your own image from a CD-ROM or your scanned picture folder, go to the **Insert** tab and click on **Picture**. In the dialogue box, scroll through and click on the location of your image. When you have located your image, click on it and then on **Insert**.

Cropping images

If you do not want to use all of the clip art image in your poster, crop out the unwanted parts. From the **Format** tab click on the **Crop** tool in the 'Size' group. Click and drag one of the picture handles in or out to cut or restore the sides of your image.

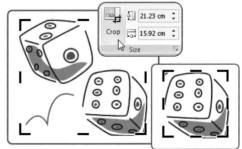

Make your fête a day

There is no aspect of a fête – except the weather – that

Project planner

*Create a folder called 'Fête'.
Add sub-folders within it for
smaller projects.*

- Fête
  - Correspondence
  - Publicity
  - Finance
  - Ideas
  - Timetable
  - Floor plan

A successful fête is all about planning ahead and good organisation. The key is to coordinate everything so that it all comes together at the right moment. It is a serious job making sure that everyone has fun on the day.

There are so many things to think about that the first job is to delegate some of the work. Form a committee and assign roles: someone to deal with drumming up publicity in the press and on the radio; someone to approach businesses for sponsorship or material help; and someone to be fête treasurer (this is particularly important if yours is a fundraising or charitable event).

Now you have to decide on a venue, and on a beneficiary if you plan to donate the proceeds of the fête to charity. Someone on the committee should keep careful notes of the discussions, and these should be typed up and circulated soon after each committee meeting. You may want to invite

in a million

you cannot plan on your computer

your community police officer, or someone from the local council, to take part in the meetings.

By now, you will have set up a timetable database on which you record the tasks that need to be carried out and when. Tick tasks off as they are completed – that way you can use the sort facility to separate completed tasks from those yet to be done, and so plan a weekly schedule.

If you are seeking sponsorship or prize donations, you might like to create an event letterhead for your correspondence. You could send out regular emails to keep

in touch with all the clubs and organisations taking part in the fête. Meanwhile, use your PC to plan the location of all the stalls on the site.

As the day approaches, you can use your PC to create posters and flyers. By now you will know what the big attractions are and you can feature these on your publicity material (if you have asked a celebrity to open the fête, make sure that their photograph is on the poster).

When the big day eventually arrives, just relax and enjoy it – by then you will have earned it.

Event organiser

- Form an organising committee. Arrange either monthly or weekly meetings
- Agree a date and beneficiaries of the profits
- Provisionally book the venue
- Approach local businesses for sponsorship
- Contact the police or local council to ensure the date and venue are suitable
- Inform local press for advance and on-the-day coverage. Agree and implement publicity ideas

Ideas and inspirations

Listed here are a selection of projects you might want to use – or customise – to help you in the organisation of a successful community event. Allocate as much work as possible to other people, but keep a record of all developments on your computer.

186 Timetable database
Leave nothing to chance – produce a helpful diary of 'to do' tasks with your database.

150 Event letterhead
Correspond with stallholders and potential sponsors in a distinctive and memorable way.

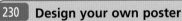

230 Design your own poster
Publicise the date, time and venue of your event locally, together with details of its attractions.

276 Accounts spreadsheet
Use a spreadsheet to keep track of all the expenditure and income arising from your event.

306 Stall planner
Create a simple, overhead 2D plan of the venue and organise your space effectively.

Also worth considering ...

If your timescale and responsibilities justify it, you may find the following project makes things easier.

168 Create a newsletter
Keep the key people involved in the event informed of developments and progress.

Create a party CD

Compile and record **your own** music compilation

Whatever the celebration, the right music can really get the party going. Make use of Windows Media Player and you do not need to spend hours trying to buy the perfect CD – you can create your own. Windows Media Player controls all the forms of entertainment you are likely to use on your PC, from playing music CDs to viewing DVDs. The Media Player really comes into its own if your PC has a CD recorder or 'burner'. Using the recorder, you can back up your files cheaply and reliably – and it even allows you to create CDs with the mix of music that suits you. So get out the CDs you already own and create a mix that will be a hit with all your guests.

Go through your CD collection and choose music for your compilation. You do not need to choose the order you want them to play in.

► BEFORE YOU START

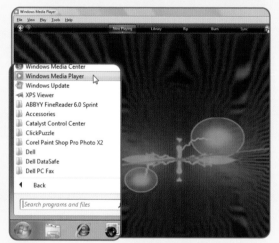

1 In the **Start** menu, click on **All Programs**, then on **Windows Media Player**. The program opens and, if it is the first time you have used it, starts playing a sample of music. Open the CD drive and insert an audio CD. The CD should start playing automatically. Click on **Copy from CD**.

Music formats

The CD that you create using Windows Media Player does not contain exact copies of the tracks on your original CDs. When it copies songs to your hard drive, the program encodes in a special space-saving format (called a .wma file), with a slight loss of quality. When you burn your CD, the files are reconverted, but the lost quality cannot be restored.

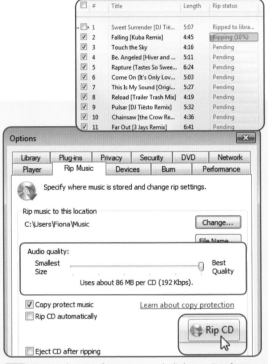

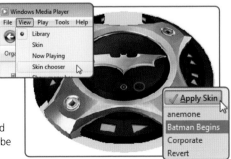

Watch out

Respect copyright: it is illegal to copy and distribute the music on most CDs. You can make a single copy for your own use, but do not share files you copy with others.

2 Go to the **Tools** menu and click on **Options**. Click on the **Rip Music** tab, set the slider to **Best Quality** (suitable for a CD) and click on **OK**. Select the tracks to copy by clicking in the boxes to their left, then click on **Rip CD**. The track will be copied to your hard drive. Eject the CD and repeat the 'rip' for all the other tracks you want to copy.

3 Click on **Create playlist**. Name your playlist in the left panel, here 'Fiona's Party', and click **OK**. Browse to the tracks to be added and drag them to your new playlist in the left-hand column. When you have finished, double-click on your new playlist to view it. You can change the order of tracks by clicking and dragging them up or down.

4 Insert a blank CD in your CD burner. With your playlist selected in the left pane, click on the **Burn** tab. Under 'Burn list' click on **Import 'Fiona's Party'** to add all the tracks to the burn list. Click on **Start burn** – a status bar displays during the burn process. When it is finished, your CD will be ejected and is ready to play.

Shedding skins

Windows Media Player lets you radically alter its appearance. From the **View** menu select **Skin chooser**. A list of different 'skins' will appear, each replacing the standard buttons and sliders with a themed look. When you find a skin that you like, click on **Apply Skin** and the program will reclothe itself – maybe in rather a surprising way!

Burn options

To set burn options, click on the **Burn options** icon (left) then on **More burn options** from the drop-down list. For example, you can select options to 'Automatically eject the disc after burning' or 'Burn CD without gaps' for smoother playing.

Digitise records and tapes

Learn how to digitise and clean up your old music collection

While they may hold some of your most treasured musical memories, cassette and vinyl recordings are delicate and do not last long. Unless you take great care, records get scratched, tapes stretch or get chewed and, before long, some of your old music can become unplayable.

It is possible, however, to record and even restore the quality of some records and tapes by recording them onto your PC. This not only means you can enjoy them for longer, but you can actually improve their sound quality by removing some of the annoying hisses, pops and crackles associated with tapes and LPs.

This project will help you to breathe life into your old music collection. The memories linked to tapes and records consigned to the attic will soon come flooding back!

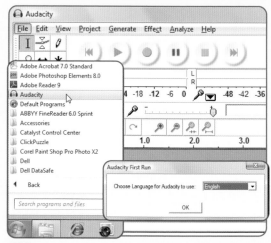

Download the Audacity software from http://audacity.sourceforge.net/ download. Select the appropriate system from the 'Stable' box.

BEFORE YOU START

1 Having connected your audio equipment (see page 239), click on the **Start** button, choose **All Programs** and then select **Audacity**. You may be asked to choose a language. Select **English** and click on **OK**. The program will launch, displaying a grey control box. You can amend the size of the box by clicking and dragging on the sides.

Other programs include Magix Audio at www.magix.com/uk and LP Recorder at www.cfbsoftware.com. Some programs have free trials, while others must be bought.

OTHER PROGRAMS

2 Now set up Audacity to record your tapes or records. Click on **Edit** and select **Preferences** at the bottom of the list. Click on the **Audio I/O** tab and, under 'Playback', select **Speakers** in the 'Device' drop-down box. Under 'Recording', select **Line In** in the 'Device' box.

3 You can choose whether you would like to record in stereo. Under the **Audio I/O** tab, select **2 (Stereo)** from the 'Channels' drop-down menu. If you would like to hear the music as it is being recorded, tick the box next to **Software Playthrough**. Click on **OK**.

4 Before you start recording your tape or record, set up a new Audacity project. Click on the **File** menu and select **Save Project As**. Add a file name and choose where you would like to save your project, and then click on **Save**.

Connecting your audio equipment

Your record deck or cassette recorder may have 'Line-level' outputs (**1**), which carry a signal of sufficient strength to be recorded properly. If so, you can connect a cable directly to your PC's soundcard – look for the 'Line-in' socket (**4**) on the back of your PC. If not, you will need to connect first to an amplifier or preamp (**2**) using standard phono connectors, then connect a cable from your amplifier (**3**) to your PC (**4**). You will need a cable with two phono plugs at one end (for the Audio Out connectors on the amp) and a single stereo mini-jack (for the soundcard's Line-in socket) at the other.

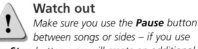

Watch out
*Make sure you use the **Pause** button between songs or sides – if you use the **Stop** button, you will create an additional Audacity track, making it difficult to edit later.*

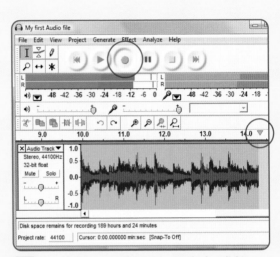

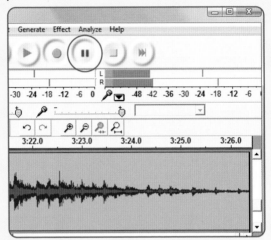

5 Now begin recording your tracks by clicking on the **Record** button (red circle) and starting your player. A red line with an arrow at the top starts to move across the screen, leaving a purple bar indicating the volume of the recording.

6 At the end of each track or, if recording a whole album, at the end of each side, click on the **Pause** button (two vertical bars). When you are ready to add another track, or side, click on the **Pause** button again to continue recording.

7 When you have added all the material you want, click on the **Stop** button (yellow square). Go to the **File** menu and select **Save Project** to add your recording to the project you created in step 4.

Clean up first

Before you start an electronic clean-up, remove any physical dirt you can see on the record or cassette tape as well as the player. Cassette player head cleaners are simple to use and effective. Consider replacing the stylus on your record deck. If you are still unhappy, a better-quality connecting cable makes a big difference.

Vinyl records can be washed in warm water with a mild detergent. Try to avoid wetting the label too much. After washing the record, rinse it in warm running water and then dry thoroughly using a soft, lint-free cloth.

Make a test recording

Audacity's automatic settings will often do the job for you, but it is a good idea to make some test recordings first and get used to the functions available. After a preliminary listen, you may find that you need to adjust the input settings or tweak the treble and bass controls on your amplifier.

Watch out

If you have recorded in stereo, make sure that you click and drag over both bars or you will only cut one element of your recording.

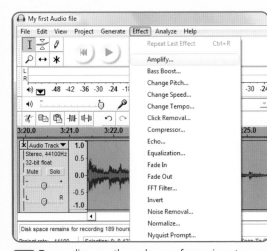

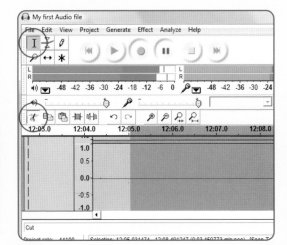

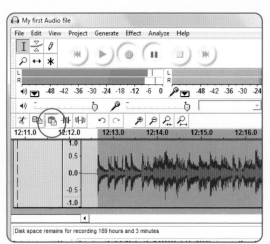

8 Depending on the volume of your input, you may find it helpful to amplify the project – this will make it easier to see where there are silent areas on your recording. Select all by holding down the **Ctrl** key and pressing **A**. Then go to the **Effect** menu and click on **Amplify**. In the dialogue box that appears, click on **OK**.

9 You may find that you have long gaps in your recording. To cut them out, first click on the **Selection Tool** on the toolbar. You can now click and hold down your left-mouse button and drag across the 'silent' area to select it. Now click on the **Cut** button.

10 Go through your whole recording, repeating the process in step 9 until all long silences have been removed. You can also re-order your recording by selecting the whole track and clicking on the **Cut** button. Select a new location on the Audacity timeline and then click on **Paste**.

Do not break the law

Always stay on the right side of the law by respecting the copyright of others. Making a single copy of a recording that you have paid for, for personal use only, is generally tolerated by record companies, although it is a bit of a grey area. Making any copy for any purpose is, strictly speaking, an offence under UK law.

Watch out

In Click Removal, do not make your Threshold and Spike width selections too sensitive as this could harm your recording as a whole.

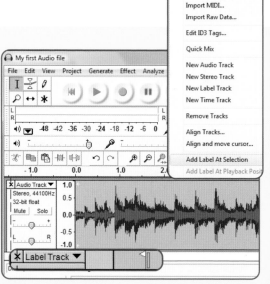

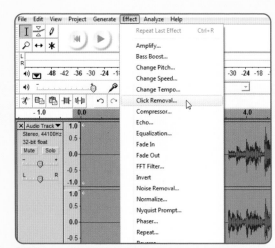

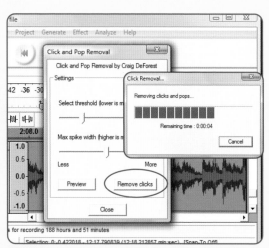

11 Audacity can also remove some of the background noise associated with tapes and records. Select your whole track by holding down the **Ctrl** key and pressing **A**. Go to the **Effect** menu and select **Click Removal**.

12 The 'threshold' slider will adjust the sensitivity of the noise detection, while the 'spike width' slider will change the length of the noise required before any modifications are applied. Alter the settings, or leave them at the preset values, and then click on the **Remove clicks** button.

13 Your recording is currently one long track, so you may like to split it into individual songs. Click on the recording line at the point where the first song starts. Go to the **Project** menu and select **Add Label At Selection**. A red flag appears with a small box ready for you to input text.

Noise removal

The 'Remove Clicks' function in Audacity is particularly useful if you are recording from old LPs. A further function is 'Noise Removal', although it will always remove some of the music with the noise. Make a selection by clicking and dragging – or select all by holding down the **Ctrl** key and pressing **A** – and then go to the **Effect** menu. Click on **Noise Removal**. In the dialogue box, click on **Remove Noise**. It is worth having a few trial runs to get used to how this function works, but it can really help to clean up older cassettes and LPs.

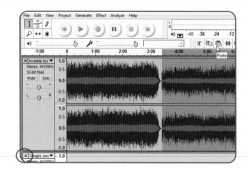

Joining tracks together

If you have stopped and restarted your recording, rather than using the Pause button, you will have created two Audacity tracks and will not be able to use the labelling function. To join the two Audacity tracks together, select the second track by clicking in its **Track Panel** (by the Mute and Solo buttons). Click on the **Cut** button. Now click in the white space at the end of the first track and click on the **Paste** button. Your first track now holds your whole recording. Delete the second track by clicking on the **[X]** at the top left of its Track Panel.

Watch out
If you edit your recording after adding labels, you may end up with labels in the wrong places. Try to complete your editing before naming the tracks.

Watch out
*If you have not named tracks, or only have one track, you cannot choose Export Multiple. Go to the **File** menu and select **Export As WAV**.*

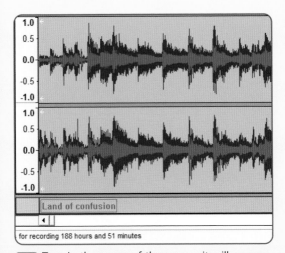

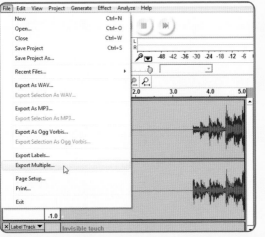

14 Type in the name of the song – it will appear underneath your first track. Now click at the start of your second track, and add a new label. Go through the entire recording, adding labels and naming the tracks as you go. If the label name does not appear, click on the box to select it and then try again.

15 When you have finished editing and naming your tracks, you need to export the recording as an audio file that you can either play on your computer or burn to a CD. To export all of your named tracks in one go, click on the **File** menu and select **Export Multiple**.

16 In the Export Multiple dialogue box, select **WAV** from the 'Export format' drop-down box. Click on **Choose** to select a location to save your files – it is probably best to select your Music folder. Click on **Export**. The Export Multiple confirmation box will tell you how many files have been exported. Click on **OK**.

Choosing file types

The most common formats for exporting music files are .wav, .aiff and .mp3. The best-quality files are .wav and .aiff but they will take up far more disc space than .mp3 – the file type used by small portable music players, such as iPods. If you intend to burn your recording to a CD, you should choose .wav when you export in Audacity. If you would like to use the files on your iPod, choose .mp3. As the project has been saved you can always export the file twice and get the most from both types of file.

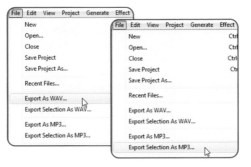

Shortcut
Media Player will automatically search the internet for an album that matches yours – if it finds one, it will add the track information and even the original album cover.

17 To test the success of your digital recording, go to the **Start** button, click on **All Programs** and select **Windows Media Player**. Windows Media Player will automatically open, displaying the contents of the folder you saved your project in. Your new files will be at the bottom of the list.

18 To listen to a track click on your new 'album' in the middle pane, then on a track in the right pane. Make sure your speakers are connected and switched on and click on the **Play** button. Use the controls either side of the play button to fast forward, pause and stop.

19 Your exported tracks can now be customised. Double-click on the album icon in the middle pane then right-click on a track and select **Edit** from the drop-down menu. Now add an album cover of your choice – find an image you like (from your 'Pictures' folder, for example) and then right-click on it. Select **Copy** from the drop-down menu.

Let Media Player entertain you

You can use your PC as more than a music player as Media Player can add moving art to your music. Click on the **Now Playing** tab and the screen will fill with imagery that moves in time to the music. To change the selection click on **Now Playing** again and hover over **Visualisations**. Click on one of the options next to **Alchemy**, **Bars and Waves** or **Battery** to change the appearance. Keep choosing until you find one you like, then sit back and relax!

Windows Media skins

Give your Media Player a new look by applying a skin. You can select a skin from the standard set or download new ones from the internet. To apply a skin, click **View** menu, then on **Skin Chooser**. In the skins list, click the skin you want and a preview of the skin appears. Click on **Apply Skin**. Now you can explore how the skin works and what it can do.

Bright idea
If you have recorded an old album that Media Player has not found, search the internet for the original album cover and paste it onto the file you have created on your PC.

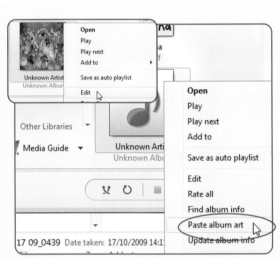

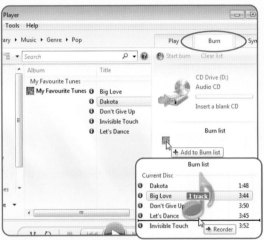

20 Go back to the Library and navigate to the new album. Right-click on it and select **Paste album art** from the menu. The new image will appear as your album cover. Right-click on the album name – currently 'Unknown' – and select **Edit**. Add your own album name.

21 You can now assemble your recorded tracks in order to burn a CD. Click on the **Burn** tab and click on each of your tracks in turn and drag them into the Burn list. To re-order the list, just click on the track and drag it to the new location. A horizontal line shows where it will be positioned. Release the mouse key.

22 Insert a blank CD in your CD drive. Ensure you have all the tracks you want and in the correct order in the Burn list. Now click on the **Start burn** button. A progress bar displays during the burn process. When finished, the CD will eject and you can enjoy your old music in its new format.

Create an album cover

Using the templates available from Microsoft Word, you can create a unique album cover for your new CD. Connect to the internet and then launch Microsoft Word by going to the **Start** menu, clicking on **All Programs** and then on **Microsoft Office Word 2007**. Click on **Templates** and type **CD cover** in the Search bar and press **Return**. Scroll through the list and click on a template to choose it. Click on the **Download** button to save it to your desktop where you can open and then edit it.

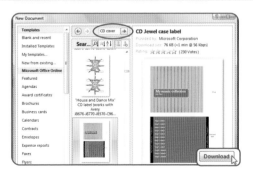

Collect music online

Find, buy, store **and** manage **your favourite** sounds online

The Apple program iTunes is a jukebox and online music store in one. It can hold your entire music collection, so there is no more hunting around the house for a particular CD or trips to the music megastore to buy the latest album. Simply connect to the iTunes Store and you can download the songs you want to hear – as well as movies, audiobooks, TV shows, podcasts and games. Then you can create your own compilations with music playlists to match your mood.

With so much music available online, choosing the right songs, and making sense of your existing collection, can be daunting prospects. This is where the iTunes Genius feature comes in. It recommends new songs and artists for you to try, and also creates playlists based on the music you have already in your iTunes library.

*Download the iTunes software free from www.apple.com/uk/itunes/. Click the **Download iTunes** button and follow the instructions to install.*

BEFORE YOU START

1 Double-click the iTunes shortcut icon on your desktop to open the program. The first time you launch iTunes you will be prompted to accept the licence agreement (see 'Know the law', page 247). Click on **Agree**. Then, if it is not already selected, click on **iTunes Store** on the left-hand panel to display the store in the main window.

Creating an iTunes Store account

To buy songs, TV shows or videos through iTunes you need to set up a new account. Open iTunes, select **Store** from the top menu, then **Create Account** and follow the onscreen instructions. You will need to fill in your email address, password, password verification, and secret question and answer, where prompted. You will also need to have your credit card or bank card details on hand to enable payment.

Shortcut
When you download iTunes from the Apple site, a shortcut icon will be added automatically to your desktop for easy launching of the software.

Key word
*Podcast A contraction of the words **iPod** and **broadcast**, a podcast is a digital sound file that can be downloaded, using free software such as iTunes, and played on a computer or MP3 player.*

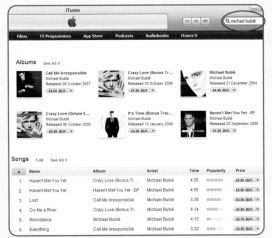

2 Here you can browse through the latest releases – of music, videos and TV shows. On the right you can see which songs are topping the download charts. Sign in to your iTunes music store account by clicking **Sign In** on the black menu bar in the top right-hand corner. Enter your details in the pop-up window and click **Sign In**.

3 If there is a particular song or artist you are looking for, the easiest way to find them is to use the 'Search Store' box in the top right corner of the screen. Enter in the box the name of the musician, band, song or album you want to find – here Michael Bublé – then press **Return**. Matching items are displayed under 'Albums' then 'Songs'.

4 Scroll down the results page, to view Music Videos, iPhone Apps, Podcasts and Podcast Episodes. To view just the song titles, click on **Music** in the FILTER BY MEDIA TYPE panel. Now you will see the albums at the top, individual songs underneath and links to Michael Bublé, and others, in the 'Artists' section below.

Know the law
When launching Apple iTunes for the first time you will see a window displaying the 'iTunes Software License Agreement', explaining the uses and restrictions related to accessing iTunes. Read the agreement and then click on **Agree** to start using the software. If you are unsure and want to read the agreement at a later time, click on **Save** to store a copy. If you disagree with the licence, click on **Decline** – this will close the window and close the software.

Watch out
*When you click **Buy** to purchase your music, the credit card you registered when you set up your Apple account is immediately charged.*

Bright idea
You can manage your family's iTunes collection by copying purchases between computers in your home – this is called 'Home Sharing'. You can set iTunes to copy automatically new purchases or you can choose which items to copy.

5 To 'sample' a track, double-click on it to listen to a 30 second preview. Do not worry – this will not commit you to buying the track. A window at the top displays the title of the track that is playing, with a progress bar below. The figure to the right of the bar shows you how much playing time remains.

6 For more information, select an album and click the cover picture. The individual tracks are listed with their playing time. A blue bar chart shows their relative popularity according to previous purchases. In the left panel is an overall rating based on customer reviews, which you can read in the main window, to the right.

7 Decide what you want to purchase and click on **£0.99 BUY** (or similar) to the right of the individual track. To buy the whole album, click the **£1.99 Buy Album** (or similar) button in the left panel. In the message box that pops up, click on **Buy** to confirm your purchase and automatically download it to your iTunes library.

Keeping up to date

Apple iTunes software is continually being updated – adding new features and embellishing existing ones. You will be prompted when a new version becomes available, but you can check for yourself. Click on **Help**, from the menu bar at the top of the screen, then on **Check for Updates** from the drop-down menu.

Help
iTunes Help
iTunes Tutorials
Keyboard Shortcuts
iPod Help
iPhone Help
iPad Help
Apple TV Help
Apple Service and Support
Provide iTunes Feedback
Check for Updates
Run Diagnostics...

Syncing with your iPod

You can synchronise, or sync, the music on the iTunes library with your iPod, so you can listen to your favourite music on the go. By default iTunes syncs with the iPod automatically each time you connect it to your PC – you can change your iTunes preferences to add items manually if you prefer. Plug the iPod into your PC using the USB cable provided and the synchronisation begins. When this has finished, a message (left) appears in the panel at the top of the iTunes window. Click on the **Safely Remove Hardware and Eject Media** icon (left), on the right of your task bar, then on **Eject Apple iPod USB Device**.

iTunes
iPod sync is complete.
Eject before disconnecting.

Open Devices and Printers
Eject Apple iPod USB Device
· FIONA'S IPOD (1)

Bright idea
Once you start buying from iTunes, you will see Genius Recommendations on the home page for 'Albums', 'Songs' and other sections. These are suggestions of similar products you might like. Initially these may not match your interests too closely, but as you purchase more from the store they will be more finely tuned to your tastes.

Key word
Playlist A collection of tracks grouped together by a theme. It may be songs by the same group or artist, or ones that match a particular type of music or mood. Apple has created a few to start you off, with playlists of 'Recently Added' songs and '90s Music'.

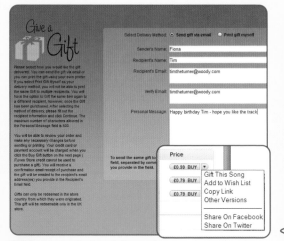

8 Alternatively, click on the arrow to the right of either **£1.99 Buy Album** (or similar) or **£0.99 BUY** (or similar) and select from the drop-down menu. To give your purchase as a present, click on **Gift This Song** and fill in the details in the form that appears. Or, click on **Add to Wish List** to purchase the album or track later.

9 Once downloaded, add the music to your own custom playlist. Click the plus sign **+** at the bottom-left of the screen. A new 'untitled playlist' is added under 'PLAYLISTS'. Type a name for it – here **Romantic** – and press **Return**. Click on **Purchased**, under 'STORE', right-click on the track and select **Add to Playlist**, then **Romantic**.

10 Based on the music you already have and love, iTunes Genius (see below) can help you to discover new music. Click **Music** in the LIBRARY panel, left, and select a track from the middle pane. The Genius Sidebar suggests 'Top Albums' that are relevant to your song and 'Top Songs' by the same artist that are not in your library.

A touch of Genius
You need to set up iTunes Genius before you use it for the first time (see step 10). Click on **Store**, at the top of the iTunes window, and then on **Turn On Genius**. The Genius menu will appear in the left-hand panel with details in the main window. Click the **Turn On Genius** button in the

main window. On the next screen, sign in to your iTunes account and click **Continue**. Agree to the terms and conditions and click **Continue** again. Apple will then look at your musical tastes in your iTunes library and compare it with information from other iTunes users to deliver the Genius results.

Genius playlists
Genius uses the collective intelligence of iTunes users to create great-sounding playlists based on your existing music. Choose a track you want to use as the basis for your Genius playlist and click the **Start Genius** button at the bottom right of the window. 'Genius' playlist appears on the left, with the tracks listed in the middle.

Learning to read music

Let your computer teach you the principles of musical notation

You do not have to read music to compose it on your computer, and it is not necessary to know the names of individual notes to be able to play them or compose a tune. But, as you become more confident and proficient at composition you may want to learn to read music. If so, a range of specialist software is available to help you.

This project uses a program called Music Ace. Aimed at the complete novice, it teaches notation through easy-to-follow lessons and related games. You will also be given the opportunity to test your knowledge by composing simple tunes. Much of the other educational music software available will follow the same basic principles.

Check that your computer meets the minimum system requirements of the program before you install the software onto your hard disk.

▶ BEFORE YOU START

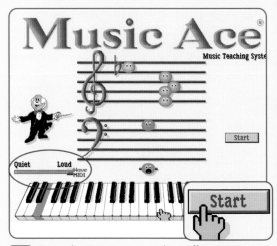

1 Go to the **Start** menu, select **All Programs** then click on your music software. The opening screen of 'Music Ace' contains musical notes playing a tune. Adjust the volume using the slide bar on the left of the screen. To begin, click on the **Start** button.

A wide range of music education programs – for all levels – can be sampled and downloaded from the internet. A good starting place is the Hitsquad Musician Network website at www.hitsquad.com/smm.

▶ OTHER PROGRAMS

Try before you buy

Music Ace software can be downloaded from www.harmonicvision.com. Here you have the choice of four versions – we have used the basic version, Music Ace. On the home page click on **About**, which takes you to a page specifying the system requirements, description of lessons and other useful product information. In the panel on the left, click on **Free Demo** to download a free demo of the latest version. Fill in the registration form, click on **Submit** and follow the on-screen prompts to download the software.

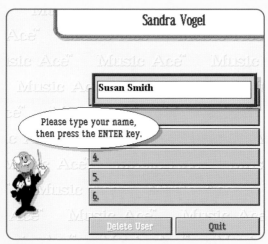

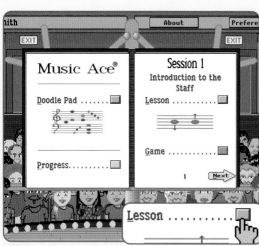

2 A little 'music maestro' will guide you through each stage of the program. Click in the first box, type your name then press the **Enter** key. Music Ace can accommodate several users, and it uses the names to keep track of each user's progress.

3 You are now presented with the Main Screen, through which you choose whether to use the Doodle Pad (a music creation tool), follow a lesson or play a music game related to the lesson. To start a lesson click on the **Lesson** button.

4 Lesson 1 deals with basic music notation. An animated tutorial teaches you about the positioning of notes. After the tutorial you will be asked questions – click on the appropriate button to respond. Continue the exercises to the end of the lesson.

Set your preferences

The screen where you elect to start a lesson or play a game also contains a Preferences button. Click on this to customise the way Music Ace works.

One set of choices, the Maestro Options, allows you to set the way in which on-screen help is delivered by the cartoon character, Maestro Max. If you wish, turn his voice or speech balloons off.

Use the Control Bar

Every lesson has a Control Bar running across the top of the screen. This provides access to basic options and settings.

To end the current lesson and return to the Main Screen click on the **Menu** button. The button to its right shows the name of the current lesson. To change the volume click on the **Vol** button. To move forwards or backwards in each lesson click on the **Skip** buttons. Click on the **Pause** button to stop the lesson at the current point (the button then changes to **Resume**). To go straight to the game that relates to the lesson, click on the **Game** button.

| Menu | 1. Introduction to the Staff | Vol | ◄◄ Skip | Pause II | Skip ►► | Game |

Watch out

*Be aware that if you click on the **Skip** buttons to move forwards or backwards within a game your score will be set to zero.*

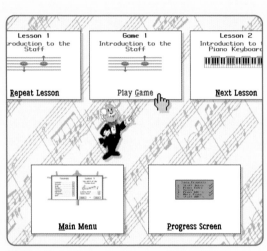

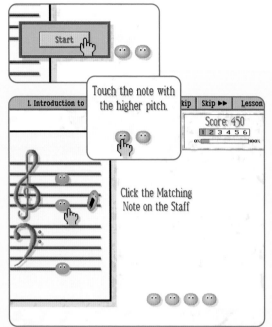

5 When a lesson ends you will be offered several options: to repeat the lesson, go to the main menu, check your progress, try the next lesson or play the related game. To play the game, click on the **Play Game** button.

6 The game will encourage you to practise what you have learned in the lesson. To begin, click on the **Start** button and follow the on-screen instructions. As you complete sections of the game your score will be displayed in the top right-hand corner of the screen.

7 When the game has finished you can choose the next lesson, another game, repeat the previous lesson or game, or view your progress. Alternatively, go to the Doodle Pad to try out what you have learned so far. Click on the **Main Menu**, then on the **Doodle Pad** button.

Assessing your progress

The lessons in Music Ace are broken down into sections. An indicator in the top right-hand corner of the screen shows you how far you have progressed through your current lesson. Completed sections are shown in green; the section you are currently working on is in red.

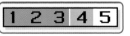

Choosing lessons

You may not want to complete lessons or games in sequence – you may want to select specific ones to work on particular areas. You can do this from the Main Menu. Click on the **Next** arrow on the lesson page to leaf through the range of lessons available. When you find the one you want, click on the **Lesson** or **Game** button to access it.

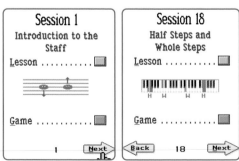

Key word

Staff *This describes the group of five lines on which notes are placed. Depending on where they are placed, the pitch of the note will change.*

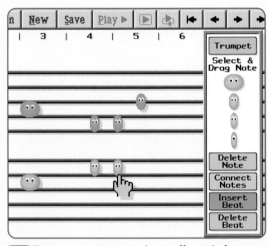

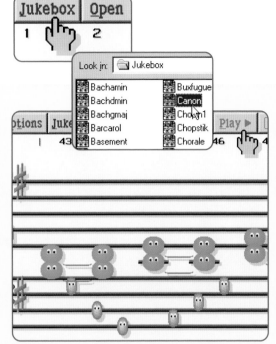

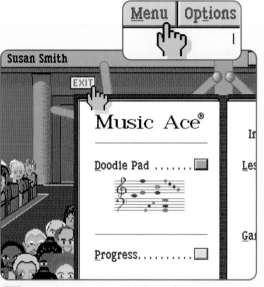

8 To move a note onto the 'staff' ready for playing, select and drag it from the box on the right of the screen. Move notes on the staff by dragging them. Each note plays as you move it. To hear your tune, click on the **Play** button on the Control Bar.

9 Music Ace has a library of songs for you to listen to and edit. To open one in the Doodle Pad, click on the Control Bar's **Jukebox** button, then double-click on a song. Click on **Play** to hear it. Edit it by moving its notes on the staff and adding new notes.

10 To end your session, click on the **Menu** button on the Control Bar, then on one of the **Exit** buttons in the Main Menu. The next time you run Music Ace, click on your name from the user list – Music Ace will remind you of your progress.

Using the Doodle Pad

To change the instrument you have chosen to compose with, click on the instrument name at the top of the box on the right of the screen. Each time you click, a different instrument name will appear – Oboe, Marimba, Trumpet, Jazz Guitar, Clarinet and Grand Piano. Stop on the instrument you want and all notes you create thereafter will sound like that instrument, and will appear in a different colour.

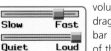

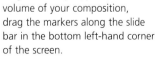

To adjust the length of a note on the staff, first delete the note (click on **Delete Note** in the box on the right of the screen then click on the note). Next, click on one of the four different note sizes and drag it onto the staff.

To change the tempo (speed) and volume of your composition, drag the markers along the slide bar in the bottom left-hand corner of the screen.

Family budget planner

Take control **of your** household's incomings **and** outgoings

Keeping track of your household budget makes good financial sense. You can keep an eye on day-to-day outgoings and also see when major expenses, such as a family holiday, lie ahead and make provision for them in good time.

One of the best ways to take care of your home accounts is with a spreadsheet program. A spreadsheet will allow you to create a set of professional-looking accounts that are easy to use – all the calculations are done for you. Once you have set up your household accounts document, you simply type in your income and expenses, and the spreadsheet updates your balances automatically.

This project is geared towards household accounts, but its structure can be used for a business accounts spreadsheet, too.

> *Gather together all the information you are going to need to create your spreadsheet. Keep details of all your income and expenditure to hand.*
>
> ► **BEFORE YOU START**

1 Go to the **Start** button, select **All Programs** and click on **Microsoft Office** then on **Microsoft Excel 2010**. To save your new document, go to the **File** tab and select **Save As**. Select a suitable folder and type in a file name, then click on **Save**.

> *You can create a budget planner in Microsoft Works. Go to the **Start** menu, click on **Microsoft Works** and then click on **Works Spreadsheet** from the 'Quick Launch' menu on the right.*
>
> ► **OTHER PROGRAMS**

You can type in text in capital letters using the Caps Lock key. Press it down before you start typing, then press it again when you have finished.

Balance carried over

Add a 'Balance carried over' row to transfer credits or debits from the previous month.

Shortcut
*To style all your section headings in the same way at the same time, hold down the **Ctrl** key and click on each of the headings in turn. Now style as usual.*

2 Click on cell **D1** and type in the heading of your spreadsheet. Click on cell **A4** and type in 'INCOME'. Click on the cells below 'INCOME' in column A and type in your sources. When you have finished, click on the cell two rows below your last entry and type in 'Total'.

3 Click on the cell two rows below 'Total' and type in 'EXPENDITURE'. Type your areas of expense in the cells below. Where appropriate, type in 'Total Household Expenditure'. You may also want to include an 'ADDITIONAL EXPENDITURE' section. Finish with 'OUTSTANDING BALANCE'.

4 To style your heading, click on cell **D1** then with the 'Home' tab selected go to the 'Font' group and click on the **Bold** button. Click on the arrow beside the font size box, scroll through and select a font size, here 18. Continue to style the rest of your text in the same way.

Changing format

When you enter data into a spreadsheet, its style is determined by the format of the cell you are entering it into. Formats can be altered by clicking on the cell and then clicking on the Font dialogue box launcher. In the Format Cells dialogue box, click on the **Font** tab, then select a font, font size, style and colour from the options.

Inserting new data

To insert a new row of expenses or income, click on the blue numbered box of the row below where you would like your new one to be placed. Click on the **Home** tab, go to the 'Cells' group and click on **Insert**. A new row will then appear above the row you initially clicked on.

To adjust the width of a column, place the mouse pointer over the right-hand edge of the blue column header. When it becomes a double-headed arrow, press the left mouse button and, keeping it pressed down, drag the column edge to the desired width.

If the range of cells that AutoSum selects is incorrect, use the mouse to highlight the correct group of cells and press Return.

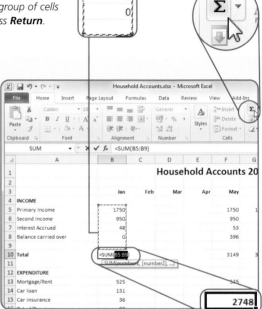

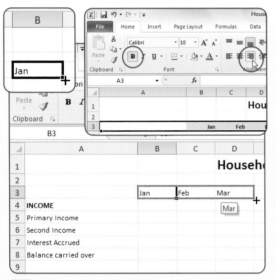

5 Adjust column widths (see top), then type 'Jan' in cell B3. Place the mouse pointer in the lower right-hand corner of B3. When it becomes a cross, click and drag to the right. The months appear in these cells. Select the row, then go to the 'Alignment' group and click on the **Bold** and **Align Right** buttons.

6 Starting in cell B5, and continuing in the cells below, enter the figures for all your income and expenditure for the month of January. In cells where there is no amount to enter, type in a zero.

7 To calculate January's total income, click on the relevant cell in column B, then click on the **AutoSum** button in the 'Editing' group. A formula appears, indicating the range of cells to add up. If the range is correct, press **Return**. Do the same for the total expenditure and additional expenditure cells.

Split the screen and freeze panes

Windows allows you to split the screen to make it easier to view figures across different columns and rows. Click on the **View** tab and in the 'Windows' group click on **Split**. Place your mouse pointer over the blue 'split' line you want to move. When it changes appearance to a double-headed arrow, hold down the left mouse button and drag the line to the desired position. You can scroll through each part of the split screen separately.

You can also freeze a pane, allowing you to select a section of data that remains static when scrolling in a sheet. For example, you may wish to keep the row and column headings visible as you scroll. Click on the **View** tab and in the 'Windows' group click on **Freeze Panes**, then select one of the three preset options. Select **Freeze Panes, Unfreeze Panes** to undo the action.

Calculating spreadsheet data can be complicated. Using Works' in-built calculation tools makes it much easier. For further help, see page 31.

▶ CALCULATING YOUR DATA

For further help, see page 31.

Shortcut
To save yourself typing in cell references to the formula in the Entry Bar, click on the relevant cell at the appropriate point in the calculation. Excel and Works automatically enter the cell reference into the formula.

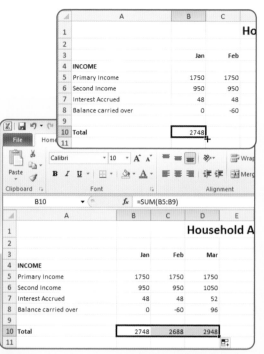

	A	B	C
1			Ho
2			
3		Jan	Feb
4	INCOME		
5	Primary Income	1750	1750
6	Second Income	950	950
7	Interest Accrued	48	48
8	Balance carried over	0	-60
9			
10	Total	2748	
11			

SUM =B10-B30-B38

	A	B	C	D	E
32	ADDITIONAL EXPENDITURE				
33	Entertainment	400			
34	Clothes	150			
35	Holidays	200		-60	
36	Savings & Investment	270			
37					
38	Total Additional Expenditure	1020			
39					
40	OUTSTANDING BALANCE	=B10-B30-B38			
41					
42					

8 To calculate January's Outstanding Balance, click on the relevant cell, then enter the formula shown above in the Entry Bar to subtract Total expenditure from your Total income. Type an '=' sign, then use cell references and minus signs to subtract expenses from income. Press **Return**.

SUM =B40

	A	B	C	D	E
1				Household	
2					
3		Jan	Feb	Mar	A
4	INCOME				
5	Primary Income	1750	1750	1750	17
6	Second Income	950	950	950	9
7	Interest Accrued	48	48		
8	Balance carried over	0	=B40		
9					
10	Total	2748		-60	

9 Type in figures for February. To carry over January's balance, click in the relevant cell (here, cell C8) then type an '=' sign, followed by the cell reference for January's Outstanding Balance. Press **Return**. Now you are ready to calculate totals for the year.

B10 fx =SUM(B5:B9)

	A	B	C	D	E
1				Household A	
2					
3		Jan	Feb	Mar	
4	INCOME				
5	Primary Income	1750	1750	1750	
6	Second Income	950	950	1050	
7	Interest Accrued	48	48	52	
8	Balance carried over	0	-60	96	
9					
10	Total	2748	2688	2948	
11					

10 Place the mouse pointer over the lower right-hand corner of the cell that holds January's Total income (here, B10). When it becomes a cross, click and drag to the right. The formula is copied to all the other months. Repeat for other totals.

Using Excel's templates

You can if you wish use one of the many budget planner templates available from the Microsoft Office online resource. Go to the **Start** menu, click on **All Programs** and select **Microsoft Excel 2010**. Click on **New**, then under 'Office.com Templates' select **Budgets**, **Home Budgets**, to view a selection of template thumbnails. Select a template and click on **Download**.

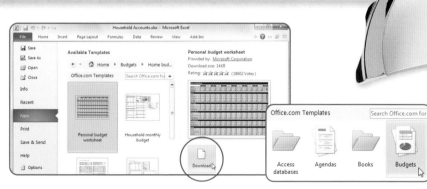

Home Contents - Fix&Fittings			
Item Type	Description	Value	Where Store
Electrical	Sharp Microwave 700w	£300.00	Kitchen
Electrical	Panasonic 26" Television	£300.00	Lounge
Electrical	BT Answerphone	£175.00	Hall
Electrical	Zeus Aquarium	£800.00	Hall
Electrical	Bose Clock Radio	£27.00	Bedroom
Electrical	Sony Video Recorder	£300.00	Lounge
Electrical	Fridge	£200.00	Kitchen
Electrical	Freezer	£375.00	Kitchen
Electrical	Kenwood Food Processor	£129.00	Kitchen
Electrical	Siebart Cooker	£400.00	Lounge
Electrical	Technic Music System	£900.00	Study
Electrical	Sony Desktop Computer	£1,500.00	Study
Electrical	Digital Camera	£400.00	
		SUM: £5,806.00	
Furniture	Two-seat Sofa	£400.00	Lounge
Furniture	Oak Table & Six Chairs	£600.00	Dining Room
Furniture	Painting - Dali Sketch	£5,000.00	Lounge
Furniture	Grandfather Clock	£6,000.00	Hall
Furniture	Vase	£900.00	Hall
Furniture	Persian Rug	£750.00	Bedroom
Furniture	Sleepeze Double Bed	£500.00	Bedroom
Furniture	Silent Night Single Bed	£300.00	Bedroom
Furniture	Silent Night Double Bed	£350.00	Bedroom
Furniture	Ikea Dressing Table	£275.00	Bedroom
Furniture	Ikea Coffee Table	£120.00	Lounge
		SUM: £15,195.00	
		SUM: £21,001.00	

Catalogue and value your home contents

Save time and money by keeping a record of your possessions

If you have ever had to look for a receipt or guarantee in order to make a claim on a faulty product, you will know how frustrating that search can be. Calculating the value of your household possessions when your contents' insurance needs renewing is just as time-consuming. So do not waste your energy sorting through endless old bills, invoices and receipts every time. Instead, create a database to catalogue your home contents. With it you can record, sort, retrieve and update vital information quickly and easily.

Collect all the information you have about your home contents, such as dates of purchase, values, guarantees and so on.

BEFORE YOU START

1 Go to the **Start** menu, select **All Programs** and **Microsoft Works**, then click on **Microsoft Works Task Launcher**. When Works has opened, click on **Works Database** from the Quick Launch taskbar on the right.

You can also create a database using Microsoft Excel. Use the spreadsheet to type in your headings, and the Filter feature to create your reports.

OTHER PROGRAMS

Shortcut
When recording items, include a serialised reference field. Your PC will automatically assign a number to each item that you enter, so you will not need to type in the numbers yourself.

Key word
Field This is a placeholder that contains a particular category of information stored within a database. Examples of database fields are Name, Address and Telephone Number.

Watch out
Do not lose information from your database – save and name it as soon as you have created it. Save it regularly as you work, and immediately after you make any updates.

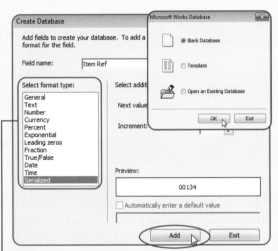

2 In the Microsoft Works Database window **Blank Database** will be selected by default – click on **OK**. In the Create Database dialogue box, input your fields (see top, middle) and specify a format for each one, such as Text or Number (enter the fields and formats listed below). When you have typed in a field, click on the **Add** button.

3 After creating your fields, click on **Done**. The database appears in List form. Click on the **Form Design** toolbar button to customise your database. To move text boxes, click on them and drag; to resize them, drag the bottom right-hand corner or the handles on the side and bottom.

4 Next add a heading. Click at the top of the page and type it in. To style your title, field names or text boxes, click on them, go to the **Format** menu and click on **Font and Style**. Select fonts, sizes, styles and colours in the Font tab. Click the **Alignment** tab and select the Left option.

Fields and formats

Field	Format
Item Ref	Serialized
Item Type	Text
Description	Text
Purchase Date	Date
Value	Number
Product Ref	Text
Guarantee	Text
Where Stored	Text
Purchased	Text

Format style

When you select Number, Date, Time or Fraction as a format, you are given a list of options in the Appearance section. Click on your preferred style.

Set date format:
- 28/11/2009
- 28/11
- 11/2009
- 28 November 2009
- November 2009
- 28 November
- November

Different views

There are four ways to view your database:

List View is best for quick reference as it allows you to view many entries at the same time.

Form View displays one entry at a time and is the best for entering data.

Form Design does not let you enter information; instead it lets you add, delete, move and resize fields, alter font styles and add colours.

Report View allows you to compile selective reports from your database.

Shortcut
*To style several text boxes in the same way at once, select them all by holding down the **Ctrl** key and clicking on each box in turn. Any style change will be applied to all boxes.*

It is possible to extract data for specific reasons. An inventory of fixtures and fittings will be useful should you rent out your property.

MAKING A REPORT

Key word
Report *This is a printed summary of information stored in a database. From your Home Contents database you could make a report on uninsured and insured household items.*

5 To enter data, click on the **Form View** toolbar button. Click on a text box and type in your data. Press the **Tab** key to move to the next field or record, and use the **Shift** and **Tab** keys together to move back a field. Click on the **List View** toolbar button to view your list.

6 To list your furniture and electrical goods, go to the **Tools** menu and select **ReportCreator**. Enter a report name. In the next box click the **Fields** tab. In the 'Fields available' pane, click the fields you want in your report (in the order you want) then click on **Add**. When finished, click on **Next**.

7 Select the Sorting tab. To sort data into similar types, click in the 'Sort by' box and select **Item Type** from the drop-down menu. Group the same item type entries by clicking on the **Grouping** tab and then clicking in the 'When contents change' and 'Show group heading' boxes.

Finding information

To search for specific data, go to the **Edit** menu and click on **Find**. Type in a key word or words for what you want to search for, select the 'All records' option, then click on **OK**. The database view changes to show only those records that match your search. To return to the full database view, go to the **Record** menu, select **Show** and then select **All Records**.

In Form View you can move through entries quickly by clicking on the arrows on either side of the Record counter at the foot of the window.

View Report

Select the report you want to view:

Fixs&Fittings
Insurance
Claim Items

Preview

Modify

*Microsoft Works automatically saves any report that you create. To print or update an old report, go to the **View** menu and click on **Report**. A list of your reports appears. Click on the relevant one then click on **Preview** or **Modify** as appropriate.*

ReportCreator

The report definition has been created.

Do you wish to preview or modify the report definition?

Preview   Modify

Filter Name

Type a name for the filter below:

Fixs&Fittings

OK

Easy Filt

Field name	Comparison
Item Type	contains
or ▾ Item Type	contains
and ▾ (None)	is equal to
and ▾	
and ▾	

Easy Filter   Filter using fo

Comparison	Compare To
contains	Furniture
contains	Electrical

ReportCreator - Fixs&Fittings

Title | Fields | Sorting | Grouping | Filter | Summary

Select a field

Item Ref
Description
Where Stored
Value

☑ Sum
☐ Average
☐ Count
☐ Minimum
☐ Maximum
☐ Standard Deviation
☐ Variance

☑ Show summary name

Display Summary Information

☑ At end of each group   ● Under each column
☑ At end of report   ○ Together in rows

< Previous   Next >   Done   Cancel

Item Type	Description	Where Stored	Value
Electrical			
Electrical	Sharp Microwave 700w	Kitchen	£300.00
Electrical	Panasonic 26" Television	Lounge	£300.00
Electrical	BT Answerphone	Hall	£175.00
Electrical	Zeus Aquarium	Hall	£800.00
Electrical	Bose Clock Radio	Bedroom	£27.00
Electrical	Sony Video Recorder	Lounge	£300.00
Electrical	Fridge	Kitchen	£200.00
Electrical	Freezer	Kitchen	£375.00
Electrical	Kenwood Food Processor	Kitchen	£129.00
Electrical	Siebart Cooker	Kitchen	£400.00
Electrical	Technics Music System	Lounge	£900.00
Electrical	Sony Desktop Computer	Study	£1,500.00
Electrical	Digital Camera	Study	£400.00
		SUM:	£5,806.00
Furniture			
Furniture	Two-seat Sofa	Lounge	£400.00
Furniture	Oak Table & Six Chairs	Dining Room	£600.00
Furniture	Painting - Dali Sketch	Lounge	£5,000.00
Furniture	Grandfather Clock	Hall	£8,000.00
Furniture	Vase	Hall	£900.00
Furniture	Persian Rug	Hall	£750.00

8 Click on the **Filter** tab and then on **Create New Filter**. Next, type in a name and click on **OK**. In the 'Field name' box select **Item Type**; in 'Comparison' select **contains**; in 'Compare To' type 'Furniture'. In the boxes below, select **or**, **Item Type**, **contains** and type 'Electrical'. Click on **OK**.

9 To add up all the figures in your Value field, click on the **Summary** tab, click on **Value** in the 'Select a field' box and then click in the 'Sum' box. In the 'Display Summary Information' section, click the options as shown above. Click on **Done**.

10 A prompt box appears asking whether you want to preview or modify your report. Click on **Modify** if you want to add any styling to your report (see below) or click on **Preview** to view your report. Finally, click on **Print** to print it out.

Reporting in style

To add a professional touch to your reports, adjust the fonts and font sizes, and add colour.

Click on the **Report View** toolbar button. Click in the cell or row you want to style. Go to the **Format** menu and click on **Font and Style**. In the Format dialogue box click the various tabs, selecting fonts, sizes, styles, colours and background patterns as you do so.

If your columns are too close together, adjust their widths. Place the cursor on the right-hand edge of the column heading, hold down the mouse button and drag to the desired width.

Report View

	A	B	C	D
			Home Contents	FixRF
	Item Type	**Description**	**Where Stored**	**Value**
	=Item Type			
	=Item Type	=Description	=Where Stored	=Value
			SUM:	=SUM(Val
			SUM:	=SUM(Val

Profit from your

Make the most of your money by using your

Investment circle

Create a folder called 'Investment circle'. Add sub-folders for each mini-project.

- Investment circle
  - Investors
  - Research
  - Accounts
  - Communications
  - Investments
  - Contacts

Investment circles have taken off around the globe, and the most successful have been known to outperform those of professional fund managers. These circles contain up to 15 people who enjoy making the most of their finances by selecting, purchasing and monitoring their own stocks and shares. They also save money by avoiding management charges.

All this has become possible in recent years because of the computerisation of the world's stock exchanges. People outside the world's financial citadels can act as their own fund managers, using their computers to access and act upon a wealth of up-to-date financial information: stock prices are updated on the internet as soon as they change.

So if you are thinking of playing the markets, make the internet your first stop. There are many sites where you can gather data on companies your group is thinking of investing in. It is easy to find out how your stock has performed, current earnings-to-share ratios, liabilities, assets and profit forecasts. In fact, you can find virtually everything you need to make an informed assessment.

There are many financial news sites listing online share price data,

investment circle

PC as a window on the financial markets

enabling you to track shares you may be interested in or have already purchased. You can then paste downloaded data into your portfolio spreadsheet – and even use it to calculate projections for your share dividends.

Once you have decided on your investments, you have to choose an online broker and open an account. You can then trade shares on the world markets without getting up from your computer.

If you set up an online bank account for your group you can also access your current financial status in a matter of seconds.

With your portfolio in place you can use your PC to administer your investment circle. You could set up

an investors' database to hold relevant information. For example, some members may prefer not to invest in certain industries or countries on ethical grounds.

Create more spreadsheets to monitor members' individual holdings and produce a newsletter to keep everyone informed.

If your group wants to diversify into other areas such as antiques trading, the internet holds much useful data. Sites that carry price guides and tips on authenticity, where to buy and what to look for are easily accessible and will help you to make informed choices. You could also participate in online bidding at some of the world's leading auction houses.

Ideas and inspirations

Adapt the following projects and exercises and then apply them to setting up your own investment circle. You may find that you do not need all of them to get things up and running, so include only the documents you need for your own requirements.

94 Searching the internet
Use search engines to locate online brokers, share price and stock performance information.

272 Build a shares portfolio
Set up a spreadsheet for your investment circle to keep track of your portfolio's performance.

Budget summary - summer pro		
Item	Estimated costs	Actua
Costumes	107.99	
Refreshments	144.24	
Props	98.00	
Printing/publicity	50.00	
Total	400.23	
Item	Estimated revenue	Actua
Refreshments	330.00	
Tickets	2,200.00	
Total	2,530.00	
Balance		

276 Keep your accounts
Use separate worksheets in a spreadsheet to keep track of individual and group holdings.

168 Create a newsletter
Produce performance updates for your group. If other members are online, email it to them.

154 Write a formal letter
Keep it professional, if you need to send a formal letter to, say, request a prospectus.

Prepare to invest

- Recruit members and agree aims, level of investment and club rules
- Appoint club officers and outline their responsibilities
- Research and select an online broker
- Open a club bank account and agree the signatories
- Set up online banking facilities
- Produce copies of initial research material for members

Also worth considering ...

If you have used most of the above to form your investment circle, you may want to refine it further.

322 Membership database
Create a record of members' details and notes on any investment preferences.

BB8652102

Calculate your bills

Keep track of your spending to help to predict future bills

A spreadsheet is ideal for keeping track of the amount you spend on household bills – and it can help you to estimate and plan for future bills. Not only can you enter details about utilities, such as gas and electricity, but you can also enter expenses that crop up once a year, such as breakdown cover and club subscriptions. These are often the bills that get overlooked.

With the spreadsheet program in Excel you can also create a pie chart to analyse your expenses. This gives a useful visual guide to spending and can help you to spot financial 'black holes' that are eating up your money.

Collect up your most recent bills, and make a note of any regular household expenses for which you have no documentation.

BEFORE YOU START

1 Click on the **Start** button, select **All Programs** and click on **Microsoft Excel 2010**. Save and name the new spreadsheet by clicking on the **Save** button on the Quick Access toolbar. You will need to select a folder to save it in and type a name into the 'File name' box. Click on **Save**.

*You can create similar spreadsheets in Microsoft Works. Open Works, then choose **Works Spreadsheet** from the 'Quick Launch' menu on the right.*

OTHER PROGRAMS

Watch out
You are in danger of losing your work if you do not save it regularly. Make a habit of saving the changes to your spreadsheet every few minutes.

Shortcut
To style several cells in the same way at the same time, press the **Ctrl** *key and, keeping it pressed down, click on each cell in turn. Style as usual.*

	A	E	F	G
1		Household Bill Calculator		
2	Bills			
3				
4	Rent			
5	Loan			
6	Phone			
7	TV			
8	Council Tax			
9	Water			
10	Gas			
11	Electricity			
12	Credit Card			
13	Car Insurance			
14				
15	Total			

2 Click in cell **E1** and type in your heading. In cell **A2** type in 'Bills'; in cell **A4** type in your first type of bill. Enter the different types of bill in the cells below. When you have finished your list, click in the cell two rows below the last entry and type in 'Total'.

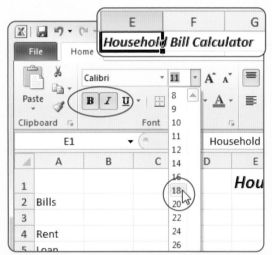

3 To style your heading, click in cell **E1** then on the **Bold** and **Italic** buttons in the 'Font' group. Click on the arrow beside the font size box and select a size. Style the rest of your entries, then adjust the width of column A to fit your text (see below, right).

4 Type 'Jan' in cell **B2**. Place the mouse pointer in the lower right-hand corner of the cell. When it changes to a black cross, click and drag along row 2 to reveal the other months, until you reach 'Dec'. Release the mouse button, then click on the **Bold** button in the 'Font' group to style your months of the year.

Inserting new data

To add a new bill, click on the blue numbered box of the row below where the new one is to be placed. Go to the 'Cells' group and click on the **Insert** button. A blank row will appear above the row you selected. Type in your text as in step 2.

7	TV
8	Council Tax
9	
10	...ter
11	Gas

To adjust the width of a column, place the cursor over the right-hand edge of the blue column header. When the cursor becomes a double-headed arrow, click and drag the edge to the desired width.

M19		Width: 15.00 (110 pixels)

	A	B	C
1			
2	Bills	Jan	Feb	M
3			
4	Rent		

Close-up
When you enter figures into a spreadsheet, they automatically align on the right-hand side of the column. This way, the decimal points align neatly above each other.

	A	B	C	D
1					*H*
2	Bills	Jan	Feb	Mar
3				
4	Rent	350.00		
5	Loan	121.00		
6	Phone	34.27		
7	TV	28.99		
8	Council Tax	36.00		
9	Water	19.65		
10	Gas	0.00		
11	Electricity	0.00		
12	Credit Card	45.00		
13	Car Insurance	37.50		

5 Starting in cell **B4**, and continuing in the cells immediately below, enter the amounts paid out in January for each type of expenditure. If you did not pay anything for a particular bill, type '0' into the relevant cell.

Σ ▾
Sort & Find &
Filter ▾ Select ▾
Editing

	A	B		M
1				
2	Bills	Jan		
3				
4	Rent	350.00		
5	Loan	121.00		
6	Phone	34.27		
7	TV	28.99		
8	Council Tax	36.00		
9	Water	19.65		
10	Gas	0.00		
11	Electricity	0.00		
12	Credit Card	45.00		
13	Car Insurance	37.50		
14				
15	Total	=SUM(B4:B14)		
16		SUM(**number1**, [number2], ...)		

672.41

6 To calculate January's total expenditure on bills, click in the cell to the right of 'Total', then click on the **AutoSum** button in the 'Editing' group. The cells to be calculated are outlined with a dotted line, and a formula appears in the Total cell. Press **Return**. The sum of your cells will then appear.

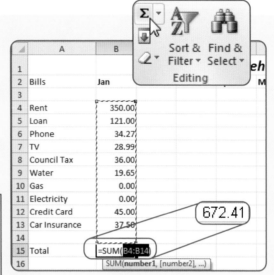

14							
15	Total		672.41				
16							

Household Bill Calculator

Mar	Apr	May	Jun	Jul	Aug	S
350.00	350.00	350.00	350.00	350.00	350.00	
121.00	121.00	121.00	121.00	121.00	121.00	
34.27	34.27	34.27	34.27	34.27	34.27	
28.99	28.99	28.99	28.99	28.99	28.99	
36.00	36.00	36.00	36.00	36.00	36.00	
19.65	19.65	19.65	19.65	19.65	19.65	
0.00	0.00	0.00	0.00	0.00	0.00	
0.00	0.00	0.00	0.00	0.00	0.00	
45.00	45.00	45.00	45.00	45.00	45.00	
37.50	37.50	37.50	37.50	37.50	37.50	
672.41	672.41	672.41	672.41	672.41	672.41	

7 To copy the formula to add up total expenditure for the other months of the year, first place the cursor in the lower right-hand corner of the cell. When it becomes a cross, click and drag until you reach December's column. Excel will automatically update all cell references.

Decimal places

For financial spreadsheets you need to format your figures so they display two figures after the decimal point. Select the relevant cells, go to the 'Number' group and click on the dialogue box launcher. In the Format Cells dialogue box the Number tab is selected. Click on **Number** in the Category pane, and set the number of Decimal places to '2'. Click on **OK**.

Format Cells

General ▾

Number | Alignment | Font | Border

% , ◄.0 .00
.00 ►.0

Number

Category:
General
Number
Currency
Accounting
Date

Sample
672.41

Decimal places: 2

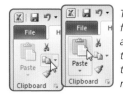

*To copy and paste a formula, click on the formula cell then go to the 'Clipboard' group and click on the **Copy** button. Highlight all the cells you want the formula to appear in, then click on the **Paste** button. The cell references automatically update themselves.*

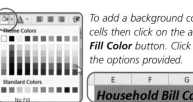

*To add a background colour, select the cells then click on the arrow next to the **Fill Color** button. Click on a colour from the options provided.*

	K	L	M	N	O	P
	Oct	Nov	Dec	Totals		
00	350.00	350.00	350.00	=SUM(B4:M4)		
00	121.00	121.00	121.00	SUM(number1, [number2], ...)		
27	34.27	34.27	34.27			
99	28.99	28.99	28.99			
00	36.00	36.00	36.00		Totals	
65	19.65	19.65	19.65			
00	0.00	0.00	0.00		4200.00	
00	0.00	0.00	0.00			
00	45.00	45.00	45.00			
50	37.50	37.50	37.50			
41	672.41	672.41	672.41			

	I	J	K	L	M	N
	Aug	Sep	Oct	Nov	Dec	Totals
	350.00	350.00	350.00	350.00	350.00	4200.00
	121.00	121.00	121.00	121.00	121.00	1452.00
	34.27	34.27	34.27	34.27	34.27	411.24
	28.99	28.99	28.99	28.99	28.99	347.88
	36.00	36.00	36.00	36.00	36.00	432.00
	19.65	19.65	19.65	19.65	19.65	235.80
	0.00	0.00	0.00	0.00	0.00	0.00
	0.00	0.00	0.00	0.00	0.00	0.00
	45.00	45.00	45.00	45.00	45.00	540.00
	37.50	37.50	37.50	37.50	37.50	450.00
	672.41	672.41	672.41	672.41	672.41	8068.92

Household Bill Calculator

E	F	G	H
			Household Bill Calculator

8 Type 'Totals' in the cell to the right of 'Dec'. Click on the cell two rows below 'Totals', then in the 'Editing' group click on the **AutoSum** button. The yearly total for your first type of bill will appear. Copy and paste this formula (see top) into the cells below to calculate the totals for your other bills.

9 Paste the same formula into the cell two rows below the final figure in the 'Totals' column. Press **Return**. The total amount you have spent on bills in the course of the previous year will appear. This completes the calculation sheet.

10 To add a pie chart, see below. To print your spreadsheet go to the **File** tab, and click on **Print**. Your spreadsheet will be previewed in the panel on the right. To make an alteration, click on the **Home** tab and edit as necessary. To print, check the options under 'Settings', then click on the **Print** button.

Make a pie chart

To make a pie chart, press the **Ctrl** key and select the cells containing your types of bill in column A, and their respective yearly totals in the Totals column (as column N above). Click on the **Insert** tab, go to the 'Charts' group and click on **Pie**, then select a chart type from the drop-down menu. Your chart will now appear in your spreadsheet. Click on it and drag it into position. To resize it, click and drag one of the corner tabs.

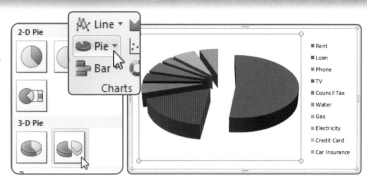

Calculate your car costs

Use your PC to help you to get the best mileage for your money

A spreadsheet is ideal for monitoring all sorts of expenditure. As well as creating a budget planner for all your household expenses (see page 254), it is also possible to keep close track of large, individual expenses – this could range from buying and running a car to building an extension to your house.

By recording all your motoring expenses you can work out annual costs and build a comprehensive analysis of your car's value for money. You can also anticipate motoring bills, and so plan a budget to accommodate them – perhaps you could put away a fixed amount of money every month. That way, if a major expense such as an emergency repair crops up, you will be better prepared.

Once you have set up the car running costs spreadsheet shown here, all the calculation work will be done for you. All you have to do is enter your monthly figures.

Write down all the costs your car incurs. Include repayments, road tax, insurance, spare parts and servicing, as well as oil and fuel.

► BEFORE YOU START

1 Click on the **Start** button, select **All Programs** and click on **Microsoft Excel 2010**. Save the new spreadsheet by clicking on the **Save** button on the Quick Access toolbar. Select a folder to save it in, or create a new one by clicking on **New folder**, and type a name in the 'File name' box. Click on **Save**.

*You can create similar spreadsheets in Microsoft Works. Open Works, then choose **Works Spreadsheet** from the 'Quick Launch' menu on the right.*

► OTHER PROGRAMS

Shortcut

If your columns are not wide enough to accommodate your text, place the cursor over the border between the column headings. When it changes to a double-headed arrow, double-click. The column will automatically resize itself to fit the text.

	A
25	Mileage
26	Month start
27	Month end
28	Monthly Total
29	
30	Cost per mile

Below the cell in which you type 'Mileage' (here, cell A25), type in 'Month start', 'Month end' and 'Monthly Total'. Two cells below that, type in 'Cost per mile'.

2 In cell **A1** type in a heading. In cell **A4** type 'Vehicle Information'. Type in the headings as shown above in cells **A5** to **A9** then fill in your car's details in the adjoining cells in column B, starting in cell **B5**.

3 Click on cell **C11** and type in 'Jan'. Place the cursor in the bottom right-hand corner of the cell. When it becomes a cross, click and drag across the spreadsheet until you reach column N, and Microsoft Excel will enter the months of the year.

4 Click on cell **A12** and type in 'Expenses'. Starting in cell **A13**, and continuing in the cells below, type in your different types of car cost. Two cells below the final entry (here, **A23**) type in 'Total costs'. Two cells below that, type in 'Mileage' (see above).

Merge and centre headings

It is possible to merge a number of cells together, then centre the contents within that larger cell. This is particularly useful for headings such as 'Car Running Costs'. To select the cells you wish to merge, click on the first one, then drag the cursor over the others. Then in the 'Alignment' group click on the **Merge & Center** button.

Bright idea

You can use your spreadsheet to calculate your fuel consumption. Enter a row for the amount of fuel bought in litres every month. Then divide the number of litres by the Total Monthly Mileage to work out how many litres your car uses per mile.

269

To copy the formula for the other months of the year, place the cursor in the lower right-hand corner of a cell. When it becomes a cross, click and drag until you reach column N. Excel will automatically update the cell references.

23	Total costs	0

Bright idea
To account for annual bills, such as insurance, on a monthly basis, click on the relevant cell in January's column, type '=', the total annual amount, then '/12' – for example (=515/12). Copy the formula to every month using the technique described left.

Shortcut
*To align all the cells containing figures, click in the first cell, then hold down the shift key and click in the last cell. Now click on the **Align Text Right** button in the 'Alignment' group.*

Σ ▾ A Z ▾ Z A ▾ 🔍
Sort & Find &
Filter ▾ Select ▾
Editing

× ✓ *fx* =SUM(C12:C21)

		C	D	E	
10					
11		Jan	Feb	Mar	Apr
12	Expenses				
13	Repayments				
14	Insurance				
15	Road Tax				
16	MOT test				
17	Service				
18	Spare parts				
19	Oil				
20	Car valet				
21	Fuel				
22					
23	Total costs	=SUM(C12:C21)			
24		SUM(**number1**, [number2], ...)			

SUM ▾ × ✓ *fx* =C27-C26

	A	B	C	D	E
18	Spare parts				
19	Oil				
20	Car valet				
21	Fuel				
22					
23	Total costs		0	0	0
24					
25	Mileage				
26	Month start				
27	Month end				
28	Monthly Total		=C27-C26		
29					
30	Cost per mile				

SUM ▾ × ✓ *fx* =C23/C28

	A	B	C	D	E
18	Spare parts				
19	Oil				
20	Car valet				
21	Fuel				
22					
23	Total costs		0	0	0
24					
25	Mileage				
26	Month start				
27	Month end				
28	Monthly Total		0	0	0
29					
30	Cost per mile		=C23/C28		
31					

5 To set the formula for working out monthly costs, click in the 'Total costs' cell for January (here, **C23**), then on the **AutoSum** button in the 'Editing' group. Click and drag over the cells to be added together and then press **Return**. Copy the formula for the other months (see above).

6 To calculate the total monthly mileage for January, click in the relevant cell (here, **C28**) and type '='. Click in the 'Month end' for January cell (**C27**), type '-', then click in the 'Month start' for January cell (**C26**). Press **Return**. Next, copy the formula to the other months.

7 To enter a formula for the total cost per mile for January, click in the relevant cell (here, **C30**) and type '='. Then click in the 'Total costs' for January cell (**C23**), type '/', and then click in the cell for January's mileage total (**C28**). Press **Return**. Copy the formula to the other months.

Styling your work

To style the text in your spreadsheet and add some colour, first select the relevant cell or cells. (To style several cells in the same way at the same time, click and drag the cursor over them, or click on the first cell, hold down the **Ctrl** key and click on the other cells in turn.)

Now go to the 'Font' group and click on the dialogue box launcher. Click on the various tabs and select a font, size, style, effect and background colour. Click on **OK**.

To create a border, select the cells then click on the **Border** tab in the Format Cells dialogue box. Select a style and colour, click on **Outline** and then on **OK**.

To align text to the left, right or centre, click on the relevant cells and then on the appropriate alignment button.

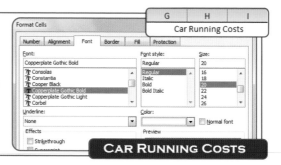

Watch out

Do not be alarmed if you see '#DIV/0!' in any of your cells. It means that Excel is trying to divide a number by zero. This will change when you enter figures for your spreadsheet and AutoSum has something to work with.

*To calculate your annual cost per mile, click on the cell to the right of December's Cost per mile (here, **O30**), type '=', then click on the cell for the Total annual costs (**O23**), then type '/' (division sign on the numeric keypad). Now click on the cell for the Total annual mileage (**O28**). Press **Return**.*

0.73
18566
19055
489 6499
0.68 =O23/O28

C	D	E	F	G
Jan	Feb	Mar	Apr	May
175.25	175.25	175.25	175.25	175.25
42.76	42.76	42.76	42.76	42.76
0	0	150	0	0
0	0	22	0	0
0	0	254.26	0	0
25.45	0	12.96	23.55	0
0	12.99	0	0	0
35	35	35	35	35
97.56	79.98	85.87	75.3	89.03

8 Now enter the values into your spreadsheet. Click on the cells and type in the relevant amounts (enter '0' if you do not have a value). For payments that remain the same every month, type the figure in once and copy it to the other months.

Dec	Annual costs
175.25	=SUM(C13:N13)
42.76	SUM(**number1**, [number2], ...)

175.25	175.25	175.25	175.25	175.25	2103
42.76	42.76	42.76	42.76	42.76	
0	0	0	0	0	
0	0	0	0	0	
0	0	0	0	0	
0	0	17.69	12.51	0	
0	0	0	0	0	
35	35	35	35	35	
88.9	91.76	99.67	78.67		
341.91	362.46	365.19	331.68		

9 Click on cell **O11** and type in 'Annual costs'. To calculate the total annual costs for your first expense, click on cell **O13** then on the **AutoSum** button in the 'Editing' group. Press **Return**. Copy the formula into the cells below, stopping at the Total costs row.

J	K	L	M	N	O
ug	Sep	Oct	Nov	Dec	Annual costs
	175.25	175.25	175.25	175.25	175.25	2103
	42.76	42.76	42.76	42.76	42.76	513.12
	0	0	0	0	0	150
	0	0	0	0	0	22
	135.55	0	0	0	0	389.81
	15.44	0	17.69	12.51	0	107.6
	0	0	0	0	0	12.99
	35	35	35	35	35	420
	86.42	88.9	91.76	99.67	78.67	1049.57
						0
	490.42	341.91	362.46	365.19	331.68	4768.09

6499

16618	17110	17566	17899	18566	
17110	17566	17899	18566	19055	
492	456	333	667	489	=SUM(C28:N28)
					SUM(number1, [number2], ...)
1.09	0.75	1.09	0.55	0.68	0.73

10 To calculate your annual mileage, click on the cell to the right of December's mileage Monthly Total (here, **O28**), then click on the **AutoSum** button in the 'Editing' group. Press **Return**. (To calculate your annual cost per mile, see above.) To print, go to the **File** menu and click on **Print**.

Calculating second car costs

You can create a spreadsheet for a second car. Right-click on the **Sheet1** tab at the bottom of the window and select **Move or Copy**. In the dialogue box, make sure your spreadsheet is selected in the 'To book' box. Click on **Sheet2** in the 'Before sheet' box, ensure the 'Create a copy' box is ticked, then click on **OK**.

Rename the sheet tab by double-clicking on it and typing the new name. Then change the text or figures as necessary.

Move or Copy
Move selected sheets
To book:
Car Costs.xlsx
Before sheet:
Sheet1
Sheet2
Sheet3
(move to end)
☑ Create a copy
OK   Ca

Rename
Move or Copy...
View Code
Protect Sheet...
Tab Color
Hide
Unhide...
Select All Sheets

eet1 Sheet1 (2) Sheet2
eet1 **Car 2** Sheet2

Styling numbers

To give your values a uniform format, select all the cells in which you enter currency figures (not mileage). Click on the **Font** dialogue box launcher and with the 'Number' tab selected, under 'Category' click on **Number**, and select **2** in the 'Decimal places' box. Click on **OK**.

Format Cells
Number Alignment Font Border Fill
Category:
General
Number
Currency
Accounting
Date
Sample
175.25
Decimal places: 2

Build a shares portfolio

Follow the stock market with your own monthly guide

A spreadsheet is an excellent tool for taking care of financial calculations, and there are few more confusing areas of finance than fluctuating share prices. Because share prices change continually, it is a good idea to assess their performance every month. Your financial adviser or stockbroker will be able to give you detailed advice about the best strategy for buying and selling shares, but using a spreadsheet means you can keep a close watch on the overall trends of all your shareholdings.

The cell references here are correct for those who hold shares in three companies. If you hold shares with fewer or more companies, you must adjust the references accordingly.

▶ BEFORE YOU START

1 Click on the **Start** button, select **All Programs** and click on **Microsoft Excel 2010**. Save the new spreadsheet by clicking on the **Save** button on the Quick Access toolbar. Select a folder to save it in, or create a new one by clicking on **New folder**, and type a name in the 'File name' box. Click on **Save**.

*You can use Microsoft Works to create similar spreadsheets. Open Microsoft Works then choose **Works Spreadsheet** from the 'Quick Launch' menu on the right.*

▶ OTHER PROGRAMS

To adjust the width of a column to accommodate your text, double-click on the right-hand edge of the blue column heading. The column will adjust to fit the widest piece of text in that column.

To style your text, highlight it then select a font, size and style from the 'Font' group.

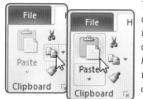

To copy and paste a formula, click on the formula cell and then, in the 'Clipboard' group, click on the **Copy** button. Highlight all the cells you want the formula to appear in, then click on the **Paste** button.

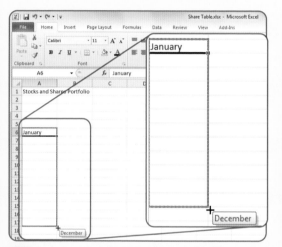

2 Type your heading in cell **A1**. Next, click on cell **A6** and type in 'January'. Place the mouse pointer over the lower right-hand corner of the cell. When it becomes a cross, click and drag down the column until 'December' appears.

3 Click in cell **B4** and type in the first company name – do not worry if the name is too long for the cell. Select **B4** and **C4** then click the **Merge & Center** button in the 'Alignment' group. In cell **B5** type 'Share price' and in **C5** type 'No. of shares'. Enter other company names in row 4.

4 Click in cell **H4** and type 'Total portfolio value (£)'. In cell **H6** (this is the row of your first month) type in '=' then your formula (see below). Press the **Return** key. Copy and paste the formula into the cells below for subsequent months.

You do not need to start your shares portfolio with January. Type in whichever month you want, then click and drag the cursor as described in step 2. The program will fill in the other months automatically.

Calculating your shares

The formula for calculating the total value of your shares portfolio needs to multiply the current share price by the number of shares for each company and then add them together (place this part of the formula in brackets).

To convert the value into pounds sterling, you must then divide by 100 (share prices are given in pence). Here, the formula is: '(B6*C6+D6*E6+F6*G6)/100'.

You do not need to type cell references into the formula – simply click on the cells to enter them.

4	Cable & Wireless		General Motors		Coca-Cola		Total portfolio value (£)
5	Share price	No. of shares	Share price	No. of shares	Share price	No. of shares	
6 January							=(B6*C6+D6*E6+F6*G6)/100
7 February							

Cells that contain formulas will display '0' until you enter figures in the relevant share price and share number cells. The calculation cells will update themselves automatically as you enter these figures.

! Watch out
Remember that the cell references here are correct for those who hold shares in three companies. For those who hold shares with fewer or more companies, you must adjust the references.

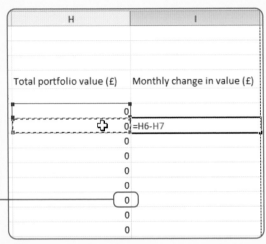

H	I
Total portfolio value (£)	Monthly change in value (£)
0	0
0	=H6-H7
0	
0	
0	
0	
0	
0	
0	

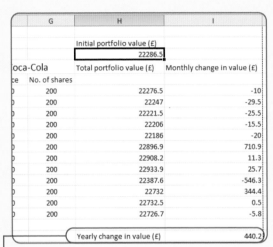

Initial portfolio value (£) 22286.5

oca-Cola	Total portfolio value (£)	Monthly change in value (£)
No. of shares		
200	22276.5	-10
200	22247	-29.5
200	22221.5	-25.5
200	22206	-15.5
200	22186	-20
200	22896.9	710.9
200	22908.2	11.3
200	22933.9	25.7
200	22387.6	-546.3
200	22732	344.4
200	22732.5	0.5
200	22726.7	-5.8
	Yearly change in value (£)	440.2

Conditional Formatting ▾   Format as Table ▾   Cell Styles ▾
Styles

			C	D
1	Stocks and Shares Portfolio			Share price
2				
3	Sell now	3632		3632
4		Cable & Wireless		3628
5		Share price	No. of shares	3622
6	January	3632	100	3624
7	February	3628	100	3603
8	March	3622	100	3597
9	April	3624	100	3626
10	May	3603	100	
11	June	3597	120	3637
12	July	3626	120	3644
13	August	3637	120	3648
14	September	3644	120	
15	October	3648	130	3653
16	November	3653	130	

5 Click in cell **I4** and type 'Monthly change in value (£)'. In cell **I7** (the row for your second month) enter a formula that subtracts the Total portfolio value in February (H7) from the Total value in January (H6). Press **Return**. Copy and paste the formula into the cells below – the cell references will update automatically.

6 In **H2** type 'Initial portfolio value (£)'. In **H3** enter the total value of the shares when you bought them. To calculate the change in value for January, click in cell **I6** and type in '=H6-H3'. Type in your share price data and the formulas will update.

7 Now create a warning for when your share value falls below the price at which you might sell (you will need to determine the price). In **A3** type in 'Sell now'. In **B3** enter the selling price for the first company. Highlight column B, go to the 'Styles' group and click on **Conditional Formatting** (see below).

Yearly change in value (£)   440.2

*Click in cell **H19** and type 'Yearly change in value (£)'. In cell **I19** type in the formula '=H17-H3'.*

Set up a warning
Click on **Conditional Formatting** in the 'Styles' group and then on **Highlight Cells Rules** and **Less Than**. Click on the cell containing your selling price, here **B3**, and then click on the arrow beside the 'with' box and select a colour scheme. Click **OK**.

Share prices that are below your selling price will appear in this colour. Repeat for all your price columns.

Conditional Formatting ▾   Format as Table ▾   Cell Styles ▾   Insert ▾   Delete ▾   Format ▾   Sort & Filter ▾   Find & Select ▾

Highlight Cells Rules ▸   Greater Than...
Top/Bottom Rules ▸   Less Than...

Less Than
Format cells that are LESS THAN:
=B3   with   Light Red Fill with Dark Red Text ▾
OK   Cancel

To highlight more than one column at a time, press the **Ctrl** key and click on each blue column heading in turn.

Stocks and Shares Portfolio

To style the heading, highlight it, right-click your mouse and select **Format Cells**. Click on the **Font** tab and select a font, size, style and colour. Click on **OK**.

To centre your heading, select cells **A1** to **I1** and click on the **Merge & Center** button. To add a background colour, click on the arrow beside the Fill Color button and select a colour from the drop-down palette.

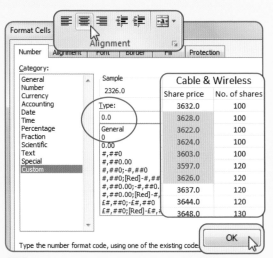

8 To style your share price columns, highlight them, then go to the 'Number' group and click on the Format Cells dialogue box launcher. Under 'Category' click on **Custom**, then in the 'Type' box click on **0** and add '.**0**'. Click on **OK**. To centre columns, highlight them and click on the **Center** button in the 'Alignment' group.

9 To style currency, select columns H and I, right-click your mouse, then select **Format Cells**. Click on the **Currency** category of the Number tab. In the 'Decimal places' box, type in '2'. In the 'Symbol' box, select to display a '£', '$' or 'None'. In the 'Negative numbers' box, click on your choice of style for negative amounts. Click on **OK**.

10 Create lines to separate your columns so you can read your data more easily. Select the cells in each 'No. of shares' column then go to the 'Font' group and click on the arrow beside the Border button. Click on the option that adds a right border.

Printing your table

Your spreadsheet will probably be quite wide, so to make it fit on a sheet of A4 go to the **File** tab and click **Print**. Your Share Table is previewed on the right-hand side. Under 'Settings' select 'Landscape Orientation' and in the Scaling section, select 'Fit Sheet on One Page' option. If you need to make any adjustments to your document, click on the **Home** tab. Click on the **Print** button to finish.

275

Manage a special event

Learn how to keep track of a budget, and raise money

Managing a budget for, say, a school play or a benefit dinner can be a complex business. Not only must you keep track of a range of expenses, but you also have to weigh up outgoings against projected income to ensure you make a profit. If that profit is earmarked for a particular use – a new computer lab, for instance – you will have a better idea of how much you need to raise, and so be able to budget accordingly.

Using a spreadsheet program on your PC will make light work of budget calculations and projections. Microsoft Excel also lets you create accounts for specific aspects of a project such as ticket sales, and incorporate these within the accounts for the whole project.

Note each area in which you will have to spend money, and all sources of income. Ask colleagues to provide figures for their projects.

▶ BEFORE YOU START

1 Click on the **Start** button, select **All Programs** and click on **Microsoft Excel 2010**. Save the new spreadsheet by clicking on the **Save** button on the Quick Access toolbar. Select a folder to save it in, or create a new one by clicking on **New folder**, and type a name in the 'File name' box. Click on **Save**.

You can create a similar spreadsheet in Microsoft Works. However, Works does not have multiple worksheets within the same document, so you must create separate documents for each area of budgeting.

▶ OTHER PROGRAMS

Watch out

You are in danger of losing your work if you do not save it frequently. Make a habit of saving the changes to your spreadsheet every few minutes.

Key word

Format *This refers to the process of setting the appearance of text (font, style, size and colour), and figures (number, currency, date and so on) in cells.*

	A	B
1	Costume Costs	
2	Item	Estimated
3	Fabric for costumes	

	Estimated costs	Actual costs

2 In cell **A1** type a heading for your first sheet; in cell **A2** type 'Item'; in cell **B2** 'Estimated costs'; and in cell **C2** 'Actual costs'. In cell **A3** type your first expense. List your expenses in the cells below. Type 'Total' under your list of expenses.

3 To style your text, right-click on the cell and select **Format Cells**. Click on the **Font** tab in the dialogue box. Select a font, style, size and colour, then click on **OK**. To style several adjacent cells in the same way at once, click and then drag your mouse over the cells and then apply styling.

4 Format the cost cells in columns B and C. Click and drag across the cells, right-click and choose **Format Cells**. Select the **Number** tab and **Accounting** in the Category window. Select **2** in the 'Decimal places' box and **None** in the Symbol box. Click on **OK**.

Estimated costs	A
35.00	
16.50	
3.99	
-	
12.50	
25.00	
15.00	

To adjust the width of a column to accommodate your text, double-click on the right-hand edge of the blue column heading. The column will automatically adjust to fit the widest piece of text in that column.

The Accounting format

When you select the Accounting format for cells, the decimal points and currency symbols (if you use them) are aligned directly above each other, making your account-keeping easier.

You should also be aware that when you type '0' into a cell to indicate that there is no cost, it will be expressed as '-' as soon as you click out of that cell.

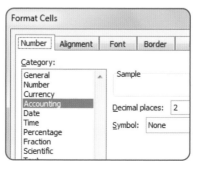

Close-up
*You may need to insert new rows of expenses. Click on the row below where you would like the new row to appear and click on **Insert** in the 'Cells' group.*

You can keep accounts for various aspects of the same project within one Excel document. Simply create a separate worksheet for each one (see bottom left).

ADD MORE WORKSHEETS

A	B	C	D
1 Ticket sales (estimated)			
2 **No.**	**Item**	**Ticket price**	**Estimated revenue**
3 500	Standard seats	3.00	
4 100	Privilege seats	4.00	
5 200	Children's seats	1.50	
6		**Total**	
7			
8			
9 Ticket sales (actual)			
10 **No.**	**Item**	**Ticket price**	**Actual revenue**
11 389	Standard seats	3.00	
12 79	Privilege seats	4.00	
13 184	Children's seats	1.50	
14		**Total**	
15			

Sheet1 **Sheet2** Sheet3

5 Enter the individual estimates then add up your figures in the 'Estimated costs' column. Click in the Total cell for column B (here, **B10**), then click on the **AutoSum** button in the 'Editing' group. Press **Return** and the total will appear.

6 To copy the formula for Actual costs, click in the Total cell for 'Estimated costs' (here, **B10**) then place the cursor in its lower right-hand corner. When the cursor turns into a cross, click and drag across to the 'Actual costs' column. The sum will adjust as you enter each cost.

7 To create a second worksheet for, say, income from tickets, click on the **Sheet2** tab at the bottom of the screen. The spreadsheet above has sections for estimated and actual revenue from sales of different seats. Name the two worksheets Costumes and Ticket Sales (see below left).

Naming and adding worksheets

For easier navigation between worksheets, rename them. To rename Sheet1, double-click on the **Sheet1** tab at the bottom of the screen and type in a title (here, Costumes), then press the **Return** key.

To add more worksheets, click on the **Insert Worksheet** button to the right of the

Sheet names. To re-order the sequence of worksheets, click on the tab of the one you want to move and drag it to its new position.

Adding grids

To enclose your worksheet details in a grid, select the relevant cells, right-click and select **Format Cells**. In the dialogue box, click on the **Border** tab. First, select a Line style and colour, then, in the Presets section, click on the **Outline** and **Inside** buttons, then click on **OK**.

To add a background colour, select the cells, right-click and select **Format Cells**. Click on the **Patterns** tab. In the 'Cell shading' section click on your choice of colour, then click on **OK**.

Watch out
If you name your worksheets you must use the new names, rather than Sheet1, 2 and so on, when referring to them in cell references. So, formulas should read "'Costumes'!B10" rather than "'Sheet1'!B10".

Ticket price	Estimated revenue
3.00	=A3*C3

Ticket sales (estimated)

	A	B	C	Estimated revenue
1	Ticket sales (estimated)			
2	No.	Item	Ticket price	Estimated revenue
3	500	Standard seats	3.00	1500.00
4	100	Privilege seats	4.00	400.00
5	200	Children's seats		
6				1500.00
7				400.00
8				300.00
9	Ticket sales (a			=SUM(D3:D5)
10	No.	Item		SUM(number1, [number2], ...)
11	389	Standard seats		
12	79	Privilege seats	4.00	316.00
13	184	Children's seats	1.50	276.00
14			Total	£1,759.00
15				

8 To estimate income from standard seat sales, click in the relevant cell (here, **D3**), type '=' then a formula for the total seats multiplied by the price (A3*C3). Repeat for other seats. Click in the Total cell (**D6**), go to the 'Editing' group, click the **AutoSum** button and press **Return**. Repeat for actual sales.

	A	B	C
1	Budget Summary		
2	Item	Estimated costs	Actual costs
3	Costumes	=Costumes!B10	
4	Refreshments		
5	Props	107.99	
6	Printing/publicity		
7	Total		
8			
9			
10	Item	Estimated revenue	Actual revenue
11	Refreshments		
12	Tickets		
13	Total		
14			
15	Balance		

9 Open a worksheet to add up costs and revenue of the individual parts of the project. Create columns as shown above. In the costs and revenue columns, enter the sheet and cell references of your totals for other worksheets. For example: "='Costumes'!B10".

	A	B	C
1	Budget Summary		
2	Item	Estimated costs	Act
3	Costumes	107.99	
4	Refreshments	144.24	
5	Props	98.00	
6	Printing/publicity	50.00	
7	Total	400.23	
8			
9			
10	Item	Estimated revenue	Actual revenue
11	Refreshments	330.00	
12	Tickets	2,200.00	
13	Total	2,530.00	
14			
15	Balance	2,129.77	

10 Now calculate total costs and revenue. Click in the Total cell for 'Estimated costs' (here, **B7**), then click on the **AutoSum** button and press **Return**. Copy the formula into the 'Actual costs' cell (see step 6). Repeat for revenue. If you wish to work out balances, see below left.

Calculating balances

To calculate Estimated and Actual balances, click in the Estimated Balance cell (here, **B15**), type '=', then a formula that subtracts the total estimated costs from the total estimated revenue (B13-B7). Press **Return**. Copy and paste the formula into the Actual Balance cell (see step 6).

	Estimated revenue	A
Total	400.23	
Item	Estimated revenue	A
Refreshments	330.00	
Tickets	2,200.00	
Total 2,129.77	2,530.00	
Balance	=B13-B7	

Printing out worksheets

To print a worksheet, first go to the **File** tab and click **Print**. Your worksheet is previewed on the right-hand side. Under 'Settings' select options for which worksheets to print, orientation and paper size. If you need to make any adjustments to your document, click on the Home tab. Click on the **Print** button to finish.

Form a Neighbourhood

Your PC can make it easier for friends and neighbours

Project planner

Create a folder called 'Neighbourhood Watch'. Add sub-folders for mini-projects.

- 📁 **Neighbourhood Watch**
  - 📁 **Membership**
  - 📁 **Contacts**
  - 📁 **Crime database**
  - 📁 **Holiday diary**
  - 📁 **Communications**
  - 📁 **Meetings & events**

Any community-based project will benefit from some sound organisation, effective communication and a high local profile. Your PC can help to make each of these objectives achievable.

Neighbourhood Watch schemes rely on volunteer members keeping an eye on each other's properties, particularly during working hours and holiday periods. Knowing who is available to patrol the area, and which houses are unoccupied, will make your Neighbourhood Watch scheme more efficient.

The ideal starting point is to create a tailored membership form using a database program. Distribute this to prospective members then, when you receive the completed forms, enter the details into a members' database.

Your database will then help to identify who is at home and who is out, and at what times. By including work and holiday schedules, and using the program's 'sort' facility, you can compile a day-to-day list of unoccupied properties – the ones most at risk. Then, using the information

Watch group

to guard against local crime

on members' availability, you can produce a rota of neighbours who can keep an eye out for suspicious behaviour.

Once you have set up your scheme, your computer can help you to log incidents of crime. Use your database's Form Design feature to create an incident report form on which members can record the date, time, place and type of any incident.

If you set up a separate crime database you will soon be able to build up a profile of the types of crime that occur in your area, and when crime is most likely to take place. You can then review your activities and patrols accordingly.

To raise the profile of your scheme, use your PC's graphics

capabilities to design a poster for members to display in their windows. You could also design a letterhead for correspondence, and produce a newsletter to keep members informed of any special events and new members, as well as raise awareness of crime trends and home security.

And if you are connected to the internet, you can take a look at the wide range of Neighbourhood Watch information on the World Wide Web. You will find messaging forums, details on training, useful contact numbers, home insurance information and lists of the type of items that most appeal to thieves. You could even join a weekly emailing list, giving tips on, among other things, home security.

Starting your watch

- Search the internet for information on setting up a Neighbourhood Watch scheme
- Canvas interest and arrange first meeting
- Appoint a group chairperson and other officials
- Invite the local police to make a presentation
- Organise press coverage of launch and use it to recruit new members
- Arrange affiliation to a national/regional organisation
- Compile a patrol schedule and holiday diary, and set up a crime database

Ideas and inspirations

Below are project ideas to help you to set up an effective Neighbourhood Watch group that the local community – and criminals – will take seriously. The projects can be adapted to your own requirements.

172 Membership database
Record members' details, including contact phone numbers and car registration numbers.

168 Create a newsletter
Design an eye-catching publication to keep your neighbours informed of developments.

230 Design a poster
Attract attention to a forthcoming meeting, or publicise your scheme.

186 Create a diary
Use this handy feature to keep track of members' travel plans, absences and availability.

150 Design a letterhead
Give your scheme's correspondence an official and business-like appearance.

Also worth considering …

No matter how successful your group is, you may benefit from the experience of others.

94 Search the internet
Find out more about established Neighbourhood Watch schemes, and correspond by email.

Record a family history

Explore **your** past **with a** database **of** relatives and ancestors

ompiling a family history can be hugely rewarding. It is astonishing how soon knowledge about a family's past is lost if no one writes it down; but, if you do, the detail you can quickly and easily find out about your ancestors will fascinate every member of your family, young and old.

The database program in Microsoft Works is ideal for making systematic records of your family's history. Dates of birth, occupations, marriages and so on can all be noted – or left blank until your research bears fruit. You can also make space to record interesting facts about your forebears: the homes in which they lived, medals they won, famous people they met, the traces they left behind. Use your PC to explore your roots – your grandchildren will thank you for it one day.

You will find the quickest way is to input all your information in one go. Do not worry if you need to do more research though, as it is easy to add information at any time.

► BEFORE YOU START

1 Go to the **Start** menu, select **All Programs** and **Microsoft Works**, then click on **Microsoft Works Task Launcher**. When Works has opened, click on **Works Database** from the Quick Launch taskbar on the right.

You can also create a family database in Microsoft Excel. This will let you input and view your data in table form, ready for sorting and styling according to your needs.

► OTHER PROGRAMS

Bright idea
Create a reference field, in which each record has its own reference number, and give it a 'serialized' format. This way, record numbers will update automatically whenever a new record is added.

Key word
Field *This is a placeholder that contains a particular category of information stored within a database. Record No, Surname and First names are examples of database fields.*

*To select more than one field at a time, press the **Ctrl** key and, keeping it pressed down, click on all the boxes you want to alter.*

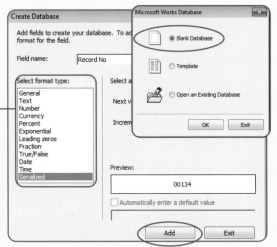

2 In the Microsoft Works Database window **Blank Database** will be selected by default – click on **OK**. In the Create Database dialogue box, input your fields (specify a format for each one, such as Text or Number). Enter the fields and formats listed below. When you have typed in a field, click on the **Add** button.

3 Your database appears in List form. Now name and save it. Then customise the look of it by clicking on the **Form Design** toolbar button. To move a text box, click on it and drag it. (To resize it, see below.) Rearrange your text boxes to leave space at the top of the page for a heading.

4 Click at the top of the page and type in your heading. To style it, highlight it, then go to the **Format** menu and click on **Font and Style**. Select a font, size, colour and style, then click **OK**. Style your field names using the same method.

Fields and formats
Consider using the following fields and formats. For an added sense of history, include a field for biographical facts.

Field	Format	Field	Format
Record No.	Serialized	Married to	Text
Surname	Text	Marriage date	Date
First names	Text	Children	Text
Date of birth	Date	Occupation	Text
Place of birth	Text	Date of death	Date
Mother	Text	Burial place	Text
Father	Text	Notes	Text

Resizing text boxes
To resize a text box, click on it. Place the mouse pointer over the side, bottom or bottom right-hand corner. When the pointer changes to a double-headed arrow, click the mouse and, keeping the button pressed down, drag it across the screen.

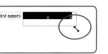

Different views
There are four ways to view your database:

List View is best for quick reference. It lets you view lots of entries at the same time.

Form View displays one entry at a time and is clearer for entering data.

Form Design lets you add and delete fields and alter their layout.

Report View allows you to compile selective reports from your database.

To move to the next field or record, press the **Tab** key. To move back, press the **Shift** and **Tab** keys.

Key word

Report A report extracts designated information from a database. For example, from your family database you could make a report on relatives who emigrated, or who fought in wars.

Form View

Record No: 00001

Family History

Surname: Potts   First names: James Brian

Date of birth: 11/10/1957   Place of birth: Putney, London

Mother: Jane Potts (nee West)   Father: Jeffrey Potts

Married to: Gillian West   Marriage date: 08/02/1982

Children: Occupation:

5 To enter information, first click on the **Form View** toolbar button. Click on the text boxes adjoining the field names and type in the relevant data. To move to the next field or record, press the **Tab** key. To move back to the previous field, press the **Shift** and **Tab** keys at the same time.

List View

Family History - Microsoft Works Database

File   Edit   View   Record   Format   Tools   Help

Arial   10

"Grimley Moore Cemetery Leeds

✔		Date of death	Burial place	Note
	19	07/03/1954	Eversham Park Crescent	Arrested mu
	20	10/12/1971	Eversham Park Crescent	
	21	09/06/1962	Grimley Moore Cemetery	Drove "The F
	22	23/09/1962	Grimley Moore Cemetery	Worked as d
	23	10/02/1943	Banbury Cemetery	Served under
	24	14/07/1940	Du Pont Cemetery	
	25	23/05/1939	Leeds Municipal Cemetery	
	26	17/01/1957	Highgate Cemetery	
	27			
	28			
	29			
	30			

6 When you have entered all your data click on the **List View** toolbar button to view your complete database. To see all the data in a particular cell, click on it. Its contents appear in the Entry bar at the top of the form.

Family History - Microsoft Works Database

File   Edit   View   Record   Format   Tools   Help

Arial   10   "Bertram

✔		Record No	Surname	First names	Date of birth	Place o
	11	00011	Bertram	Jim Bruce	29/11/1959	
	12	00012	Bertram	Sandra Kim	25/02/1960	
	14	00014	Bertram	Jamie Stuart	13/08/1985	
	15	00015	Bertram	Hayley Sonia	13/08/1985	
	27					
	28					
	29					
	30					
	31					
	32					
	33					
	34					
	35					
	36					
	37					

Find and Replace

Find   Replace   Go To

Find what: Bertram

Match:
○ Next record
● All records

OK   Close

7 To find a record or piece of information – such as everyone who has the same surname – go to the **Edit** menu and click on **Find**. Type a key word in the 'Find what' box, select the 'All records' option, then click **OK**. Works will display all the records containing the key word.

Sorting your records

You can 'sort' or prioritise information within your database. For example, you may want to rank family members from the oldest to the youngest. In the ReportCreator dialogue box (see step 8, p285), click on the **Sorting** tab. Click on the arrow beside the first 'Sort by' box, scroll through and select the field you want – in this case 'Date of birth'. Select the Ascending option, then click on **Done**.

ReportCreator - Report 1

Title   Fields   Sorting   Grouping   Filter   Summary

Sort by:
Date of birth   ● Ascending   ○ Descending

Then sort by:
(None)   ● Ascending   ○ Descending

< Previous   Next >   Done   Cancel

Showing all

To see all your records after you have done a search or created a Report, go to the **Record** menu, select **Show** then click on **All Records**.

Record   Format   Tools   Help

Insert Record
Delete Record

Insert Field
Delete Field

	Mother	
	otts (nee West)	Jeffre
Sort Records...	Vest (nee ?)	Willia
	West (nee ?)	Ernes
	Norris (nee ?)	Harol
Mark Records	Potts (nee ?)	Jacob
Mark/Unmark All	romley (nee ?)	Henn

Show ▶ | 1 All Records
Hide Record | 2 Marked Records
| 3 Unmarked Records

You may want to create a report – in other words, print out all or parts of your database – for the family to see or to help you in your research.

CREATING A REPORT

*If the report's contents are too close together, click on **Modify** and adjust the column widths. Place the mouse pointer on the right-hand edge of the column heading, then click and drag to the right.*

Bright idea
To print all the records in your database, select the 'All records' option.

What to Print
⦿ All records
○ Current record only

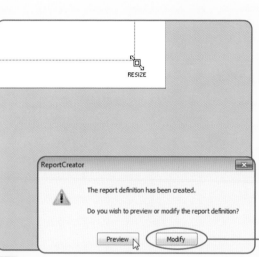

Report Name
Type a name for the report below:
Family_History
OK   Cancel

ReportCreator - Family_History
Title | Fields | Sorting | Grouping

Fields to Display
Fields available:
Place of birth
Mother
Father
Married to
Marriage date
Children
Occupation
Date of death
Burial place

Add >
< Remove
Add All >>
<< Remove All

Field order:
Surname
First names
Date of birth
Father
Mother
Children

Display Options
☑ Show field names at top of each page
☐ Show summary information only

< Previous | Next > | Done | Cancel

RESIZE

ReportCreator
⚠ The report definition has been created.
Do you wish to preview or modify the report definition?
Preview   Modify

Form View

Print Preview

Record No: 000

Family History

Surname: Potts   First names: James Brian

Date of birth: 11/10/1957   Place of birth: Putney, London

Mother: Jane Potts (nee West)   Father: Jeffrey Potts

Married to: Gillian West   Marriage date: 08/02/1982

Children: Robert and Emily   Occupation:

8 To create a printed record, go to the **Tools** menu and click on **ReportCreator**. Type in a name for your report and click on **OK**. Click on the **Fields** tab. Click each field you want to print in turn, clicking on **Add** as you do so. When you have finished click on **Done**.

9 A prompt box appears. Click on the **Preview** button to see how your report looks. If you are satisfied with it, click on **Print**. If you would like to make some style changes, press the **Esc** key, highlight the text you would like to change, go to the **Format** menu and click on **Font and Style**.

10 Click on the **Form View** button, then on the **Print Preview** button to see how a record will look when printed. If you are happy, click on **Cancel**. Go to the **File** menu and select **Print**. Under 'What to Print' select the 'Current record only' option. Click on **OK**.

Date of birth: 25/11/1959
Mother: Sally Bertram (nee Brown)
Married to: Sandra Potts
Children: Jamie & Hayley
|◀ ◀ Record 11 ▶ ▶| Zoom 100% − + ◀ ▶

Scrolling
You can scroll through your records quickly by clicking on the arrows either side of the Record counter located at the bottom left of the Form View window.

Create a family tree

Put faces to names with your own photo family tree

Researching your family's history can provide unexpected insights into the lives of your ancestors. You will not only discover who they were, but where they lived, what they did, and the personal and historical events that shaped their lives. There is a wealth of research resources that you can take advantage of – much of this is online, including government files of family records.

When you have completed your research, this project will help you to put together a comprehensive, illustrated family tree. Using Microsoft Excel, it is straightforward to create a clear guide to your ancestry in which you can include family photos. Once you have finished, why not print it out and frame it for the rest of your family to learn about their personal history?

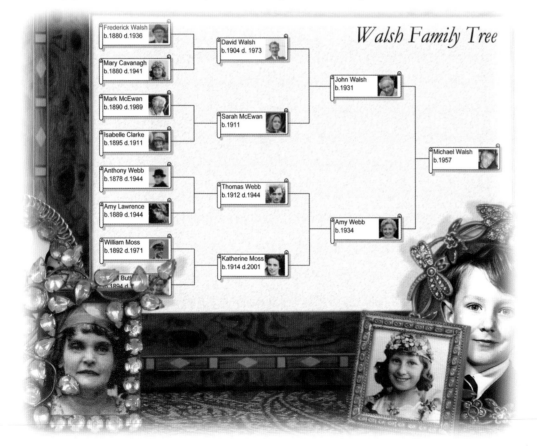

Walsh Family Tree

Frederick Walsh
b.1880 d.1936

Mary Cavanagh
b.1880 d.1941

Mark McEwan
b.1890 d.1989

Isabelle Clarke
b.1895 d.1911

Anthony Webb
b.1878 d.1944

Amy Lawrence
b.1889 d.1944

William Moss
b.1892 d.1971

David Walsh
b.1904 d. 1973

Sarah McEwan
b.1911

Thomas Webb
b.1912 d.1944

Katherine Moss
b.1914 d.2001

John Walsh
b.1931

Amy Webb
b.1934

Michael Walsh
b.1957

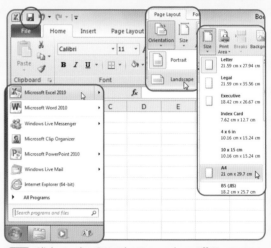

1 Click on the **Start** button, select **All Programs** and click on **Microsoft Excel 2010**. A new blank workbook appears. To change it to landscape format, click on the **Page Layout** tab, then on **Orientation** and select **Landscape**. Next click on **Size** and choose **A4**. To save the workbook, click on the **Save** button on the Quick Access toolbar.

Highlighting the cell range as specified in step 2 should cover your whole A4 page – there are dotted lines showing the page area. Make sure your coloured background covers the whole A4 page even if you have to select more cells than stated in step 2.

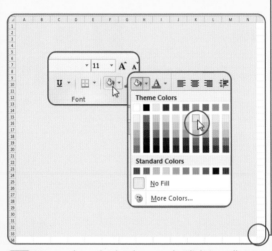

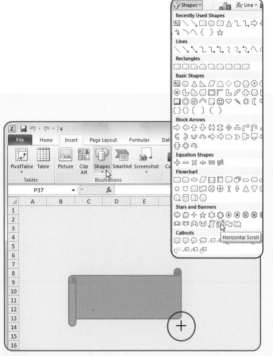

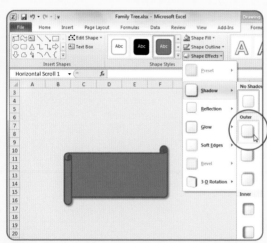

2 Now colour the background. Click in cell **A1** and then, holding down the **Shift** key, click in cell **N33**. Click on the **Home** tab and, in the 'Font' group, click on the arrow next to the **Fill Color** button. Select a pale colour from the palette by clicking on it.

3 To add a scroll shape, click on the **Insert** tab and then on **Shapes** from the 'Illustrations' group. Under 'Stars and Banners' click on the **Horizontal Scroll** and then click and drag on your page to draw the shape. Do not worry about the size for now, but for a four-generation family tree you will need to fit 15 of these on the page.

4 To give your scroll more effect, add a drop shadow. Click on the shape to select it and then click on the **Format** tab. In the 'Shape Styles' group, click on **Shape Effects** and choose **Shadow** from the menu. Click on the first shadow under 'Outer' to apply a drop shadow.

Research begins at home

It Is best to start with what you already know: the names and dates of birth of your immediate family. You may already have copies of birth, marriage and death certificates that can tell you facts you might not be aware of. For example, your mother's birth certificate will tell you the maiden name of her mother and so your grandmother's surname. Also, talk to your older relatives about what they remember of their parents and grandparents.

Watch out
*Make sure your text is aligned to the
left to leave space for the family photo.
Go to the 'Alignment' group and click on the*
Left Align *button.*

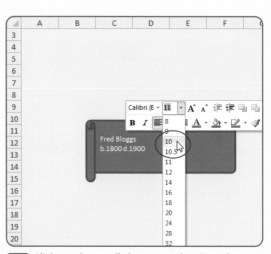

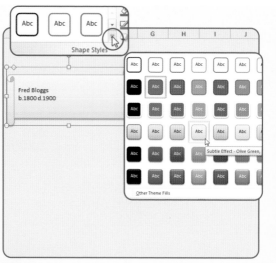

5 Click on the scroll shape to select it and then type a sample name in. It Is fine to use dummy text at this stage. Highlight the typed name to select it, then right-click and choose a font and type size from the drop-down options. Unless your family has particularly long names, try **10pt** text.

6 To change the standard colour of your scroll box click on it to select it, and then click on the **Format** tab. In the 'Shape Styles' group, click on the **More** button to the right of the 'Abc' images. In the dialogue box that opens, click on a colour that contrasts softly with your background.

7 Click outside the scroll box, and then click on the **Insert** tab. Click on **Picture** and browse your hard disk to find the first of your family photos. Click on **Insert**. If you need to resize the photo, see page 289. Position the photo inside the scroll shape to the right of the text. Use the **arrow keys** on your keyboard to nudge it into position.

Preparing your photos

Crystal-clear high-resolution images of relatives and ancestors are not essential for your family tree, but it is worth adjusting colours and contrast so that the small images stand out clearly when you incorporate them. It can be worth opening the image in a photo-editing program such as Photoshop Elements to adjust the brightness and contrast levels for the best result. Also, when you scan in old prints, set the scanner resolution to 600dpi (dots per inch) or greater, especially where the original is small. See pages 200 and 210 for more information on scanning and editing images.

Watch out

When selecting grouped items to be moved, make sure you click on the outer group frame. If you do not, you might select just one component and move that, leaving the other elements behind.

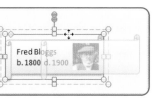

Watch out

You are in danger of losing your work if you do not save it frequently. Make a habit of saving the changes to your family tree every few minutes.

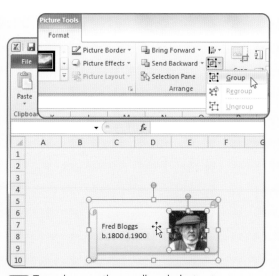

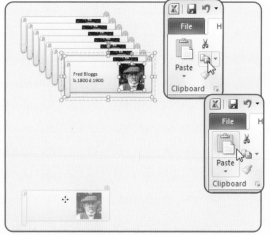

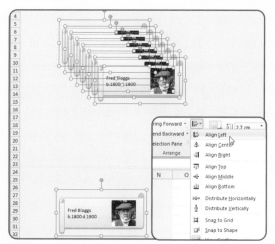

8 To make sure the scroll and photo stay together, hold down the **Shift** key and then click on both the photo and the scroll shape. Click on the **Format** tab and then, in the 'Arrange' group, click on **Group**. Select **Group** from the menu. The photo and the scroll will now stay together, which makes it easier to move them.

9 Now add the rest of your family tree. Click on the scroll/photo group to select it and choose **Copy** from the 'Clipboard' group. Now click on **Paste**. Click on **Paste** a further six times so that you have eight scroll boxes. Select the final scroll and drag it to the bottom left of the coloured background, roughly aligned with the top box.

10 Your scroll boxes are currently positioned on top of one another. To separate them neatly, first click on one of the scrolls and then hold the **Ctrl** key and press **A** to select them all. Click on the **Page Layout** tab and, in the 'Arrange' group, click on **Align**. Choose **Align Left** from the menu.

Resize your images

As the images need to be quite small, you may need to resize your pictures. Right-click on an image and choose **Size and Properties** from the pop-up menu. Under the **Size** tab, the 'Lock aspect ratio' box should be ticked – this means the image dimensions are kept if you make a change (that is, if you amend the height, the width will also change).

   If you would like to crop an image, go to the 'Size' group and click on **Crop**. Click on the black corners or on the black side bars – wait for the cursor to become a black cross-hair – then drag with the mouse to crop out areas you do not need to show. Click on **Crop** again to finish.

Bright idea
*To position the 'child' correctly
between its two 'parents', look
at the vertical cell references and work out
the midpoint.*

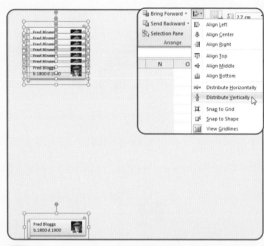

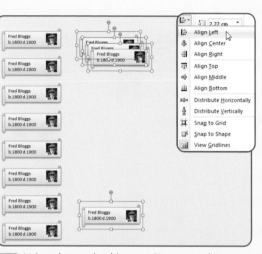

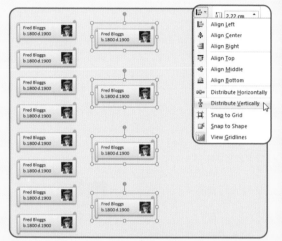

11 The scroll boxes are now aligned along their left edges, but still piled together. With all of the boxes still selected, click on **Align** again and choose **Distribute Vertically**. The eight scroll boxes will be distributed equally down the left-hand side of the page, to form the column that will hold the details of your great-grandparents.

12 Using the method in step 9, copy and paste four more scroll boxes – these will hold the details of your grandparents. Click on the fourth box and drag it to the bottom to form a column to the right of the others, positioned vertically to sit between its 'parent' boxes in the left-hand column.

13 Ensure the four boxes are still highlighted. If not, hold down the **Shift** key and click on each of the boxes to select them. To arrange them neatly, click on the **Page Layout** tab and, in the 'Arrange' group, click on **Align** and **Align Left**. Then click on **Align** again, this time selecting **Distribute Vertically** as you did in step 11.

Different tree types

The family tree in this project is an 'ancestor tree'. This means that the subject, usually you, appears at the top, or to one side, and preceding generations branch out from that point. Another popular format is a 'descendant tree' (right), also known in the UK as 'dropline' format, in which an ancestor appears at the top and descendants branch off, down to the present generation.

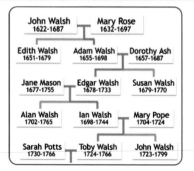

Shortcut
*To constrain an object so that it moves only horizontally or vertically, press and hold **Shift** while dragging it. To move an object in small increments, press and hold **Ctrl** while pressing an arrow key.*

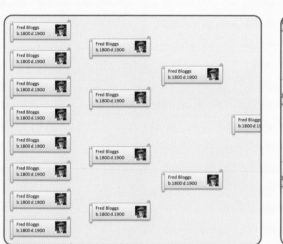

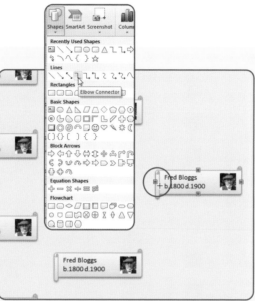

14 Repeat the process from steps 12 and 13, pasting new scroll boxes and aligning them, to produce two more columns with two and one boxes respectively in each column. You now have 15 boxes (from left to right – eight, four, two and one) arranged over four columns, covering your great-grandparents through to yourself.

15 To start linking your scroll boxes, click on the **Insert** tab, then on **Shapes**. Choose the **Elbow Connector** shape under 'Lines'. Place the cursor over the first generation scroll/photo box on the far right – the cursor will change to a small cross and red dots will appear on the object showing where you can attach the line.

16 Click on the connection site on the left side of the first generation box and drag to one of the parent boxes to the left. The cursor will change to the small cross target again and red dots will appear on the parent box. Let go of the mouse when the cursor is over the connection site on the right-hand side of the parent box.

Online research

You can always start to create your family tree without having all the information to hand, and then add details as you find them. Generally, where you look for information about relatives will focus on where they were born, lived and died, but searching more generally online can produce great results.

A good starting point for births, marriages, deaths and adoptions is the government website www.direct.gov.uk, under the 'Government, citizens and rights' heading. For census returns, wills and military records, go to www.nationalarchives.gov.uk. Other useful research and advice websites include the BBC family history site (www.bbc.co.uk/familyhistory), Ancestry.co.uk (www.ancestry.co.uk), RootsWeb.com (www.rootsweb.com), Genuki (www.genuki.org.uk), Findmypast.com (www.findmypast.com), FamilySearch (www.familysearch.org) and Genes Reunited (www.genesreunited.co.uk).

Adjusting the connecting lines

It is not always easy to put the connecting lines in exactly the right space. However, you can amend them afterwards by clicking on the line and then pulling the round handles that appear. You can also move them around by clicking on the line to select it and then pressing the arrow keys on your keyboard. To make sure the lines connect neatly to your boxes, go to the 'View' group and click on **Zoom** to choose a higher magnification. You will then be able to have a really close look.

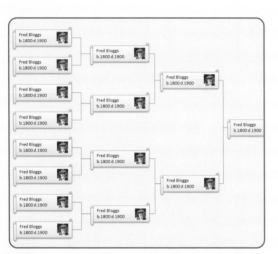

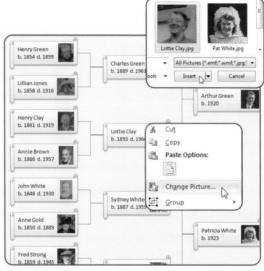

17 Repeat steps 15 and 16, adding connectors between each child box and its two parent boxes. The lines may need some adjustment, see above. If you accidentally move a scroll box, hold down the **Ctrl** key and press **Z** to undo the action and return the box to its original position.

18 Now make your family real. Highlight the default 'Name' text and type in the correct name. Then right-click on the photo and select **Change Picture**. Browse your hard disk to find the correct picture, and click on **Insert**. Repeat for all the other members of your family tree.

19 To add further interest, you could replace the plain background with a texture or picture. Click in cell **A1** then on the **Insert** tab and then on **Picture**. Search for a suitable image and then click on **Insert**. The image will initially appear on top of everything else.

Online resources from Office

The Microsoft Office Online website has family history templates. These include a family-tree template in Excel and Word templates for requesting family records from churches and other organisations. Launch Excel, click on the **File** tab then on **New**. In the search bar to the right of 'Office.com Templates' type **family tree** and press **Return**. Any templates that match your search criteria for your program, here Excel, will be displayed in the middle pane. Click on a template to see it displayed more fully in the pane on the right. Make your selection and then click on **Download** at the bottom of the window.

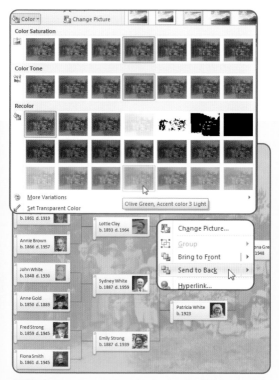

Bright idea
If you have a family coat-of-arms –
or would like to create one – scan
in an image and add it to your family tree for
a bit of extra colour.

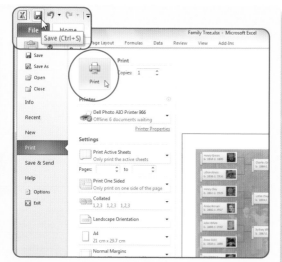

20 If necessary, resize the image to fit your page (see page 289). To place the image behind your family tree, right-click on the image and select **Send to Back**. Your family scroll boxes will now appear on top of the image. To soften the background click on **Color** in the 'Adjust' group and select a light variation or washout.

21 Now add a title. Click on the **Insert** tab and click on **Text Box** in the 'Text' group. Click and drag to create a text box, then type in your title. Highlight the text to select it and then click on the **Home** tab. Go to the 'Font' group and choose a font, size and colour.

22 Make sure you save your finished family tree by clicking on **Save** on the Quick Access toolbar. If you are ready to print it out, click on the **File** tab and then **Print**. Check the options under 'Settings' and when ready click on the **Print** button. You could then frame your printed history to show to the rest of your family.

Professional finish

You could take your finished family history file to a print shop for printing and also for laminating. Save the file as normal and also onto a CD (compact disc) or DVD (digital versatile disc).

Place a formatted disc in the CD/DVD drive and, with your document open, click on the **File** tab and select **Save As**. In the Save As dialogue box, select **Computer** and then click on **DVD RW Drive (D:)** (or another destination for saving your document), before clicking on **Save.**

Share it on the web

Having made your family tree in Excel, you can print it out and even frame it. But one way many people can get to see it and explore the information and pictures is to save it as a web page. If you have web space supplied by your internet provider, save the file as a web page to upload. Go to the **File** tab and choose **Save As**. In the 'Save as type' drop-down menu, select **Web Page**. Excel creates a web page document and a folder containing images for the web page that you can upload.

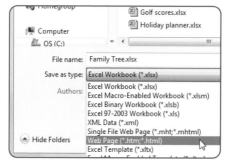

Make a recipe collection

Keep all your family's favourites together in a database

Most people keep recipes in different places – in books, on bits of paper or cut out from magazines. Tracking them all down can take time.

Save yourself the trouble by creating a recipe database. This allows you to keep all your recipes together, and lets you sort them to find the right recipe for the occasion. When you have found the recipe you want, you can print it out to use or make copies for friends. Once you have created your database, you can add new recipes as you discover them.

Give some thought to the type of information you want stored in your database. Do not worry if you cannot find all your recipes when you start – add them at a later date.

► BEFORE YOU START

1 Go to the **Start** menu, select **All Programs** and click on **Microsoft Works**. Click on **Works Database** from the Quick Launch menu on the right. In the Microsoft Works Database window select **Blank Database** then click on **OK** to open a new blank database document.

You can also create a recipe collection in Microsoft Excel. This will let you input and view your recipes in table form, ready for sorting according to your needs.

► OTHER PROGRAMS

Bright idea
Always include a serialised reference number field in your database so that each record will have a unique reference number. Works will automatically update the numbers.

*To select more than one field at a time, press the **Ctrl** key and, keeping it pressed down, click on all the boxes you want to alter.*

2 The Create Database dialogue box will open, where you can input your field names and specify a format for each field. When you have typed in your field name, click on **Add**. When you have entered all your fields, click on **Done**. Save your document by clicking on the **Save** toolbar button.

3 Your database appears in List form with the field names at the top of columns. To structure your database go to the **View** menu and select **Form Design**. You can now adjust the position and size of text boxes to make sure your recipe details are visible.

4 Click on the text box adjoining each field name. Keeping the mouse button pressed down, drag it into position. When positioning text boxes, rearrange them so that there is about 8 cm of space at the top of the page for your heading.

Fields and formats
Consider using the following fields and formats.

Field	Format
Recipe Ref	Serialized
Recipe type	Text
Recipe name	Text
Date of entry	Date
Calories	Number
Number served	Number
Cooking time	Time
Ingredients	Text
Instructions	Text

Sizing field boxes
To increase the size of fields, click on the field box to highlight it then move the mouse pointer over the bottom right-hand corner. When the cursor changes to a double-headed arrow, click the mouse and, keeping the button pressed down, drag the box to the size you require.

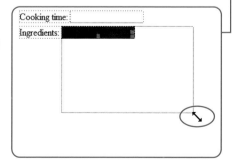

Key word

Field *This is a placeholder that contains a particular category of information stored within a database. Recipe Ref, Calories and Ingredients are examples of database fields in this project.*

Close-up

When you type words into each field they will appear in the Entry Bar above your form. You can correct any typing mistakes and edit your text there.

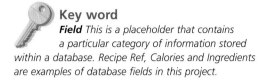

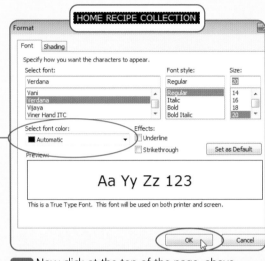

5 Now click at the top of the page, above your first field name, and type your heading. Highlight your heading then go to the **Format** menu and select **Font and Style**. In the dialogue box select a font, font size, colour and style. Click on **OK**.

6 Style the field names and the adjoining text boxes, perhaps using different fonts for each field to make them distinguishable. When you type in the empty boxes the text will appear in the style you have set.

7 To input recipes, go to the **View** menu and select **Form**. Type the information into the fields you have made. Press the **Tab** key to go to the next field or record, and **Shift** and **Tab** to move back. When you have typed in all your recipes, click on the **List View** toolbar.

*If you have a colour printer, why not add colour to your recipes? In the Format dialogue box select white as your font colour then click on the **Shading** tab. Now select a foreground colour and pattern. Click on **OK**.*

Shortcut

*To style several field names or text boxes in the same way, click on the first box, press the **Ctrl** key and, keeping the Ctrl key pressed down, click on all the boxes you want to style. Go to the **Format** menu and select **Font and Style**. Now style as you wish.*

Bright idea
You can view your database at different levels of magnification by using the Zoom tool at the bottom of the screen. Simply click on the '+' and '-' buttons.

Key word
***Report** A report extracts designated information from a database. For example, from your recipe database you could make a report on chicken dishes or meals that take 30 minutes to cook.*

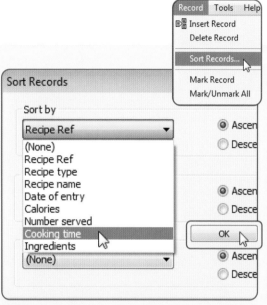

8 When it comes to selecting a particular recipe, click on it in List form then go to the **View** menu and select **Form**. The recipe will then appear in its fully formatted form.

9 To sort recipes by, say, cooking time, go to the **Record** menu and select **Sort Records**. Click on the arrow beside the 'Sort by' box and scroll down to select the field by which you would like the records sorted. Click on **OK**.

10 To list your sorted records, go to the **Tools** menu and select **ReportCreator**. Name your report and click **OK**. Then click on the **Fields** tab, select the fields to be included and the order in which they are to appear. When you have finished, click on **Done**. You can then print your list.

Scrolling recipes
You can scroll through all the records on your database by clicking on the arrows in the record counter at the foot of the Form View window. This moves you through each formatted recipe to adjacent records or to the first or last in the database.

Amending a report
To amend a report go to the **View** menu and select **Report**. Select the report to be changed and click on **Modify**. You can increase space between columns by adjusting their width. Click on the right-hand edge of the column header and drag to the right.

Design a baby book

Keep a special book of memories for all the family to enjoy

Watching children grow up is one of the greatest pleasures in life, and creating a record of their early years allows you to relive the experience time and again. By designing a baby book on your PC you can use as many photographs as you like, and you can also print copies of the book for your relatives instead of paying for expensive photographic reprints. It is straightforward to add a few personal design touches that will make your baby book a delight for generations to come.

Decide which photographs you want to include in your book and download them from your digital camera (see page 206) or scan them in (see page 200).

BEFORE YOU START

1 Go to the **Start** button, click on **All Programs** and select **Microsoft Word 2010**. Go to the **Page Layout** tab and click on the **Page Setup** dialogue box launcher. Click on the **Margins** tab to set your orientation and on the **Paper** tab to select your paper size. Click on **OK**. Now save and name your document.

You can create a baby book using Microsoft Works. To import scanned photographs or digital camera images, make sure the files have been saved in JPEG or TIFF formats.

OTHER PROGRAMS

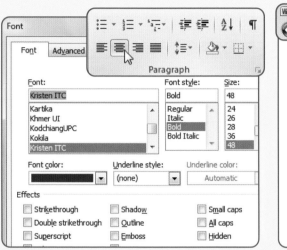

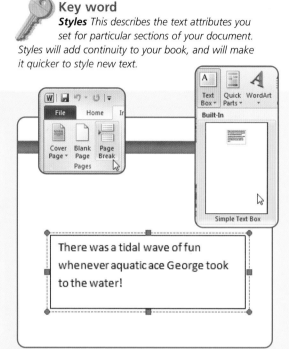

2 First, make a title page. Type in the title then highlight it and click on the **Font** dialogue box launcher. Click on the **Font** tab and select a font, style, size, effect and colour. Click on **OK** when you have finished. To position the title on the page, select it again and click on the **Center** button in the 'Paragraph' group.

3 To insert a photo, go to the **Insert** tab and click on **Picture** in the 'Illustrations' group. Locate your image – try looking in your 'Pictures' folder – and click on a photo to select it, then click on **Insert**. To position photos, see below.

4 To add a new page, go to the **Insert** tab and click on **Page Break**. You might like to add text in a text box for easier positioning. From the **Insert** tab click on **Text Box**, then on **Simple Text Box** from the options given. Move and resize the box in the same way as pictures (see below left).

Placing your pictures

To ensure you can move and resize pictures with ease, click on your image, go to the **Format** tab and select **Wrap Text** from the 'Arrange' group. In the 'Layout' dialogue box, click on the **Text Wrapping** tab. In the 'Wrapping style' section, select **In front of text**, then click on **OK**.

Move a picture or text box by clicking on it and dragging it. Resize a picture by clicking on a corner handle and dragging it diagonally.

Page and picture borders

To add a border around a page, go to the **Page Layout** tab and click on **Page Borders** in the 'Page Background' group. Click on the **Page Border** tab and choose the type of border you want. Click on the arrow beside the 'Apply to' box and scroll down to 'This section – First page only'. Then click on **OK**.

To put a frame around a photo, double-click on it and then click on **Picture Border** in the 'Picture Styles' group. Select a colour, weight and style. Click on **OK**.

Bright idea
You could also create a table of milestones, so that you can note when your baby started smiling, crawling, talking and so on.

*When you reach the last cell of your table, press the **Tab** button to create a new row. Continue to enter measurements.*

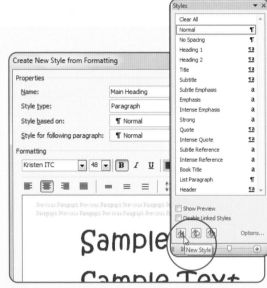

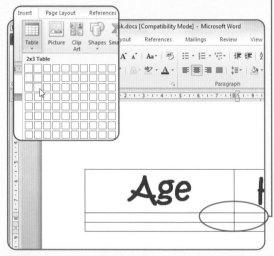

5 Now create consistent styles for your book. Click on the **Home** tab, then on the 'Styles' dialogue box launcher. Click on the **New Style** button at the bottom of the 'Styles' panel on the right. In the dialogue box, name your style (Main Heading, for example). Select a font, size, colour and alignment. Click on **OK**.

6 To apply your new style, highlight the relevant text and then click on the formatting style in the panel to the right of the document window. Use the same processes to create and apply styles for all your other text elements, such as captions and body text.

7 To add a height chart, go to the **Insert** tab and click on **Table**. Hover your mouse over the grid and click to set the number of columns and rows. Type 'Age' into the first cell, press the **Tab** key and type 'Height' into the second cell. Style the headings in your table using the new set of styles you created.

Font: Kristen ITC, 48 pt, Bold, Font color: Text 2, Do not check spelling or gra
Quick Style
   Based on: Normal
   Following style: Normal

In the 'Create New Style from Formatting' dialogue box, under the preview of your new style, is a description of the style. Showing font name, size, colour and alignment.

Using pictures within text

If you would like your text to run around a photograph, double-click on the image and click on **Wrap Text** in the 'Arrange' group. Select the wrapping style of your choice, here **Tight**, from the drop-down menu.

Bring Forward
Send Backward
Selection Pane

- In Line with Text
- Square
- Tight
- Through
- Top and Bottom
- Behind Text

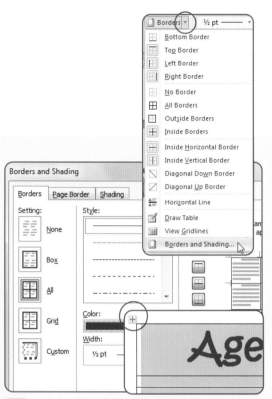

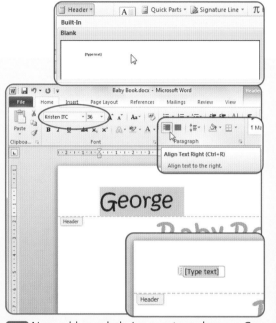

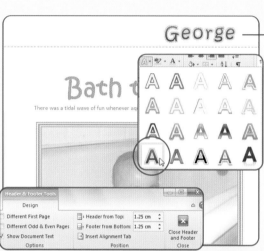

*If you do not want your header to appear on the title page, go to the **Page Layout** tab and click on the **Page Setup** dialogue box launcher. Select the **Layout** tab and, in the 'Headers and Footers' section, click in the 'Different first page' box, then click on **OK**.*

8 To style your table with coloured borders, click on the table move handle (upper-left corner) to select it. Go to the **Design** tab and click on the **Borders options** button in the 'Table Styles' group, and then on **Borders and Shading**. In the Borders and Shading dialogue box select a setting, line style, colour and width. Click on **OK**.

9 Now add your baby's name to each page. Go to the **Insert** tab and click on **Header** in the 'Header & Footer' group and select **Blank**. Type a name to replace the default '[Type text]', here 'George'. Highlight the text, click on the **Home** tab, select a font and size from the 'Font' group and **Align Text Right** from the 'Paragraph' group.

10 To further style your text, click on the **Text Effects** button in the 'Font' group, and select from the drop-down options. Click on the **Design** tab then on **Close Header and Footer**. The name will appear in the same place on every page of your baby book.

Print Preview

Once you have added all the elements to your book, click on the **File** tab and then select **Print**. Your book is previewed on the right. Check your options under 'Settings' and if you are happy, click on the **Print** button. If you need to make adjustments to the page, click on the **Home** tab to return to your page layout.

Watch your health

Keep a detailed record of your family's medical history

Everyone values their health, and that of their family, above all things. Yet few people keep accurate records of their own illnesses and treatments.

This information can be useful in establishing patterns of illness, providing up-to-date records for healthcare workers, and in keeping an account of medical and dental expenses.

With your PC, you can create a database that keeps detailed records of your family's health: what medications have been prescribed; dates of inoculations, check-ups and operations; allergies suffered. You can extract specific data when someone gets ill (for example, the name of a medicine that helped last time), and you can print out lists of future appointments.

Family Health Records

Name: John
Consult type: Optician
Consult date: 29/07/2010
Appoint time: 11:30 AM
Details: Regular check up
Comments: John's been complaining his eyesight is getting worse

Family Health Records

Name: Rosie
Consult type: GP
Consult date: 22/06/2010
Appoint time: 11:00 AM
Record ref: 00001
Appoint type: Runny nose
Treatment cost: N/A
Details: Rosie unable to go to playschool today as she was feverish and had a streaming nose
Comments: Dr prescribed antibiotics, advised stay off school for the week and come back if it hadn't cleared up by Sunday

Gather all the information you have about your family's health records, such as dates of check-ups, details of consultations and so on.

BEFORE YOU START

1 Go to the **Start** menu, select **All Programs** and click on **Microsoft Works**. Click on **Works Database** in the Quick Launch menu on the right. In the Microsoft Works Database window select **Blank Database** then click on **OK** to open a new blank database document.

*You can create a family health database in Excel. Go to the **Start** menu, select **All Programs** and click on **Microsoft Office Excel 2007**. Enter your data into the empty grid.*

OTHER PROGRAMS

Some format types, such as Date and Time, give a choice of additional formatting. Click on your choice from the list displayed.

To resize a text box, click on it then place the mouse pointer over the bottom right-hand corner. When the cursor changes to a double-headed arrow, click the mouse and drag the corner until the box is the right size.

Bright idea
When styling your fields and text boxes, use different fonts for each one to make them stand out.

2 In the Create Database dialogue box input your field names. Type the name of your first field in the box, select a format for the field, then click on the **Add** button. Continue to add all the fields you want and then click on **Done**. Your document will appear in List form.

3 Name and save your document. To ensure your details are visible and appear as you wish, adjust the design of your file. Click on the **Form Design** toolbar button. Click and drag on the text boxes to move them. To adjust the size of text boxes, see top.

4 To add a general heading to appear on each record, click at the top of the form and type in your heading. Highlight it, go to the **Format** menu and select **Font and Style**. Select a font, size, colour and style. Click on **OK**. Use the same method to style all the field and text boxes.

Fields and formats

For a family health database, you might want to create these fields, together with these formats.

Field	Format
Record ref	Serialized
Name	Text
Date of birth	Date
Consult type	Text
Consult date	Date
Appoint time	Time
Appoint type	Text
Details	Text
Comments	Text
Treatment cost	Number

Using Works templates

Microsoft Works has several health records templates already set up.

Go to the **Start** menu, select **All Programs** then click on **Microsoft Works**. Click on the **Templates** icon and choose **Home & Money** from the categories on the left. Select **Medical records** from the list that appears, choose a style to preview it, then click on **Use this style** to start your database project.

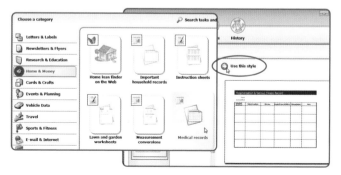

In Form View you can move through entries quickly by clicking on the arrows either side of the Record counter at the foot of the window. To change the magnification of the screen, click on the '+' or '-' signs beside the Zoom tool.

`|◄ | ◄ | Record 16 | ► | ►| | Zoom | 100% | − | + |`

You can extract and print data from your database. It is a good idea, for example, to print out a list of future appointments to put on display.

▶ SORTING AND PRINTING

Family Health Records - Microsoft Works Database

File Edit View Insert Format Tools Help

Times New Roman ▾ 12 ▾ | ☐ 🖙 🖫 🖨 🖺 | ✄

17.9cm 15.6cm

Form View

Family Health Records

Name: Gill

Consult type: GP   Record ref: 00017

Consult date: 01/10/2010   Appoint type: Check

Appoint time: 02:00 PM   Treatment cost:

Details:

5 Change the background colour if you wish (see below) then begin entering your records. Click on the **Form View** toolbar button. Click on the text boxes and type in the data. Press the **Tab** key to move to the next field, and **Shift** and **Tab** at the same time to move back to the previous field.

List View — ...cords - Microsoft Works Database

...w Record Format Tools Help

▾ 10 ▾ | ☐ 🖙 🖫 🖨 🖺 | ✄

"Rosie unable to go to playsch

✔		Record ref	Name	Consult type	Consult da
	1	00001	Rosie	GP	22/02/2010
	2	00002	John	GP	01/03/2010
	3	00003	John	Dentist	15/03/2010
	4	00004	Robert	Dentist	11/04/2010
	5	00005	Robert	Dentist	16/04/2010
	6	00006	Robert	Dentist	23/04/2010
	7	00007	John	Optician	23/04/2010
	8	00008	Gill	Dentist	08/05/2010
	9	00009	John	GP	09/05/2010
	10	00010	Gill	GP	09/05/2010
	11	00011	Robert	GP	09/05/2010

6 To see all your records at a glance, click on the **List View** toolbar button. If you cannot see all the information in a particular cell, click on it then view the contents in the Entry bar at the top of the screen.

Find and Replace

Find   Replac

Find what:

Match:

○ Next record

● All records

[OK]   [Close]

Record ref	Name	Consult type	Consult date
00002	John	GP	01/03/2010
00003	John	Dentist	15/03/2010
00007	John	Optician	23/04/2010
00009	John	GP	09/05/2010
00013	John	Optician	28/07/2010
00015	John	Dentist	10/09/2010

Robert	Dentist	15/08/2010	10:00 AM	Check up
John	Dentist	10/09/2010	09:45 AM	Check up
Robert	GP	18/09/2010	03:45 PM	Blood test
Gill	GP	01/10/2010	02:00 PM	Check up

7 To search for specific data in List View, go to the **Edit** menu and click on **Find**. Type in a key word for your search (here, records involving John), select the 'All records' option, then click on **OK**. All records concerning John will then appear in a list.

Background colour

You can give the background of your form a colour and pattern. In Form Design click on an area of white space outside a field or text box, go to the **Format** menu and click on **Shading**. Select from the pattern colour and other choices available, then click on **OK**.

Format

Font | Shading

Specify shading options you want for the selected cells.

Select color:	Pattern color:	Pattern:
Automatic	Violet	☐ 25%
Black	Dark Red	☐ 20%
Dark blue	Red	☐ Light Vertical
Blue	Turquoise	☐ Light Horizontal
Teal	Bright Green	☐ Down Diagonal
Green	Pink	☐ Up Diagonal
Violet	Yellow	☐ Light Grid

Preview:

Aa Yy Zz 123

Showing all

To see all your records after you have done a search or created a Report, go to the **Record** menu, select **Show** then click on **All Records**.

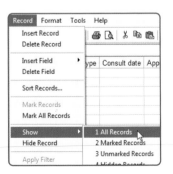

Record	Format	Tools	Help

Insert Record
Delete Record

🖨 🖺 | ✄ 🗐 🖺

Insert Field ▸
Delete Field

...ype Consult date App

Sort Records...

Mark Records
Mark All Records

Show ▸   1 All Records
Hide Record   2 Marked Records
    3 Unmarked Records
Apply Filter

Bright idea
To make an appointments list you probably will not need all your fields. Choose Consult date, Name, Consult type, Appoint time and Appoint type in that order.

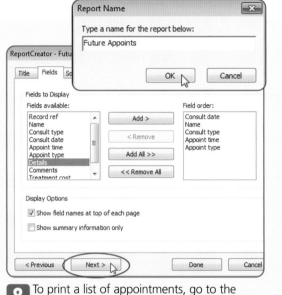

8 To print a list of appointments, go to the **Tools** menu and click on **ReportCreator**. Enter a report name in the dialogue box and click on **OK**. In the next box, click on the **Fields** tab. Click on each field you want in turn (in the order you want them), then click on **Add**. Click on **Next** when you have finished.

9 The Sorting tab is now selected. Scroll through and click on **Consult date** in the first 'Sort by' box. In order to print out future appointments only, click on the **Filter** tab and then on the **Create New Filter** button. Type in 'date' as your filter name and click on **OK**.

10 In the first 'Field name' box click on **Consult date**, then scroll through the 'Comparison' box and click on **is greater than**. Type today's date in the 'Compare To' box and click on **OK**, then click on **Done** to see a Summary. You are now ready to print your list.

Family Health Records - Future Appoints

Consult date	Name	Consult type	Appoint time	Appoint type
28/07/2010	John	Optician	11:30 AM	Check up
15/08/2010	Robert	Dentist	10:00 AM	Check up
10/09/2010	John	Dentist	09:45 AM	Check up
18/09/2010	Robert	GP	03:45 PM	Blood test
01/10/2010	Gill	GP	02:00 PM	Check up

Plan a new kitchen

Try out a variety of room designs to find the one that suits you

Drawing up a plan for your new kitchen helps you to decide how best to arrange all the elements for ease of use and optimum storage. You can create a two-dimensional plan on your PC using Microsoft Word. The plan can be easily adjusted as you make new additions, and you can create several alternative versions for comparison. When you are planning your kitchen think about how you will use it. If you do a lot of cooking, make sure you have plenty of work surfaces and that the three key elements (cooker, fridge and sink) are close to each other and easily accessible.

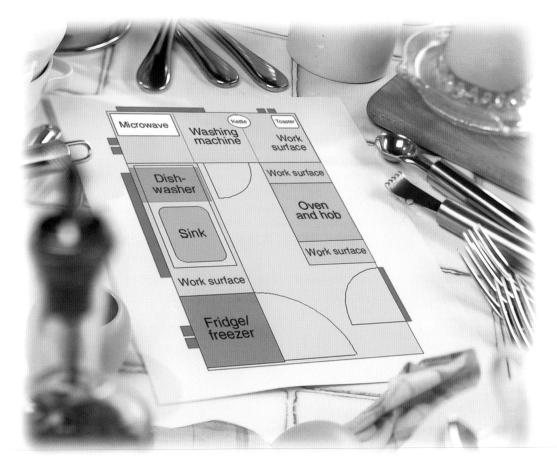

Measure the dimensions of your kitchen, including all doors, windows and appliances. Also note the position of electrical sockets and plumbing outlets.

► BEFORE YOU START

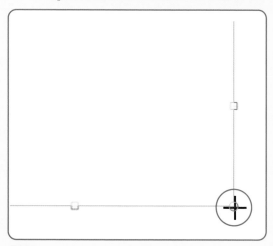

1 Go to the **Start** button, click on **All Programs** and select **Microsoft Word 2010**. Go to the **Insert** tab and click on **Text Box** in the 'Text' group, and then on **Draw Text Box** at the bottom of the menu. Click and drag the mouse diagonally to create a text box that will act as the outline for your kitchen.

*It is not possible to create a detailed plan to scale in Microsoft Works, but specialised interior design programs are available. IKEA offers a free planner on its website (www.ikea.com/gb/en/). Click on **Kitchens** then scroll down and click on **3D PLANNING TOOL**.*

► OTHER PROGRAMS

As soon as you have opened your new document, save and name it. Click on the **Save** *button on the Quick Access toolbar and save the document in a suitable folder.*

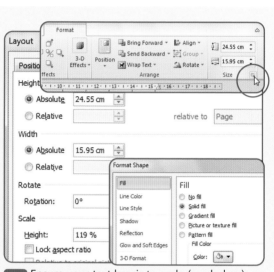

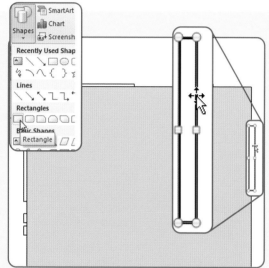

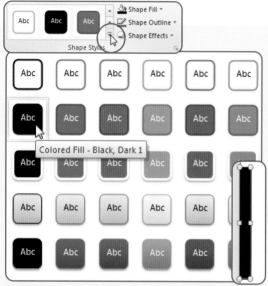

2 Ensure your text box is to scale (see below). Go to the **Format** tab and click on the **Size** dialogue box launcher. In the 'Layout' dialogue box click on the **Size** tab. Specify the height and width of your box. Click on **OK**. Click on the **Shape Styles** dialogue box launcher. Select a colour in the 'Fill' and 'Line Color' sections. Click on **Close**.

3 Now create boxes for all your fixed features, such as doors, windows and electrical sockets. Go to the **Insert** tab, click on **Shapes** and from 'Basic Shapes' select **Rectangle**. Click and drag in your document to create the shape. To move a shape, click on the edge of the box and drag to the required position.

4 It is a good idea to colour all the fixed features in the same way. To select all the boxes at once, hold down the **Shift** key while clicking on each of them in turn. Click on the **Shape Styles More Options** arrow and select a colour and line style from the presets.

Drawing to scale

Measure your kitchen, then scale it to fit onto an A4 page. If your kitchen measures 650cm x 450cm, divide each of the figures by the same number to calculate measurements that will fit on the page. Dividing the real measurements by 25, for example, would create a box of 26cm x 18cm. Design to real-world standards by scaling down 30, 60 and 90cm kitchen units and appliances in the same way, and using the same number.

Avoid clashes

To indicate the space needed to open a door, draw an arc. Go to the **Insert** tab and select **Shapes**.

Click on the **Arc** icon in the 'Basic Shapes' section, then click and drag on your document to draw the shape. Now add a straight line to form a complete segment. Adjust the arc's shape and size by clicking on a handle and dragging it.

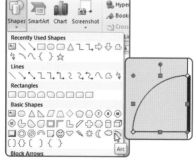

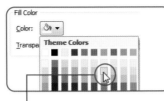

Use different colours for each appliance to make them distinguishable.

Bright idea
Write down some ground rules for planning your kitchen. For example: 'Don't put the sink below electrical sockets' and 'Appliances should be placed in positions where their doors can be opened safely'.

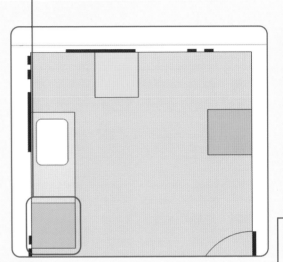

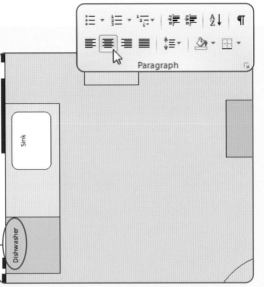

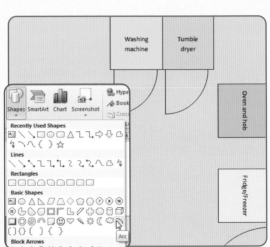

5 You now have the basic structure of your kitchen in place. Create more text boxes to represent your floor-standing appliances, such as a washing machine and cooker. Remember to scale them down in size in the same way that you scaled your kitchen dimensions.

6 To name an appliance, click in the box and type the name. To move the text down, click at the start of the word and press the **Return** key. To position it centrally within the text box, highlight it and click on the **Center** button in the 'Paragraph' group.

7 Move your appliances into position by clicking on the edge of the boxes and dragging them. Remember to allow for the space needed to open appliance doors. If you wish, draw arcs to indicate how far they will extend.

Style changes

To change the size and font of your text, highlight it, click on the **Font** dialogue box launcher, then click on the **Font** tab. Select a font and size then click on **OK**. To rotate text, go to the **Format** tab and click on **Text Direction**. Each time you click, your text will rotate 90 degrees clockwise.

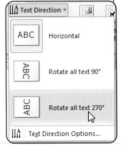

*You may find it easier to position items on your plan by increasing the magnification of your page. Click on the current zoom value (here 100%) found to the left of the slider at the bottom right of your window and, in the Zoom panel that opens, select **Whole page** and then click on **OK**. Alternatively, click and drag on the slider to select a suitable viewing value.*

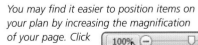

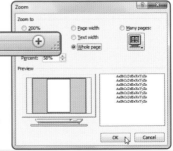

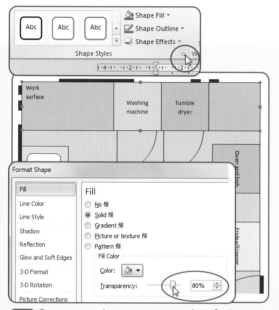

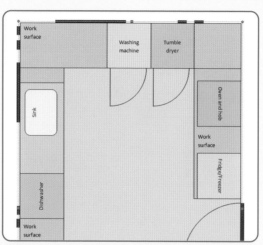

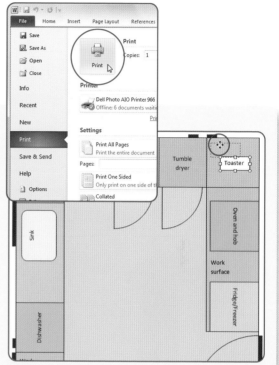

8 Create a semi-transparent text box for your work surface. This will allow you to see the floor-standing items below. Click on the **Shape Styles** dialogue box launcher. In the 'Fill' section, select a colour and then click and drag the slider on the **Transparency** bar to choose a transparency value of around 80%. Click on **OK**.

9 Continue to add and position as many elements as you need, working with spaces that match standard cupboard sizes. Take into account the space needed for doors and allow enough room to move around comfortably. Experiment with several alternative plans.

10 Finally, add smaller items, such as a toaster and microwave to show you whether your design is feasible in terms of your electric sockets. To print out a copy of your plan, click on the **File** tab, then on **Print**, check the options under 'Settings' then click on the **Print** button.

Creating different plans

You do not need to start from scratch to create different versions of your plan – you just save them as you go along.

When you want to save a version of what you have done, go to the **File** tab and click on **Save As**. Give the plan a different name from the original (Kitchen Plan 3, for example) then click on **Save**.

Take the effort and stress out

Finding, buying and moving to a new property is hard work – make sure

Moving house can be one of the most exciting events of your life, but also one of the most stressful. Big decisions and large amounts of money are involved, and you will need all the help you can get to make the process go smoothly.

You can get your PC involved as soon as you start looking for a new home. Use the internet to look for property, gather information about mortgages, find a solicitor and investigate the local amenities in the place you would like to move to.

Before deciding which is the best mortgage for you, you could input the details of different packages into a spreadsheet program and compare the costs. All the various and confusing factors such as cashback offers, varying interest rates, compulsory

# of moving house

your computer is the last thing you pack

life cover and indemnity guarantee premiums can be built into the equation, so you can see the best deal at a glance. Keep another spreadsheet for outgoings such as search fees, stamp duty, deposit and estate agent's fees.

When you find the right house for you, create folders for all the correspondence with solicitors, lenders, estate agents and surveyors. You do not even need to print off a copy for yourself: the file on the PC is your record.

Once the deal is complete there is, of course, the whole matter of moving. The keys to a successful move are sound budgeting and effective planning – and here too you should make the most of your PC. Create a spreadsheet to track the cost of a removal van and other moving expenses. You might also make a checklist of tasks to do – have you cancelled the milk, transferred the TV licence and your phone account, and arranged to have the utility meters read?

Before moving day, you can get ready by printing off labels for the packing boxes. Then, once you are safely installed in your new home, remember to send a card (which you have designed yourself) or an email to all your friends, to let them know your new address.

Countdown to moving

- Book time off work for the move
- Inform friends, bank, work and schools of your move
- Re-catalogue and value home contents
- Set up a budget document for the move
- Source removal firms and insurance (request quotes)
- Purchase or hire packing boxes and materials
- Plan packing schedule
- Arrange final readings and closing accounts for utilities: gas, electricity, phone and water
- Arrange house clearance for unwanted items
- Design invitations for house-warming party

Ideas and inspirations

Below are some suggestions to get your house move started. The projects can be adapted to your particular circumstances. You may want to give various tasks to different family members. Plan early to avoid the last-minute rush that plagues most home moves.

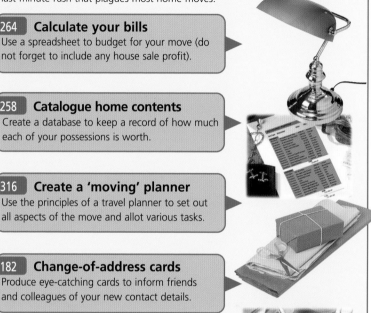

264 Calculate your bills
Use a spreadsheet to budget for your move (do not forget to include any house sale profit).

258 Catalogue home contents
Create a database to keep a record of how much each of your possessions is worth.

316 Create a 'moving' planner
Use the principles of a travel planner to set out all aspects of the move and allot various tasks.

182 Change-of-address cards
Produce eye-catching cards to inform friends and colleagues of your new contact details.

176 Packing labels
If your boxes are clearly marked you will be able to unpack items at your own pace, as you need them.

Also worth considering …

Once you have moved into your new house, put your own stamp on it by designing your dream kitchen.

306 Plan a new kitchen
Create a simple, overhead 2D plan of your new kitchen and organise your space effectively.

Beginner's Running Log

Devise a fitness plan

A simple spreadsheet can help you to schedule regular exercise

Along with your training shoes, stop-watch and sheer determination, your computer can play an integral part in devising and maintaining an effective fitness plan. Using a spreadsheet program, such as the one in Microsoft Works, you can create a fitness log to keep track of your progress, using both figures and written comments. Getting in shape can involve many forms of exercise so, while these pages show you how to put together a jogging schedule, you can adapt the project to suit any fitness plan.

Keeping a log of your progress can help you to see how well you are doing, or how far you have to go to achieve your goals. It also lets you make changes if you have miscalculated your time and abilities – and you can note down sessions missed due to illness or injury.

It is important that the schedule you devise is appropriate for your level of fitness. If you do not exercise regularly, consult your doctor first.

BEFORE YOU START

History

Quick Launch

Works Word Processor
Create documents

Works Spreadsheet
Perform calculations

Works Database
Organize information

Save As

Save in: Leisure

Name
Letters

Save

File name: Fitness Plan
Save as type: Works 6.0-9.0 (*.xlr)

1 Go to the **Start** menu, select **All Programs** and click on **Microsoft Works**. Click on **Works Spreadsheet** in the Quick Launch menu on the right to start your spreadsheet project. From the **File** menu click on **Save**. Now name the document, choose an appropriate folder and click on **Save**.

You can create a similar fitness schedule using Microsoft Excel, perhaps setting up a new worksheet for each week.

OTHER PROGRAMS

Key word

Formatting *This term describes the collection of style elements – including fonts, colours, effects and alignment – that determine how a cell looks.*

2 Cell A1 is automatically selected in your spreadsheet. Type a title for your plan into this cell. Highlight it, go to the **Format** menu and click on **Font**. Select a font, style, size and colour in the Format Cells dialogue box. The row height will automatically adjust to include your text.

3 Starting in cell **A2**, and continuing in the cells along the same row, type in headings as shown. In cell **A3** type in 'Monday'. Drag the bottom right-hand corner of the cell down so that the rest of the days of the week appear in the cells below. In cell **A10** type in 'Total'.

4 To change the position of text within cells, select a cell or block of cells with the mouse, then click on your choice of alignment toolbar button. Click on **OK**.

Adjusting column widths

Some of the text that you enter into cells may not be visible. To adjust the width of cells in a single column to accommodate your text, place the mouse pointer on the right-hand edge of the beige lettered column header. When the mouse pointer changes to a double-headed arrow, hold down the left mouse button and drag the column edge to the required width. Or double-click on the column header and it will resize automatically.

Your jogging schedule

When you start your schedule, concentrate on running continuously for a certain time, rather than covering a certain distance. Do not push yourself too hard. In the early sessions, alternate between brisk walking and running.

Before each jogging session warm up by walking briskly for 10 minutes. Cool down afterwards by walking for 5 minutes then stretching. Hamstring stretches are especially important.

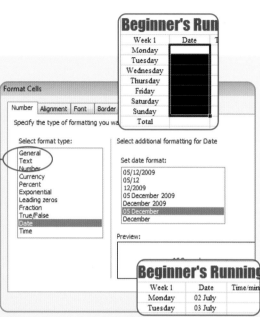

5 To style your text, select the relevant cells, go to the **Format** menu and click on **Font**. In the Font tab of the Format Cells dialogue box, select a font, style, size and colour. Click on **OK**.

6 Give your dates a uniform look. Select the cells beneath the Date heading, go to the **Format** menu and click on **Number**. Select the **Date** option in the 'Select format type' box and a style from the 'Set date format' box. Click on **OK**.

7 To assign colours to text, select the relevant column or section, go to the **Format** menu and click on **Font**. Select a colour then click on **OK**. Mark the end of your plan by adding a divider below the last row (see below).

Number formats
You need to select a format for the 'Time/mins' column. Go to the **Format** menu and select **Number**. Click on the **Number** option in the 'Select format type' box. Select a style from the additional formatting section – here, two decimal places.

Adding a divider
To add a divider beneath your weekly schedule, click and drag your cursor along the required number of cells in the row below the Total row. Go to the **Format** menu and click on **Shading**, then, in the Shading tab, click on your choice of colour and pattern. Click on **OK**.

Key word

Template A template is created to use as the basis for further documents that share the same basic features. To create a new document, open the template, edit it, then save it under a different file name.

When you paste your fitness plan in this way, you need to clear the information in the pasted log and change the weekly heading.

Week 1	Date	Time/mins	Weight/st
Monday	02 July	20.00	12st 11lb
Tuesday	03 July	0.00	
Wednesday	04 July	21.00	12st 11lb
Thursday	05 July	0.00	
Friday	06 July	0.00	
Saturday	07 July	0.00	

Format Cells

Number | Alignment | Font | Border | Shading

Specify how you want the border lines to appear.

Select border color: | Line type: | Border location:

Automatic
Black
Dark blue
Blue
Teal
Green
Violet
Dark Red
Red
Turquoise

None | Outline | Inside

Text

1		
2		
3		
4		
5	Wednesday	04 July
6	Thursday	05 July
7	Friday	06 July
8	Saturday	07 July
9	Sunday	08 July
10	Total	
11		
12	Week 1	Date	Time/mins

Beginner's Running log

Week 1	Date	Time/mins	Weight/st	
Monday	02 July	20.00	12st 11lb	Walk/r
Tuesday	03 July	0.00		Rest d
Wednesday	04 July	21.00	12st 11lb	Walk/r
Thursday	05 July	0.00		Rest d
Friday	06 July	0.00		Had a
Saturday	07 July	0.00		Rest d
Sunday	08 July	21.00	12st 10lb	Walk/r
Total				

Walk/run - started too fast
Rest day
Walk/run - found it hard going
Rest day
Had a brisk walk at lunch
Rest day
Walk/run - thoroughly enjoyed it

Beginner's Running log

Week 1	Date	Time/mins	Weight/st	Not
Monday	02 July	20.00	12st 11lb	Walk/run - started to
Tuesday	03 July	0.00		Rest day
Wednesday	04 July	21.00	12st 11lb	Walk/run - found it h
Thursday	05 July	0.00		Rest day
Friday	06 July	0.00		Had a brisk walk at lu
Saturday	07 July	0.00		Rest day
Sunday	08 July	21.00	12st 10lb	Walk/run - thoroughl
Total		62.00		

Week 1	Date	Time/mins	Weight/st	Not
Monday	09 July			
Tuesday	10 July			
Wednesday	11 July			
Thursday	12 July			
Friday	13 July			
Saturday	14 July			
Sunday	15 July			

8 To place lines between sections, select a section, go to the **Format** menu and click on **Border**. Select where you would like the border and choose a line colour, style and location. Click on **OK**. To remove the gridlines, go to the **View** menu and click on **Gridlines**.

9 Your fitness schedule is finished – now the hard work really starts! Fill in the relevant data every day and monitor your progress. Remember to build in rest days.

10 Use your plan as a template for subsequent weeks. Starting in row 2, select the cells in the plan and click on the **Copy** toolbar button. Place your cursor at the start of the row beneath the divider under Week 1. Go to the **Edit** menu and click on **Paste**.

Adding up totals

To calculate, say, the total number of minutes you have run in a single week, use the Works AutoSum facility.

Click in the cell below the cells containing your times, then click on the **AutoSum** toolbar button. Press the **Enter** key. For AutoSum to work, you must enter times into all the cells in the week, even if that time is zero.

	Beginner's R		Σ 🗐 🖩 📊
1			AutoSum
2	Week 1	Date	
3	Monday	02 July	20.00
4	Tuesday	03 July	0.00
5	Wednesday	04 July	21.00
6	Thursday	05 July	0.00
7	Friday	06 July	0.00
8	Saturday	07 July	0.00
9	Sunday	08 July	21.00
10	Total		=SUM(C3:C9)

Make a holiday planner

Keep all your family's travel details up to date and in order

Holidays are a time to relax and forget the stresses and strains of everyday life. To get the most out of them, however, there are some things you need to plan in advance, especially if you are going abroad. Do you have the right visas? Is your passport still valid? Have you had the immunisations you need? What must you remember to pack?

Your computer can help with much of your holiday planning. Spreadsheets are ideal for preparing lists of things that need to be done, and checking them off as they are completed. It is simple to draw up your lists using separate spreadsheets in the same document. Before long, you will be ready to jet off without any last-minute stress.

Ensure that all the information you are putting into your spreadsheet is correct. This is especially important when using formulas.

▶ BEFORE YOU START

1 Click on the **Start** button, select **All Programs** then click on **Microsoft Excel 2010**. A new spreadsheet opens. Click on **Save** button on the Quick Access toolbar and name and save your document. Now type your spreadsheet heading into cell A1, which is automatically selected. Add the rest of your checklist into column A as above.

You can also make a holiday planner in Microsoft Works, which has several useful travel templates. Follow the steps detailed at the bottom right of page 317.

▶ OTHER PROGRAMS

To adjust the width of a column, place the mouse pointer over the right-hand edge

	A	+	B
1	HOLIDAY PLANNER		

J24 | Width: 17.57 (128 pixels)

of the blue column header. When it becomes a double-headed arrow, drag the edge to the desired width.

Watch out
The currency converter does not take into account the commission you will be charged when you exchange cash or buy travellers' cheques.

=E9*E10

*To enter a multiplication sign, press the **Shift** key and **8** simultaneously.*

	A	B	C
1	HOLIDAY PLANNER		
2			
3	Destination: Orlando, Florida, USA		
4			
5	Departure date:	01-Apr	
6	Time:	9.15am GMT	
7	Check-in:	5.15am GMT	
8	Airport:	Heathrow	
9	Terminal:	Terminal 4	
10	Flight no:	BA507	
11	Local arrival time:	12.15pm EST	
12			
13	Return date:	15-Apr	
14	Time:	6.15pm EST	
15	Check-in	2.15pm EST	

	A	B	C	D
1	HOLIDAY PLANNER			
2				
3	Destination: Orlando, Florida, USA			
4				
5	Departure date:	01-Apr		
6	Time:	9.15am GMT		
7	Check-in:	5.15am GMT		Currency converter
8	Airport:	Heathrow		
9	Terminal:	Terminal 4		Sterling:
10	Flight no:	BA507		Exchange rate:
11	Local arrival time:	12.15pm EST		Foreign currency =
12				
13	Return date:	15-Apr		Foreign currency:
14	Time:	6.15pm EST		Exchange rate:
15	Check-in	2.15pm EST		Sterling value =
16	Airport:	Orlando International		
17	Terminal:	Main		
18	Flight no:	BA607		
19	Local arrival time:	7.15pm GMT		
20				

	B	C	D	E
	ida, USA			
	r			
	m GMT			
	m GMT		Currency converter	
	hrow			
	inal 4		Sterling:	1000.00
	7		Exchange rate:	1.61
	pm EST		Foreign currency =	=E9*E10
	r		Foreign currency:	
	m EST		Exchange rate:	
	m EST		Sterling value =	

2 Adjust the width of column A so that your text, except for your title and subtitle, fits neatly within the column (see above). Type your travel details into the relevant cells in column B. If necessary, adjust the width of this column, too.

3 You can now create a currency converter. This will automatically work out how much foreign currency your sterling buys, and vice versa. Type the text shown above into column D, starting in cell D7 and continuing in the cells below.

4 To calculate the foreign currency you can buy, add the amount of sterling you want to spend and the latest exchange rate into the relevant boxes. Now click in **E11** and type in '=E9*E10'. Press **Enter**. To convert an amount into sterling, click in **E15** and type in '=E13/E14'. Press **Enter**.

Formatting your cells

You will be entering different types of data into column B, including dates and times. You can select a style for each by clicking on the cell in question, then right-clicking and selecting **Format Cells** from the menu. In the 'Category' pane click on the type of information to be entered, or choose the **Custom** option. In the 'Type' pane, select your preferred style. Click on **OK**.

Format Cells

| Number | Alignment | Font | Border | Fill |

Category:
General
Number
Currency
Accounting
Date
Time
Percentage
Fraction
Scientific
Text
Special
Custom

Sample
01-Apr

Type:
dd-mmm
0.00E+00
##0.0E+0
?/?
??/??
dd/mm/yyyy
dd-mmm-yy
dd-mmm

Using Works

Microsoft Works has templates that can help you to plan your holiday. Open Works and click on the Templates icon, then select **Travel** from the list on the left. Click on the **Travel planning tools** icon and choose a style, then click **Use this style**. A customised spreadsheet will appear for you to start your travel project.

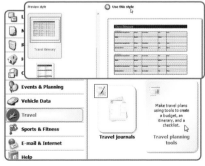

Close-up
When you choose a large font size for text, the spreadsheet row automatically adjusts to accommodate it.

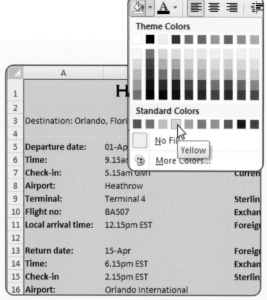

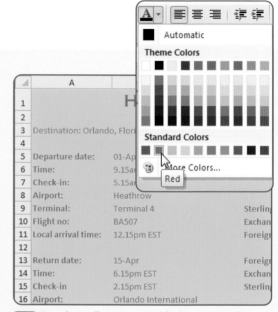

5 To style your heading, click in the cell, here **A1**, then click on the **Font** dialogue box launcher. Choose a font, style, size and effect, then click on **OK**. Style the rest of your text in the same way. To select a number of adjacent cells at the same time, click on the top cell and then drag over the others.

6 To add a background colour, select the cells and click on the arrow beside the **Fill Color** button in the 'Font' group. A drop-down colour palette appears. Choose a colour and click on it to apply it.

7 To colour all your text with the same colour, select the cells and click on the arrow beside the **Font Color** button in the 'Font' group. As before, a colour palette appears. Click on a colour to apply it.

Centre your heading

To position the heading in the centre of your page, click on cell **A1** and drag your cursor along the top row of cells until the full width of your form is covered (here, to column F). Then click on the **Merge & Center** button in the 'Alignment' group.

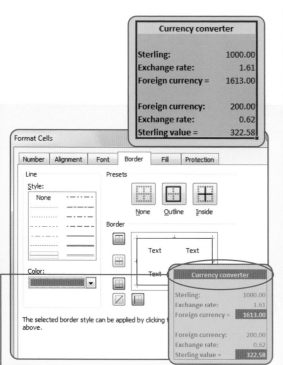

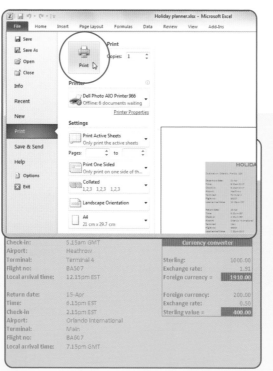

Bright idea
*If you want to add another page to your spreadsheet, go to the **Insert** tab and click on **Worksheet**. Another sheet tab will appear at the bottom of your screen.*

HOLIDAY PLANNER

Packing list

	Mum	Tick	Michael	Tic
4	Underwear (7)		Underwear (7)	
5	Socks (5)		Socks (7)	
6	T-shirts (6)		T-shirts (6)	
7	Shorts (4)		Shorts (4)	
8	Trousers (3)		Trousers (4)	
9	Tops (8)		Shirts (4)	
10	Dresses (4)		Tie	
11	Swimsuit (2)		Shoes (3)	
12	Sun hat		Hat	
13	Jackets (2)		Jacket	
14	Blouses (3)		Tops (5)	
15	Shoes (4)		Jumper	
16	Skirt (3)		Swim shorts	
17	Jumper			

8 To separate your currency converter from the rest of your travel details, place a border around it. Highlight the relevant cells, right-click with the mouse and select **Format Cells** from the menu. Click on the **Border** tab, select a line style, colour and outline for your border and then click on **OK**.

9 Before printing your planner, check the layout. Click on the **File** tab and select **Print**. Your planner is displayed on the right. If it needs adjusting, click on the **Home** tab and edit the layout accordingly. If you are happy with it, check the options under 'Settings' and click on the **Print** button.

10 Using the same process, it is possible to create a packing list and a list of tasks to complete before going on holiday. At the bottom of the window you will see a series of tabs. Click on the **Sheet 2** tab. A blank spreadsheet page appears, ready for your next list.

Currency converter

*To make your headings really stand out, reverse your 'fill' and 'font' colours. In this case, the background has been coloured red, and the text yellow. Finally, click on the **Center** button in the 'Alignment' group.*

Setting up your page
You may need to adjust the page settings of your document. Click on the **Page Layout** tab then on the **Page Setup** dialogue box launcher. In the 'Page Setup' dialogue box, click on the **Page** tab to check that Orientation is set to **Landscape**. Also, ensure **A4** is selected in the 'Paper size' box. To centre the page, click on the **Margins** tab and, under 'Center on page' options, tick both **Horizontally** and **Vertically**. Click on **OK**.

319

Plan a holiday you will

Do not leave your holiday enjoyment to chance –

Project planner

Create a folder for the entire project, called 'Holiday'. Add sub-folders for each element.

- 📁 Holiday
  - 📁 **Research**
  - 📁 **Preparation**
  - 📁 **Flights**
  - 📁 **Accommodation**
  - 📁 **Dining**
  - 📁 **Overall budget**

Everyone dreams of escaping from their day-to-day routine. For some, the ideal escape is a beach and a book on a desert island; for others it is a hectic round of entertainment and shopping in a cosmopolitan city. Whatever your dream, your PC can help you to make it a reality.

With your computer you can access websites on the internet to check out national, regional and resort destinations. You can look up weather forecasts to help you to decide which clothes to pack. You can even find out about wider weather patterns to ensure your visit does not coincide with monsoon or hurricane seasons. You may also be able to read

remember forever

your PC can help it to go smoothly

about local events listings such as carnivals or exhibitions scheduled to happen during your stay.

Through the internet you can order brochures, buy travel guides and check whether any inoculations or other health precautions are needed. Once your destination has been chosen, you can book flights and accommodation, hire cars and organise excursions. You could even check train timetables, ferry services and bus routes for destinations on the other side of the world, and pick up tips from fellow travellers.

In short, every aspect of your holiday arrangements can be researched, sourced and paid for via your computer.

Once everything is booked, your computer is also the ideal tool for holiday planning. You can create a database to organise all the tasks that need to be undertaken before your departure, and set up a spreadsheet to project costs and a budget. You can then create a diary to organise your trip and take a printed copy with you.

On your return you will be able to scan in or, if you have a digital camera, download your holiday pictures and produce your own photo album, which you can either display on a website for your friends to see or email/post to them. You could even send a holiday newsletter to friends with stories and pictures from your trip!

The adventure starts here

- 6 months: book time off work
- 5 months: check whether inoculations are required
- 4 months: budget for holiday
- 3 months: confirm booking/itinerary
- 1 month: organise travel insurance
- 2 weeks: buy currency/travellers' cheques

Ideas and inspirations

Below are project ideas to make your holiday run as smoothly, and be as memorable, as possible. All the projects can be adapted to your own circumstances and will give you further ideas of your own. Just alter the wording, layout or search details of each exercise as you work.

94 **Find information on the net**
Research destinations and weather conditions, and book accommodation and tickets online.

254 **Travel budget planner**
Spreadsheet software on your PC helps you to plan the finances for any purchase or project.

316 **Make a holiday planner**
Produce a document containing all the practical details of your trip, from time zones to car hire.

216 **Create an online photo album**
Make sure your trip is one you will remember with a pictorial souvenir created on the internet.

Also worth considering ...

Once you have finished, do not let your research go to waste. You can use information again and again.

172 **Create a contact database**
You can produce address and contact lists specific to transport, accommodation and new friends.

A collector's database

Keep a detailed record on every addition to your collection

Whatever you collect, whether it is rare stamps, coins, wine or music albums, it can be useful to keep a log of each item you own. As your collection grows, it becomes necessary to keep a check on its contents, its value and even the whereabouts of each item. You can use a database program on your PC to keep such records.

Creating a database is straightforward and, once you have entered all your details, you can find any information you need quickly and simply. Not only do you have all the information about your collection in one place, but a database is also a way of spotting 'gaps' in your collection and can help you to plan future purchases.

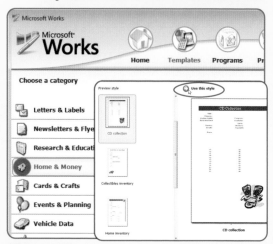

For a music database, gather together all your CDs, records and cassettes. If you have kept receipts for them, have these to hand too.

BEFORE YOU START

1 Go to the **Start** menu, select **All Programs**, then **Microsoft Works**. Click on the **Templates** icon and select the **Home & Money** category from the left-hand pane. Select **Home inventory worksheets** and choose **CD collection**, then click on **Use this style**.

You can also make a record of your collection using Microsoft Excel. Use the spreadsheet to type in your headings and data, then the Filter feature to create your reports.

OTHER PROGRAMS

Key word

Field A field is a space allocated for a particular item of information. For example, in a database of contact details there might be different fields for names, addresses and phone numbers. Fields appear as columns of data in a database. Several fields about a single subject make up a 'record'.

Shortcut

To style several field names or text boxes in the same way, click on the first box, press the **Ctrl** key and, keeping the Ctrl key pressed down, click on all the boxes you want to style. Go to the **Format** menu, click on **Font and Style** and make your style changes.

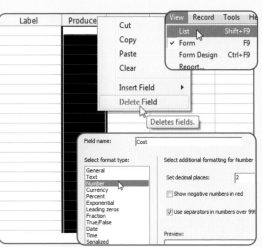

2 The CD Collection database opens up. It is quite comprehensive, but you may want to change some fields to suit your needs. For instance, we are going to change 'Producer' and 'Copyright' to the purchase cost of the item, and its estimated collector's value now.

3 To delete fields and add new ones, go to the **View** menu and click on **List**. Click on the column header entitled 'Producer', then right-click and select **Delete Field**, then **OK**. Right-click again and select **Insert Field**, then **Before**. Name your new field 'Cost' and select **Number** in the 'Format' section. Click on **Add**, then on **Done**.

4 Repeat the actions in step 3 to delete the 'Copyright' field and add a 'Value' field. Go to the **View** menu and select **Form Design**. The new fields appear in place of the deleted ones. To style them, see box below. (Note that 'Copyright' may still appear in this view – click on it, then press the **Delete** key.)

Fields and formats

Before you build a database, take some time to familiarise yourself with the various field formats.

You can preset data fields to style numbers, dates and text, applying font characteristics, rounding decimal places and so on. It is a good idea to include a serialised reference number to automatically update each record with a new number.

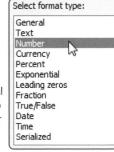

Styling fields

You can assign fonts, colours, effects and styles to your fields and their adjoining data boxes. Click on the **Form Design** toolbar button, then on a field name or adjoining data box. Go to the **Format** menu and click on **Font and Style**. Select a font, size, style and colour. To make changes to the position of data within the data boxes, click on the **Alignment** tab. When you are finished, click on **OK**.

Fields that have been formatted as 'serialized' will automatically update themselves as you enter new records. Set this option before you enter any data.

*To move to the next field or record, press the **Tab** key. To move back, press the **Shift** and **Tab** keys.*

To extract and display specific information from your database – for an insurance valuation, perhaps – you need to create a report.

CREATE A REPORT

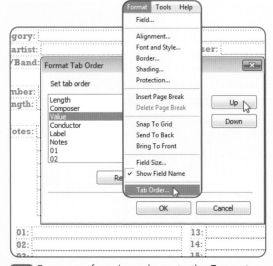

5 Once your form is ready, go to the **Format** menu and select **Tab Order**. When you create records you can move from field to field using the tab key – setting a logical order will speed up data entry. To change the order, click on a field name and then click on the **Up** or **Down** buttons to move it through the list. Click on **OK**.

6 To enter data, go to the **View** menu and click on **Form**. Enter the data for the first item and, when it is complete, click on the next record arrow in the bottom left-hand corner or hold down the **Control** key and press the **Page Down** key. To see all your entries at once, go to the **View** menu and click on **List**.

7 Go to the **Tools** menu and click on **ReportCreator**. Give your report a title, then click on **OK**. In the next box click on the **Fields** tab. In the 'Fields available' pane click on each field you would like to print, clicking on **Add** as you do so. Click on **Next** when you have finished.

You can move through your records quickly in Form View by clicking on the arrows on either side of the Record counter at the bottom of the window.

Searching for information

To search for specific data – say, all the music you have by a particular orchestra – go to the **Edit** menu and click on **Find**. Type in a key word, or words, for what you want to search for, select the 'All records' option, then click on **OK**.

The database changes to show only those records that match your search. To return to the full database view, go to the **Record** menu, select **Show** and then click on **All Records**.

View Report

Select the report you want to view:

Category
Artist
Insurance

[Preview] [Modify]

Works automatically saves all reports. To print or update an old report, go to the **View** menu and click on **Report**. A list of reports appears. Click on the relevant one then click on **Preview** to view it (then go to the **File** menu and select **Print** to print it), or **Modify** to update it.

ReportCreator

⚠ The report definition has been created.

Do you wish to preview or modify the report definition?

[Preview] [Modify]

ReportCreator - Insurance

Title | Fields | Sorting | Grouping | Filter | Summary

Sort by:

(None) ▼
(None)
Title
Category
Featured artist
Orchestra/Band
Composer
Conductor
Label

○ Ascending
○ Descending

○ Ascending
○ Descending

ReportCreator - Insurance

Title | Fields | Sorting | Grouping | Filter | Summary

Group by: Composer

☑ When contents change   ☑ Show group heading
☐ Use first letter only   ☐ Start each group on a new

8 The Sorting tab is now selected. To organise your data in order of, say, composer, click on the arrow to the right of the 'Sort by' box, scroll down and select **Composer**. Click on **Next** to select the Grouping tab and click in the 'When contents change' and 'Show group heading' boxes. Click on **Next** twice.

ReportCreator - Insurance

Title | Fields | Sorting | Grouping | Filter | Summary

Select a field

Title   ☑ Sum
Cost   ☐ Average ☑
Notes   ☐ Count
Composer   ☐ Minimum
            ☐ Maximum
            ☐ Standard Deviation
            ☐ Variance

☑ Show summary name

Display Summary Information
☑ At end of each group   ○ Under each column
☑ At end of report   ○ Together in rows

[< Previous] [Next >] [Done] [Cancel]

9 The Summary tab is now selected. To add up all prices for each composer, in the 'Select a field' pane click on **Cost** and then in the **Sum** box to the right. In the 'Display summary information' pane select the options as shown above. Finally, click on **Done**.

Title	Cost	Notes	Composer
Bach			
Preludes and Fug	£14.99	No sleeve notes.	Bach
Brandenburg Con	£12.99		Bach
	SUM:		
	£27.98		
Beethoven			
5th Symphony	£3.00	Rare LP	Beethoven
Piano Concerto 5	£8.99	Deleted rarity	Beethoven
Symphony no.5 in	£14.99		Beethoven
5th	£14.99		Beethoven
	SUM:		
	£41.97		
Chopin			
Miniatures	£22.00		Chopin
Nocturnes / Schm	£22.00		Chopin
	SUM:		
	£44.00		
Corbetta			
Guitar Music	£9.99		Corbetta
	SUM:		
	£9.99		
Handel			
Water Music	£14.99		Handel

10 A prompt box appears asking whether you want to preview or modify your report. Click on **Modify** if you would like to add any styling to your report (see below). Click on **Preview** to view your report. When you are happy with it, click on **Print** to print it out for your own records.

Styling a report

In the same way that it is possible to style forms, you can also adjust the fonts and sizes, and add colour and effects in your reports.

Click the **Report View** toolbar button. Select the cell or row you want to style, go to the **Format** menu and click on **Font & Style**. In the Format dialogue box click the

various tabs, selecting your fonts, sizes, styles, colours and background patterns as you do so.

To adjust column widths, place your cursor on the right-hand edge of the column heading. When the cursor changes appearance, click and drag to the desired width.

CD Collection - Microsoft Works Database

File | Edit | View | Insert | Format | Tools | Help

Arial ▼ 10 ▼

Report View

	A	B
F		
Title		
Title		
Headings	**Title**	**Cost**
Headings		
Intr Composer	=Composer	
Record	=Title	=Cost
Summ Composer		SUM:
Summ Composer		=SUM(Cost
Summary		

Organise a reunion and relive

Whether bringing distant family members together, or catching up with

Project planner

Create a folder called 'Reunion'. Then add sub-folders for each area of the project.

- Reunion
  - People
  - Communications
  - Event logistics
  - Finance
  - Suppliers
  - Design and logos

It is all too easy to lose touch with the people who used to be part of our lives. All of us have friends we would like to see more often. That is why a reunion is so special – and your PC can help to bring together people separated by the years and even by continents.

Start by setting up an event planner database. Record what tasks need to be taken care of, by when and by whom. Add details of each guest, such as address, email address and phone numbers, as well as contact information for caterers and other professionals you may need to recruit to make the reunion a success.

The increasing popularity of the Friends Reunited website (www.friendsreunited.co.uk) means old school chums can be easy to trace. There are also worldwide email directories of people who are online.

Once you have compiled your initial guest list, try searching

the good old days

old schoolfriends, your PC can help you

online for those you have not yet been able to trace. Some people – as well as your old school or workplace – might be easier to contact by email. For letters and emails you could create an attention-grabbing 'reunion' letterhead, then adapt it for subsequent gatherings.

Use your word-processing program to produce a newsletter to keep everyone updated on the arrangements.

This could be a 'missing persons bulletin', to encourage others to help you to trace 'lost' invitees.

When you have a rough idea of how many people will be attending the event, book the venue and arrange catering and entertainment, at the same time as keeping track of expenses through a spreadsheet.

One item you will not have to pay for is the invitations. Just design and print them on your PC – personalise the design and create a stir from the start.

Ideas and inspirations

Coordinating guests, possibly from all over the world, requires military-style planning. Make sure you dip into your armoury of PC-based skills to cover as much of the hard work as possible. Adapt the following projects as required, then prepare for a truly memorable occasion.

94 **Searching the internet**
Locate people anywhere in the world via email address databases and make contact with them.

316 **Event planner database**
Set up a document to handle the logistics of your reunion, and delegate jobs to others.

172 **Compile a guest list**
Make a database to incorporate people's address, phone and email details.

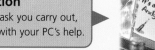
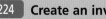
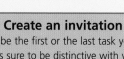

168 **Create a newsletter**
If the timescale for planning your event is long, you may wish to update guests on progress.

224 **Create an invitation**
It may be the first or the last task you carry out, but it is sure to be distinctive with your PC's help.

Get old friends together

- Contact your old company or school for a list of previous employees or students
- Conduct research over the internet
- Draw up a guest list
- Mail or email a proposal to potential guests
- Start to compile a reunion database
- Design and send final invitations
- Scan in photos or download digital images and email photos of the event

TROUBLE

Frozen screens, printing errors, corrupt programs and malevolent computer **viruses** can befall any PC user. But in most cases these and many other problems are **easy** to solve. Wherever the fault lies – in Windows, in any application or in the computer hardware – this section will help you to **identify** the symptoms, **diagnose** the problem and come up with a **remedy**.

SHOOTING

Problems sometimes occur with the physical machinery of your computer – its cables, components and 'moving parts'. The advice on these pages will help you to fix most common hardware difficulties.

Windows is the element of your system that allows communication between your hardware and your programs. Without it, your PC is useless. So deal with any problems as soon as they arise to be sure that your computer stays in peak condition.

When a program behaves in an unexpected way, you may be inclined to think that you have done something wrong, but programs do malfunction. Software Solutions can help you to understand and overcome the most common program faults.

My computer will not start up

There are steps you can take when you cannot get your PC to start working

A start-up problem is the most serious and worrying of hardware hiccups. It is hard to cure the sickness if the patient cannot tell you what is wrong and it is difficult to assess how serious the problem might be. Thankfully start-up problems are rare with Windows 7, but if you are unable to start up your computer there are a number of steps you can take to diagnose the problem. Then, even if you cannot solve the problem yourself, you can at least give some useful pointers to a specialist PC repairer.

Are you connected?

If your computer does not react at all when you turn it on, the first thing you should do is to check whether the power lights on the system unit and monitor are on. If not, check that both units are plugged into the mains, that the sockets are working and turned on and that the fuses in the plugs have not blown. Also, check that the brightness control on the monitor has not been turned down. Finally, you should also check the cable that connects the monitor to the PC.

Try resetting

If none of this helps, turn your computer off and then leave it for a minute before switching it back on again. If the screen stays blank, note down the number of beeps given out by the computer during the start-up routine as this might be helpful for a PC specialist in diagnosing the problem.

Hard-disk problems

If your computer will not start, it may be due to problems with the hard disk. This vital part of your PC stores Windows files and all of your documents. The hard disk consists of a 'read/write' head that hovers over magnetised disks. If the read/write head touches the disk, the result is a 'head crash' – a damaging collision between the head and the fast-spinning platters. This can destroy large amounts of data on the hard disk, including the data needed to make Windows operate. A hard-disk failure of this type is difficult to solve and should be dealt with by your PC's manufacturer (or your supplier if the computer is still under warranty).

Key word

POST The POST (Power On Self Test) routine checks that your most vital hardware components are working correctly. If the POST messages move up the screen too fast for you to read them, press the **Pause** key on the top right of your keyboard. Press **Return** to continue.

Windows 7 repair tool

There are many different problems that might prevent your computer from starting up. Thankfully, Windows 7 has a recovery tool called Startup Repair that can diagnose and fix many problems for you. If it cannot fix a problem, it will give you the necessary details to pass on to a specialist.

Startup Repair

The Windows 7 recovery tool Startup Repair can fix many problems that might prevent Windows from starting up correctly, such as missing system files, drivers, boot configuration settings, or damaged registry settings and disk metadata (information about your hard disk). When you run Startup Repair, it scans your computer for the problem and then tries to fix it so your computer can

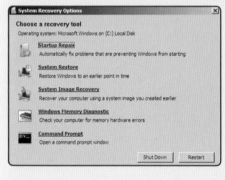

start correctly. If a startup problem is detected, it launches automatically a troubleshooter that will attempt to resolve the issue with little or no intervention from the user. If successful, the computer will reboot and an 'event' will be written to the 'event log', providing information about the problem. Where Startup Repair cannot repair the problem without user intervention, it will help you through the process to manually deal with the fault. If Startup Repair is unsuccessful in its attempt to identify or fix the problem, it will re-start the computer, reverting to the settings and configuration used before the problems occurred.

Startup Repair cannot fix hardware failures, such as a faulty hard disk or incompatible memory, nor can it protect against virus attacks. Also, it is not designed to fix Windows installation problems. If repairs are unsuccessful, you will see a summary of the problem. You can view a log of this and any earlier problems by accessing the Event Viewer (see page 363). For further information on Startup Repair and how to use it, see page 356.

Start with your Windows disk

If all else fails, you may need to use your Windows 7 disk to start up the computer.

If you have checked the connections and power supply and Windows still will not start up, locate your Windows 7 installation DVD. Insert it into your CD/DVD drive and switch your PC off. Then switch it back on again to start your system from the Windows 7 disk. You can then go to the installation menu and select the 'Repair Your Computer' option to try to correct the fault.

Some older PCs may not support start-up from the CD/DVD, in which case you will not be able to use the Windows 7 DVD as a rescue disk. If this is the case, you should consult an expert.

If Windows 7 was pre-installed

If you are using a pre-installed edition of Windows 7, you may not have an installation DVD. In this case, ask your PC supplier how to access the 'Repair Your Computer' option.

Your supplier might have provided a special 'boot disk' with the system, or supply instructions on how to make a boot disk that contains all the files necessary to repair your installation.

Watch out

Do not move your system unit, which houses the hard disk, when it is switched on. This could cause the hard disk's read/write head to touch the disk platters, which would destroy a great deal of data. When the computer is turned off, the head moves away from the platters. However, you should still be careful when moving the unit in case any other components become loose.

My printer is not working

Check your hardware and software to solve printing problems

Nothing is more frustrating than to put the finishing touches to a document, only to find that you cannot print it out. But do not worry. While printing problems are the most common of hardware hiccups, they are also among the easiest to solve.

Printers are usually good at telling you what has gone wrong. Sometimes it is simple: is there paper in the tray? Has the ink (or the toner) run out? Otherwise, there is a limited number of things that can go wrong: paper jams, loose connections, and mistaken set-up commands cover most difficulties. The steps on this page should lead you to the root of problems. After a while, you will develop a feel for what has gone wrong with your own printer. In the meantime you can use the excellent Help and Support files in Windows 7.

In the hardware

If you send a document to print, and it fails to do so, the first thing you should check is that the printer is switched on – is the power light on? Check that it is switched on at the mains socket, too.

Next, make sure there is paper in the printer paper tray, and that none of it has become jammed as it has been fed through. If the printer runs out of paper you should get an error message on your computer screen. If your printer is quite old and is jamming frequently, getting the rollers replaced may help. Otherwise, you may need to buy a new printer.

When your computer recognises that you have a printing problem, Windows will alert you by bringing up an error message suggesting certain actions that you can take.

Is the printer connected?

Most modern printers connect to the PC through a USB connection. USB cables plug into a free USB socket. Problems with USB printers can often be cleared simply by unplugging and then reconnecting the cable from the socket on the computer. Older printers use serial and parallel connections. With these types of cable, make sure all connections are secure and screwed in firmly.

Dell Photo AIO Printer 966: USB003

Communication Not Available

The printer cannot communicate with the computer.

Try These Solutions:

- Ensure the printer is powered on
- Disconnect and reconnect the USB cable
- Disconnect and reconnect the printer's power cable
- Restart your computer

OK

Start again

One way of quickly solving a printer problem is to try resetting the printer. To do this, just turn it off, wait a few seconds, then turn it on again.

Getting ready to print

The first step to successful printing is making sure you have selected the correct settings.

Page Setup

Occasionally, a page will fail to print, or will print out wrongly, if your page is not 'set up' correctly. Get into the habit of checking your Page Setup before you print. To do this, go to the **Page Layout** tab and click on the **Page Setup** dialogue box launcher.

Page Setup
Margins | Paper | Layout
Paper size:
A4
Width: 21 cm
Height: 29.7 cm

In the Page Setup dialogue box, set the parameters for the way the document will print. If you want A4 size, click on the **Paper** tab and select **A4** in the 'Paper size' box. Check you have the correct orientation, too: with Portrait the page's width is the shorter dimension; with Landscape, the page's height is the shorter.

Print Preview

In many programs you can look at how the page will appear before you print it. To do this, click on the **File** tab, then on **Print**. You will be able to see any set-up

problems in the right pane, such as if text runs over to other pages because the orientation is wrong.

Paper source

Your printer may have more than one feeder tray for paper, such as a manual feed tray needed to print envelopes. If so, make sure that you have selected the correct tray to print from. In the **Page Setup** dialogue box, click on the **Paper** tab and select the tray under 'Paper source'. Then check that the tray you want to print from has the right size of paper.

Paper source
First page:
Default tray (Automatic)
Automatic
Tray 1/Bypas
Tray 2
Other pages:
Default tray (Automati
Automatic
Tray 1/Bypas
Tray 2

Troubleshooting

If none of the above solutions works, you may have a software problem. Windows 7 has an extensive set of help files that can help to solve problems with your printer.

Go to the **Start** button, click on **Help and Support**, then **Troubleshooting**, and then type 'printer' in the search box at the top of the window. Now choose from the options presented to you, here **Open the Printer troubleshooter**. These help files can identify whether problems with printing are being caused by the printer itself or by a piece of software.

Windows Help and Support
printer
Best 30 results for **printer**
1. Install a printer
2. Share a printer
3. Rename a printer
4. Install a printer on a home network
5. Why can't I print?
6. Change your default printer
7. Getting started with printing
8. Why can't I change the printer properties?
9. Open the Printer troubleshooter
10. Find and install printer drivers

Printer tools

Many printers come with a set of tools on a CD-ROM disc that checks for common printer faults and may even try to fix them. If you do not have the original CD-ROM, try downloading the utility from the manufacturer's website.

Reinstalling your printer

If all else fails, you could try reinstalling your printer. Go to the **Start** button, select **Control Panel** then **Printer** from the 'Hardware and Sound' group. Click on **View installed printers or fax printers**. Right-click on your printer's icon and select **Remove device** from the drop-down options to uninstall the printer. Click on **Yes** to confirm. Click on **Add a printer** and follow the on-screen instructions to identify the type of printer you are installing and install its driver. Click on **Next** as you move through the steps.

Add a printer

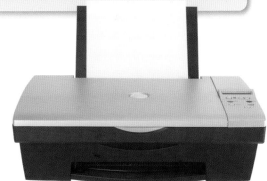

Add Printer
Install the printer driver
Choose your printer from the list. Click Windows Update to see more models.
To install the driver from an installation CD, click Have Disk.

Manufacturer | Printers
Brother | Epson EPL-6200
Canon | Epson EPL-6200L
Dell Inkjet Drivers | Epson EPL-N2050
Epson | Epson EPL-N3000

This driver is digitally signed.
Tell me why driver signing is important
Windows Update | Have Disk...
Next | Cancel

Checking ink levels

If the printer is printing your work but the printed text is faint or invisible, check that the ink or toner has not run out. Most printers will have a light on the front that will indicate if either is running out, and may also have software that warns you when levels are getting low. Sometimes with colour inkjet printers, the cartridge for one colour gets blocked or runs out sooner than the others. This can lead to strange colours being printed. It may be possible to clear a temporary blockage – check the printer's manual for details. If this does not work out, you will have to replace the cartridge.

My keyboard is not working

Hardware or software may be at fault if your keyboard is playing up

Your keyboard is perhaps the most vulnerable part of your computer. It gets the heaviest wear and tear; it is more likely to be moved and dropped; it takes a physical pounding every single time you key in a letter; and it is also exposed to dust, dirt and the occasional spillage. Fortunately, most modern keyboards are hardwearing and can take a lot of punishment before they start to malfunction.

The best way to avoid problems in the first place is to look after your keyboard (see page 63). But even if you take good care of your equipment, you may find keys start to stick or fail to respond when you press them. The problem may be due to a faulty connection or (more rarely) to a software error. Check every possibility before you buy a new keyboard: the remedy could be as simple as giving the keys a quick clean.

If the whole keyboard fails

If none of the keys on your keyboard is responding, check whether your PC has crashed. Try using your mouse to move the mouse pointer on screen. If it moves as usual and the PC responds, the problem must lie with your keyboard.

First check the connections. Most modern keyboards connect to the PC via a USB socket. Try unplugging and plugging the keyboard in again as this can sometimes restore a lost connection. On older keyboards that connect via a serial or parallel port, make sure the keyboard is plugged into the right socket in the system unit (it is possible to plug the keyboard into the mouse port by mistake). Also check the lead for signs of damage.

If a key will not respond

If one of the keys on your keyboard is not working properly, check whether dirt has built up between the keys. Use a dust spray, or work cleaning cards dipped in cleaning solution between the keys, to solve the problem. As a final measure, gently lever off the offending key and check for debris trapped underneath.

If this does not work, and you know the software is not to blame (see opposite), it is often less expensive to buy a new keyboard than to have the current one repaired.

Dealing with a spillage

If you spill a drink on your keyboard, unplug the keyboard, wash it using a clean sponge and a bowl of soapy water and leave for a day or two to dry thoroughly. Modern keyboards can be washed without suffering ill-effects.

Solving keyboard software problems

Windows has several settings that can affect the use of your keyboard. Check these if you are having problems with the keyboard or if the settings do not suit your special needs.

Select the correct language

Sometimes, a new PC will be set up for a different country, so that keyboard letters produce unexpected symbols on screen. Also dates and numbers may appear with unfamiliar formats.

To check this, go to the **Start** button, click on **Control Panel**, then on **Change keyboards or other input methods** under 'Clock, Language, and Region'. In the Region and Language dialogue box, click on the **Formats** tab. Ensure the correct country is selected in the drop-down box. Next, click on the **Keyboards and**

Languages tab and then on the **Change keyboards** button. If the correct language is not displayed in the pane – English (United Kingdom) for the UK; English (United States) for the US – click on the arrow to the right of the 'Input language' box, scroll down and select the correct language. To add a language, here German (Germany), click on the **Add** button. Then on the '+' to the left of 'German', then again on the '+' to the left of 'Keyboard' to expand the available options. If you have changed any of the settings, click on **Apply**, then on **OK**. Note that you will need to restart your computer before the settings can take effect.

Make your keyboard easier to use

If you have difficulty using your keyboard because of a disability, Windows 7 has a special Accessibility function that will make it easier. You can set up your PC so that you do not have to press more than one key at a time (StickyKeys). You can also set it up to ignore multiple presses of the same key (FilterKeys), or to warn you when you have pressed an important key, such as the Caps Lock (ToggleKeys).

To customise the keyboard in this way, go to the **Start** button, click on **Control Panel**, then on **Ease of Access**. Click on **Change how your keyboard works** and choose options under 'Make the keyboard easier to use' for how you want your keyboard to work.

⚠️ **Watch out**
If you press a key and an unexpected character appears, it may not necessarily mean the language your PC is using is incorrect. You may simply be using the wrong font. Some fonts, such as Zapf Dingbats and Wingdings, are entirely composed of unusual characters. Highlight the character then look at the font box on the toolbar to view the font used.

My mouse is not working

If your mouse stops responding, it is not necessarily broken

Do not be alarmed if something goes wrong with your mouse. There are many ways of working out where the problem lies.

If your cursor starts to move in a jerky way, or stops moving altogether, there are a few likely causes. Most of the latest types of mouse use an infrared light to track the mouse's movements. They may be wired or wireless. They are less likely to malfunction as they have no ball and rollers to get dusty or sticky. If this type of mouse does malfunction, check the surface you are using it on – it should be smooth and clean – and that the infrared transmitter is clean (see page 63). If the mouse is wired, check the connection (see opposite). If all else fails, the problem is likely to be the software and will require specialist attention.

If you have an older mouse with a ball and rollers, check if the inside of the mouse needs to be cleaned (see page 63) and whether it is properly connected (see opposite).

Different types of mouse

The traditional type of mouse connects directly to the system unit via a lead. However, many other styles of mouse are available today.

● Infrared mice track your hand's movement using infrared light. They may be wired or wireless. The only maintenance they need is gentle cleaning of the lenses and the small pads underneath them.

● Trackballs contain a ball and rollers on top of the mouse and need maintenance and cleaning just like conventional mice.

● Touchpads and tiny joysticks used on laptop computers cannot be cleaned easily. If you experience problems, take it back to the shop you bought it from (if still under guarantee), or a specialist repair shop.

Trackball

Touchpad

Bright idea
If you want to shut down your computer but your mouse is not working, press one of the **Windows** *keys on your keyboard (to either side of the space bar). This will bring up the Start menu. Now press the* **U** *key twice to shut down.*

Watch out
If your mouse is not plugged in properly when you turn on your computer, Windows will give you a warning message and you will find that the mouse will not respond to your hand movements.

Pointing you in the right direction

If you are having problems with your mouse, first check that the hardware is connected and in working order, then check for software trouble.

Check your connection

If your mouse stops responding while you are working, first check that the cable, or receiver if cordless, is plugged in properly to the system unit, and that it is in the correct port. The different types of mouse connections are explained below:

USB

All modern input devices connect to a computer using a USB port. Such devices include tablets – touch-sensitive pads that you write or draw on with a pen-like tool – and a wide variety of joysticks. Most problems with input devices that are connected via USB ports can be solved by simply unplugging and then reconnecting the device in the socket.

PS/2 and serial ports

Older computers used PS/2 ports or serial ports for the mouse and keyboard. If you are using these connections and your mouse stops responding while you are working, check that the cable is plugged in properly to the correct port. Mice are connected to PS/2 ports using a round 5 or 6-pin plug and to serial ports using a large 9-pin 'D' type plug. Switch off the PC then disconnect and reconnect the mouse in the correct port. Then switch the PC back on.

Infrared

This type of connection uses an infrared light to transmit mouse movements from the mouse to your PC. Infrared mice can be wired or wireless. A wireless infrared mouse transmits mouse movements to a receiver attached to your PC. Both the mouse and its receiver need to be in 'line of sight' in order to work properly. Check this and check the infrared lasers are clean (see page 63). If the mouse is wired, check the connections. You should also try restarting the PC.

Bluetooth

Typically a cordless device, which requires a receiver (attached to the PC) and a transmitter (the mouse). Bluetooth uses similar technology to infrared except that mouse movements are transmitted via radio signals from the mouse to the receiver. This technology offers freedom of use, but may suffer interference from microwave ovens or cordless phones. If you are encountering problems with a Bluetooth mouse, check the connection for the receiver and try restarting the PC. If this does not solve the problem, the software may be at fault and will need to be looked at by a specialist.

If all else fails …

If none of the solutions offered above work, try borrowing a mouse that definitely works from another computer. Make sure the mouse has the same connector as yours. If the borrowed mouse works on your computer, there must be something wrong with the mechanics of your mouse. If you are sure your mouse is broken and it is not under guarantee, then you will have to buy a new one.

Check your mouse properties

Strange mouse behaviour may be caused by settings in the Mouse Properties dialogue box. To open this dialogue box, go to the **Start** menu, click on **Control Panel**, then **Hardware and Sound**. Under 'Devices and Printers', click on **Mouse**.

The Buttons tab lets you switch the functions of the left and right buttons (to suit a left-handed user, for example). You can also set the interval between the two clicks of a double-click.

If you have a scroll wheel you can change the way it works under the Wheel tab. To investigate other mouse problems, click on the **Hardware** tab, and then on **Troubleshoot**. Follow the steps to discover where the trouble lies.

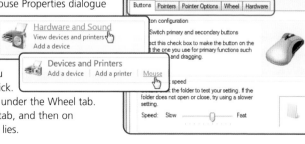

My speakers do not work

What to do if the only sound coming from your PC is silence

Computer speakers will generally give many years of use without any need for maintenance, apart from regular cleaning. Over time – years, in fact – the sound computer speakers generate may become increasingly crackly. This is merely a sign of wear and tear, and the most economical solution is to replace them. So seldom do computer speakers malfunction that,

if you are using your computer and no sound comes out of them, the likelihood is that the problem lies not with the speakers but with the way they have been connected to the PC, or with the software you are using.

A little knowledge of how speakers connect to your computer and interact with your software should help you to get to the bottom of the problem fast.

Some sound advice

It may seem obvious, but first check that the volume control is turned up. Next, check that the speakers are plugged into a mains socket and switched on – is there a power light? Also check that they are plugged into the correct socket on your sound card in the system unit. There are usually

a number of connectors, for microphones as well as speakers. Sometimes these are colour-coded – the speaker socket is often green. Swap the speaker plug around until you hear the speakers. If you have stereo speakers, you need to make sure they are connected to each other.

Software options

Another user may have disabled the sound facility on the piece of software you are using. Many games allow you to turn off the sound, out of consideration to those who share your space. If you can find no reference to sound in the program, check that sound is actually supposed to come from the software you are using (look in the manual).

⚠ Watch out

The sockets on a sound card can be difficult to tell apart, so it is easy to plug your speakers into the wrong one. This could be the cause of your speakers failing to work – but make sure the volume is turned down when you connect them to the correct socket.

Checking your volume control

If none of the checks to your connections and external controls reveals the fault, then you probably have a software problem. First of all check that the speaker volumes are not turned off.

Locate the small speaker icon that appears on the right-hand side of the

Windows Taskbar. (If you cannot see it, click on the white **Show hidden icons** arrow.) Hover your mouse pointer over

the speaker icon to reveal a pop-up message identifying your current speaker volume. Click on the speaker icon to display the Volume Control settings. Check that the 'Mute' box underneath the volume slider does not have an icon (red circle with a diagonal line) next to it and that

the volume slider is near the top of its scale. Click on **Mixer** to display an additional volume control setting for your system sounds under 'Applications'. These are sounds that your computer plays when certain events happen – for example, when you log on to your computer or when a new email arrives in your inbox. Again, check

that the 'Mute' box does not show a red icon next to it, and also check that the volume slider for 'Windows Sounds' is near the top of its scale.

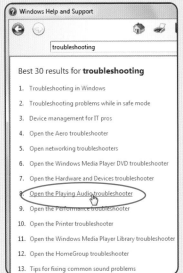

Extra help

Remember that Windows has its own built-in help and support pages, which explain how it works and what to do when things go wrong. Go to the **Start** button and click on **Help and Support**. In the search box type 'troubleshooting' and press **Return**.

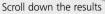

Scroll down the results list and click on **Open the Playing Audio troubleshooter**. Now click on the **Click to open the Playing Audio troubleshooter** link. In the Playing Audio dialogue box, click on **Next** and the software will identify the problem and offer options to fix it.

💡 Bright idea

If you cannot borrow a pair of speakers to check the connection, you may be able to use your Hi-Fi speakers. Use a cable to connect between the speakers port on your system unit and the auxiliary jack socket of your amplifier (you may need to get a special cable). Do not place your Hi-Fi speakers too close to your PC as they are magnetic and may corrupt your hard disk and affect the picture quality on your monitor. Proper computer speakers are magnetically shielded to avoid these problems.

Types of speakers

Most PCs emit sound through their own separate, free-standing speakers. It is possible, though, that your PC's speakers are built into the monitor, one on either side of the screen. These speakers also connect by cables to the main system unit.

Ensure your speakers are part of your regular cleaning routine (see page 62), and that their cables are kept clear of any obstruction.

My modem is not working

How to solve problems linking to the internet or sending email

On some occasions, a piece of software or hardware that has been functioning well for months can suddenly go wrong or stop working altogether. If something like that happens with your modem, do not panic. There are a number of reasons why your modem might not be working, and most of the problems are easily resolved.

Problems with your ISP

You should first check whether the problem is at your end. Try to connect to your Internet Service Provider (ISP). If you have a dial-up modem and you hear a series of loud, high-pitched tones (the sort you hear when you connect to a fax machine) then you know your modem is trying to make a connection. If the connection process does not complete, the cause could well be with the service provider's equipment rather than yours. If you have a broadband modem, it is more tricky to find out where the problem lies. In either case, call your ISP to find out if other customers are having problems and, if so, when the fault will be fixed.

Modem checks

If you are still having problems connecting and it is nothing to do with your ISP, the problem may be with the modem set-up on your computer – the modem might not be properly installed, for example. Sometimes, if you add a new piece of hardware or software to your computer, it can affect the way your modem is set up. Run through the set-up procedure in the modem manual to check that everything is arranged correctly. Alternatively, Windows 7 has a number of helpful tools that will diagnose and repair problems, including an interactive modem troubleshooter (see opposite).

Plugs and switches

Although it may seem obvious, check that the modem is properly connected. If you have an internal modem, check that the cable that connects it to the phone socket is plugged in at both ends. If you have an external modem, check that all its cables are firmly plugged in, and that the right cables are plugged into both the PC and the mains supply. Check that the modem and the mains power are switched on.

If you are sure that your modem is set up correctly, that your phone line is working and that all your cables are correctly fitted, but you still cannot make a connection, it is possible that the delicate head of the modem cable that connects the modem to the phone line is damaged. This is a standard cable, so simply buy a new one from a computer shop and reconnect your modem (see opposite).

Key word

Modem On Hold *(MOH) is a feature that allows a dial-up modem to work with call waiting. If you have Modem On Hold running and receive a call on the line that the modem is using, the modem can go into a hold state and pick up where you left off after you have finished with the call.*

To use this feature you need your modem as well as your ISP to support it. Contact your ISP and check your modem settings to determine if you can use Modem On Hold.

Watch out

*Never leave your wireless network unsecure – do not be tempted to let your router work without wireless security – someone **will** hack into it before long!*

Modem troubleshooting

If your ISP and your connections seem fine, try using the help facility available in Windows 7.

Before troubleshooting

Establish what type of modem you have. Most modems built into computers are dial-up modems and connect to the internet through a telephone line.

Go to the **Start** button and click on **Control Panel**. Select **Hardware and Sound**, then **Phone and Modem Options**. Click on the **Modems** tab and check that your modem is listed (this means your computer recognises it as installed).

If your modem is not listed, it may have been accidentally removed by another installation. Reinstall it by clicking on **Add** to bring up the Add Hardware Wizard dialogue box. Work through the simple steps suggested by the Wizard to reinstall your modem.

Broadband modems

If you have broadband internet access through an ISP, then you will have a broadband modem (see pages 88-89). This is usually connected to a cable or ADSL line, which in turn is connected to your computer through an ethernet cable and network adapter.

If you are unable to connect to broadband, look at the lights on your modem. There are four options:

1. Power light is on and the ADSL light is flashing. Shut down your computer and, after one minute, restart. Once the computer has completely re-booted, check the lights again and also the cabling.

2. Power light is on and the ADSL light is off. More than likely this is caused because the modem cable (RJ11) is not plugged in properly. Check the cable at both ends and check that the cable is plugged into an ADSL filter and not directly into a main phone socket.

3. Power light and ADSL light are off. Shut down your computer and re-check all connections. Remove all USB devices, wait one minute and restart. Reconnect the modem, and if there are still no lights on, try uninstalling and then re-installing your modem software.

4. Power light and ADSL light are on. You could be mistyping your username or password. Check that they are correct, and if the problem persists, consult a computer expert.

Networks

Broadband routers (wired or wireless) enable computers to communicate with each other and also the internet. If you have multiple computers, a router is an ideal way for them to access the internet via one modem. They also typically provide built-in 'firewall' security.

Wired

A wired router has numbered lights corresponding to each computer connected to it, so if a connection is 'down' the router light for that connection will be off. This probably means that there is a fault with that computer's ethernet cable.

If none of your computers are able to get internet access, you will need to unplug the ethernet cables from the router, disconnect the router from the phone jack and remove the router's power supply cable. Wait for one minute, then reconnect the router, then each of your computers in turn.

Wireless

Make sure the router is positioned away from anything else electrical. Wireless routers ideally should be placed on a high shelf in a midpoint of the house, say the hallway. Do not place them on the floor or behind a TV. Choose the best wireless channel and do not use the same channel as a neighbour. Finally, make sure your drivers and adapter are up to date.

Using Windows Help and Support

Go to the **Start** menu and click on **Help and Support**. In the Windows Help and Support dialogue box, type 'modems' into the search bar at the top of the screen. Scroll through the list of options and click on one of the links – here we have chosen 'Why can't I connect to the Internet?'. In the next box, click on **Click to open the Network troubleshooter** link. This in turn opens the Windows Network Diagnostics box, which starts the detection process. If this does not help you, click on **Explore additional options**, or click on the back arrow button at the top left of the window, and choose another option.

Upgrading your hardware

Improve the capabilities of your PC by adding or replacing a component

As your computer gets older you may find that it does not run as quickly as you would like, particularly when you add new software applications. The easiest way to resolve this problem is often to add more RAM (Random Access Memory). RAM is the place where your PC stores the program you have open and the data you are currently working on.

Installing more RAM will help your computer to function better, but it will not get the best performance from newer programs. If, for example, you load the latest computer game onto an old machine, you may find that the quality of graphics and sound effects is not what you were hoping for.

While it is possible to upgrade individual components, you may find that if there are several items requiring replacement it might be more cost-effective to buy a new PC. As time passes it will become more expensive to 'match' upgrades to the capabilities of your old PC.

Before installing new components, create a System Restore Point (see page 350) and back up your hard disk (see page 357), so you can revert to a properly functioning system if anything goes wrong.

Watch out
As with all mains-powered devices, treat your PC with caution. Switch the electricity off at the socket and then pull the plug out in case the switch is faulty. If your PC is an 'all-in-one', take care – components in your monitor can give you a painful shock, even if the machine is unplugged.

Bright idea
Computer developments come thick and fast. It is hard to know whether this month's hot new item will be next month's white elephant. Wait for new products to establish themselves before you buy; successful devices will improve in quality and fall in price.

The basics of upgrading

Upgrading your PC will often involve opening up the system unit. Here we show you how to fit a graphics card – use the instructions as a guide to fitting a sound card or internal modem.

Fitting a new graphics card

A graphics card generates the picture signal and sends it to the computer monitor. The latest graphics cards generate faster and smoother 3D graphics, and many support DVD and television playback. These cards will be designed to fit into a PCI or AGP slot at the rear of your system unit. To make sure you buy the appropriate card for your PC, consult your PC's manual or contact the manufacturer.

Switch off the PC, remove the power cables from the back of the system unit, then take the cover off (consult your PC's manual to find out how to do this). Locate your existing graphics card – this is the card your monitor cable will be attached to at the rear of the unit.

Unplug the monitor cable and then remove the screw that holds the card in place and put it to one side. Carefully but firmly ease the card out of the slot, then gently insert the new card in its place, making sure the socket for the monitor cable is facing outward from

the back of the unit. Secure the card by replacing the screw, then replace the system unit's cover.

Replace all the cables and turn on your PC. Windows will automatically detect the change to your components and, if it can, will install drivers for the device and configure it for use.

If Windows does not have the required drivers it will run the Add Hardware Wizard so you can tell Windows where to find them (see below). If you have an internet connection, Windows 7 will automatically search the Windows Update internet site for an up-to-date driver. If all else fails, you may find a suitable driver on the manufacturer's website.

Remove the existing graphics card to make space for the new one

Gently insert the new card, pushing it firmly, if necessary, to make sure it is in place

When the card is in place secure it with the screw

Adding new hardware

All modern hardware devices are 'Plug and Play', which means they will work immediately, without requiring you to manually install a device driver. A driver is the piece of software that Windows uses to run or access the device, and these days many drivers come pre-installed. When you add older hardware devices, Windows will usually detect the additional hardware when you start your PC and automatically install the appropriate driver if it is available. If not, Windows will prompt you to insert

the software disc that came with your device. If you are still struggling to install your additional device, use Windows Help and Support. To do this, go to the **Start** menu and click on **Control Panel**. Type 'add new hardware' in the search box at the top of the window. Under 'Administrative Tools' click on **How to add new hardware**, then in the next window click on **What to do when a device isn't installed properly** to display a list of options to try to resolve the problem.

Installing new hardware: recommended links

You can install most hardware or mobile devices just by plugging them into your computer. Windows will automatically install the appropriate driver if it's available. If it's not, Windows will prompt you to insert a software disc that may have come with your hardware device.

- Install a USB device
- Install a printer
- What to do when a device isn't installed properly
- Install, view, and manage your devices and printers

⚠ Watch out

Modern PCs use DIMMs (dual inline memory modules), older ones use SIMMs (single inline memory modules). They each have different size and pin configurations and SIMMs need to be fitted in pairs of the same capacity.

What to get and why

Think carefully before you upgrade. Be sure the new hardware will make a real difference.

Upgrading memory

Installing extra RAM in your PC is one of the most cost-effective upgrades you can make. Windows 7 (Home Premium) needs at least 1Gb of RAM, but will perform much better with 2Gb. If you find that your PC operates very slowly, or that your hard-disk light flickers constantly as you use your PC, you will almost certainly benefit from additional RAM.

Fitting memory is easy. Remove the cover from the system unit and 'clip' the chip into the appropriate slot (your PC's manual will show you the exact location). Make sure you fit the correct type of memory for your machine (see above). If in doubt, take your PC to a dealer to have your RAM fitted correctly.

Sound cards

Although PCs have come equipped with perfectly adequate stereo sound cards for some time, the higher-quality devices now available provide a richer audio experience. High-definition digital sound cards can provide a surround-sound environment for the latest computer games or for setting up a digital home cinema. Some cards also create realistic instrument sounds and 'acoustic environments' that make it seem as though sounds are coming from some distance away. They may also allow recording from several sources to enable mixing, which is useful for video editing, as well as for musicians.

Fitting a sound card is almost the same procedure as replacing your graphics card (see page 343). The sound card is easy to identify – it is the card your speakers are attached to at the rear of the system unit.

Graphics cards

Modern computers are sold with a graphics card that will handle most programs with ease. But if you work on very large scanned images, or if you want to run 3D games at top speed and high resolution, you might find that you need to upgrade to a faster graphics card.

Some graphics cards will also improve the picture when viewing DVD movies on your computer screen (see below), and may allow the use of a second monitor.

DVDs

Digital Versatile Discs (DVDs) store video as well as audio and computer data. There are five recordable formats of DVD: DVD-R, DVD-RW, DVD+R, DVD+RW and DVD-RAM. Often referred to as 'dash' and 'plus' formats, R means a write-once format, RW is rewritable and RAM can be single or double-sided. R, RW and RAM single-sided formats hold 4.7Gb of data while RAM double-sided can hold 9.4Gb. Most computer DVD drives, though, use only one laser, so a double-sided disc cannot be read. But this is hardly a problem when a DVD can store seven times as much data as

a CD. As well as the ability to play DVD films and software, a DVD drive will also play audio CDs and CD-ROMs.

If you want to fit a DVD drive to an older system you should consider buying an 'all-in-one' kit. This adds an MPEG-2 decoder, which is required for DVD movies, unless you already have a suitable card. Check the manufacturer's specifications for your graphics card if you are unsure.

Adding a DVD player will expose any weaknesses in your current graphics and sound cards and you may need to make further upgrades to get the most out of your system.

 ## Watch out

When buying pre-recorded DVDs online, make sure that you select the correct region. There are eight region codes worldwide, but the majority of DVDs fall into two regions: 1 for US and Canada and 2 for Europe, with a few exclusions. A DVD player bought in the UK will play only DVDs encoded for region 2.

Bright idea
Software manufacturers have a vested interest in encouraging you to buy products that might mean having to upgrade hardware. So, if in doubt, read product reviews in computer magazines for impartial advice on whether such an item is worth buying.

CD-RW Drive

Virtually all software supplied by computer manufacturers and software sellers comes on a CD or DVD. If you work with graphics or video on your Desktop you are going to want a device capable of holding hundreds of megabytes of data. A CD-RW (rewritable) disc can be used over and over again and can hold up to 750Mb of data. If you are upgrading your PC, get your dealer to fit and configure the new drive for you.

Monitors

Buying a bigger or better-quality monitor will not make your PC run any faster, but in conjunction with a modern graphics card it will improve the quality of images you see on the screen. Most PCs are sold with 15 or 17-inch monitors. Buying a 19 or 21-inch monitor will make using your PC more fun, especially for games and DVD movies.

Hard disks

Modern programs take up a lot of hard-disk space, especially if they use graphics, sound or videos. If your hard disk is nearly full, your PC will run more slowly (for guidance on how to check its capacity and available space, see page 52). Adding a new hard disk, and keeping your current one for extra storage, is one solution. Installing a new hard disk and making the necessary adjustments to the old hard disk is a job for a PC dealer.

New processors

You can even upgrade the central processing unit (CPU) of your PC. This is the main chip on the motherboard, through which signals between all the other circuit boards are routed. A faster processor will improve the speed of computer games and other processor-intensive activities, such as video editing, as well as making your computer simply 'feel' faster. Buying a new processor can be expensive, and there may be a variety of options to consider. Your motherboard may also need upgrading to maintain compatibility. To really get processors to perform at their best, you will need an appropriate amount of RAM (Random Access Memory) available for the processor to use. Your PC dealer will advise on the

best match with your current set-up and will be able to install it for you. If your PC is old, you may well be better off buying a whole new system.

Speakers

The standard speakers supplied with most PCs are adequate for normal use. However, if you want the loudest, Hi-Fi quality sounds, and you have a new sound card, you may want to upgrade your speakers. Changing speakers is easy – simply plug the new speakers into the sound card at the rear of the system unit.

Only buy speakers intended for a PC – they are specially shielded to stop their magnetic components from damaging your computer.

Problems after upgrading

How to solve hitches encountered with new hardware

Upgrading your computer system with new hardware will rarely present you with a problem. Usually, after you connect any additional hardware to your computer, Windows will detect it automatically and install the relevant software files for operating it. The process is designed to be straightforward and you should be able to complete it yourself. However, if you are concerned, you can ask a dealer to carry out the upgrade for you. If problems do arise, these may often stem from using an incorrect or outdated driver, and Windows 7 can resolve them with very little fuss. Faulty connections or incorrectly fitted cards also cause difficulties – do not be brutal, but fit all components and cables firmly, and ensure they are plugged into the correct socket.

Troubleshooting new hardware

Take precautions to help things to run smoothly when you tackle problems with new hardware.

Before you begin

In most cases installing new hardware is a relatively straightforward process. But there are some important preparations you can make.
● Make a System Restore Point (see page 350 for details).
● Always check the requirements of your new hardware. For example, are you running the correct version of Windows? Do you have enough RAM? Do you need any other components – if you want to use a new widescreen monitor, for instance, can your graphics card drive it? If you want to add a new surround-sound speaker set, does your sound card actually support it?

● Always check the manufacturer's website to see if there are updated drivers you should download. New software may have been tweaked soon after its release to improve compatibility.

Why upgrades can be a problem

Hardware and software upgrades can cause difficulties. With hardware you may have been supplied with an incorrect part – for instance, the wrong kind of RAM. Software glitches are more common and fall into two camps. The first camp is simply that the software you are adding is incompatible with your existing set-up and therefore will not work – an example might be installing a graphics program that is not compatible with Windows 7. The second camp is where the new software conflicts with existing programs and causes a system crash.

View basic information about your computer

Windows edition

Windows 7 Home Premium

Copyright © 2009 Microsoft Corporation. All rights reserved.

Get more features with a new edition of Windows 7

System

Manufacturer:	Dell
Model:	Inspiron 545
Rating:	3.7 Windows Experience Index
Processor:	Intel(R) Celeron(R) CPU 450 @ 2.20GHz 2.19 GHz
Installed memory (RAM):	3.00 GB
System type:	64-bit Operating System
Pen and Touch:	No Pen or Touch Input is available for this Display

Dell support

| Website: | Online support |

Computer name, domain, and workgroup settings

Memory problems

If your computer is unable to locate a new memory chip, it may be because it is not plugged in properly. To check the memory, go to the **Start** menu, right-click on **Computer** and click on **Properties** in the pop-up menu. The dialogue box will tell you how much memory your PC thinks it has. If your RAM memory has increased, your memory card is fitted correctly.

If a series of error messages mentioning memory problems and 'parity errors' are displayed, your memory may be of the wrong type. In that case, check with your PC manufacturer to discover the correct specification.

Hard drives

Your PC may not recognise a new hard drive. If so, take the computer back to your dealer. There are several possible solutions, but they require specialist knowledge.

External drives

If a new external drive – such as a hard disk, CD or DVD writer – is not recognised by your PC, first check that the cables are properly connected. Then ensure that any new driver card, such as a SCSI card, is correctly seated in its slot. If the problem persists, you may be using the wrong driver or have a hardware conflict (see page 348).

Sound cards

If you cannot get any sound from your computer after fitting a new sound card, first check that the card has been fitted properly, that your speakers are plugged in, and that all the connections have been made, including the cable that joins the CD/DVD-ROM to the sound card. If this does not solve the problem, or the sound from the speakers is poor, you may have a driver problem.

Monitor problems

If your new monitor does not work, first check that it is properly plugged into the power supply and the graphics card. Check the settings by turning up the brightness and contrast controls. If it still does not work, connect another monitor that you know works (this may be your old one). If this one works, then the new monitor is faulty and should be taken back to your dealer. If the other monitor does not work either, the fault lies with the graphics card.

Key word

Expansion card *This is a circuit board that adds certain functions to a computer. Expansion cards can be installed for improved or additional features. For example, a sound card gives a PC the ability to record and play sound.*

Graphics cards

If the graphics card is not working at all, you will not see anything on your screen, but you should still hear your hard disk 'whirring' when you turn on your PC. The most likely explanation is that the card is not connected properly. Switch the PC off at the mains, open the system unit and make sure the card is seated along its full length.

If your screen is 'snowy' or your Windows display looks strange, you have a graphic-driver problem. Make sure you use the latest driver – you can visit the card manufacturer's website to obtain the latest version.

A driver problem may also be the cause if the standard 640 x 480 with 16 colours is the only screen resolution available. To view the resolution settings, go to the **Start** button, click on **Control Panel**, then on **Personalization**, and select **Display Settings**. The current resolution and colour depth is displayed in the **Monitor** tab.

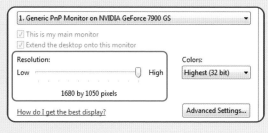

1. Generic PnP Monitor on NVIDIA GeForce 7900 GS

☑ This is my main monitor

☑ Extend the desktop onto this monitor

Resolution:

Low ————————— High

1680 by 1050 pixels

Colors:

Highest (32 bit)

How do I get the best display?

Advanced Settings...

'Plug and Play' upgrades

Most new hardware is described as 'Plug and Play' and installs automatically, or with minimum involvement from you. Most Plug and Play devices are external and have a USB-type connector: you just plug them in and let Windows do the rest.

USB connection has replaced most earlier peripheral connections, and appears to be immune to the kind of hardware conflicts that plagued older systems. However, to ensure future Plug and Play compatibility it is essential that you keep your system up to date.

Bright idea

*Always install the manufacturer's software supplied with your new device. Carefully read the instructions that accompanied the device to see if you need to install a driver **before** connecting the device. In most cases, Windows will find functioning drivers for you when you connect a new device, although some devices require you to install the drivers manually.*

Troubleshoot hardware conflicts

If you install a lot of hardware, particularly devices that are not Plug and Play (see page 347), you may encounter problems such as a piece of hardware that has functioned well for a long time suddenly refusing to work.

You can check to see what hardware you have, and its 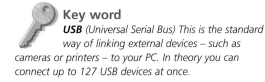 settings, in the Device Manager. Click on the **Start** button, **Control Panel**, then double-click on **Device Manager**.

In the Device Manager dialogue box, click on the plus signs to see more detail about any of the devices attached to your PC, and double-click on a particular item to bring up a dialogue box that shows its properties in greater detail.

An exclamation mark indicates some kind of a problem – perhaps the device is not fitted correctly, or your driver is out of date.

System Information

You may also find it useful to use System Information to help to resolve persistent problems. Click on the **Start** button, choose **All Programs**, **Accessories**, **System Tools** then **System Information**. Now click on the **+** sign next to **Hardware Resources**, then **Conflicts/Sharing**. The information here looks quite complex, but it can help you to quickly identify hardware that is sharing important system resources. Factory-fitted items that share resources – such as your central processor and video card – are unlikely to cause problems, but devices you have fitted yourself might be at the root of any difficulties. If you discover a particular item is conflicting, contact its manufacturer's technical support department for advice.

Keep your system up to date

It is not only owners of newer computers who can experience problems. If your computer is a little old and you buy new hardware for it, there may be problems. The cause might include existing software or hardware, or even the operating system itself.

It is a good idea to try to keep your operating system and all your hardware drivers as up to date as possible, in order to avoid any problems.

Windows Update

Windows 7 includes a feature called Windows Update that keeps your operating system up to date. It will automatically find online software updates for your computer whenever you launch it.

Go to the **Start** button and click on the **Control Panel** button, and then double-click on **Windows Update**. When Windows Update has connected to the internet, choose **Check for updates** from the panel on the left.

Reviewing the situation

To review previously installed updates, click on **View update history**. Here you can see important information regarding the name, status, importance and date of installed updates. Click on **Troubleshoot problems with installing updates** for solutions to common problems with installing updates.

Review your update history

Check the Status column to ensure all important updates were successful. To remove an update, see Installed Upd
Troubleshoot problems with installing updates

Name	Status	Importance
Definition Update for Windows Defender - KB915597 (Definition 1.71.992.0)	Successful	Important
Definition Update for Windows Defender - KB915597 (Definition 1.71.833.0)	Successful	Important
Definition Update for Windows Defender - KB915597 (Definition 1.71.700.0)	Successful	Important
Update for Microsoft Office Outlook 2007 Junk Email Filter (KB976884)	Successful	Important
Windows Malicious Software Removal Tool x64 - December 2009 (KB890830)	Successful	Important
Update for Microsoft Office InfoPath 2007 (KB976416)	Successful	Important

Key word

Hardware conflict *This occurs when your PC is unable to recognise a piece of hardware. This can happen when the hardware is set up incorrectly, or because it is incompatible with your particular PC or the software you are attempting to use it with.*

Wait while the checking process is in progress – this may take some time if you have a dial-up connection. If there are updates available, you can choose which updates to install by clicking on **important updates are available** (a number will precede this if relevant). The simplest option is to accept all the updates by clicking on **Install updates** and follow the prompts. You can review previously installed updates by clicking on **View update history** (see above). Many updates will be designed to fix security lapses – software developers and computer hackers are engaged in a continual battle, so it makes good sense to use each security advance as soon as

it becomes available. You need to authorise downloads if they are not Microsoft Certificated, and you will also need to re-boot your computer after update installations are completed – you will be informed of this by on-screen messages.

Automatic updates

Better still, set Windows to search for updates by itself. Click on the **Start** button, then on **Control Panel**, then double-click on **Windows Update**. When the Windows Update box appears, choose **Change settings** from the panel on the left. This option is particularly handy if you have an always-on internet connection such as an ADSL or cable line. If you leave your PC running all the time (something that most computers are designed for), you will always be up to speed on updates.

Manufacturers' websites

Visit manufacturers' websites and check them for new information or updates for your hardware and software.

Generally, new drivers will be located in a section of the site known as Support, Software Updates or Downloads. Work systematically through the options available to find the right driver for your operating system and hardware device, and do not forget to check the version of your existing driver first. You can find out what driver you already have by right-clicking on the device in Device Manager, selecting **Properties** and then choosing the **Driver** tab.

If you do encounter a problem after installing new hardware and software, go straight to the manufacturer's website. It is likely you will not be the only person to have encountered the problem, so you may find a 'patch' to fix it or suggestions of things to try.

Your consumer rights

In Britain you have a number of legal rights that a UK-based retailer must abide by. One example given by the government's Office of Fair Trading is that if you specifically request products for one particular computer system and are supplied with goods that only work with a different set-up, you are entitled to return the goods and ask for your money back. You may also be entitled to compensation if the goods cause damage to your machine.

Troubleshoot using System Restore

If an upgrade results in a problem, here is one way of solving it

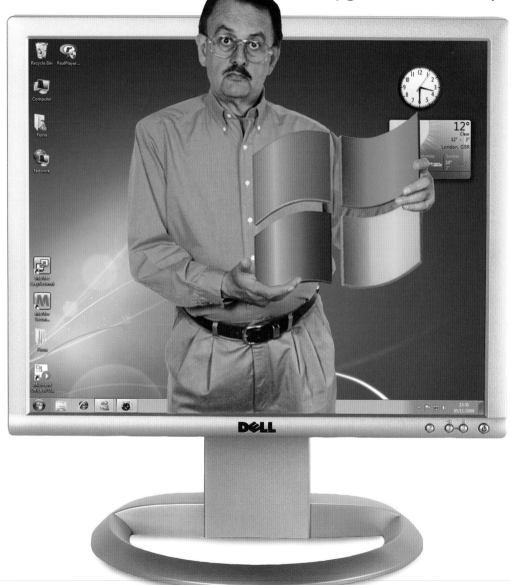

Windows 7 is designed to be user-friendly, versatile and robust. Even professional users making complex videos or animations find crashes are rare. Windows will not leave you on your own even if a crash does occur. Indeed, it has one of the most reliable and comprehensive recovery and diagnosis tools available: System Restore.

Use 'time travel' to fix problems

System Restore is a clever utility that lets you take 'snapshots' of the state of your system at regular intervals. If something goes wrong when you install new software or hardware, you can use System Restore to quickly put your machine back into a working condition – effectively stepping back in time to a point before your PC became unstable.

In addition, System Restore can be used for much more. With a little logical thought you can diagnose and track down the source of any problems so you can repair them.

The process involves trial and error – you start from a point where you know your PC works, add in suspect software and devices, making 'System Restore Points' as you go, until your PC crashes again. You then roll back to your last 'Restore Point'. The chances are that the last piece of software or hardware you added caused the crash. Often problems are caused by a conflict between two programs. If this is the case, an additional Windows system tool called 'Conflicts/Sharing' can help.

Using System Restore to diagnose a conflict

Your computer might crash for a variety of reasons, such as a power surge or cut. System Restore gets you up and running again quickly. Persistent failures, however, may have deeper roots.

Properties dialogue box as before, then click on **System Restore**, then on **Next**, and then choose which Restore Point you want to revert to. Continue selecting options and clicking on **Next** until you finally click on **Finish**. Windows 7 will automatically create Restore Points whenever you install files or hardware so, even if you have not set many manual Restore Points yourself, you may have a long list to choose from.

Use the System Restore procedure to move through subsequent Restore Points, restarting the PC each time, to locate the point at which problems develop.

First steps

Before you install new hardware, use System Protection to create a Restore Point. Click on **Start**, **Control Panel**, then double-click on **System**. In the left pane click on **System Protection** (you may be asked for an administrator password or confirmation). In the System Properties dialogue box, ensure the System Protection tab is selected, and click on **Create** next to 'Create a restore point right now for the drives that have system protection turned on'. In the System Protection dialogue box, give your Restore Point a name and click on **Create**. A progress bar displays during this process. Click on **OK** when finished. Next install your new items. A subsequent crash indicates that one or more items, or their drivers, are causing problems.

Reverting to an earlier state

After a crash you can revert back to your Restore Point where the PC worked well. Open the System

Focusing on the suspects

Once you have established the point at which your system became unstable, you can find out why. For hardware, check that all cards are firmly seated in their slots and that cables are securely attached. Then check that you have the latest drivers – either by visiting the manufacturer's website or by using the Add Hardware install process.

Go to the **Start** menu, click on **Control Panel**, then double-click on **Device Manager** (you may be prompted for an administrator password or confirmation). Click on the + sign next to the category matching your new device. Right-click on your device and choose **Update Driver Software** from the drop-down list. In the Update Driver Software window, select from the options presented. Follow the steps to search for an up-to-date driver for your device (you may need to connect to the internet during the process). If these measures fail to remove the instability, go to **All Programs**, **Accessories**, **System Tools**, **System Information**, then click on the + sign next to **Hardware Resources**, then **Conflicts/Sharing** to see if your suspect device is clashing with any others. If it is clashing with a device you can do without, remove that item. If it is clashing with a built-in system component, contact the device's manufacturer for advice.

What System Restore does not do

System Restore is a clever piece of software. If you tried to do manually what it manages automatically you would spend long hours undertaking detailed work.

It gets better, though. A basic piece of software would simply take a snapshot of your system and, when a failure occurred, would revert to exactly that. System Restore does not do more than this. It recognises that there will be many files that you *do not* want to dispense with – such as your recent emails and word-processing documents.

System Restore will not affect items like documents, email messages, your web browsing history and passwords. All these are saved when you revert to an earlier state.

Furthermore, you can ensure that System Restore protects all your personal files, no matter what type they might be, by keeping them in the Documents folder. By default, System Restore leaves that untouched. Also, it does not overwrite or remove any files created with everyday programs such as Microsoft Word or Excel.

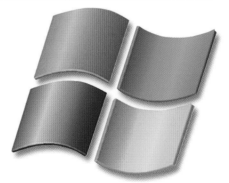

Windows will not close down

This is what to do **when your operating** system freezes

Occasionally, Windows will appear to freeze on screen – a condition known as 'hanging'. You will realise this may have happened when the cursor does not respond to your mouse movements, and you cannot issue any keyboard commands.

If your computer has these symptoms but you are still not sure whether Windows has hung,

press the **Num Lock** key (found above the numeric keypad on the right of the keyboard) a few times. If the Num Lock light above the key does not go on and off, then you know the system is definitely frozen.

The remedy for dealing with a hung program is fairly straightforward as you can still access Windows' help facilities. If Windows itself hangs

however, it is a little more difficult to deal with. This is because Windows governs everything you do on your PC – including accessing help facilities. If it seizes up, therefore, you will find you cannot carry out any of your normal actions.

First steps to closing Windows

When Windows hangs, you will not be able to restart by going to the Start menu as usual. Instead, press the **Ctrl** + **Alt** + **Del** keys together. You will then have several choices presented to you – either click on the red **Shut Down** button located at the bottom right of your screen or, if you had programs running when Windows hung, click on **Start Task Manager** to shut them down and save any changes you made. Select each in turn in the **Applications** tab of the Windows Task Manager window and then click on **End Task**. The second column will display the current status of a program. A dialogue box will appear asking if you want to save changes. Click on **Save**. If you had Internet Explorer open, close this last as it does not have active documents.

Sometimes, closing programs in this manner can unfreeze Windows. If it does not, then restarting Windows usually does the trick.

Bright idea
If you cannot solve the problem using Windows Help and Support you should consider reinstalling Windows. This is not as daunting a process as it sounds. See page 354 for more details.

Key word
Definitions *These are files that act like an ever-increasing database of potential software threats. Windows uses these definitions to alert you to potential unwanted software installed on your PC.*

Close-up
Whenever possible, make sure you restart or shut down your computer through the Start menu. This will mean that all current information is saved and that each program closes before Windows.

My computer will not turn off, or on, quickly

If your computer seems to shut down slowly, or not at all, it is possible that a program or device driver is interfering with your Windows power settings.

A slow turn-off

If your computer takes an age to turn off, go to the **Start** button and click on **Control Panel**, then click on **Performance Information and Tools**. In the panel on the left, click on **Advanced Tools**.

Under 'Performance issues', click on any issues that are listed for information regarding which programs or drivers are causing problems. If a program is preventing your PC from turning off quickly, try closing the program before shutting Windows down. It is possible that the problem only occurs if a particular program is running.

Alternatively, check with the program supplier for an update. A newer version may resolve the problem. It is possible that the program or driver might be incompatible with Windows 7.

A slow turn-on

Some programs begin automatically when you start Windows. Too many programs starting at the same time can slow your computer down. To rectify this, click on the **Start** button, **Control Panel**, then on **Performance Information and Tools**. In the panel on the left click on **Advanced Tools**. Under 'Performance issues', click on **Startup programs are causing Windows to start slowly. View details**. Now the 'Performance Information and Tools' dialogue box will open displaying details of any problem programs. Read the information and then click on the **Remove from list** button.

Use Windows Help and Support

To see all of the programs and processes that run when Windows starts, go the **Start** button and click on **Help and Support**. In the search bar at the top, type in **What programs are running when Windows starts** and press **Enter**. Click on **Stop a program from running automatically when Windows starts**. The next window explains about 'Autoruns for Windows', which is a free tool from the Microsoft website. Click on the link to go to the Microsoft website. Then click on **Download Autoruns and Autorunsc (581 KB)**. When the download is complete, launch the software and accept the licence agreement. Click on the **Logon** tab in the Autoruns window to display all the programs that are running during start-up. To disable an entry next time you start up, click on its tick to uncheck it.

Windows Defender

When you connect to the internet or install programs from a CD or DVD, spyware can install itself on your PC without your knowledge. This could potentially be triggered to run when you start up or close down your computer, causing either or both procedures to run slowly or stop completely.

Windows Defender is anti-spyware software that is included with Windows and runs automatically when it is turned on. Make sure you have Windows Update 'on' (see page 348) – this will automatically keep Windows Defender definitions up to date at the same time.

If all else fails

*If you cannot shut down Windows by pressing the **Ctrl** + **Alt** + **Del** keys, use the **Power on** button. Press and hold in the power switch for a few seconds until you hear the fan stop whirring. Wait for 30 seconds and switch on again.*

Reinstalling Windows

If you cannot repair a fault with the operating system, reload it

Reinstallation is the last resort for solving problems with Windows. The process leaves almost all your work unaffected, and returns Windows to its original state.

Complete reinstallation may be necessary if, for example, you keep experiencing serious crashes. All you need to begin reinstallation is your Windows 7 disk. For safety, back up your work before you start (see page 357).

If you do need to reinstall Windows, there are risks. It should only be tackled after you have tried all other remedies, and when you are sure that the problems relate to the Windows operating system, rather than an individual application. Windows 7 should reinstall without losing critical system data, such as internet settings, but make a note of these first, just in case.

Generally you will be able to reinstall from the Windows 7 disk, as shown here. However, if Windows will not start up, you must restart with the disk in the drive (see page 356).

◄ IF REINSTALLATION FAILS

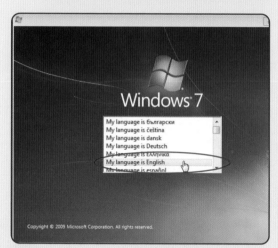

1 Put your Windows 7 disk into the CD/DVD drive of your PC. The disk will run automatically and begin leading you through the installation process. If it does not, see 'Close-up' below. First you are invited to choose a language. Scroll through the list and click on **My language is English**. This will take you to the next window.

🔍 Close-up

*If your Windows 7 installation disk does not automatically run, click on the **Start** button, then on **Computer**. Double-click on your DVD drive to open the Windows 7 installation disk and double-click on **setup.exe**.*

Bright idea
*Making screen grabs is a good way to note system settings. Open the relevent panels – for instance, ISP settings. On your keyboard press **Print Screen**, then open a graphics program such as Paint and paste the grab into it. Print it out as a permanent record.*

Close-up
If you have an internet connection, make sure it is active during installation as it will be used to check for Microsoft updates to Windows 7 – this means that you may get a newer system than that on your disk.

Watch out
During the set-up procedure you will be asked to enter your Windows 7 product key or serial number (you will find this on your Windows installation disk sleeve or manual cover). Be careful to input the number correctly and not to lose it.

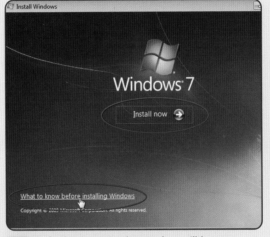

2 Click on the down arrow next to 'Time and currency format' and select **English (United Kingdom)** from the drop-down list. 'Keyboard or input method' should automatically change to **United Kingdom**. Click on **Next**. The installation program will examine your pc and automatically work out the best configuration for it.

3 To find out more about what will happen when you reinstall windows click on **What to know before installing Windows**, at the bottom of the screen. When you are ready, click on **Install now**. Windows will now copy temporary files and collect information about your system in preparation for the reinstall process.

4 Click on **Go online to get the latest updates for installation (recommended)** to ensure you get the latest available security updates and hardware drivers. Follow the on-screen instructions to finish the reinstall. Progress information is displayed at the bottom of the screen as this happens.

Getting expert help
If you are worried about the reinstallation process, consider getting expert guidance. For extra help during reinstallation, go online and visit http://windows.microsoft.com/en-GB/windows7/Installing-and-reinstalling-Windows-7, call the Microsoft technical support line or, if Windows 7 came pre-installed, your PC's manufacturer.

Explorer favourites
Internet Explorer is tightly integrated with Windows 7 – so much so that it is reinstalled at the same time as the operating system. Losing your Explorer favourites can be frustrating, so do not be caught out, and preserve your data first. In Explorer go to **File** and click on **Import and Export** to open Import/Export Settings. Follow the on-screen instructions and click on **Next** at each stage, to export your favourites. For added safety, export them to a file and save it on a CD. After your system reinstall, simply insert the disk, open Internet Explorer, go to Import/Export again and this time import the file. Your favourites will appear as before.

Create a system repair disc

Click on the **Start** button, **Control Panel** then on **Backup and Restore**. In the panel on the left click on **Create a system repair disc**. Select your CD/DVD drive from the drop-down list, insert a blank disc and click on **Create disc**. Follow the prompts to create the disc. Remove the disc, label it and keep it in a safe place.

Watch out

To restart your computer from the Windows 7 installation disk, your computer must be configured to do so. Check with your manufacturer if you are unsure.

How to reinstall when Windows will not load

If Windows will not start up, you need to start from your Windows 7 installation disk and deal with any problems from there. Here is how.

If you bought a copy of Windows 7 and installed it on a PC yourself, the disk you used will contain all the files required to start Windows again. In addition, a new feature called Startup Repair is accessible from the disk. This can fix some problems, such as missing or damaged system files, that might prevent Windows from starting correctly. There are also some other tools, stored under the System Recovery Options menu, that can help in repairing or restoring data.

If you bought your computer with Windows 7 pre-installed, the Startup Repair option may have been saved to your hard disk. In some cases, manufacturers do not then also add it to the reinstallation disk they provide. If this is the case, follow the 'Pre-installed method' outlined on the right of this panel.

If you have a hardware failure, Startup Repair will not be able to fix it. However, it will give a summary of the problem and links to contact information for support. Your computer manufacturer might also offer additional assistance and information.

If you upgraded to Windows 7 from XP, you should have a 'boot disk' (sometimes called a start-up disk).

This boot disk – generally a CD – will have been provided with your PC and holds copies of the Windows start-up files that were installed on your PC. If the files on your hard disk become corrupt, you should use this boot disk to get Windows started again.

Starting up from your installation disk

If Windows does not load normally when you switch on your PC you should be able to start your system from the original Windows 7 installation disk by placing it in your disk drive before starting the computer. Your PC will automatically detect that a disk is present in the disk drive and attempt to use the files held on it, allowing you to access the Startup Repair recovery tool.

To start the process, place the disk in the drive and then click on the **Start** button, then on the arrow next to the 'Shut down' button, and click on **Restart**. When you are prompted, press any key to start Windows from the installation disk. Choose your language settings and then click on **Repair your computer**. Select the operating system you want

to repair – you can check this on your installation disk box. From the System Recovery Options menu, click on **Startup Repair**. During this process you may be prompted to make choices as the program tries to fix the problem. You may also find that it is necessary to restart your computer during, or at the end of, Startup Repair.

Finally, it is most important to keep your Windows 7 installation disk in a safe place as reinstalling the system can often solve PC problems.

Using the pre-installed method

If your manufacturer loaded Startup Repair on your hard disk, then it should start automatically and try to fix the problem. If the problem is so severe that Startup Repair does not start by itself and you cannot access the System Recovery Options menu, then you must use the method previously described. Alternatively, if you created a system repair disc, switch off your computer, insert the disc into the CD/DVD drive and swich the computer back on and follow and respond to the prompts.

Give your hard disk a check-up

If your computer is having difficulty in loading Windows, you might have a hard disk problem. Use Windows 7's built-in disk utility to examine and repair any flaws.

Go to the **Start** button, click on **Computer** and then right-click on your hard-disk drive – normally 'C:'. Click on **Properties** and then on the **Tools** tab. In the Error-checking panel, click on **Check Now**. In the next panel, click in the boxes next to 'Automatically fix file system

errors' and 'Scan for and attempt recovery of bad sectors', then click on **Start**. The utility will ask if you want to schedule the disk examination for the next time you start your computer – click on **Yes**. Then restart your machine and let the utility check your disk.

A full check will take some time – do not cancel the examination half way through. If it does find errors, follow the on-screen instructions and you should be able to make repairs.

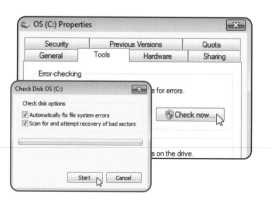

Close-up
For the earliest PCs, floppy disks were suitable for backing up data; later, Zip disks were used. Today, recordable CDs, DVDs and external hard disks have taken on the role of back-up devices. For larger networks, fast tape drives or banks of hard disks are used to store data.

Bright idea
*In the 'Set up backup' window (see below), click on the first option **Let Windows choose (recommended)** to ensure all data files saved in libraries, on the desktop and in default Windows folders, for all users on your computer, are backed up.*

Making and storing back-ups
Windows 7 Backup and Restore Center is automatically installed, but you need to tell it where to place your copied files and schedule it to do its work automatically.

Initiating Back-up
Click on the **Start** button, then on **Control Panel**. Now click on **Backup and Restore**. The 'Back up or restore

your files' options window will open – click on the **Set up backup** link. The 'Starting Windows Backup' window opens while it gathers information about your PC. If a 'User Account Control' permissions message appears, click on **Continue**. In the 'Set up backup' window, select where you want to save your back-up, normally, your CD or DVD drive. If your hard disk has been partitioned, then that will be the first option in the list. Make your selection and click on **Next**.

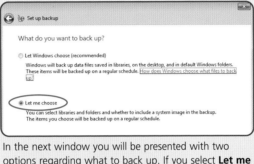

In the next window you will be presented with two options regarding what to back up. If you select **Let me choose**, you will be presented with a checklist of options covering the types of files to back up. Click in the box to the left of an option to add a tick and select it. Click in a ticked box, to deselect. Make your choice and click on **Next**. In the 'Review your backup settings' window click on **Save settings and run backup** to finish.

Set a schedule
Backing up can be a slow process – many people leave their computer on and set it to back up during the night or at the weekend. In the 'Review your backup settings'

window click on **Change schedule**, select the frequency of automating your back-ups, using the drop-down options next to 'How often', 'What day' and 'What time', and click **OK**. Click on **Save settings and run backup** to start the process. If this is the first time you have backed up, Windows will create a new full back-up. For later back-ups, updated or new files will simply be added on.

Choose a back-up medium
Before you back up you need to decide what you want to save and how often. It is worth planning in advance because you might need to buy new hardware or storage media. Your circumstances will probably govern your choices – for instance, how critical is your data? If you are running a small business, it is vital to protect accounts on a day-by-day basis. If, on the other hand, you use your PC for creating a quarterly newsletter, then a weekly back-up might be adequate. Also, how much time do you want to devote to this?

Use a CD for data under 700Mb, or a DVD disk if the amount of data to be backed up is less than 4.7Gb. However, these options are still not large enough to be able to back up even the basic files installed by Windows, so if you want to back up your entire system you will need to invest in an external hard disk of at least equal capacity to your existing one. Click on **Computer** in the **Start** menu to check on the size of your hard disk and how much space you have used. External hard disks are available with capacities of more than 80Gb – large enough to store multiple back-ups.

My program has crashed

If an application **stops responding** to your **commands, here is** what to do

When a program crashes, your mouse pointer will appear as an hourglass and you will not be able to type or access menus. It may seem that your PC has stopped working – but if the hourglass pointer changes back to an arrow when you move it onto your Desktop, this means Windows is still working. Windows runs each program in its own protected memory space, so problems with one active program do not usually affect the others.

It is possible to exit the crashed program using keyboard commands, and then to open it again. If you have not saved changes in the document you were working on before the crash, you will lose some of your work when you exit the program. This is why it is vital to make a habit of saving your work regularly, and why it is also worth remembering to save work in other programs that are running.

Closing a crashed program

When a program crashes you will not be able to close it in the usual way – for example, by going to the **Office** button and clicking on **Close**. In this case, you should press the **Ctrl + Alt + Del** keys simultaneously.

This brings up a list of options, the last one of which is 'Start Task Manager'. Click on it and, under the 'Applications' tab, you will see a list of all the programs currently running on your PC. Under the 'Processes' tab you will also see system programs that run invisibly on your computer. Under the Applications tab, scroll down the list until you see the name of the program that has crashed – it will be labelled 'Not Responding' in the status column. Click on it to highlight it and then click on the **End Task** button.

The crashed program window should then close. If it does not, another dialogue box will open, giving you the option of either waiting for the program to close by itself or terminating it immediately by clicking on the **End Task** button. Windows 7 will not usually ask you to restart your machine but, if more than one program has crashed, you should probably restart.

Close-up
*If you cannot exit from the crashed program by pressing the **Ctrl + Alt + Del** keys, you must press, and hold down, the **Power on** button on your system unit until it shuts down. Wait 30 seconds or so and then press the **Power on** button again.*

Bright idea
*Some programs allow you to save data automatically at set intervals. In Word, for example, click on the **Office** button and select **Word Options**. In the left pane, click on **Save**. In the right pane, under 'Save documents', click in the box by 'Save AutoRecover information every'. Now set a time – say, 15 minutes – from the drop-down box and click on **OK**.*

What to do when a program crashes
Windows records and reports the problem and searches online for a solution. When you restart, check your PC and reinstall any troublesome programs.

How to check for problem solutions
When problems occur and a program stops working or responding, Windows creates a problem report so you can check for a solution.

Go to the **Start** button and click on **Control Panel**, then on **Action Center**. Any problems found on your computer are listed in the right pane. Click on

Maintenance. Under 'Check for solutions ...', click the **Check for solutions** button. Windows will notify you if there are solutions to problems available for your computer. A progress window appears as an online solution to the problem is sought.

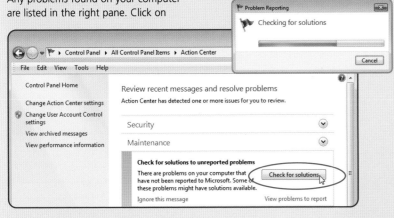

Reinstalling a problem program
If a program persistently crashes, the easiest remedy is to reinstall it. To do this, place the program's installation disk in the drive, click on **Computer**, then double-click on the CD/DVD drive icon. A warning message will appear, asking if you will allow an unidentified program to access your computer. Click on **Allow** to confirm. Click on 'Setup' or a similar start icon or link. Most programs will install over an older version of themselves without losing any alterations.

If this does not solve the problem, uninstall the program first. To do this, go to the **Start** button, click on **Control Panel**, then under 'Programs' click on **Uninstall a program**. Select the relevant program from the list, click on **Uninstall** and follow the on-screen instructions. Restart your PC and install the program from scratch.

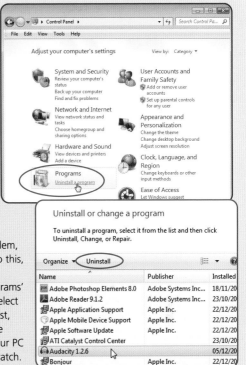

Remove unwanted files
When a program crashes it can leave behind temporary files (with filenames ending in '.TMP') that are usually deleted when you exit the program normally. Windows 7 comes with a tool called Disk Cleanup designed to remove these unwanted files.

To access it, go to the **Start** button and select **All Programs**, **Accessories**, **System Tools** and then **Disk Cleanup**. Disk Cleanup then calculates how much space you will be able to free up. In the Disk Cleanup dialogue box, click to add a tick in the check box next to the file types you wish to delete and click on **OK**. A message asks you to confirm you want to permanently delete these files. Click on **Delete Files** to continue. A progress bar is displayed during the cleanup process.

I cannot read a document

Find out how to open and read **seemingly** impenetrable files

As a rule, if you receive a file from another source, such as the internet, and you do not have the program in which it was created, then you will not be able to open the file.

There are, though, ways around this problem. Sometimes your software may recognise the type of document and be able to convert it. If not, you can ask the sender to supply it in a 'neutral format'. For example, a text document saved as 'Text Only' should be read by any word-processing program (though text styling will be lost with this 'no-frills' format). Here we show you some other ways you can access 'unreadable' files.

Find out what type of file it is (word processor, spreadsheet and so on), which program created it and if it can be sent to you in a different format.

▶ BEFORE YOU START

1 If Windows does not know how to open a particular file, it displays it with a plain icon. Select the file, click on **Open** in the menu bar and in the 'Open with' dialogue box that appears, select a program to open your file from the list offered. Click on **OK**.

A quick guide to file extensions

File extensions are letter combinations (usually three) that indicate which program created a file. To display the extensions on your files, go to the **Start** menu, then **Documents**. In the **Tools** menu, select **Folder Options**. In the **View** tab, untick the 'Hide extensions for known file types' box. Some common file extensions are:
- **Text file** .asc .doc .htm .html .msg .txt .wpd
- **Image file** .bmp .eps .gif .jpg .pict .png .tif
- **Sound file** .au .mid .ra .snd .wav

Just as Windows sometimes cannot open a document created on another operating system, other systems can have difficulty reading files created in Windows. To reduce the risk of this happening, save documents as 'Plain Text' or 'Rich Text Format'. To do this, scroll down the 'Save as type' menu in the Save As dialogue box and select one of these formats. Note that this will mean you will lose any complex formatting.

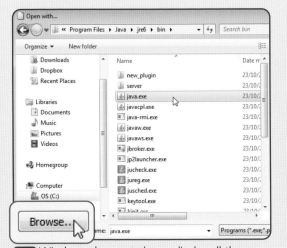

2 Windows does not always display all the programs installed on your PC in the 'Open with' dialogue box. If you would like to choose a program that is not shown, click on **Browse** to see all of those in your 'Program Files' folder. Scroll through and select from the list, then click on **Open**.

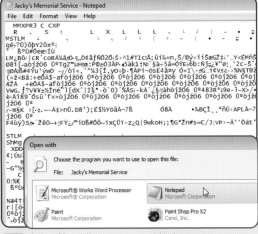

3 If the file will not open with the program you have selected, try another one – Notepad is able to open many types of file. However, you may still see an unreadable mass of code and symbols. If this happens, close the file without saving.

4 Another option is to launch a program such as Microsoft Office Word and try to open the file by going to the **File** tab and clicking on **Open**. Navigate to the folder containing the file, then choose **All Files** from the file type list. Select the file and click on **Open**. If this works, go to **Save As** to save the file in the appropriate format.

Opening compressed documents

To reduce the amount of space a file takes up on a hard disk or as an email attachment, many people 'compress' files. If you receive a compressed file (with the file extension '.zip') you will need the same compression program in order to decompress it and then open it. WinZip is a common compression program. You can download it from the internet at www.winzip.com free of charge.

If you do not have the relevant program to decompress a file, ask the sender to mail it again in an uncompressed version.

Open Office files without Microsoft Office

If you receive files created in Microsoft Office programs – Word or Excel, for example – and you do not have Office software, you can open these files – for free! Log on to the internet and in your web browser address bar type **www.openoffice.org** and press **Enter**. This will take you to the OpenOffice.org website. Click on the **Download** tab, then on **Download OpenOffice.org** and follow the prompts.

I am getting error messages

What to do when **your computer warns you** there is a problem

When your PC has difficulty carrying out one of your commands it will display an error message. Generally, error messages include a description of the error, a possible reason for it and, if appropriate, a way to resolve the problem. Some error messages are easier to understand than others.

Do not ignore error messages. If you do, you may lose your work or, at worst, make your computer unusable. Follow the on-screen advice, which may mean exiting from the program you are using or restarting your computer. There are many error messages – the ones described here are the most common.

Storage problems

One of the most common error messages appears when Windows detects that your hard disk is getting full and storage space is becoming limited. This can seriously affect the performance of your PC and may prevent you saving files. It will also limit the amount of space System Restore can use to back up critical data and will disable Virtual Memory.

If 'Not enough disk space' messages appear, use Disk Cleanup to delete unnecessary files and create more space. Click on the **Start** button and select **All Programs**, **Accessories**, then **System Tools** and **Disk Cleanup**.

Disk Cleanup will then automatically calculate how much space can be regained. Click in the tick box next to the items you want to delete and click on **OK**. Finally, click on **Delete Files** to confirm your choice.

Understanding error messages

Although the wording may vary, most error messages will fall into one of these categories.

Error messages caused by hardware

● Hardware conflicts
With the stability and improvement of Windows 7 over older versions of Windows, and the advent of 'Plug and Play' devices, hardware conflicts should now be limited. However, if your hardware seems to be working properly but you still get error messages, a defective or conflicting driver may be the cause. (See page 351 for possible solutions.)

If your computer freezes – or 'hangs' – when you try to use a particular device, or if a device refuses to work, this, too, could be the result of a hardware conflict, which a new driver might remedy.

● Problems with your memory?
Memory problems can cause your computer to lose information or stop working. If you get an error message, Windows will ask you if you want to run 'Windows Memory Diagnostic' immediately or the next time you start your computer.

Make your selection and follow the prompts. You will need to press **F10** to start the test; it is best to keep the tool's default settings. If the Memory Diagnostics Tool detects problems, contact your computer or memory manufacturer for information on how to resolve them.

You can start the Memory Diagnostics Tool manually, if you wish. To do this, go to the **Start** button and click on **Control Panel**, then on **Administrative Tools** then double-click on **Windows Memory Diagnostic**.

Error messages caused by software

● This file is being used by another user
The message occurs when you try to open the same document in different programs at the same time. You can either close down the document before opening it in a second program, let Windows tell you when the file is available for editing, or 'Open a Read Only copy'.

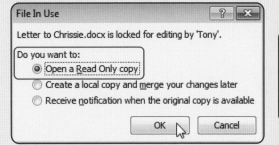

● This file is write protected
You cannot delete, rename or sometimes even copy write-protected files. To remove the protection, right-click on the file's icon, go to **Properties** and uncheck the box next to **Read-only** in the General tab.

● Error Deleting File
This happens when you try to delete a file that is open. Close the file and then try to delete it again.

● Sharing Violation/You don't have permission to open this file
This can be caused by having a file open in two programs at the same time, or by a program trying to open a file that is either corrupted or missing.

● File Corruption
Sometimes, a file gets 'mangled' by Windows. The best solution is to replace it from your back-up copy.

● Missing or Out-of-Date Files
This message appears if somebody deletes a file by mistake, or if a program overwrites, deletes or renames a file as it is installed or uninstalled. If the problem is with a program, you need to reinstall it.

What to do if you cannot understand messages

● Windows 7's Help and Support Center will explain most error messages and suggest solutions. Click on the **Start** button and select **Help and Support** from the right-hand menu.

● Save any opened files. Shut down the program that prompted the message, then restart it.

● If the message reappears, shut down the program (and any others running) and restart your computer (go to the **Start** button, select **Restart**).

● If the message occurs again, make a note of what it says and seek expert advice. If the error is prompted by Windows rather than a program, contact your PC dealer. If a program is causing the problem, contact the software manufacturer.

Use Event Viewer

Event Viewer is an important diagnostic tool that runs in the background and logs information about any hardware and software problems. While the tool cannot remedy the problems, the information can be useful when discussing the issues with a PC engineer or the manufacturer. To use it, go to the **Start** button, click on **Control Panel**,

then double-click on **Administrative Tools**. Finally, double-click on **Event Viewer**.

Under the 'Level' column, log entries for serious problems are displayed with a white '!' in a red circle, warnings appear with a black '!' in a yellow triangle, and information entries have a blue 'i' in a grey circle.

Using anti-virus software

Run specialist packages to preserve or restore your PC's health

Although the spread of computer viruses is often reported in the media, the problem is not as widespread or difficult to deal with as most people think. Simple preventative steps (see page 56) will help you to reduce the risk of getting a virus and put you in a better position to eradicate any that you may get.

Anti-virus software

Many packages are available. In general, they detect viruses on storage discs, such as CDs, and files downloaded from the internet. Such programs stop viruses infecting your PC in the first place.

Most anti-virus packages can be set up to scan every item downloaded to your system, but it is also a good idea to run the program every week or so to examine your whole system.

If a virus does make its way onto your computer, the software will alert you by bringing up a warning on screen. At this point you must use the disinfecting function in the anti-virus program, which will attempt to repair the infected file. This is normally a straightforward process, performed by following the on-screen instructions given by the program. Sometimes, the infected item cannot be repaired. In this case you should delete the file or, in the case of a program, uninstall and then replace it.

Keeping up to date

It is vital to keep your software defences up to date. This does not mean having to buy new software. The best anti-virus packages allow you to stay current by downloading new information from their websites. Check your software for details on how to do this. It is best to set the software to do this automatically.

> *A good anti-virus package such as McAfee VirusScan or Norton AntiVirus is essential. Ask at a computer store for advice on which package is best for your needs.*
>
> **▶ BEFORE YOU START**

Bright idea
*There are several useful websites that offer information about viruses. Some also provide software updates to help you to defend your PC. Try http://www.symantec.com/en/norton/index.jsp then click on **Viruses & Risks**, and choose from the list of options.*

Key word

Virus *A virus is a computer program whose sole purpose is to get into your PC and cause unwanted and unexpected behaviour, such as erasing files, displaying messages and attacking your PC's set-up.*

Make the software do the work
Without the right software you might never know your PC is infected until it is too late.

The main types of viruses that are likely to infect your computer are called 'file viruses', 'macro viruses' and 'boot and partition sector viruses'. Each one of these viruses attacks different parts of your computer, including your hard disk, programs and document files. Some websites may also place small applets (mini-programs) on your system that can have similar highly destructive effects.

Stopping viruses at source
McAfee VirusScan, part of McAfee Security Center, is typical of the effective anti-virus programs that are now available to buy. You can configure McAfee VirusScan to examine every file downloaded or read from all forms of recordable media, such as CDs and DVDs. It continually checks for known viruses and other harmful software on your system and will alert you to any it finds.

You can also set the software to regularly check on the internet for software updates, so you will always be protected against new viruses. If an infected file is located it is 'quarantined' on your system and you will be notified of the best steps to take.

Disinfecting your system once a virus is found
If your software detects a virus you should use the disinfecting or cleaning function in the software to remove or isolate it. If it is a new virus, some anti-virus programs may even send the file to their laboratory for examination.

If an infected file cannot be repaired then it will generally be renamed to prevent it being used again. You will then have the option of deleting it. Files that you delete may need to be replaced. If these are system files (the files that make up Windows) then you will definitely need to do so.

To reinstall program software, see page 359; or to reinstall Windows, see page 354.

Viruses affect computers in different ways. Some contain messages that appear on screen.

Worst-case scenario
With proper use of an anti-virus program, you should be able to detect and remove any viruses before they cause really serious damage. Without taking such precautions it is possible, although not likely, that a virus could destroy the contents of your hard disk.

In such a case you will have to restore the hard disk from your original system disks. This is like restoring your computer to its original state, as it was on the day you bought it. The original settings for it will therefore be restored, but you will probably have lost all your documents, pictures, emails, internet favourites and data files.

Hit back at hackers
Top-level security packages like Norton's and McAfee's also protect your computer against the threat of hacking – unauthorised entry to your machine using the internet. With the spread of 'always on' broadband connections, hacking has become much easier and more widespread. Setting up a 'firewall' – a barrier to hackers – is simple with these two products. Persistent attackers can also be tracked, providing evidence for possible prosecution.

Windows security
Windows 7 provides its own firewall to help to protect your PC against malevolent attacks from others on the internet. To check it is activated, click on the **Start** button, select **Control Panel**, then click on **Windows Firewall**. For further information about your protection status click on **Advanced settings** in the panel on the left. If you are running anti-virus software such as McAfee, it will be controlling your protection settings for you.

My text does not look right

If your fonts look odd **on screen or when printed,** the solution is easy

Font problems are rare nowadays, largely because the leading software developers have come together to create new user-friendly technologies such as TrueType and OpenType. Windows 7's default fonts should display and print faultlessly.

Difficulties only arise when additional fonts are installed, either by other software programs or manually – from a free CD, for instance. You may find that a font that looks fine on screen prints badly or not at all. Alternatively, your screen display could be terrible, but a document might print superbly.

Do not worry – by using Windows 7's Help and Support utilities you can solve most typographical problems with ease.

Do you have a problem?

If a font looks strange on screen or when printed, first check whether there really is a problem. Some fonts are specifically designed to look unusual. Wingdings and Zapf Dingbats are made up entirely of quirky characters.

To check how a font should look, click on the **Start** button, select **Control Panel**, then double-click on **Fonts**. Initially all the fonts installed on your PC will be listed. If you view the Fonts folder as either Extra Large, Large or Medium Icons, a small display of the font can be seen above the font name. Double-click on the font in question to bring up a sample of what it should look like.

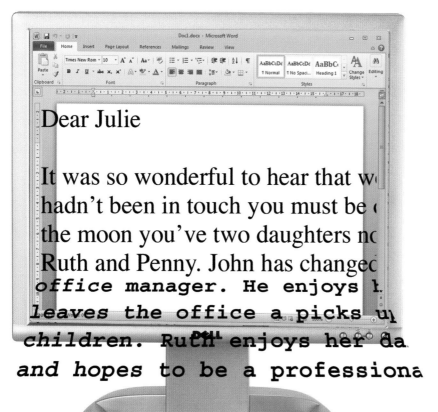

If the sample text shown looks the same as the text in your document, you have simply chosen an unusual-looking font.

In the font viewer window, the font heading at the top also shows the kind of font displayed – OpenType and TrueType will be the most common, but you may also have some PostScript fonts. PostScript fonts require special software – Adobe Type Manager (ATM) – to display correctly. If a PostScript font's screen appearance is irregular or jagged, check the Adobe website at www.adobe.com/products/atmlight/download.html for the latest version of ATM.

Bright idea
*Windows 7 has a great Printing Troubleshooter. Click on the **Start** button and select **Help and Support**. Then type 'printing' into the search bar at the top and press **Return**. In the results list, click on **Open the Printer troubleshooter**, and follow the prompts.*

Solving font software problems

Understanding what different font files do and where they are located is the first stage of problem-solving.

Types of font

The type of font you are using may affect the way it appears on screen or when printed. TrueType fonts are designed to print as they look on screen. This is also the case with OpenType fonts, which are in fact a newer kind of TrueType file.

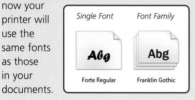

PostScript fonts and printer-only fonts can look slightly different on screen to how they appear when printed. PostScript fonts used on a PC that does not have Adobe Type Manager (ATM) installed will often display jagged edges, particularly at larger point sizes (see left).

Some printers (notably laser printers) use printer fonts, which are stored on the printer itself. Problems can develop when the font you are using on screen, and its equivalent on the printer, do not match. To fix this, most printer driver options will allow you to override the printer fonts. Click on the **Start** button, then **Control Panel**, and double-click on **Printers**. Right-click on your printer driver icon and select **Printing Preferences**. All printers are different but you should find an option marked **Download as softfont**. Select that, or check the box next to it – now your printer will use the same fonts as those in your documents.

Single Font — Forte Regular
Font Family — Franklin Gothic

Common difficulties

You have been emailed a Word document that prints badly

Look in the font box on the Ribbon to note the name of the font that prints incorrectly. Then click in a section of text that does not use that font, or add a few words in a system font such as 'Arial'. Return to the font box, click in it and scroll down to check whether the name of the problem font appears. If it does not, then the font is not installed on your system. Either install the font on your system (see right) or highlight the text and select a new font from the font box.

You cannot print the Euro symbol

Some older fonts may not contain the Euro symbol. You can access it on a standard European keyboard by pressing and holding **Alt Gr** (to the right of the space bar) and pressing **4**. Three font families that consist of only the Euro symbol are available for free from www.adobe.com/type/eurofont.html. Click on the site's **free download** link.

Managing fonts

Removing fonts

Fonts may become damaged, or non-standard fonts may have been incorrectly constructed initially. If all documents using a particular font have problems, remove the suspect font. Click on the **Start** button, select **Control Panel**, then double-click on **Fonts**. Right-click on the font and select **Delete**. Your system will ask 'Are you sure you want to delete this font permanently?' Click on **Yes**.

Delete Font
Are you sure you want to delete this font permanently?
ADMU3Lg
If you delete this font, some text might not appear as you intended.
Yes | No

Installing fonts

To install or reinstall a font, it must first be available either in a folder on your PC or on a disk or CD. Browse to the font file, then right-click on it and then on **Install** from the list of options.

Viewing foreign text

Multilingual users will probably want to view foreign websites – in the past, any language using unusual characters or pictograms, such as Russian or Japanese, could cause problems. Nowadays, Internet Explorer, used in conjunction with Windows 7, will breeze through any linguistic complexities, even in reading 'right-to-left' languages.

In most cases Windows 7 will automatically set up your system to view international texts such as Japanese, Russian or Hebrew. If it has not, when you load a web page with unusual characters in Internet Explorer you will see the Language pack installation dialogue box. This will ask you to install the required files. If the files are not available on your installation disc, Explorer may suggest downloading them from the Microsoft website.

Problems with passwords

You can unlock your computer even if you forget your password

In Windows 7 it is easy to let several people use the same PC, each with their own set of files and folders, and preferences for Windows' appearance. You can set a password to protect your files, but the level of security is not so great that forgetting a password becomes a disaster. As long as a user with administration rights knows their password, they can get you back in. You can also create a special password reset disk that gives you access. Even if you have not created the reset disk, technical support helplines can talk you through relatively simple ways to get back into your PC.

If you need real security for your work, there are plenty of reasonably priced programs you can buy that offer much stronger password protection. However, they are not as forgiving if you forget your password!

Create a password reset disk
Use Windows 7's utilities to create this handy back-up device.

Getting started
Once you have started a new user account, and chosen a password, you can create a password reset disk. This disk can be used at a later stage if your forget your log-in password.

Click on the **Start** button, select **Control Panel**, then double-click on **User Accounts**. In the panel on the left you will see **Create a password reset disk** – you can only create a disk for the user currently logged in.

Click on **Create a password reset disk** to start the Forgotten Password Wizard. Insert a blank CD or DVD or use a flash drive to store the file that will be created. Click on **Next** and follow the Wizard's prompts to create a disk that you can use as a 'key' to unlock your PC.

Tips for effective passwords

An effective password is one that cannot be easily guessed. For this reason make sure your password adheres to several of the following:

● It is at least six characters long.
● It contains a mix of capital letters and lowercase letters.
● It contains at least one digit or special character such as a punctuation mark.
● It cannot easily be guessed (for example, do not use your child's, spouse's or pet's name).
● It is changed frequently.

⚠ Watch out

Using one password for many applications is convenient, but it means that a single breach of security could render all your protection useless.

What to do if you forget your password

There is no need to panic if you forget your password. Load your password reset disk and you will be up and running in no time.

If you have a reset disk

Simply start your PC as usual. When asked for your password, type in a few random letters, then click on the blue circled **white arrow**. When you see the message 'The user name or password is incorrect', click on **OK**. Your login window will open again displaying your 'Password Hint' and the 'Reset password...' link. If your hint does not remind you of your password, click on the link **Reset password** and follow the instructions on screen. At this point you will be asked to insert the reset disk that you have previously created.

If you do not have a reset disk

There are other ways to enter a password-protected system. If another user has an account set up on the machine you use, ask them to log on then go to **Start**, **All Programs**, **Accessories**, then **Run**, and enter 'control userpasswords2', then click on **OK**. Click on your User Name, and then click on **Reset Password** and choose a new password. The user that does this must have administrator rights to be able to change passwords.

Password Reset Wizard

Welcome to the Password Reset Wizard

If you forget the password for this user account and are unable to log on, this wizard helps you reset the password.

Note: To use this wizard, you must have first created a password reset disk.

Password for Fiona
To change the password for Fiona, click Reset Password.

[Reset Password...]

To continue, click Next.

[< Back] [Next >] [Cancel]

Forget your passwords safely

Even a relatively light user of a computer and the internet soon finds that they build up a long list of passwords and usernames for banking, shopping and logging on to websites. There are shareware programs (ones you can download and try before you buy) that can help out. The programs store all your passwords for you, and are activated by one single password – the only one that you will have to remember.

Two of the best-known utilities are Password Tracker, available from www.clrpc.com, and Password Agent from www.moonsoftware.com. Both programs are modestly priced and each is approved by Microsoft.

Shortcut	User ID	Password
http://www.chicagot... C:\Program Files\In...	lindasman	cubs&sox
http://www.irnet.co... C:\Program Files\M... C:\Program Files\M...	david87	Gv4z?%W
http://edit.my.yaho... C:\QUICKENW\QW...	dave	linda457 mYfinancE
http://www.digits.co... C:\WINNT\Profiles...	dave@t... davidsp	gFtCwo4l dave-linda

Beef up security

If you want to hide your files and applications from prying eyes, at home or in the office, there are a number of programs that offer differing levels of protection.

User management systems replicate Windows 7's own password-protected log-in system, but add much tougher controls. Passwords are non-recoverable and different levels of access can be permitted for different users. System use can also be monitored and recorded.

File and folder encryption systems do not block users out – they simply allow you to encrypt specific parts of your disk so that no one can read your personal files and folders. Different levels of encryption are available – the strongest is practically unbreakable, so be sure to remember your password. Travellers please note: the possession and use of strong encryption software is lawful throughout the EU and North America, but is strictly controlled in much of the Middle East, the former USSR, China and other countries.

Password Vault

Built into McAfee Security Center is an effective mechanism for protecting your passwords called Password Vault. To utilise this feature, launch the Security Center and click on **Internet & Network**, then on **Configure**. In the Password Vault panel click on **Advanced**. Type a password into the first box and then re-enter it in the second box and click on **Open**. This one password will give you access to all your passwords. Click on **Add** and in the Manage Password Vault dialogue box type a name, say 'eBay', into the Description box, then click in the Password box and type in the password you use to access 'eBay'. Click on **OK** when finished. Continue to add entries and their passwords in the same way and finally click on **OK** to close the Password Vault. Remember, no one else can access your Password Vault without knowing the password to it.

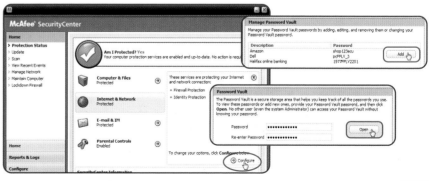

A

Accessories Mini-programs, such as Calculator, Notepad or Wordpad, built into Windows to perform simple tasks.

Active window The window you are working in. To activate a window, click on it and it will jump to the front of your screen, in front of any other open windows. See *Window*.

ADSL Asymmetric Digital Subscriber Line. A way of getting broadband internet access through a normal phone line. See *Broadband*.

Aero A Windows feature that allows you to view open documents, with a 3D display and 'thumbnails' above the file name shown on the Taskbar.

All-in-one (AIO) A single hardware device that does the job of a photocopier, scanner, printer and fax machine.

Alt key A key on the keyboard that gives commands when pressed in combination with other keys.

Application program A piece of software that performs specific kinds of tasks. For example, Microsoft Word is a word-processing application program. See *Program*, *Software*.

Archive To transfer files to a separate storage system, such as a CD-R.

Attachment A file such as a picture or spreadsheet that is sent with an email message.

Audio file A file containing a digital recording of sound. In Windows, audio files usually have '.wma' after their file name. See *Digital*.

B

Back-up A duplicate copy of a file, made in case of accidental loss or damage to the original. Back-ups can be made onto a second hard drive either fitted internally or attached externally to the computer, or on removable media such as CD or DVD.

BIOS Basic Input/Output System. Instructions that control the computer's hardware at the most basic level. The BIOS tells the operating system which hardware to expect to come into operation and how it is arranged.

Bitmap An on-screen image made up of tiny dots, or pixels. See *Pixel*.

Blog A diary or log that you store on a website and update regularly. Blogs can include photos as well as links to other blogs or websites, and are usually free to set up.

Bluetooth A wireless connection between mobile phones, computers and PDAs over short ranges. See *PDA*.

Boot or **boot up** To switch on the computer.

Broadband High-speed internet access via either an ADSL, cable or satellite connection.

Browser Software application for retrieving or presenting information on the internet.

Bug An accidental error or fault in a computer program. Bugs may cause programs to crash, which can lead to data loss.

Button An on-screen image that can be clicked on using the mouse. Clicking on a button performs a function, such as opening a dialogue box or confirming an action.

Byte A unit of computer memory, made up of eight bits. It takes one byte of memory to store a single character, such as a letter of the alphabet.

C

C: The hard drive of a PC, where programs and documents are stored. In speech, it is referred to as the 'C drive'.

Cable Broadband internet access that is delivered via a cable television network.

Cache A section of high-speed memory that stores data recently used by the PC's processor, thereby increasing the speed at which that data can be accessed again.

CD-R/CD-RW Compact Disc Recordable/Rewritable. CDs that can be written to in a special type of disc drive (sometimes called a 'burner'). CD-Rs can only be written to once, CD-RWs can be rewritten many times over.

CD-ROM Compact Disc Read Only Memory. A removable storage device, identical in appearance to a music CD. Some software programs come on CD-ROM. CD-ROMs are usually inserted into and accessed from the 'D drive' on the computer.

Cell A small rectangular section of a spreadsheet or database, into which text or figures are entered. Click on a cell to make it active, ready for entering or editing data.

Click To press and release the left mouse button once. Used to select menu and dialogue box options and toolbar buttons. See also *Right-click*.

Clip art Graphic images that can be inserted into text-based documents from the Clip Art gallery and then resized and manipulated.

Clipboard When text is cut or copied from a document it is stored on the Clipboard. The Clipboard has a viewer option that enables you to store several items of cut or copied data. You can put the current Clipboard material back into as many documents as you like using the paste command. See *Copy*, *Cut* and *Paste*.

CMOS Complementary Metal Oxide Semiconductor. A type of memory chip that stores the computer's configuration settings and the date and time. To protect its data, this memory is maintained by battery. See *Configuration*.

Compressed files Files that have been temporarily condensed so they use less memory and can be copied or downloaded in a fraction of the time it would take for the full-sized version.

Computer An option found in the Start menu of a PC running Windows. Select it to access everything stored in the system on the hard drive and CD/DVD drive.

Configuration The settings used to ensure hardware or software runs as the user requires.

Control Panel Adjustments made to your system or its settings are made through the Control Panel. You can change the look of your Desktop, add new hardware or alter your PC's sound output via the Control Panel's functions.

Copy To make a duplicate of a file, folder, image or section of text.

CPU Central Processing Unit. The brain of your PC, which carries out millions of arithmetic and control functions every second.

Crash Your PC has crashed if it has stopped working, the screen has 'frozen' and there is no response to keyboard or mouse commands. A crash usually requires you to restart the computer.

Cursor A marker, usually a flashing vertical line, that indicates where the next letter or digit typed in will appear in the document.

Cut To remove selected text and/or images to the Clipboard, where they are stored for later use.

D

D: The CD/DVD drive on a PC. In speech it is referred to as the 'D drive'. See *CD-ROM* and *DVD*.

Database A program used for storing, organising and sorting information. Each entry is called a record and each category of information held in a record is called a field.

Default Settings and preferences automatically adopted by your PC for any program when none are specified by the user.

Defragmenter A program that 'tidies' files on the hard disk. When a file is saved to the hard disk, Windows may split it up into fragments that are stored in different locations on the hard disk. This makes the retrieval of the file much slower. The 'defrag' program solves this problem by regrouping all related data in the same place.

Delete To remove a file, folder, image or piece of text completely. If you accidentally delete something from a document you can undelete it using the Undo button on the Quick Access toolbar in Office 2010 programs or the Edit/Undo function in Windows Explorer or Works.

Desktop The screen displayed when Windows has finished starting up. Any icon on screen, together with the Taskbar and Start button, are known collectively as the Desktop. See *Icon* and *Taskbar*.

Desktop Gadgets Windows mini programs that provide up-to-date information about weather, exchange rates and news headlines, for example.

Dialogue box A window that appears on screen displaying a message from the program currently in use. This usually asks for preferences or information to be input by the user.

Dialogue box launcher A small arrow to the bottom right of a group on the Ribbon in Office 2010 programs that you click on to launch a dialogue box providing more options related to the group.

Dial-up connection The process of accessing another computer via a phone line.

Digital Data that exists in binary number form as 0's and 1's. Computers process digital data.

Digital camera A camera that can store many high-quality digital images on a memory card, removing the need for film. Images can then be downloaded onto a computer and edited, emailed or printed.

Digital image An image stored in number format, that can be transferred to hard disks or removable storage disks, displayed on screen or printed.

Disk cleanup A program that will find and remove unwanted files from your hard disk, freeing up memory.

Disk tools Programs that manage and maintain the hard disk, ensuring data is stored efficiently and that the hard disk runs at optimum speed.

Document A single piece of work created in a program. Also referred to as a file. See *File*.

Documents A folder option found in the Start menu. Each user has a Documents folder for their files.

Dots per inch (dpi) The number of dots that a printer can print on one square inch of paper. The more dots, the greater the detail and the better the quality of the printout.

Double-click To press and release the left mouse button twice in quick succession.

Download To copy a file or program from another computer to your own. For example, when you collect email from an internet service provider, you are downloading it.

Drag A mouse action used to highlight text, reshape objects or move an object or file. To move an object with the mouse pointer, for instance, click on it and, keeping the left mouse button held down, move the mouse pointer.

Drive A device that holds a disk. The drive has a motor that spins the disk, and a head that reads it – like the stylus on a record player.

Driver Software that translates instructions from Windows into a form that can be understood by a hardware device such as a printer or scanner.

DVD Digital Versatile Disc. Identical in appearance to a CD, but with a much greater storage capacity. Often used for storing film or video footage. Rewritable DVDs are also available.

E

Email Electronic mail. Messages sent from one computer to another through the internet.

Error message A small window that appears on screen warning the user that a fault has occurred and, where appropriate, suggesting action to remedy it.

F

Field A category of information in a database, such as Name, Address or Phone Number.

File Any item stored on a computer. This includes, for example, a program, a document or an image.

File extension A code, usually of three letters, at the end of a file name to indicate its format (the type of file). Windows uses this to identify the relevant program. ▶

File format The way in which files created by different programs are saved. This differs from program to program, so that one program may have difficulty reading files created by another. Common file formats are listed below:

Text	.asc .doc .htm .html .msg .txt .wpd
Image	.bmp .eps .gif .jpg .pict .png .tif
Sound	.aac .au .mid .ra .snd .wma .wav
Video	.avi .mpg .wmv
Compressed	.arc .arj .gz .hqx .sit .tar .z .zip
Program	.bat .com .exe

File tab The coloured tab located at the top left of Office 2010 programs that gives access to functions, such as print and save. It is also the route to accessing some online, program-specific extras such as templates.

Firewall Software or hardware that limits the access that can be gained to your PC through an internet connection.

Flash A plug-in that enables animations and games to play within a browser window.

Flash drive Small, portable storage device used for easily transferring files from one PC to another.

Folder An electronic storage compartment used to keep related files and relevant documents in the same place on the hard disk.

Font A particular style of type, such as Helvetica, Arial or Times New Roman. Most fonts can be displayed and printed in different sizes. They can also be styled in bold or italic, or with other effects.

Format To alter the appearance of a document – for example, its typography or layout.

Freeware Programs, usually produced by hobby programmers, for which users do not pay a fee. Freeware can often be downloaded from the internet.

FTP File Transfer Protocol. Program used to transfer a copy of a file between computers over the internet. One is the client the other the server. It requires you to log in with a username and password.

Function keys The 12 keys (labelled F1, F2 and so on) at the top of the keyboard. Their function depends on which program is in use. So, for instance, Shift + F7 in Word calls up the Thesaurus, and F12 calls up the Save As dialogue box.

G

.GIF file Graphics Interchange Format. This is a commonly used format for storing images and bitmapped colour graphics, especially on the internet.

Gigabyte (Gb) A unit of memory capacity. A single gigabyte is 1000 megabytes. See *Kilobyte*, *Megabyte* and *Terabyte*.

Graphics Any illustrative file, including pictures, photographs and clip art.

Group The categories into which certain tasks have been placed in Office 2010 for ease of use on the Ribbon. See *Ribbon*.

H

Hard disk A computer's high-speed storage device. It contains the operating system, the programs and your files. The hard disk is referred to as the 'C drive'.

Hardware The physical parts of a computer, including the system unit, monitor, keyboard, mouse and other devices such as the printer, scanner and speakers.

Header The area at the top of a page in a document. Text entered in the header (such as a title) appears on every page of the document unless you specify otherwise.

Help key Usually the F1 key. Pressed to access advice and information on how to perform the task the user is currently engaged in.

Highlight To select a word, a section of text or a group of cells, by clicking and dragging over them using the mouse.

I

Icon A graphic representation of a file or a function, which is designed to be easily recognisable as the item it represents. For example, the printer icon on the toolbar accesses the print function.

Import To bring an element from another file, such as a photograph, illustration or clip-art image, into the active document.

Inkjet printer A printer that works by squirting tiny drops of ink onto the surface of the paper.

Install To copy a program onto the hard disk and then set it up so it is ready for use. Programs are usually installed from a CD-ROM.

Internet Millions of computers throughout the world linked together via phone and cable lines. Computer users can communicate with each other and exchange information over the internet for the price of a local phone call.

IP address Logical address assigned to every computer, printer and router on a network.

ISP Internet Service Provider. A company that provides connection to the internet – this can be via your phone line, cable or satellite.

J

JPEG Joint Photographics Experts Group. A compressed format for storing images so that they take up less space on a computer.

K

Keyboard shortcut A method of issuing a command using a combination of keystrokes. This is quicker than using the mouse.

Kilobyte (Kb) A unit of memory capacity. A single kilobyte is equivalent to 1000 bytes. A short letter created in Word uses about 20 Kb. See *Gigabyte*, *Megabyte*, *Terabyte*.

Kilobytes per second (kbps) A measurement for the speed with which data can be sent to or from a computer via a modem.

L

Landscape See *Orientation*.

LAN Local Area Network. Network that operates within a small area, usually in a building or office.

Laptop A portable computer, usually with the functions of a full-size PC.

Laser printer A printer that uses a laser beam to etch images onto a drum and then transfers the image to paper. The reproduction quality is usually higher than with an inkjet printer. See *Inkjet printer*.

Launcher A window in some software suites, such as Microsoft Works, through which the suite's various programs and 'mini programs' can be opened.

Logging on The process of accessing computers or files using a username and password or other instructions. Some websites also require users to log on.

M

Maximise To increase the size of a window so that it fills the screen. The Maximise button is the middle button in the set of three in the top right-hand corner of a window. Once used, this button becomes a Restore button. Click on it to restore the window to its original size.

Megabyte (Mb) A unit of memory capacity. A single megabyte is 1000 kilobytes.

Memory A computer's capacity for storing information. See also *RAM* and *ROM*.

Menu bar The line of menu options that runs along the top of a Works window. When a menu is selected, you can access its list of options through a drop-down menu.

Minimise To reduce a window to a button on the Taskbar. The Minimise button is the left button in the set of three in the top right-hand corner of a window. To restore the window to the screen, click on its button on the Taskbar.

Modem A device that converts electronic signals from a computer into sound signals that can be transmitted by phone then reconverted by another modem into the original electronic data. An ADSL 'modem' is misnamed: it really works as a router. See *Router*.

Monitor The viewing screen on which you see your computer's files. Images are made up of thousands of tiny red, green and blue dots, called pixels, that combine to form colours.

Motherboard The circuit board that houses a PC's central processing unit (see *CPU*), some memory and slots into which expansion cards can be fitted. See *Memory*.

Mouse pointer A small arrow on screen that moves when the mouse is moved. Other representations of the pointer, depending on the program being used, include a pointing hand, a pen, a cross and a double-headed arrow. When you click in a text document, the cursor will appear. See *Cursor*.

MP3 Format used for storing audio files digitally in a compressed form. These files can be played on a computer or transferred to a portable device called an MP3 player. An Apple iPod is an example of an MP3 player.

N

Network The connection of several computers and printers so that they can share files and messages.

O

Online The status of a computer that is actively connected via a modem to the internet. Also used as a term for people who are able to connect to the internet. See *Internet*.

Open To look inside a file or folder to view its contents. To open a file or folder, either double-click on it, or right-click on it and select Open from the menu. In Works, you can also use the File menu and in Office 2010 programs, the File tab.

Operating system The software that controls the running of a computer, allowing, for example, programs to communicate with hardware devices such as printers. Windows is the most popular operating system for PCs.

Orientation An option available when creating a document. Users can choose to set up a page as either Landscape (of greater width than height) or Portrait (of greater height than width), depending on how they want the final version of the document to appear.

P

Page break The point at which one page ends and another begins. Insert a page break into a Microsoft Word document by pressing the Ctrl key and, keeping it pressed down, pressing the Enter key.

Paste The insertion into a document of text or other data that has previously been cut or copied.

PC-compatible Software or hardware that will work on a standard PC.

PCI slot A spare space inside a PC for extra expansion cards, such as a sound or graphics card.

PDA Personal Digital Assistant. Touch-screen hand-held computer.

PDF Portable Document Format. A file type that can be read on any computer. A free PDF reader can be downloaded at www.adobe.com.

Peripheral A device such as a scanner that can be connected to a PC, but is not vital to its function.

Phishing Attempting to acquire sensitive information fraudulently via email or phone, by pretending to be a trustworthy party.

Pictures The default folder in Windows for storing photos and other images.

Pixel An individual dot on a computer screen. The number of pixels horizontally and vertically on the screen determines the level of detail and quality of image that can be displayed. This can be set and altered by the user.

Plug and play Where extra items can be added to your PC without the need for loading new software.

Plug-ins Programs that are needed to open and run certain files, such as video clips or sound files. Websites often provide plug-ins for visitors to download, so that they ▶

are able to view the entire site. See *Download*.

Point size Measurement used to describe the size of fonts. For example, this page is in 9 point; newspaper headlines are usually between 36 and 72 point.

POP3 Post Office Protocol version 3. Email service that allows clients to access their mailboxes from a remote messaging server. See *SMTP*.

Port A socket at the rear of the system unit that allows users to connect a peripheral device to the PC.

Portrait See *Orientation*.

Printer driver A piece of software that helps Windows to communicate with the printer. See *Driver*.

Print Preview On-screen display that shows how the active document will look when printed. Accessed from the File tab, Print option in Office 2010 programs and the File menu in Works.

Processor The central processing unit (CPU) of a PC. See *CPU*.

Program A product installed on a computer that allows the user to interact with the computer's hardware to perform a specific type of task. For instance, a word-processing program allows the user to direct the computer in all aspects of handling and presenting text. See *Application program*, *Software*.

Prompt A window that appears on screen to remind users that additional information is required before an action can proceed.

Properties The attributes of a file or folder, such as its creation date and format.

R

RAM Random Access Memory. The memory used for the temporary storage of information on active documents and programs.

Record An individual entry in a database comprising several categories of information. For example, an address book database comprises 'records', each with a name, address and phone number.

Recycle Bin A Desktop feature that allows you to delete files. To rescue or 'recycle' a file, drag it back out of the bin. To delete a file completely, right-click on it and select Empty Recycle Bin.

Resolution The degree of detail on a screen or a printed document. It is measured in dots per inch (dpi). The more dots per square inch, the greater the detail.

Ribbon A toolbar-driven way of working in Office 2010. Clicking on the tabs at the top of the Ribbon gives easy access to associated tasks, collected into 'groups'.

Right-click To press and release the right mouse button once. Right-clicking often calls up a pop-up menu and is often a shortcut to various actions. See *Click*.

ROM Read Only Memory. Memory chips used by the computer for storing basic details about the PC, such as the Basic Input/Output System (BIOS) instructions. See *BIOS*.

Router Device that links a network

of computers to a remote network, such as the internet. See *Internet*.

S

Save To commit a document to the computer's memory. To do so, press the Ctrl + 'S' keys, or click on the Save button on the Quick Access Toolbar in Office 2010.

Save As A way of saving a file under a different name or format. If the file was previously saved under a different name or format, that version will remain unchanged. This is useful for saving an edited file, while still keeping the original.

Scanner A device for converting images on paper, such as photos, into electronic images that can then be manipulated and reproduced by a PC. See *Digital*, *Digital image*.

Screensaver A picture that appears on-screen when the PC is left idle for a specified time. You can choose to use one of your own images as a screensaver.

Scroll To move through the contents of a window or menu, using the arrows on the scrollbars at the top and/or foot of the item.

Search A program that searches a PC for a file. Searches can be carried out on various information, such as the file name, author or the date on which it was last modified.

Search engines Huge databases on the World Wide Web that are used to locate information on the internet. They can look for key words or phrases, or for categories, then sub-categories.

Select To choose a file, folder, image, piece of text or any other item by

clicking on it or highlighting it, before manipulating it in some way. For example, selecting some text before styling it.

Shareware Programs, or reduced versions of programs, that can be sampled for free for a limited period. Users must then buy the program to continue to use it.

Shortcut An icon on the Desktop that links to a file, folder or program stored on the hard disk. It provides quicker access to the file, and features the icon of the linked item, with a small arrow in the bottom left-hand corner, and its name below.

SMTP Simple Mail Transfer Protocol. Email service to send outgoing messages. See *POP3*.

Software Programs that allow users to perform specific functions. Microsoft Excel and Microsoft Outlook are examples of software. See *Application program*, *Program*.

Software suite A collection of programs that come in a single package. For example, Microsoft Works is a software suite that includes word-processing, database and spreadsheet programs.

Sound card A device that lets users record, play and edit sound files. Fits into an expansion slot within the system unit. See *Sound file*.

Sound file A file containing audio data. To hear the sound, double-click on the file (you will need speakers and a sound card).

Spreadsheet A document for storing and calculating numerical data. Spreadsheets are used mainly for financial planning and accounting.

Start button The button on the left of the Taskbar through which users can access the Start menu and its options, including programs.

Status bar A bar that appears in some program windows, giving users information about the document being worked on.

Styling Altering the appearance of the content of a file. For example, by making text **bold** (heavier-looking and more distinct) or *italic* (slanting to the right), or by changing its colour and size. See *Format*.

System software The software that operates the PC, managing its hardware and programs. Windows is the system software for PCs.

System unit The rectangular box-shaped part of the PC that contains the hard disk, the CPU, memory and sockets for connections to peripheral devices.

T

Tab A function used for setting and pre-setting the position of text.

Tab key A key on the keyboard used to tabulate text, to move between cells in spreadsheets, or to move from one database field to the next.

Taskbar A bar usually situated along the bottom of the screen in Windows that displays the Start button and buttons for all the programs and documents that are currently open.

Template A format for saving a document, the basic elements of which you regularly want to use. When you open a template, a copy of it appears for you to work on, while the template itself remains unaltered for further use.

Terabyte (Tb) A unit of memory capacity. A single terabyte is 1000 gigabytes.

Tile To reduce in size a group of open windows and then arrange them so that they can all be seen on screen at once.

Toolbar A bar or window containing clickable buttons used to issue commands or access functions. For example, spreadsheet programs have a toolbar that contains buttons that are clicked on to perform calculations or add decimal places. See *Taskbar*.

U

Undo A function in some programs that allows you to reverse tasks. Word, for example, also has a Redo option.

Uninstall To remove programs from the PC's hard disk. Software is available for uninstalling programs that do not contain an inbuilt uninstall option.

Upgrade To improve the performance or specification of a PC by adding new hardware, such as a higher-capacity disk drive or the latest version of software. See *Hardware, Software*.

URL Uniform Resource Locator. A standard style used for all internet addresses on the World Wide Web. The first part of the URL, such as www.yahoo.com, indicates the location of a computer on the internet. Anything that follows, such as /myhome/mypage.htm, gives a location of a particular file on that computer.

USB Universal Serial Bus. A hardware connector that allows users to plug a wide range of USB devices into a computer without having to restart. See *Hardware*.

Utilities Software that assists in certain computer functions, such as uninstalling and virus-scanning.

V

View A menu through which users can change the way a file is displayed on screen. For example, in a Works database users can choose to see a document in List, Form or Form Design View.

Virus A program designed to damage a computer system. Viruses can be 'caught' through portable storage devices or through programs downloaded from the internet.

VoIP Voice over Internet Protocol. Voice conversations over the internet.

W

WiFi Popular name for IEEE 802.11b, a standard for wireless networks suitable for use in the home.

Window Each program or individual file on your PC can be viewed and worked on in its own self-contained area of screen called a Window. All windows have their own menu bar, through which users can issue commands. Several windows can be open at once on the Desktop.

Windows The most popular operating system for PCs, which allows users to run many programs at once and open files on screen. The latest version is Windows 7. See *Operating system*.

Windows Explorer A program that allows users to view the contents of a PC in a single window.

Windows Live Messenger A Microsoft program that enables you to 'chat' online, and share folders and files with others logged onto Live Messenger.

Wizard A tool that guides users step by step through processes such as installing software and adding new hardware.

WordArt A graphic text image that can be customised and imported into a document.

Word processing Text-based tasks on the PC, such as writing letters.

WWW World Wide Web. System of interlinked documents held on the internet, that can be viewed using web-browsing software. Other functions of the internet such as email do not count as part of the World Wide Web. See *Internet*.

Z

Zip file A file that has been compressed with the WinZip compression program.

*Numbers shown in **bold** type indicate pages dedicated to the subject listed.*

ACKNOWLEDGMENTS

We would like to thank the following individuals and organisations for their assistance in producing this book.

Additional writing
Roger Laing

Photography
Steven Bartholomew, Steve Tanner, Karl Adamson, Tim Course

Styling
Mary Wadsworth

Picture agencies
L=left, R=right, T=top, C=centre, B=bottom
56 iStockphoto.com; 79 R iStockphoto.com/ Gustaf Brundin, B iStockphoto.com/ Nick Schlax; 80 T iStockphoto.com/ Daniel Halvorson, B iStockphoto.com/ Dan Wilton; 98 PhotoAlto/Lucas Racasse; 158-159 ShutterStock, Inc/Neale Cousland; 168 T iStockphoto.com/Jason Stitt, B iStockphoto.com/Greg Cerenzio; 170 R iStockphoto.com/Jason Stitt; 171 C iStockphoto.com/Greg Cerenzio; 180 ShutterStock, Inc/Forest Path; 190-191 ShutterStock, Inc/Elwynn; 200 C www.sports-photos.co.uk, BL www.sports-photos.co.uk/George Herringshaw, BC Colorsport/Andrew Cowie, BR www.sports-photos.co.uk/Nigel French; 205 BC www.sports-photos.co.uk/Ed Lacey; 224 iStockphoto.com/Jaroslaw Wojci; 227 iStockphoto.com/Jaroslaw Wojci; 228-229 ShutterStock, Inc/Audrey Burmakin; 234-235 ShutterStock, Inc/Natural Digital; 262-263 ShutterStock, Inc/Ralf Siemieniec; 280-281 Corbis/Al Francekevich; 310-311 Corbis/Gary D Landsman; 320-321 ImageState/ Ethel Davies; 326-327 Getty Images/Lonny Kalfus; 364 iStockphoto.com/Duck Do

Equipment and photographs courtesy of
Microsoft Corporation, Epson Corporation, Fujifilm, Dell Computer Corporation, Canon (UK) Ltd, D-Link Systems Inc., Alcatel, Nokia, Carrera Technology Ltd, Logitech, Iomega, Yamaha Kemble Music Ltd, Bite, KYE Systems UK Ltd, PMC Electronics Ltd

Software
Microsoft Corporation, Steinberg Media Technologies AG, Guildsoft Ltd, Focus

Windows 7 and Office 2010 Edition

Editor
John Andrews and Jon Kirkwood

Art Editor
Conorde Clarke

Designer
Wai Sing Tang

Technical Editor and Consultant
Tony Rilett

Proofreader
Barry Gage and Sarah Kaikini

Indexer
Marie Lorimer

Reader's Digest General Books

Editorial Director
Julian Browne

Art Director
Anne-Marie Bulat

Managing Editor
Nina Hathway

Trade Books Editor
Penny Craig

Picture Resource Manager
Sarah Stewart-Richardson

Pre-press Accounts Manager
Dean Russell

Production Controller
Jan Bucil

Product Production Manager
Claudette Bramble

HOW TO DO just about ANYTHING ON A COMPUTER
Microsoft® Windows® 7™ and Office® 2010™ Edition

Published in 2011 in the United Kingdom by Vivat Direct Limited (t/a Reader's Digest),
157 Edgware Road, London W2 2HR.

How To Do Just About Anything On A Computer, Microsoft® Windows® 7™ and Office® 2010™ Edition is owned and under licence from The Reader's Digest Association, Inc. All rights reserved.

Based on *How To Do Just About Anything On A Computer* (first published 2000) and subsequent updates.

We are committed both to the quality of our products and the service we provide to our customers. We value your comments, so please do contact us on **0871 351 1000** or via our website at **www.readersdigest.co.uk**

If you have any comments or suggestions about the content of our books, email us at gbeditorial@readersdigest.co.uk

Website addresses and the contents of websites change constantly; websites may disappear without warning. The publishers accept no responsibility for the accuracy of any of the information given in this book concerning websites, their contents or any of the views expressed in them.

Every effort has been made to establish ownership of copyright material depicted in this book. All queries regarding copyright issues should be directed to Sarah Stewart-Richardson at: sarah.stewart-richardson@readersdigest.co.uk

Origination: FMG

Printed in China

Concept Code IE 0055/G
Book Code 400-561 UP0000-1
ISBN 978 1 780 20048 4